RISK MANAGEMENT IN SOCIAL WORK

D1736278

Risk Management in Social Work

PREVENTING PROFESSIONAL MALPRACTICE, LIABILITY, AND DISCIPLINARY ACTION

Frederic G. Reamer

Legal review by Michael J. Racette, Esq.

 COLUMBIA UNIVERSITY PRESS   NEW YORK

COLUMBIA UNIVERSITY PRESS
Publishers Since 1893
New York   Chichester, West Sussex

cup.columbia.edu

The first and second editions of this book carried the title
Social Work Malpractice and Liability: Strategies for Prevention

Library of Congress Cataloging-in-Publication Data

Reamer, Frederic G., 1953– author.
  [Social work malpractice and liability]
  Risk management in soical work : preventing professional malpractice, liability,
and disciplinary action / Frederic G. Reamer; legal review by Michael J. Racette,
Esq. — [Updated edition].
      pages cm
  Includes bibliographical references and index.
  ISBN 978-0-231-16782-6 (cloth : alk. paper) — ISBN 978-0-231-16783-3 (pbk. : alk. paper) —
  ISBN 978-0-231-53843-5 (e-book)
  1. Social workers—Malpractice—United States. 2. Social workers—Legal status,
law, etc.—United States. I. Title.

KF3721.R43 2015
344.7303′13—dc23

                                                                    2014014581

Cover design: Jordan Wannemacher

References to websites (URLs) were accurate at the time of writing.
Neither the author nor Columbia University Press is responsible for URLs
that may have expired or changed since the manuscript was prepared.

FOR DEBORAH, EMMA, AND LEAH

CONTENTS

LET'S START WITH THE GOOD NEWS: Relatively few social workers are named as defendants in lawsuits or respondents in licensing board complaints. The vast majority of social workers practice ethically and competently, adhering to widely embraced standards of ethics and social work practice designed to protect clients.

And then there's the bad news: Some social workers—a distinct minority, to be sure—practice social work outside established standards, thus posing significant risk to clients and to their own careers. These social workers are much more likely to have lawsuits and licensing board complaints filed against them. And even the most conscientious, principled, earnest, and ethical social workers run the risk, however small, that disgruntled clients will file complaints against them, even when no evidence of wrongdoing exists.

That there is a need for this book is unfortunate. After all, what social worker wants to spend time reading and thinking about being sued or being named in a licensing board complaint? Sadly such formal complaints are a fact of modern life, and the costs are significant. I am not referring only to the financial cost, mind you. I am also referring to the emotional cost. Even when a social worker has done nothing wrong, being named in a lawsuit or licensing board complaint is psychologically taxing. Moreover the social worker will need to consult (and pay) a lawyer, answer interrogatories, produce documents, attend depositions and hearings, and repair or preserve her reputation. Under the best of circumstances this arduous process is a miserable experience. Under the worst of circumstances it can be devastating.

Unfortunately social workers get little training to help them avoid malpractice claims and licensing board complaints. Professional education typically includes little on the subject of what has come to be known in the trade as "risk management." Although more and more social workers are learning about professional ethics, professional and continuing education rarely includes a systematic introduction to risk management and ways to prevent formal complaints. My hope is that this book will help remedy the situation.

Since the early 1980s I have had the privilege of speaking to thousands of social workers throughout the United States, Canada, Europe, and Asia about professional ethics. When I started to receive invitations to deliver lectures and workshops on the topic, my focus was primarily on ethical issues in social work and the nature of ethical decision making when confronted with difficult dilemmas.

Over time, however, I noticed a distinct trend. During conference breaks and after my presentations I began to get more and more questions that started along the lines of "I was wondering if I can get sued for _____?" or "Can I get in trouble with my licensing board if I _____?" (Fill in the blanks.) It did not take me long to figure out that while I was preoccupied with perplexing and conceptually complex philosophical issues related to social work ethics, many in my audiences were understandably consumed with more pragmatic concerns about potential lawsuits and other complaints. This should not have been much of a surprise because many ethical issues that I was presenting broached complicated legal questions as well.

What this meant, of course, was that I found myself learning more and more about the malpractice and licensing board risks associated with social work practice. Over the years I have collected scores of case examples from conference participants, colleagues, and more than one hundred court and licensing board cases in which I have served as an expert witness and consultant.

It is sad, in a way, that the profession has generated so much concern about risk management. It distracts from the principal mission of social work, and the concern often is out of proportion to the statistical risk of being named in a lawsuit or licensing board complaint. From my point of view, however, this also represents an important opportunity to educate social workers about good practice and good ethics, which ultimately prevent lawsuits and licensing board complaints. My hope is that this book will provide social workers with an in-depth and practical guide to help them recognize, prevent, and cope with risks they encounter in their work.

The book is designed to assist social workers involved in direct practice (especially clinical work with individuals, couples, families, and small groups) and in social work supervision, management, and administration. After I introduce the concepts of negligence, malpractice, liability, and risk management (chapter 1), I turn to a series of discrete topics. These include problems related to privacy and confidentiality (chapter 2), improper treatment and delivery of services (chapter 3), impaired practitioners (chapter 4), supervision (chapter 5), consultation and referral (chapter 6), fraud and deception (chapter 7), and termination of service (chapter 8). I conclude the book with a series of practical suggestions for social workers who are named as defendants in lawsuits and licensing board complaints, and some observations about the role of good practice and good ethics in managing and reducing risk (chapter 9).

This book contains considerable case material. I drew the cases from several sources, including legal texts, law reporters (published summaries of legal cases), court documents, newspaper accounts, and my own involvement in a wide variety of court and licensing board cases. Some case illustrations come from publications that provide periodic updates of litigated cases. I found other case examples in textbooks and original court opinions published in various state, federal, and regional reporters. Most cases that I cite are a matter of public record; in some instances I could not provide dates for the decisions because I found descriptions of these cases only in secondary sources and the cases themselves were not published. In several instances I report case-related details in disguised form to protect the privacy of the parties involved.

It is important to note that I am not an attorney, and I am not offering legal advice in this book. Although this book includes information and commentary about legal concepts and cases, readers who believe they need or want legal advice should consult an attorney with expertise in professional malpractice and risk management.

I have noticed that when I speak to social workers about this subject, their anxiety tends to increase. Contemplating being named in a lawsuit or licensing board complaint is not exactly fun. What I have found, however, is that whatever anxiety this topic produces can stimulate determined efforts to enhance the quality of social work practice. Perhaps the most effective way for social workers to protect themselves from formal complaints is to offer competent and ethical service to clients. Sometimes anxiety can serve a useful purpose by inspiring constructive action. As the nineteenth-century Scottish writer Thomas Carlyle said, "Talk that does not end in any kind of action is better suppressed altogether."

RISK MANAGEMENT IN SOCIAL WORK

1

Professional Risk Management

AN OVERVIEW

IMAGINE THAT YOU ARE A social worker employed at a community mental health center. For three months you have been counseling a twenty-six-year-old man who was referred to you by the staff of a local psychiatric hospital, following the young man's inpatient treatment for depression.

Your client has made considerable progress. He is holding down a job for the first time in five years, is living independently in his own apartment, and is romantically involved with a young woman who is also a client at the mental health center; the couple met while participating in group therapy. Your client reports that he is happier than ever.

Your telephone rings one afternoon, and your client says, in a fearful voice, that he needs to see you as quickly as possible. He explains that he does not want to discuss the matter over the telephone, and you agree to meet him early the following morning.

Your client arrives on time. His affect is flat, and he seems unusually distressed. After you usher him into your office, your client explains that his physician has just informed him that he has tested positive for HIV, the virus that causes AIDS. He explains that he is shocked by the diagnosis and needs help dealing with the terrible news.

Your client is convinced that his lover infected him with HIV. Your client is furious and makes a number of disparaging comments about her. After several minutes of this ranting, your client erupts and says, "She's going to pay for this. She's *really* going to pay for this." Your client then storms out of your office, leaving you to wonder whether he intends to harm his lover imminently.

You pause to collect your thoughts: To what extent do you have an obligation to protect the client's lover, who is also a client at your agency, from harm? Did your client forfeit his right to confidentiality by threatening his lover? Are you permitted to disclose confidential information about the client without his consent to protect the lover, and, if so, how much information can you disclose and to whom should you disclose this information? What specific ethical standards and laws govern the disclosure of this confidential information? What steps do you need to take to make a sound decision and minimize risk to everyone involved?

All contemporary social workers need to be acquainted with the nature of risk management, specifically the ways in which their decisions and actions can expose them to lawsuits and licensing board complaints, in addition to exposing clients and others to harm. What kinds of claims are clients filing against social workers? With what frequency? What constitutes negligence and malpractice? How can social workers avoid liability and licensing board complaints? These are the principal questions that will concern us.

PROFESSIONAL MALPRACTICE AND LIABILITY

Risk management is a broad term that refers to efforts to protect clients, practitioners, and employers (Carroll 2011). Risk management includes the prevention of lawsuits and licensing board complaints. Lawsuits allege professional malpractice; licensing board complaints allege violation of standards of practice set forth in licensing laws and regulations. Lawsuits can result in monetary judgments against social workers; licensing board complaints can result in fines, revocation or suspension of a professional license, probation, mandated supervision and continuing education, reprimand, or censure.

Professional malpractice is generally considered a form of negligence. The concept applies to professionals who are required to perform in a manner consistent with the legal concept of the standard of care in the profession, that is, the way an ordinary, reasonable, and prudent professional would act under the same or similar circumstances (Austin, Moline, and Williams 1990; Barker and Branson 2000; Bernstein and Hartsell 2004; Cohen and Mariano 1982; Meyer, Landis, and Hays 1988; Schutz 1982). Malpractice in social work usually is the result of a practitioner's active violation of a client's rights (in legal terms, acts of commission, misfeasance, or malfeasance) or a practitioner's failure to perform certain duties (acts of omission or nonfeasance).

Some malpractice and liability claims result from genuine mistakes or inadvertent breaches of confidentiality on the part of social workers (a social worker sends an e-mail message containing confidential information to the wrong recipient, or a passenger in an elevator overhears a social worker talking with a colleague about confidential aspects of a case); other claims arise from a deliberate decision to risk a claim (a social worker decides to divulge confidential information about a client in order to protect a third party from harm). A social worker's unethical behavior or misconduct (sexual contact with a client or embezzling a client's money) also triggers claims.

In general malpractice occurs when evidence exists that

1. At the time of the alleged malpractice, the practitioner had a legal duty to the client (as in the opening example concerning the obligation to keep confidential information shared by a client).
2. The practitioner was derelict in that duty, either through an omission or through an action taken by the practitioner (divulging confidential information to the client's lover without the client's consent).
3. The client suffered some harm or injury (the client alleges that he suffered emotional distress and required additional psychiatric care after the unauthorized disclosure, that he lost time and wages at work, and that he was deprived of his lover's affection and companionship).
4. The professional's dereliction of duty was the direct and proximate cause of the harm or injury (the client's injuries were the result of the social worker's unauthorized disclosure of confidential information).

In contrast in making their decisions licensing boards need not require evidence that social workers' actions (commission) or inactions (omission) caused harm. Rather social workers can be sanctioned based simply on evidence that their conduct violated standards contained in licensing statutes and regulations.

KEY CONCEPTS IN RISK MANAGEMENT

Complaints filed against social workers fall into two broad groups (Reamer 2001a, 2002, 2013a). The first includes claims that allege that social workers carried out their duties improperly or in a fashion inconsistent with the profession's standard of care (so-called acts of commission or misfeasance/malfeasance). Examples include flawed treatment of a client (incorrect treatment), sexual impropriety or other boundary violation, breach of confidentiality or privacy, improper referral to another service provider, defamation of a client's character (as a result of slander or libel), breach of contract for services, improper civil commitment of a client (false imprisonment/arrest), wrongful removal of a child from a home (loss of child custody), assault and battery, improper termination of service (abandonment), improper licensing of staff, and improper peer review.

The distinction between misfeasance and malfeasance is an important one. *Misfeasance* is ordinarily defined as the commission of a proper act in a wrongful or injurious manner or the improper performance of an act that might have been performed lawfully. Examples include flawed informed consent procedures or inadvertent disclosure of confidential information. *Malfeasance* is ordinarily defined as the commission of a wrongful or unlawful act. Examples include embezzlement of a client's money, sexual contact with a minor client, and violation of a client's civil rights (Bernstein and Hartsell 2004; Bullis 1995; Gifis 2010).

The second broad category includes claims that allege that social workers failed to carry out a duty that they are ordinarily expected to carry out in accordance with the profession's standard of care (so-called acts of omission or nonfeasance). Examples include failure to conduct a proper biopsychosocial assessment, failure to prevent a client's suicide, failure to supervise a client properly, failure to protect third parties from harm, failure to treat a client successfully or at all (sometimes known as failure to cure—poor results), and failure to refer a client for consultation for specialized treatment. In subsequent chapters I shall explain more fully the specific allegations contained under these broad headings.

Of course, not all claims have merit. Some are frivolous or lack evidence of professional malpractice or misconduct. However, many claims do have merit or are settled out of court (or, in the case of licensing board complaints, settled with consent agreements) in order to minimize loss and legal expenses. In either case the result may be costly.

As I noted earlier, malpractice is a form of negligence that occurs when a practitioner acts in a manner inconsistent with the profession's standard of care—the way an ordinary, reasonable, and prudent professional would act under the same or similar circumstances. Suits that allege malpractice are civil suits (in contrast to criminal proceedings). Ordinarily civil suits are based on tort or contract law, with plaintiffs (the individuals bringing the suit) seeking some form of redress for injuries that they claim to have incurred (Bernstein and Hartsell 2004; Hogan 1979). These injuries may be economic (lost wages or the cost involved in seeking psychiatric care), physical (resulting from a suicide attempt or a practitioner's attempt to restrain an impaired client), or emotional (depression or anxiety brought about by the inappropriate disclosure of confidential information). Although this allegation is much less common, a plaintiff may also allege denial of constitutional rights (individuals hospitalized against their wishes may allege abridgement of their rights to liberty and due process).

As in criminal trials, defendants in civil suits are presumed blameless until proved otherwise. In ordinary civil suits the standard of proof required to find defendants liable for their actions is preponderance of the evidence. This is in contrast to the stricter standard of beyond a reasonable doubt used in criminal proceedings. In the exceptional civil case (such as a contract between family members to pay for services), the court may expect clear and convincing evidence, a standard of proof that is greater than preponderance of the evidence but less than for beyond a reasonable doubt (Gifis 2010).

In principle tort law—which entails rules allowing injured parties to seek compensation through the courts from those responsible for the harm—performs three important functions in society. First, it deters behavior that causes injuries, in that it exacts a price for injuring another party. Second, tort law provides opportunity for retribution against those responsible for the injury. Finally, tort law provides a mechanism for compensating the injured party (Antler 1987; B. Bernstein 1981; Bernstein and Hartsell 2004; Edwards, Edwards, and Wells 2012; Litan, Swire, and Winston 1988).

Most legal actions against social workers involve tort law, or law involving private or civil wrongs or injuries resulting from a breach of a legal duty (as opposed to contract or criminal law). Torts may be unintentional (negligent) or intentional. Unintentional torts, which include the various forms of negligence and malpractice discussed elsewhere in this book, concern allegations that the social worker's performance fell below the standard of care for the profession. Intentional torts—such as defamation of character or assault and battery—do not require evidence of negligence.

Most tort claims against social workers allege some form of malpractice (unintentional torts). The malpractice suit has its origins in early English common law. In fact mention of physicians' professional liability dates to the thirteenth century (Hogan 1979). Since then a variety of landmark court cases have clarified the nature of malpractice. In a classic eighteenth-century case involving medical malpractice, for instance, the King's Bench stated in *Slater v. Baker and Stapleton* (1767), "He who acts rashly acts ignorantly; and although the defendants in general may be as skillful in their respective professions as any two gentlemen in England, yet the Court cannot help saying that in this particular case they have acted ignorantly and unskillfully, contrary to the known rule and usage of surgeons" (Hogan 1979:8).

The first malpractice case on record in the United States was *Cross v. Guthry* in 1794. In this case a physician was found liable in a negligence case related to surgery performed on a woman who later died (Hogan 1979).

THE ELEMENTS OF MALPRACTICE AND LIABILITY

A malpractice claim must meet four conditions to be successful in court. These include evidence that the practitioner owed a duty to the injured party, the practitioner was derelict in that duty, the plaintiff suffered some sort of harm or injury, and the injury was the direct and proximate result of the breach of that duty.

The first element—evidence that the practitioner had a legal duty to the injured party—is often the easiest to satisfy. In the example I presented at the beginning of this chapter, for instance, the social worker employed at the mental health center unquestionably had a legal duty to the client. The duty was established when the client sought and obtained a service from the formally trained social worker, who provided that service in the context of a professional agency.

Determining whether the practitioner was somehow derelict in that duty typically is much more complex. Here questions ordinarily arise that relate to the prevailing standard of care in the profession. The standard of care requires the practitioner to do what a "reasonable person of ordinary prudence" would do in the practitioner's place (Edwards, Edwards, and Wells 2012; Gifis 2010:460; Woody 1997).

For many years courts defined standard of care by comparing a practitioner's actions with those of similarly trained professionals in the same community—what is generally known as the locality rule. The assumption here was that levels of expertise and training varied from community to community, as a function of local training programs and access to technology and treatment techniques. One practical consequence of the locality rule was that expert witnesses in a malpractice case usually came from the local community.

Over time, however, many jurisdictions have overturned the locality rule, either by judicial decision or legislation (Edwards, Edwards, and Wells 2012; Schutz 1982:4). The rationale has been that changes in modern communication (especially the Internet), transportation, and education have provided practitioners with much greater access to updated information about developments in their profession. Consequently courts now typically permit out-of-state expert witnesses to testify in malpractice cases. That is, the standard of care tends to be based on national, rather than local, norms in a profession.

A plaintiff may find it exceedingly difficult to demonstrate that a social worker behaved in a manner inconsistent with the standard of care. Some departures from the standard of care are relatively easy to show, of course. A social worker who discloses confidential information about a client to a client's neighbor, in casual conversation and without the client's permission, has clearly departed from the profession's standard of care. A social worker in a residential setting who neglects to record in case notes a client's obvious suicidal symptoms has clearly departed from the standard of care. These are the easy cases.

Far more common, however, are those cases in which reasonable people may disagree about the appropriateness of the practitioner's actions, that is, whether they in fact constituted a departure from the standard of care. The social worker in the opening example, for instance, might argue that disclosing confidential information was essential to protect the client's lover from potential harm. This social worker might argue that the benefit of the disclosure, to which the client did not consent, outweighed the breach of the client's right to privacy.

Other social workers might find such an argument unpersuasive. They might argue that the social worker had an obligation to respect the client's right to confidentiality and that, without his explicit consent, disclosure to a third party was unacceptable and constituted a departure from the profession's standard of care.

Further, it is not hard to imagine that expert witnesses drawn from the social work profession might disagree with one another. A jury hearing this case might have to deal with thoughtful, experienced experts who offer dia-metrically opposite views about the social worker's actions. One might sup-port the social worker's claim to a duty to protect a third party from serious harm and say that a breach of confidentiality under such circumstances is justifiable. Another expert witness might contend that the social worker's disclosure constituted a clear violation of professional ethics, particularly because the client never uttered an actual threat against his lover.

Courts recognize that professionals subscribe to various, sometimes competing, schools of thought. The idea that different schools of thought are permissible emerged in the nineteenth century, when physicians sub-scribed to different philosophies of practice, or schools, each with its own assumptions, principal concepts, and standards. Rather than try to determine which school of thought is most appropriate, courts have generally acknowl-edged the legitimacy of different schools, so long as they are supported by a "respectable minority of the profession" (Hogan 1979:9). When it is difficult to determine whether a respectable minority of a profession endorses a par-ticular school of thought, a judge is likely to explore whether a professional association, relevant standards of practice, and ethical guidelines exist.

Thus practitioners are judged according to the principles and doc-trine endorsed by the school of thought to which they subscribe (*Force v. Gregory* [1893]; *Nelson v. Dahl* [1928]). As Slovenko notes with respect to psychotherapy,

> The courts tend not to pass judgment on the appropriate therapy or the efficacy of different forms of treatment (except sterilization, electroshock, and psychosurgery), a reflection of Justice Cardozo's observation that the law treats medicine with diffidence and respect. Thus, the court has refused to consider which "of two equally reputable methods of psychiatric treatment"—psychoanalysis as against a physiological approach—would prove most efficacious in a particular case. In *Tribby v. Cameron,* for example, the U.S. Court of Appeals for the District of Columbia said: "We do not suggest that the court should or can decide what particular treatment this patient requires. The court's function here resembles ours when we review agency action. We do not decide whether one agency has made the best decision, but only make sure it has made a permissible and reasonable decision in view of the relevant information and within a broad range of discretion."
>
> (1978:61–62)

This is a profoundly important observation, in that it suggests that reasonable minds may differ with regard to the most appropriate intervention or course of action. What matters is whether a social worker's conclusion in particular circumstances was a permissible and reasonable decision in light of the relevant information, recognizing that some colleagues may have reached a different conclusion.

Note that if social workers present themselves as specialists within the social work profession—specializing in, for example, treatment of depression, marital conflict, eating disorders, substance abuse, or posttraumatic stress disorder—they will be held to the higher standards of a specialist, even if the social worker's claim of expertise is a misrepresentation (Edwards, Edwards, and Wells 2012; Schutz 1982:4).

Ordinarily the plaintiff has the burden of producing the evidence in a negligence case. However, in some cases the plaintiff introduces the doctrine of *res ipsa loquitur* (the thing speaks for itself) to shift the burden of proof to the defendant. Under res ipsa loquitur the plaintiff argues that the negligence is so self-evident that any reasonable person can see it (Edwards, Edwards, and Wells 2012; Schutz 1982:4–5). Imagine, for example, a suit filed on behalf of a child who was injured by an abusive foster parent; the suit proffers evidence that the social service agency placed the child in the foster home without screening the foster parents, who had a known record of abuse.

The 1865 British case of *Scott v. London and St. Katherine Docks Co.* (Hogan 1979:9–10) established the doctrine of res ipsa loquitur. Several sacks of sugar fell out of a warehouse window and hit an English customs officer on the head. The judges concluded that sacks of sugar do not fall out of second-story windows and hit pedestrians unless negligence is involved (Hogan 1979:318).

Courts require that suits based on the doctrine of res ipsa loquitur must meet three criteria: the injury sustained does not ordinarily occur in the absence of negligence; elements within the exclusive control of the defendant must have caused the injury; and the injury must not have been the result of any voluntary action or contribution on the plaintiff's part (although states that recognize the concept of comparative negligence, described later, may dispose of the third criterion and apportion liability according to the percentage contributed by the plaintiff and defendant). The procedural effect of successfully invoking the doctrine of res ipsa loquitur is to shift the burden of producing the evidence, which normally belongs to the plaintiff, to the defendant, who must then introduce evidence to refute the presumption of negligence (Gifis 2010).

Demonstrating the third element—that the client suffered some harm or injury—can also be difficult in social work. Unlike medicine, for example, where injuries resulting from malpractice are sometimes easy to document (when a fracture is set improperly and evidence of this appears on an X-ray or a physician mistakenly operates on the wrong body part or prescribes a clearly excessive dose of medication), in social work the injuries alleged are often difficult to document empirically. In many instances plaintiffs claim that they have experienced some form of emotional injury or harm, as opposed to some form of physical injury. In these cases the plaintiff may have some difficulty substantiating the injury. Compelling expert testimony may be required in order to present a strong case.

This suggests of course that a plaintiff can find it difficult to satisfy the fourth element—that the social worker's dereliction of duty was the direct and proximate cause of the harm or injury. Even plaintiffs who can document that they sustained some sort of injury—emotional distress or depression, physical harm—may have difficulty demonstrating that the social worker's alleged dereliction of duty was the direct and proximate cause of the injury (Edwards, Edwards, and Wells 2012; Slovenko 1978:61–63). For example, strong evidence may exist that a client manifested symptoms of depression after a social worker inadvertently released confidential information without the client's permission. The social worker's attorney might argue, however, that this client had a long-standing history of depression and that a variety of other stressful events in the client's life at the time of the inadvertent disclosure may account for the depression.

As Rothblatt and Leroy observe in relation to demonstrating the causal connection between a psychiatrist's breach of a duty and the injury of emotional harm:

> Besides proving that the psychiatrist has breached the requisite standard of care in some specific detail, the plaintiff must also demonstrate causation and damage. Because the natural pathological development and prognosis of mental disease is not well known, it is frequently difficult to state to a reasonable degree of medical certainty whether the application or omission of a particular procedure at a specified time caused mental injury to the patient. Thus, it is often difficult for the plaintiff to prove the element of causation.

The task is simplified, however, if the alleged negligence in some manner caused or encouraged the patient to sustain or inflict tangible physical injuries upon himself or others. Indeed, this characteristic is typical of almost every successful suit. In this situation, proof of the injuries in addition to proof that ordinary prudent therapeutic techniques would have prevented the damage may sustain the burden of proof.

The plaintiff who complains of exclusively mental injuries may also have a difficult time proving the element of damages. Not only are his allegations intangible and difficult to demonstrate to the judge and jury, but they also tend to be somewhat speculative because of the state of knowledge about mental illness. Even where improper procedures have been used to institutionalize a person in need of mental care, the courts may absolve physicians from liability by finding that the patient was not injured by receiving the treatment he needed.

(1973:264, quoted in R. Cohen 1979:49–50)

Consider the opening example. Assume for the moment that the client sues you and your agency, alleging that you violated his right to confidentiality. Through his attorney your client (now presumably your former client) claims that you had a duty to respect his right to privacy and breached this duty by disclosing to his lover details about comments made by the client in a confidential counseling session. In particular your former client asserts that you violated standard 1.07(c) in the National Association of Social Workers' *Code of Ethics,* which states that "social workers should protect the confidentiality of all information obtained in the course of professional service."[1]

In addition your former client claims that, as a result of your disclosure of confidential information about him, he suffered significant harm. Specifically he alleges that he suffered serious emotional distress and symptoms of depression and anxiety. He spells out how he never intended to harm his lover, you misinterpreted his comments, his lover fled the relationship following your disclosure, and he had to seek psychiatric help at considerable expense as a result. Finally, your former client claims that he lost time at work and wages as a result of this emotional injury.

You can imagine how controversial your former client's claims would be. In his mind, perhaps, is a clear, direct, and unambiguous connection between your alleged violation of his right to privacy and the emotional injury that he claims to have suffered. From your point of view serious questions can be raised about this connection. In your defense your attorney may argue that your former client has a history of depression and anxiety symptoms and that he has missed work in the past as a result of his emotional difficulties. Further, at the time of your disclosure to the lover of your former client—which you do not deny—your former client also complained of significant stress in his life because of conflict with his supervisor at work and financial problems. Hence your attorney might argue that your former client cannot demonstrate conclusively that disclosure of the information was the direct cause of his subsequent symptoms of depression and anxiety, missed work, or lost wages. A number of other factors could account for these difficulties.

Your lawyer also might question whether your former client's claims of injury are valid. Although missed days of work and lost wages are easy to document—recognizing that the cause may be uncertain—claims of emotional injury can be difficult to substantiate, because emotional injuries do not show up on X-rays or laboratory tests. Evidence often takes the form of self-report and evaluations conducted by mental health professionals. As social workers know quite well, even seasoned practitioners may disagree about the validity of evidence presented to substantiate claims of emotional injury.

In many cases involving liability risks, social workers are vulnerable to a lawsuit no matter what course of action they take. In the case example, for instance, the social worker might be sued for disclosing confidential information without the client's permission. A social worker also could be sued for *failure* to disclose confidential information without a client's permission (here the distinction between acts of commission and acts of omission is clearly relevant). Imagine that you decide to honor your client's request for privacy. Perhaps you concluded that your client's comments did not pose a serious threat of harm to his lover. Moreover you do not believe that violating your client's right to privacy without his permission would be ethical.

Shortly thereafter your client gets involved in a vicious argument with his lover, brings up the HIV infection, accuses his lover of being unfaithful and deceptive, and stabs her. Your client's lover knows that he was in counseling with you and has reason to believe you were aware of his threatening comments. The lover is so distressed and feels so betrayed that she consults an attorney, who sues you, alleging that you were obligated to take steps to protect your client's lover. Specifically her attorney argues that you violated standard 1.07(c) of the NASW *Code of Ethics:* "The general expectation that social workers will keep information confidential does not apply when disclosure is necessary to prevent serious, foreseeable, and imminent harm to a client or other identifiable person." The attorney claims that the risk to her client's safety clearly constituted a compelling professional reason to violate confidentiality and that you were remiss in not taking steps to protect her.

PROCESS VERSUS OUTCOME AND THE STANDARD OF CARE

Some malpractice cases in social work are relatively clear cut. A social worker in a residential setting who simply forgot to enter into the record that a client displayed evidence of suicidal ideation may clearly be liable if staffers on the next shift, unaware of the suicide risk, consequently failed to monitor the resident closely, and the client was injured seriously in an actual suicide attempt. Similarly a social worker in private practice who neglects to discuss informed consent with a client, fails to have the client sign a consent form, and then discloses diagnostic information to the client's employer clearly may be liable if the employer then fires the client. In these instances malpractice and negligence may be relatively easy to establish.

In general social workers will agree that a practitioner should never strike a client physically (except perhaps in extreme cases requiring self-defense when a client is out of control) and that a practitioner should always obtain informed consent from a client before disclosing confidential information (except in rare cases involving genuine emergencies). The opening case example, however, illustrates a common phenomenon—reasonable practitioners disagree about what the social worker should have done and whether those actions departed from the standard of care in the profession. Some social workers might argue, for example, that you were ethically obligated to take steps to protect your client's lover from harm and that this might include disclosing confidential information about his threats. They probably would cite the well-known case of *Tarasoff v. Regents* (1974, 1976), discussed more fully later in this book, to support their argument.

Other social workers might argue with equal force that you had an obligation to respect your client's right to privacy, that you did not have sufficiently compelling evidence to warrant disclosure of confidential information against his wishes, and that disclosure without the client's consent would violate state law. Thoughtful, experienced social workers have in fact presented such conflicting arguments about this very set of circumstances (Reamer 1991a, 1991b, 2013a).

What this suggests is that in many liability cases a judge or jury can find it quite difficult to determine what, exactly, constitutes the standard of care in the profession with regard to a social worker's actual decision and actions. The same holds for licensing board cases, where board members may have difficulty reaching consensus. Attorneys and expert witnesses often present strong arguments in conflicting directions.

What can happen, however—and this is a remarkably important point—is that debate about the standard of care may shift away from the social worker's actual decision and actions related to the substantive issue at hand or the outcome of the decision (in this instance whether the social worker should have divulged confidential information to the client's lover against the client's wishes) and toward the process and procedures that the social worker followed in order to make the decision. That is, the line of questioning may focus instead on the steps that the social worker took (or did not take) to make a sound decision.

In my view the procedural standard of care—the steps an ordinary, reasonable, and prudent social worker should take in order to make a sound decision in complex circumstances that may lead reasonable social workers to reach different conclusions—includes seven key elements, which I will explore in detail throughout the book:

1. *Consult colleagues.* Social workers who face difficult or complicated decisions should consult colleagues who have specialized knowledge or expertise related to the issues at hand. Social workers in private or independent practice should participate in peer consultation groups. Social workers employed in settings that have ethics committees (committees that provide staff with a forum for consultation on difficult cases) should take advantage of this form of consultation when they face complicated ethical issues (Reamer 1987b, 2013a). Moreover social workers who are sued can help demonstrate their competent decision-making skills by showing that they sought consultation.

2. *Obtain appropriate supervision.* Social workers who have access to a supervisor should take full advantage of this opportunity. Supervisors may be

able to help social workers navigate complicated circumstances. And social workers who are sued can help demonstrate their competent decision-making skills by showing that they sought supervision.

3. *Review relevant ethical standards.* It is vitally important that social workers become familiar with and consult relevant codes of ethics, especially the current code of the National Association of Social Workers (see Reamer 2006, 2013a). The current NASW code provides extensive guidelines concerning ethical issues that often form the basis for malpractice claims and lawsuits, for example, confidentiality, informed consent, conflicts of interest, boundary issues and dual relationships, client records, defamation of character, and termination of services (Reamer 2006). The code includes 155 specific ethical standards of care in the profession. In addition the code's standards provide the basis for adjudication of ethics complaints filed against NASW members; many state licensing boards use the code, or portions of it, when reviewing complaints filed against licensed social workers.

4. *Review relevant regulations, laws, and policies.* Social workers who make difficult judgments that have legal implications should always consider relevant federal, state, and local regulations and laws. With respect to the opening case, for example, social workers should review state laws concerning the disclosure of confidential information by clients during counseling sessions. Many regulations and laws have direct relevance to social work; prominent examples concern the confidentiality of alcohol and drug treatment records, the confidentiality of students' educational records, and the confidentiality of health care and mental health treatment records. In addition to state laws, key federal laws and regulations may be relevant to social workers' ethical decisions (such as the regulation Confidentiality of Alcohol and Drug Abuse Patient Records, the Health Insurance Portability and Accountability Act, better known as HIPAA, and the Family Educational Rights and Privacy Act, better known as FERPA). Social workers employed in military settings must be cognizant of confidentiality provisions in the Military Rules of Evidence. Social workers employed by the U.S. Veterans Administration must be familiar with unique legal regulations pertaining to management of confidential information, especially pertaining to substance abuse and HIV.

5. *Review relevant literature.* Social workers should always keep current with their professional literature, especially that pertaining to their specialty

areas. When faced with challenging decisions, social workers should make every reasonable effort to consult pertinent literature in an effort to determine what authorities in the field say about the issues and whether they agree or disagree. Such consultation can provide useful guidance and also provides helpful evidence that a social worker made a conscientious attempt to comply with current standards in the field. That a social worker took the time to consult pertinent literature looks good, as a defense lawyer might say. In addition social workers can expect that opposing lawyers will conduct their own comprehensive review of relevant literature in an effort to locate authoritative publications that support their clients' claims. Lawyers often submit as evidence copies of publications that, in their opinion, buttress their legal case. Lawyers may use the authors of influential publications as expert witnesses.

6. *Obtain legal consultation when necessary.* Social workers often make decisions that have legal implications (although many ethical decisions do not require legal consultation, for example, whether to accept a modest gift from a client or accept the client's invitation to attend the client's wedding). This is particularly true with respect to a number of ethical decisions, where statutes, regulations, and court decisions may address, for example, confidentiality, privileged communication, informed consent, conflicts of interest, digital technology, and termination of services (Dickson 1995; Madden 2003). In addition a social worker's taking the time to obtain legal consultation provides additional evidence of having made conscientious, diligent efforts to handle the situation professionally. Consultation with skilled lawyers familiar with health care law and risk management can be extraordinarily helpful.

7. *Document decision-making steps.* Careful and thorough documentation enhances the quality of services provided to clients. Comprehensive records are necessary to assess clients' circumstances; plan and deliver services appropriately; facilitate supervision; provide proper accountability to clients, other service providers, funding agencies, insurers, utilization review staff, and the courts; evaluate services provided; and ensure continuity in the delivery of future services (Kagle and Kopels 2008; Madden 2003; Sidell 2011; Wilson 1980). Thorough documentation also helps to ensure quality care if a client's primary social worker becomes unavailable because of illness, incapacitation, vacation, or employment termination; colleagues who provide

coverage will have the benefit of up-to-date information. In addition thorough documentation can help protect social workers who are named in ethics complaints and lawsuits (for example, documentation is evidence that a social worker obtained consultation, consulted relevant codes of ethics and ethical standards, referred a high-risk client for specialized services, obtained a client's informed consent for release of confidential information, or competently managed a client's suicide risk).

The extent to which a social worker engaged in these steps when making a decision may become a key issue during a lawsuit. For example, during a deposition (a method of pretrial discovery that consists of a witness's statement and responses to questioning under oath) or actual trial, an opposing attorney in the case might ask which supervisors the social worker consulted about the decision. Were these supervisors the most appropriate ones to consult, given their areas of expertise? Did the social worker bring the issue up in peer consultation? Did the social worker consult a lawyer about the legal implications of the decision? Did the social worker consult the NASW *Code of Ethics* and professional literature for guidance? Did the social worker document these various steps? Does the case record include evidence that the social worker actually took these various steps?

What I am suggesting here is that the standard of care in social work can be viewed in two ways. First, the standard of care may focus on a social worker's specific decisions or actions pertaining to the professional duty, such as the handling of confidential information, entering into friendships with former clients, physical contact with clients, informed consent, and suicide prevention. Second, the standard of care may focus on the process and procedures that the social worker followed in making the relevant decision or pursuing the controversial course of action (i.e., the social worker's use of supervision, consultation, research).

With regard to the process and procedures, documenting any supervision or consultation that social workers obtain or research that they conduct is extremely important. Should some question arise about a social worker's particular decision or actions, being able to demonstrate the kind of prudent supervision or consultation that the social worker obtained can be quite useful. I have heard many malpractice attorneys say, "If it's not written in the case record, it didn't happen."

DAMAGES IN LIABILITY CASES

If the social worker loses the suit, courts can award two kinds of damages, compensatory and/or punitive. In general damages include monetary compensation, which the law awards to the party injured by the action of another. Compensatory, or actual, damages include those directly related to the breach of duty and cover losses that can be readily proved to have been sustained and for which the injured party should be compensated as a matter of right, such as past or future earnings lost or the cost of mental health care.

Punitive, or exemplary, damages provide compensation in excess of compensatory or actual damages. They essentially constitute a form of punishment to the wrongdoer and extra compensation to the injured party. They are ordinarily awarded in instances of reckless, malicious, or willful misconduct (Edwards, Edwards, and Wells 2012; R. Cohen 1979; Gifis 2010). Courts award punitive damages much less frequently than compensatory damages (Meyer, Landis, and Hays 1988:14).

Courts may adjust monetary awards against social workers based on the concepts of joint liability, comparative negligence, contributory negligence, or assumption of risk. Under the doctrine of joint liability a court might find that a social worker and another party are responsible for the injury to the plaintiff. Imagine a social worker who is sued by a former client who alleges that he was placed in a psychiatric hospital against his wishes, in part because of inaccurate information that the social worker provided to the committing psychiatrist. If the plaintiff's claim has merit, a finding of joint liability could result—both the committing psychiatrist and the social worker who interviewed the client are held responsible.

For example, in an Oregon case a man whose baby died sued the state and a county mental health agency; he alleged negligent treatment of the infant's mother. The agency had removed the infant from the care of his mentally ill mother after she inappropriately gave him some of her own medication. After about six weeks the agency returned the infant to the mother, who several months later shot and killed the baby and then committed suicide. The court awarded the father $150,000, split between the state and the county mental health agency ("Inadequate Psychiatric Treatment" 1994:2).

In a Wisconsin case a woman who had been the victim of sexual abuse was admitted to a hospital psychiatric unit after she learned that a neighbor had sexually abused her son. The patient met a psychiatric nurse at the hospital and later left her husband and two children to live with the nurse. The woman subsequently sued the nurse, claiming the nurse had seduced her into a lesbian relationship and that the nurse caused the disruption of the plaintiff's marriage. The jury found the nurse 75 percent negligent and the hospital 25 percent negligent ("Psychiatric Nurse Seduced Woman" 1995:3).

This is in contrast to comparative negligence. According to the doctrine of comparative negligence, the court can distribute responsibility for damages between the plaintiff and defendant, based on the relative negligence of the two, particularly when the plaintiff's conduct contributed to the injury sustained as a result of the professional's negligence (known as contributory negligence; the client's own actions fell below the standard of self-care that an ordinary and reasonable person would exercise under the same or similar circumstances). As a result the court may reduce the amount of damages awarded to the plaintiff. Over the years the rather strict standard associated with the doctrine of contributory negligence—where a plaintiff who acted negligently may be barred from recovering damages—has given way to the broader doctrine of comparative negligence, where negligent plaintiffs may find their damages reduced by the proportion by which their negligence contributed to their injury (Edwards, Edwards, and Wells 2012; Litan and Winston 1988). (In some jurisdictions the court will reduce an award proportionately if a plaintiff was as much as 50 percent at fault, but the plaintiff who is equally or more than 50 percent at fault is awarded nothing.)

Imagine a client who sues a social worker, claiming failure to provide adequate protection in a group home. Another resident assaulted the client, who claims that the social worker—the group home director—should have had at least one other staff person working on that shift to provide the supervision necessary to prevent such an assault. The court could find the social worker liable in failing to have an adequate staff-to-client ratio but might also find that the plaintiff was negligent because his behavior provoked the assault. Damages may be awarded accordingly, taking into account the comparative negligence of the parties involved.

A number of court cases involving human service professionals and clinicians have resulted in findings of comparative negligence. For example, in a California case the surviving son of a man who committed suicide sued his father's therapist. The son claimed that the therapist failed to prevent his father's suicide by not hospitalizing him. The court awarded the son $602,000 but found that the decedent father was 40 percent negligent; the net award was $363,000 ("Plaintiffs Claim Failure to Continue Hospitalization" 1994:2).

In a Michigan case a man who had been admitted to a psychiatric hospital sustained serious injuries after he knocked out the window in a seclusion room in which he had been placed, made a rope with sheets, and jumped from the third floor. The man claimed that the hospital staff failed to supervise him properly and placed him in a room that was not escape-proof. The award in the case was $100,000, but it was reduced to $75,000 because of the plaintiff's 25 percent comparative negligence ("Man Claims Inadequate Observation" 1994:3).[2]

Several cases illustrate how awards for damages can address issues of both joint liability and comparative negligence. In a Colorado case a patient at a psychiatric center became involved sexually with an unlicensed mental health worker on the staff ("Sexual Relationship" 1995:3). The patient alleged that the relationship destroyed her marriage. The suit named the mental health worker, the medical director of the center, and the center itself. The award for the plaintiff was $29,145, but the court considered the plaintiff 30 percent negligent (comparative negligence). The court found that the unlicensed worker was 60 percent negligent and the medical director was 10 percent negligent (joint liability).

In a Missouri case a patient sued a physician for sexual misconduct during therapy ("Alleged Sexual Misconduct" 1994:6). The lawsuit also claimed that the physician was practicing psychotherapy without a license. The gross award in the case was $260,000. The court considered the plaintiff 5 percent negligent (comparative negligence) and split the remaining joint liability between the physician (60 percent) and the physician's employer (35 percent).

The concept of assumption of risk can also influence the outcome of a liability claim. In tort law defendants can use assumption of risk to claim that plaintiffs were aware of a condition or situation obviously dangerous to them yet voluntarily exposed themselves to the hazard or failed to take steps to avoid known danger. Thus contributory negligence arises when a plaintiff fails to exercise due care, while assumption of risk arises regardless of the care used and is based on the concept of consent (Gifis 2010).

Consider, for example, a client who, while being admitted to an inpatient psychiatric treatment program, voluntarily signs a statement that acknowledges that the discussion of personal problems during treatment might trigger emotional distress, depression, and other psychiatric symptoms. If the client subsequently sues the treatment staff and program, alleging that their treatment approach created more psychological symptoms than it alleviated, the defendants might argue that the client assumed the risk.

State legislatures use statutes of limitation to restrict the time period during which someone can file a negligence suit and seek damages. In some cases the period specified in the statute of limitations may begin at the date of the actual injury, while in other cases it may begin at the date that the person learned of the injury. Typically the statute of limitations applicable to minors begins to run when they reach the age of majority. Minors are not able to sue on their own behalf until they reach the age of majority; until a minor reaches the age of majority, a parent, guardian, or "next friend" of the minor can sue on his or her behalf. Thus adults can sue for injuries sustained during their childhood for a significant number of years after they reach the age of majority. The effective statute of limitations, as applied to the treatment of minors, is age of majority plus the relevant state's statute (Madden 1998, 2003; Schutz 1982:8).

Relatively few lawsuits actually reach court. Most malpractice and other professional liability claims (85 to 90 percent) are settled out of court (Edwards, Edwards, and Wells 2012; Meyer, Landis, and Hays 1988:14). Settlement of a case does not imply that the defendant admitted responsibility or was in any way culpable. Defendants may simply decide to cut their losses and settle out of court to avoid further legal and other expenses.

For those cases that actually reach court, rulings can be based on statutory law and constitutional law but are often based on common law. Previous court decisions establish common law, which is frequently known as case law.[3] Under the doctrine of stare decisis (Latin: to stand by decided matters), a judge determines whether a particular case falls within the ruling set forth in the earlier case. The judge may also generate a new law, or precedent, based on this particular case (Edwards, Edwards, and Wells 2012; Hogan 1979).

Social workers can obtain comprehensive liability insurance that offers legal defense coverage and indemnifies practitioners against liability. Policies are available that cover individual practitioners, social service agencies, corporations, social work students, and schools or departments of social work. These liability policies typically contain options with regard to the amount of coverage (for example, the amount of coverage for each wrongful act, or series of related wrongful acts, and the amount of aggregate coverage during a given policy period), coverage during extended reporting periods (that is, coverage for claims filed against a social worker after the end of the policy period), and coverage of employees (as in a private group practice). A typical social work policy is known as a claims-made policy, which means that the coverage is limited to liability for only those claims that are first made against the policy holder and reported to the company *during the period the policy is in force.* Social workers who also want to be insured for claims made after terminating the policy need to pay an additional premium for extended reporting period protection.

Professional liability policies also typically contain certain exclusions. Many policies exclude coverage for any dishonest, criminal, fraudulent, or malicious act or omission; fee disputes; a variety of wrongful acts of a managerial or administrative nature; any claim arising from any business relationship or venture with a former or current client; and a number of other specific activities enumerated in the policy. In addition most policies contain a special provision regarding coverage for sexual misconduct. Under this policy the company places a ceiling on the amount that it will pay for damages arising from actual or alleged sexual misconduct.

Even social workers employed in settings that provide group liability coverage should seriously consider obtaining their own individual coverage. When a liability claim names both the social worker and the worker's employer, the employer could argue that the social worker, and not the employing agency, was negligent. Individual coverage would thus protect workers who find themselves at odds with their employers in relation to a liability claim, particularly if the employer is not willing to retain separate legal counsel for the social worker. Also, most policies include a provision that will cover legal expenses if a social worker retains an attorney to assist in responding to a complaint filed with a state licensing board. Further, individual coverage protects individual social workers if claims against their employer's insurance policy exceed that policy's limits (for example, if a case involving client suicide leads to a $2.75 million judgment against an employer's insurance policy that has a $2 million limit).

Although liability claims and lawsuits filed against social workers are relatively rare, contemporary social workers must have a keen understanding of legal concepts related to malpractice, negligence, and liability. Licensing board complaints filed against social workers are more frequent. Most claims are preventable.

2

Confidentiality and Privileged Communication

THE CONCEPT OF PRIVACY

The concept of privacy is central to social work practice. In clinical work especially, social workers have always had a deep-seated respect for their clients' need for confidentiality. The trust between social worker and client, so essential to effective help, typically depends on the worker's assurance of privacy. Clients' willingness to disclose intimate, deeply personal details about their lives is understandably a function of their belief that their social worker will not share this information with others.

But privacy is also relevant in other social work domains. Social work administrators need to understand the limits of confidentiality as they pertain to personnel matters or sharing of information with colleagues in other agencies and organizations (insurance companies, accrediting bodies, utilization review representatives, human services departments, court and law enforcement officials). Protective service workers need to avoid excessive invasion of privacy while investigating reports of child or elder abuse and neglect. Social workers involved in community organizing need to appreciate the nature of privacy when they meet with local residents who air grievances about public officials. Social workers in social policy positions need to understand the tension between confidentiality rights and local open-meeting statutes, which may allow the public and media to attend sensitive high-level meetings.

The concept of privacy in professional practice to a great extent is rooted in pronouncements by the Pythagoreans in the fourth century B.C.E. and was later incorporated in the Hippocratic oath: "Whatever I see or hear, in the life of men, which ought not to be spoken of abroad, I will not divulge, as reckoning that all such should be kept secret." The concept of privacy was also an important component of ancient Jewish law, as conveyed in the Talmud. Early English common law also acknowledged the right to privacy associated with the concept of honor among gentlemen (Meyer, Landis, and Hays 1988:51).

The new American states legally codified privacy rights in 1791 in the Fourth and Fifth Amendments to the U.S. Constitution. However, medical privacy had no legal basis until 1828, when the State of New York established the physician-patient privilege. In the United States the first formal statement of the legal concept of privacy appeared in an 1890 essay, "The Right to Privacy," by Samuel Warren and Louis Brandeis. This germinal journal article ultimately served as the foundation for many court decisions and statutes. Warren and Brandeis defined *privacy* as the right to be left alone or elect not to share information about private matters, habits, and relationships (Meyer, Landis, and Hays 1988). Since then the concepts of privacy and confidentiality have assumed a prominent place among clients' most venerable rights (Donnelly 1978; Fisher 2013; Meyer, Landis, and Hays 1988).

Clarifying the meaning of, and differences between, *privacy* and *confidentiality* is important. *Privacy* refers to the right to noninterference in individuals' thoughts, knowledge, acts, associations, and property. Thus social workers' clients have a right to decide whether to share information about their emotional and behavioral challenges, sexual orientation, religious beliefs, and political ideology. Confidentiality rights arise when individuals entrust others with private information, usually because of a "vital need to share. It requires the explicit or implicit mutual understanding that this second individual will use it only for the first individual's vital need, and not make it available to a third party without the first person's consent" (Grossman 1978:139).

Schutz argues further that an invasion of privacy "is a violation of the right to be left alone. It requires that private acts be disclosed to more than a small group of persons, and such disclosure must be offensive to a reasonable person of ordinary sensibilities" (1982:11).

Contemporary social workers recognize that confidentiality cannot be absolute; clients' confidentiality rights have many exceptions. Widely accepted exceptions related to protection of third parties (for example,

mandatory reporting of child or elder abuse or neglect) and clients'
threats to harm themselves sometimes require disclosure of confidential
information. Hence clients have a right to relative (versus absolute) confidentiality (R. Cohen 1979; Dickson 1998; Fisher 2013; Meyer, Landis,
and Hays 1988).

Many of the earliest legal actions against professionals alleging breach
of confidentiality involved physicians. The first recorded appellate decision in the U.S. courts involving a physician's alleged breach of a patient's
confidence was decided in 1920 (*Simonsen v. Swenson*). In this instance the
Nebraska court ruled that the doctor had a privilege to disclose information
required to prevent the spread of a contagious disease (M. Lewis 1986:594).

Over time most jurisdictions in the United States have recognized legal
actions against psychotherapists and other social service professionals
in breach-of-confidence cases. Courts have varied, however, with respect
to the legal theory on which they have based their rulings. Suits alleging
wrongful disclosure of confidential information have been based on theories of (1) invasion of privacy, (2) express or implied statutory violations,
(3) breach of implied contract, and (4) tortious violation of the duty to
maintain confidentiality (M. Lewis 1986). In *Hammonds v. Aetna* (1965) a
federal district court in Ohio stressed the necessity of privacy in therapeutic relationships when it concluded that "the preservation of the patient's
privacy is no mere ethical duty upon the part of the doctor; there is a
legal duty as well. The unauthorized revelation of medical secrets or *any*
confidential communication given in the course of treatment, is tortious
conduct which may be the basis for an action in damages" (243 F. Supp. at
801–2). In *Horne v. Patton* (1974) an Alabama court was even more explicit
about invasion of privacy; it concluded that disclosure of confidential
information concerning a patient's mental health may constitute "unwarranted publicization of one's private affairs with which the public has no
legitimate concern such as to cause outrage, mental suffering, shame or
humiliation" (M. Lewis 1986:597). The concept of invasion of privacy was
also cited in *Doe v. Roe* (1977), in which a New York court found that a
therapist violated a patient's privacy rights by publishing a book containing
verbatim information that the patient disclosed during therapy sessions.

Some courts have also ruled that wrongful disclosure of confidential
information can be based on the theory of express or implied statutory violations, specifically statutes related to licensing, testimonial privilege, and

limiting the availability of medical information. In *Berry v. Moench* (1958) a Utah court ruled that patients may sue physicians when they disclose confidential information in violation of a statute that implicitly mandates confidentiality. In *Alberts v. Devine* (1985) the Supreme Judicial Court of Massachusetts ruled that a psychiatrist could be held liable for breach of confidence, based in part on a state statute limiting the availability of hospital records.

Several court decisions have cited the theory of breach of an implied contract (M. Lewis 1986; Meyer, Landis, and Hays 1988). In *Hammonds,* for example, the federal district court ruled that a physician's disclosure of confidential information constituted a breach of an implied contract between physician and patient. The court held that a simple contract is formed whenever a doctor and patient establish a relationship and that one condition of this contract is that information that the doctor learns during the course of the relationship will not be disclosed without the patient's permission. The court also said that within the context of such a relationship patients have the right to rely on the professional's "warranty of silence." Similar references to the theory of implied contract appear in *Horne* and *Doe v. Roe.*

Finally, some courts have cited the theory of breach of fiduciary duty in their opinions in cases involving wrongful disclosure. In *Alexander v. Knight* (1962), *Hague v. Williams* (1962), and *MacDonald v. Clinger* (1982), for example, state appellate courts held that medical professionals have a fiduciary duty to their patients that entails protecting confidential information and that a breach of that duty is actionable as a tort (a wrongful act or an infringement of a right leading to a legal liability). State courts also recognized tort actions in breach of confidentiality in *Vassiliades v. Garfinckel's* (1985), *Alberts v. Devine* (1985), and *Fedell v. Wierzbieniec* (1985).

Liability and malpractice problems related to privacy and confidentiality in social work usually fall into two broad categories. The first includes deliberate disclosure of confidential information, such as sharing with a third party threats that a client made against that person or filing a report of child or elder abuse against a client's wishes. The second includes inadvertent or accidental disclosure of confidential information, as in disclosing confidential documents without a client's authorization, posting sensitive information about a client on a social networking site (such as Facebook), leaving sensitive information about a client exposed on a table in a semipublic area, or discussing a client's circumstances in the hallway of the agency.

COMMON CONFIDENTIALITY ISSUES

Social workers encounter many instances when they have to make decisions about whether to disclose confidential information to third parties, such as personnel in other social service agencies, clients' family members or employers, law enforcement officials, or managed care organizations. Key issues include the disclosure of information to protect clients and third parties.

Protecting Clients and Third Parties

Judy S. was a social worker at the Ocean State Family Service Agency. Her client, Alan F., had sought treatment three months earlier for symptoms of depression. Alan F. reported that he has had low self-esteem for years, ever since his bitter divorce. He has struggled with alcoholism and has been hospitalized on three occasions following suicide attempts and suicidal ideation.

Alan F. was particularly agitated during one recent session. He told Judy S. that he and his former wife were in the middle of a big dispute about visitation and custody rights. Alan F. claimed that despite provisions in their divorce settlement, his former wife has been "doing everything she can to keep me from seeing the kids."

During the counseling session Alan F. went on and on about how his former wife was tormenting him. He was clearly distraught. Toward the end of the session Alan F. said, "I can't begin to tell you how much I hate that woman. She's ruining my life. You have no idea how much I'd like to get rid of her. Maybe I just ought to do it."

Nearly every clinical social worker can identify with the general circumstances presented in this case, a client who may pose a threat to a third party. In some instances the threat is clear and unambiguous, such as when a client explicitly announces an intention to harm a third party. By now there is considerable consensus that social workers and other mental health professionals need to take steps to protect such third parties, and this may entail disclosure of confidential information against the client's wishes.

In other instances, however, the validity of the threat is less clear. Many clients make vague threats during an intense therapy session. Often such threats are nothing more than blowing off steam. Yet, as we have learned all too well in recent years, such threats sometimes are genuine and purposeful.

The Tarasoff *case.* By now most social workers are acquainted with what is widely recognized as the red-letter precedent in so-called duty-to-protect cases: *Tarasoff v. Regents* (1976). In 1969 Prosenjit Poddar, an outpatient at Cowell Memorial Hospital at the University of California—Berkeley, informed his psychologist, Dr. Lawrence Moore, that he was planning to kill an unnamed young woman (easily identified as Tatiana Tarasoff) upon her return to the university from her summer vacation. After the counseling session in which Poddar announced his plan, the psychologist telephoned the university police and requested that they observe Poddar because he might need hospitalization as an individual who was "dangerous to himself or others." The psychologist followed the telephone call up with a letter requesting the help of the chief of the university police.

The campus police took Poddar into custody temporarily but released him based on evidence that he was rational; the police also warned Poddar to stay away from Tarasoff. At that point Poddar moved in with Tarasoff's brother in an apartment near where Tatiana Tarasoff lived with her parents. Shortly thereafter the psychologist's supervisor and the chief of the department of psychiatry, Dr. Harvey Powelson, asked the university police to return the psychologist's letter, ordered that the letter and the psychologist's case notes be destroyed, and directed that no further action be taken to hospitalize Poddar. No one warned Tatiana Tarasoff or her family of Poddar's threat. Poddar never returned to treatment. Two months later he killed Tatiana Tarasoff.

Tarasoff's parents sued the university's board of regents, several employees of the student health service, and the chief of the campus police, along with four of his officers, because their daughter was never notified of the threat. A lower court in California dismissed the suit, saying that sovereign immunity protected the multiple defendants. The court dismissed the civil action against the university, finding that Tarasoff's parents had no basis on which to sue because the university owed no duty of care to Tatiana, as she was not the patient. The California Supreme Court reversed the decision of the lower court and allowed the Tarasoffs to sue the university for failure to warn, returning the case to the lower court for retrial. In its 1976 ruling the California Supreme Court held that a mental health professional who knows that a client plans to harm another individual has a duty to protect the intended victim.[1] In the court's oft-cited words,

> We recognize the public interest in supporting effective treatment of mental illness and in protecting the rights of patients to privacy and the consequent public importance of safeguarding the confidential character of psychotherapeutic communication. Against this interest, however, we must weigh the public interest in safety from violent assault. . . . We conclude that the public policy favoring protection of the confidential character of patient-psychotherapist communications must yield to the extent to which disclosure is essential to avert danger to others. The protective privilege ends where the public peril begins.
>
> (551 P.2d at 336–37)

This landmark case was ultimately settled out of court for an undisclosed sum.

Since *Tarasoff* a number of important duty-to-protect cases have clarified the thinking of courts and legislatures about the circumstances under which mental health professionals are obligated to disclose confidential information against clients' wishes (National Conference of State Legislatures 2013; Simone and Fulero 2005). Some cases embrace and reinforce the court's reasoning in *Tarasoff*. Others challenge, extend, or otherwise modify the conclusions contained in the *Tarasoff* opinion. For example, in *McIntosh v. Milano* (1979) Lee Morgenstein, a patient of Dr. Michael Milano's, killed Kimberly McIntosh, a young woman with whom Morgenstein once had had a relationship but who no longer wanted to be involved with him. Morgenstein was fifteen when he entered treatment with Milano; a school psychologist had referred Morgenstein's parents to Milano because of their son's drug use. In treatment Lee Morgenstein had discussed how overwhelmed he was by his relationship with McIntosh and his intense feelings of jealousy since McIntosh had become involved with another boyfriend. Morgenstein had threatened McIntosh on a number of occasions, by firing a gun at her or her boyfriend's car and verbally threatening her and her dates. In addition Morgenstein had brought a knife into a therapy session and had discussed fantasies of violent retribution against people who frightened him. One day Morgenstein approached McIntosh, forced her to enter his car, took her to a park, and shot her.

In suing Milano, McIntosh's parents argued that by not warning their daughter, the therapist had departed from the standard of care in the profession. An expert witness, a psychiatrist, supported the parents' position.

The defense argued that the *Tarasoff* guidelines should not be applied because the State of New Jersey did not have a duty-to-protect statute. In particular the defense maintained that

> there is no such duty by a therapist to third parties or potential victims, and that *Tarasoff II* should not be applied, and was wrongly decided in that it (a) imposes an "unworkable" duty on therapists to warn another of a third person's dangerousness when that condition cannot be predicted with sufficient reliability; (b) will interfere with effective treatment by eliminating confidentiality; (c) may deter therapists from treating potentially violent patients in light of possible malpractice claims by third persons; and (d) will result in increased commitments of patients to mental or penal institutions.
>
> (Austin, Moline, and Williams 1990:98)[2]

Consistent with *Tarasoff*, however, the New Jersey Superior Court held that a therapist "may have a duty to take whatever steps are reasonably necessary to protect an intended or potential victim of his patient when he determines, or should determine, in the appropriate factual setting and in accordance with the standards of his profession that the patient is or may present a probability of danger to that person" (1982:56).

In *Davis v. Lhim* (1983) the Michigan courts also reinforced the logic of *Tarasoff*. Ruby Davis, administrator of the estate of Mollie Barnes, sued Dr. Yong-Oh-Lhim, a staff psychiatrist at Northville State Mental Hospital. Barnes, who was shot and killed by her son, John Patterson, had not been warned of a threat against her. Patterson had committed himself to the state hospital voluntarily several times during a three-year period. His problems included depression, insomnia, and schizophrenia. On September 2, 1975, Patterson asked Lhim to release him from the hospital. Lhim complied and released Patterson to the custody of his mother. Patterson initially stayed with his aunt, Ruby Davis, because his mother was visiting her brother, Clinton Bell. As time passed, however, the mother found her son too hard to handle and drove him to Bell's home. Patterson entered the Bell home, found a handgun, and began firing it. Patterson shot and killed his mother when she tried to take the gun from him.

The Wayne County Circuit Court concluded that Mollie Barnes was a foreseeable victim because Lhim knew of a threat that Patterson had made against her. The court found in favor of the plaintiff and ultimately was upheld on appeal.

The *Tarasoff* decision also clearly influenced the outcome of *Chrite v. United States* (1983). In this case Warner Chrite sued a Veterans Administration (VA) hospital in Massachusetts; he alleged that no one had warned his wife, Catherine, about a threat posed by a VA patient, Henry O. Smith, who was her son-in-law. Smith was released from the hospital under a state law that does not permit a patient to remain under supervision, without court permission, for more than sixty days. On the day he was released, Smith wrote a note stating, "Was Henry O. Smith Here Yesterday. He is wanted for murder Mother in Law." Hospital staff recorded the note in Smith's chart but did not warn his mother-in-law, Catherine Chrite. Smith carried out his threat after being released. The U.S. District Court ruled in favor of Warner Chrite, concluding that hospital staff had an obligation to warn Catherine Chrite about the threat. Because of the details in the note, the court ruled, Catherine Chrite should have been considered a foreseeable victim.

Tarasoff also had a direct influence in *Jablonski v. United States* (1983). In this case Meghan Jablonski sued the Veterans Administration hospital in Loma Linda, California, in the death of her mother, Melinda Kimball. Phillip Jablonski, Kimball's son-in-law, killed her; he was a patient at the hospital at the time of the slaying. Phillip Jablonski had gone to the VA hospital voluntarily for a psychiatric examination, after threatening Isobel Pahls, Kimball's mother, with a knife and attempting to rape her. The police spoke with the head of psychiatric services at the hospital and informed him of Phillip Jablonski's criminal record, including his obscene telephone calls to Pahls, and encouraged the medical staff to place Phillip Jablonski in an inpatient unit. In addition Kimball informed another physician that Phillip Jablonski had served a prison term for a rape conviction and said that four days earlier Phillip Jablonski had attempted to rape her mother. The federal district court found the government liable, saying that the staff should have concluded, based on the information and previous records available, that Kimball was a foreseeable victim.

In *Mavroudis v. Superior Court* (1980) the California courts further spelled out that the danger of violence to others must be an "imminent threat of serious danger to a readily identifiable victim" in order to justify a duty to warn. In *Thompson v. County of Alameda* (1980) the California courts narrowed the requirement even further by suggesting that a duty to warn exists only when someone has made specific threats against identifiable victims. In this case a chronic juvenile sex offender, "James," informed authorities that he intended to kill whatever child he next accosted. Nonetheless a juvenile counselor, who was also a licensed therapist, released the youngster, who ultimately carried out his threat. The parents of the slain youth, a five-year-old boy, sued the county authorities, alleging negligence because a dangerous juvenile was released into the community; they further claimed that the county authorities' supervision of James's legal custodian (his mother) was improper and that no one had warned the local police, neighborhood parents, or James's mother about his violent tendencies. The Superior Court of Alameda County ruled that because county officials could not have identified and warned a specific victim, the county had no duty to protect the child who was killed. The court dismissed the case, and the parents appealed. The Supreme Court of California affirmed the lower court's decision (Austin, Moline, and Williams 1990:100).[3]

The federal courts further stressed the importance of foreseeable harm and an identifiable victim in *Leedy v. Hartnett* (1981). Harrison and Gertrude Leedy sued the Veterans Administration hospital in Lebanon, Pennsylvania, after no one warned them that a patient, John Hartnett, had a tendency to get violent when drinking. Hartnett, a disabled veteran who received treatment at the hospital between 1956 and 1978, had been diagnosed with paranoid schizophrenia and chronic alcoholism. Hospital staffers apparently were familiar with Hartnett's violent tendencies during a period of at least ten years. On September 26, 1977, Hartnett discharged himself from the hospital and told hospital staffers that he would be staying with the Leedys. On March 31, 1978, Hartnett and the Leedys went to a club to celebrate Hartnett's birthday. Hartnett drank twenty-four 12-ounce bottles or cans of beer. Early the next morning at two, Hartnett assaulted the Leedys at their home.

The Leedys sued the hospital, claiming negligence because no one warned them of Hartnett's violent tendencies. The hospital argued that it could not be held responsible for Hartnett's actions because he never informed the staff of his intent to harm the Leedys. The federal district court ruled in favor of the hospital, concluding that the Leedys were in no greater danger than anyone else who came into contact with Hartnett. The court ruled that Hartnett did not make *specific* threats at the time of discharge and his actions therefore were not foreseeable (Austin, Moline, and Williams 1990:101).

A federal district court in Colorado used similar reasoning when it dismissed *Brady v. Hopper* (1983), in which victims of John Hinckley's assault on President Ronald Reagan sued, alleging negligence. Hinckley's parents had brought him to Dr. John Hopper after Hinckley attempted to commit suicide. During his treatment with Hopper, Hinckley never specifically mentioned his intention to kill the president. Moreover, the defense argued, Hinckley had no history of violence and no previous hospitalizations because of violence. The court determined that Hinckley's therapist, Hopper, did not have a duty to protect the victims because Hinckley did not make explicit threats against these specific victims (Meyer, Landis, and Hays 1988:44).

The absence of specific threats against victims also influenced the decision in *Cairl v. State* (1982). In this case Steven J. Cairl, who owned a small apartment building, sued Minnesota, the Ramsey County Welfare Department, and Bruce Hedge, the community reentry facilitator at the Minnesota Learning Center, because residents of the building, including Mary Ann Connolly and her two daughters, were not warned of the dangerous tendencies of Connolly's son. Tom Connolly, a resident at the Minnesota Learning Center who had an IQ of 57, was released to his family's home for the Christmas holiday; such home visits were consistent with the center's treatment philosophy. Learning Center staffers knew that Tom Connolly had set fires but concluded that "the fires Mr. Connolly had set while at the center were not sufficient to cause concern" (Austin, Moline, and Williams 1990:107). Mary Ann Connolly had been informed of the home visit plan, and on December 21, 1977, Hedge drove Tom Connolly to her home. On December 23, 1977, Tom Connolly set fire to the living room couch; one of his sisters was severely burned, another died of her injuries, and Cairl's property was destroyed.

At the initial trial in the District Court of Ramsey County, the court ruled that the hospital staff was not negligent in failing to warn the building's residents because Tom Connolly had not specifically stated that he would injure any of them; further, the court concluded, Mary Ann Connolly was aware of her son's fire-setting history. Cairl appealed the ruling, which was affirmed by the Supreme Court of Minnesota.[4]

The absence of a specific threat also influenced the outcome of *Rogers v. South Carolina* (1989). A woman had been admitted to psychiatric hospitals on nine occasions. She had a substantial record suggesting a long-standing delusion of persecution by her family. After her release from one of her hospitalizations, the woman claimed that her sister was trying to poison her. Two weeks later she shot and killed her sister. The personal representative of the sister's estate filed a wrongful death suit against the patient's psychiatrist, alleging that the doctor had a duty to warn the sister that the patient might harm her. The South Carolina Court of Appeals concluded in part that because there was no evidence that the patient had made specific threats against her sister while being treated by the psychiatrist, the psychiatrist had no duty to warn the sister ("Psychiatrist Did Not Owe" 1989:3).[5]

Social workers should be aware, however, that some courts have not insisted on evidence of an identifiable victim to justify disclosure to protect a third party. In *Carr v. Howard, Massachusetts* (1996), for example, a Massachusetts Superior Court judge rejected the traditional *Tarasoff* guidelines that require evidence of "specific threats to specific easily recognizable victims" (Lambert 1996:228). In this case a hospital employee was injured by a psychiatric patient who attempted to commit suicide by leaping off the upper level of the hospital's parking garage. According to Lambert,

> The reach of *Tarasoff* has been steadily stretched by other courts to encompass more than "specific threats to specific victims." See, e.g., *Hamman v. County of Maricopa*, 775 P.2d 1122 (Ariz. 1989), 32 ATLA L. Rep. 182–85 (June 1989) (going beyond *Tarasoff*, Arizona rejects specific threat to specific limit of *Tarasoff* and holds that therapist's or doctor's duty may run to and encompass non-privity third parties who are endangered by a violence-prone patient, here the enraged son's stepfather).
>
> (1996:230)[6]

At least one case suggests that therapists may have a duty to hospitalize potentially dangerous clients to protect potential victims. In *Currie v. United States* (1986) a patient at a VA outpatient clinic who was in treatment to address posttraumatic stress disorder threatened to blow up a building owned by IBM, his former employer. The therapist involved in the case believed that the patient posed a threat and contacted IBM, the FBI, local police, and the U.S. attorney's office. The therapist did not, however, believe that the patient met the commitment criteria under North Carolina law. Some time later the patient took homemade explosives and a gun to an IBM office and killed an employee.

The victim's estate sued the VA, claiming that it had not warned all potential victims and alleging negligence in not seeking the man's commitment. The defense argued that the duty to protect did not pertain because the victim was one of many IBM employees and hence could not have been identified. The defense also argued that the therapist had no duty to commit because "the patient did not meet the involuntary commitment criteria. The U.S. District Court held that patients who act out at random or in only broadly predictable ways do in fact create a duty for therapists. The court also ruled that the therapist wrongly interpreted the state's commitment criteria and that the patient was indeed committable" (Meyer, Landis, and Hays 1988:45–46).

Similar issues were raised in *Lipari v. Sears* (1980). Ruth Ann Lipari sued Sears, Roebuck because a psychiatric patient, Ulysses L. Cribbs, had bought a gun at a Sears store; also named in the suit was the federal government because Cribbs was a patient at a VA hospital. One night Cribbs entered an Omaha nightclub and fired shots into the room, killing Dennis Lipari and seriously wounding Ruth Ann Lipari. After Lipari filed her suit, Sears, Roebuck and Lipari joined forces in *Sears v. U.S.,* suing the VA hospital because Cribbs had not been detained or committed. Court papers disclosed that Cribbs had been committed to a mental institution and started treatment in a day program at the VA hospital approximately two months before the shooting. The federal district court denied the government's motion for a summary judgment and ultimately agreed with the plaintiffs' argument that the Veterans Administration was negligent because it had failed to commit Cribbs.

Many states have adopted the guidelines, in the form of statutes and regulations, that were established in *Tarasoff* and other duty-to-protect cases; some state laws require mental health professionals to disclose confidential information to protect a potential victim, while others permit disclosure to protect a potential victim (Dickson 1998; Fisher 2013; Kopels and Kagle 1993; National Conference of State Legislatures 2013; Simone and Fulero 2005). However, a Maryland court did not accept the reasoning in *Tarasoff* in *Shaw v. Glickman* (1980). In this case Leonard Billian; his wife, Mary Ann; and her lover, Dr. Daniel Shaw, were all in treatment with a team led by Dr. Leonard Gallant, who died after the events at issue occurred (Glickman was named as a defendant because he was the personal representative of Gallant's estate). While in treatment Mary Ann Billian left her husband. One night Leonard Billian entered Shaw's home at 2 A.M. and found Shaw and Mary Ann Billian both nude and asleep in the same bed. Leonard Billian shot Shaw five times. Shaw survived and sued Gallant, the team leader, arguing that he was negligent because he had not warned Shaw of Leonard Billian's "unstable and violent condition and the foreseeable and immediate danger that it presented to Dr. Shaw." The Superior Court of Baltimore City ruled in Gallant's favor—concluding that Gallant did not have a duty to warn—and granted him a summary judgment. Shaw appealed. The Maryland appellate court affirmed the lower court decision, concluding that because Leonard Billian never stated his intent to kill or injure Shaw, and Shaw assumed the risk of injury when he went to bed with Mary Ann Billian, Gallant did not have a duty to warn. Moreover the court argued that it would have been "a violation of the statute for Dr. Gallant or any member of his psychiatric team to disclose to Dr. Shaw any propensity on the part of Billian to invoke the old Solon law and shoot his wife's lover" (Schutz 1982:57).

A Florida court too apparently challenged the *Tarasoff* doctrine in *Boynton v. Burglass* (1991). In this case the plaintiff sued a psychiatrist, alleging that the psychiatrist had a duty to warn and did not do so. A patient of the psychiatrist had killed the plaintiff's son. The suit alleged that the psychiatrist had a duty to warn the intended victim, the victim's family, or law enforcement officials of the threat of violence and that the slaying resulted from the breach of that duty. The suit stated that the patient had threatened to kill the plaintiff's son during a therapy session.

The Florida trial court dismissed the suit because it failed to state a claim (i.e., the plaintiff failed to set forth sufficient facts to entitle recovery against the defendant, should the plaintiff win the case); the plaintiff appealed. The appellate court affirmed the trial court's decision, concluding that "it would be fundamentally unfair to impose a duty to warn upon psychotherapists because psychiatry is an inexact science and a patient's dangerousness cannot be predicted with any degree of accuracy" ("Psychotherapist Has No Duty to Warn" 1992:3). In addition the appellate court concluded that the psychiatrist would have violated both his duty to his patient and Florida's statutory psychotherapist-patient privilege had he disclosed any threat by the patient to harm the victim. The court opinion also expressed concern about the possibility that patients' trust and confidence would be undermined if a clinician were required to warn potential victims whenever a patient expressed hostile feelings toward a third party.[7]

A widely publicized and controversial Connecticut case, *Almonte v. New York Medical College* (1994), raised several novel duty-to-protect issues. The plaintiff, who was ten years old at the time, was brought to a hospital as a suicide risk. A physician completing his residency in child psychiatry treated the boy. As part of his training, the resident was also in treatment with a psychiatrist, with whom he shared a fantasy about having sex with children—and an unsuccessful trip to Mexico to find a child. The Connecticut boy alleged that the psychiatry resident fondled and attempted to sodomize him during treatment sessions. The psychiatry resident was found negligent ("Psychiatry Resident" 1999). In addition the federal district court in Connecticut held that the Manhattan-based doctor who treated the resident had a duty to warn or otherwise prevent the resident from sexually abusing the boy (*Garamella v. New York Medical College* (1998)). The court held that "even without breaching the confidentiality of the resident's communications, the instructor was authorized to notify the medical college that . . . the resident had revealed information that made him unsuitable for psychoanalytic training . . . and . . . the college would be advised to review whether the resident should remain in the residency program practicing child psychiatry" ("Doctor Who Conducted Training" 1999:4).

Courts have been reluctant to extend the *Tarasoff* reasoning to cases involving suicide. In *Bellah v. Greenson* (1978), for instance, a therapist's patient committed suicide, and the family members claimed that they should have been warned of this possibility. The California courts held, however, that the clinician had no duty to warn unless there was a risk of "violent assault to others" (Meyer, Landis, and Hays 1988:43). Although the ruling did not conclude that therapists *cannot* provide such warnings, it did assert that therapists are not *required* to violate confidentiality.

Clearly the *Tarasoff* decision unleashed considerable debate and controversy concerning the limits of clients' right to confidentiality. Proponents argue that it is naive to believe that the right to confidentiality is inviolable. Public safety, they assert, sometimes must trump privacy rights, particularly when a third party is at risk of serious or violent harm.

Critics, however, argue that *Tarasoff*-like guidelines are like the camel's nose under the tent. Once the perimeter has been breached, the entire structure is at risk. One commonly cited concern is that mental health practitioners have relatively poor records of predicting clients' violent behavior (Dickson 1998; Kopels and Kagle 1993; Quinsey, Harris, Rice, and Cormier 2005; Schutz 1982:55, 59–60). Thus it makes little sense to base a practitioner's obligation to disclose confidential information to protect third parties on the assumption that professionals are in fact able to predict future violence accurately. Grossman (1978) has been one of the most ardent critics. Referring to the California Supreme Court's ruling in *Tarasoff*, Grossman states,

> The court also keeps using statements such as "to *predict* that Poddar presented a serious danger of violence . . . [and] did in fact *predict* that Poddar *would* kill." It indicates that the *amicus* brief introduced by national professional organizations did bring to their attention from the authoritative source of the treating professions that therapists can *not* predict a violent act. The statistics of studied experiences ran approximately one eventual violent act out of 100 "predictions." None of these studies compared these to the average population incidence of violence. Nor was mention made that therapists can detect thought and emotional processes having a violence theme. At times they may detect a weakening of the ordinary restraints that keep such themes from overt expression, but they certainly cannot predict the future external events that may trigger such an increased weakening of control of the violent emotion or thought that leads to either a verbal or physical assault. They cannot predict whether an act that may take place, should control break, will be verbally or physically assaultive.
>
> (1978:159–60)

In addition critics question the assumption that providing a warning to a potential victim is likely to, in and of itself, prevent a violent act. According to Grossman, the belief that such warnings are likely to provide real protection is naive:

> Approximately 50 people interested in *Tarasoff* were informally asked, "If you were warned under these circumstances—a psychiatric patient on the loose, who had threatened your life during therapy—how would you

protect yourself?" Most first answered, "I'd call the police." When told of the above cases [where warnings seemed not to be effective], they gave one of these replies: "I would hate going into hiding"; "I don't know"; and "I'd kill him if he came near." The warning offers no protection and may well harm the supposed victim.

(1978:163)

Over time the influence of *Tarasoff* as a legal precedent has become more limited because many jurisdictions have adopted specific statutes addressing duty-to-protect issues. Social workers should determine whether their state has such a statute and understand its provisions, which can vary from jurisdiction to jurisdiction. For example, in some states a social worker may have a duty to disclose confidential information, whereas in others social workers may be permitted to disclose. This is an important distinction.

Balancing confidentiality and protection. The litigation in the various duty-to-protect cases over the years has helped to clarify the precarious trade-offs between social workers' obligation to respect clients' right to confidentiality and therapists' simultaneous duty to protect third parties from harm. Although some rulings in these cases are inconsistent and contradictory, the general trend suggests that four conditions ordinarily justify disclosure of confidential information to protect a third party from harm. First, the social worker should have evidence that the client poses a threat of violence to a third party. As the court said in *Tarasoff,* "When a therapist determines, or pursuant to the standards of his profession should determine, that his patient presents a serious danger of violence to another, he incurs an obligation to use reasonable care to protect the intended victim against such danger" (551 P.2d at 340 (1976)). Although courts have not provided precise definitions of *violence,* the term ordinarily implies the use of force—by use of a gun, knife, or other deadly weapon—to inflict harm.

Second, the social worker should have evidence that the violent act is foreseeable. That is, the social worker should be able to present evidence that suggests significant risk that the violent act will occur. Although courts recognize that social workers, and other human service professionals, cannot make foolproof predictions, social workers must be able to demonstrate that they had good reasons for believing that their client was likely to carry out the violent act.

Third, the social worker should have evidence that the violent act is imminent. That is, the social worker should be able to present evidence that the act was impending or likely to occur relatively soon. Here too the courts have not provided clear, unambiguous guidelines. *Imminence* may be defined differently by different practitioners, ranging from minutes to hours to weeks from the moment of decision. Ultimately social workers need to be able to make a strong case to defend their definition of *imminence*.

Finally, a number of court decisions—although not all (see, for example, the discussion of *Lipari v. Sears* (1980))—suggest that a practitioner must be able to identify the probable victim. The rationale here is that disclosure of confidential information against a client's wishes should not occur unless the social worker has specific information about the client's apparent intent. This would include knowledge of an actual potential victim. As M. Lewis observes,

> Though not stated in either opinion, it appeared that both *Tarasoff* and *McIntosh* required that there be a particular or readily identifiable potential victim in order to impose liability for negligent failure to warn. In *Thompson v. County of Alameda,* the California Supreme Court clarified this requirement. The *Thompson* court found no cause of action where the threats uttered by a juvenile offender to county officials did not constitute specific threats against particular individuals, but rather, were directed to an entire class. The court concluded that the county could not be liable for negligent failure to warn or to take other steps to protect an entire class of children to whom the juvenile posed a threat.
>
> (1986:588–89)

Note, however, that when a social worker can infer the identity of a foreseeable victim from case-related material—even if the client has not specifically named the potential victim—a duty to protect may exist (Austin, Moline, and Williams 1990:119).

These guidelines generally are reflected in the National Association of Social Workers' *Code of Ethics:*

> Social workers should protect the confidentiality of all information obtained in the course of professional service, except for compelling professional reasons. The general expectation that social workers will keep

information confidential does not apply when disclosure is necessary to prevent serious, foreseeable, and imminent harm to a client or other identifiable person. In all instances, social workers should disclose the least amount of confidential information necessary to achieve the desired purpose; only information that is directly relevant to the purpose for which the disclosure is made should be revealed.

(standard 1.07[c])

The ambiguity of "duty to protect." Despite the rulings in *Tarasoff* and subsequent duty-to-protect cases, practitioners and lawyers continue to disagree about the wisdom of the general guidelines for disclosing confidential information and about their application to various cases (National Conference of State Legislatures 2013; Simone and Fulero 2005). By now they generally agree that a social worker whose client makes a clear threat to violently injure an identifiable victim within the next several hours has a duty to take steps to protect the potential victim. This may include disclosing confidential information against a client's wishes. Other cases, however, are less clear.

Consider, for example, a case in which a social worker's client is HIV positive and seems to pose a threat to his sexual partner, who is not aware of the client's infection. The social worker does her best to encourage the client to disclose his health status to his sexual partner, but for a variety of complex clinical reasons the client does not share this information with his partner. This set of circumstances is complicated, and there has been considerable disagreement about the relevance of the *Tarasoff* and other duty-to-protect guidelines that have evolved since that decision. When the *Tarasoff* case was decided, no one anticipated its eventual application to AIDS cases. In fact the final *Tarasoff* decision in 1976 preceded by five years the first AIDS case identified in the United States. Since then, however, the debate about the relevance of *Tarasoff* to AIDS cases has been vigorous (Chenneville 2000). Some argue, for example, that *Tarasoff* is not an adequate precedent because people with AIDS may not specifically and explicitly threaten a third party with an act of violence. People who are HIV positive usually are concerned about their partners and willing to practice safer sex, although they may be unwilling to disclose their HIV-positive status to their partners. In addition the threat to third parties may not always be imminent, and the victim may not be identifiable (Kain 1988). As Francis and Chin argue, "Maintenance of confidentiality is central to and of paramount importance for the control of AIDS. Information regarding infection with a deadly virus, sexual activity, sexual contacts and the illegal use of IV drugs and diagnostic information regarding AIDS-related disease are sensitive issues that, if released by the patient or someone involved in health care, could adversely affect a patient's personal and professional life" (1987:1364).

However, some claim that the HIV-positive status of an individual, which merely *poses* a threat to another party, is sufficient to rely on *Tarasoff* and related cases as precedents (Chenneville 2000; Dickson 2001; Lamb et al. 1989). As Gray and Harding conclude, "A sexually active, seropositive individual places an uninformed sexual partner (or partners) at peril, and the situation therefore falls under the legal spirit of the *Tarasoff* case and the ethical tenets of 'clear and imminent danger'" (1988:221). As the president of the American Professional Agency, a major malpractice insurer of social workers, said, "We can pay for breach of confidentiality, but we can't bring the dead back to life" ("Malpractice" 1997).

Although precise, unequivocal guidelines governing disclosure of confidential information to protect third parties do not exist, social workers can minimize their liability risks (Austin, Moline, and Williams 1990; Schutz 1982). For example, faced with a client who may pose a threat to a third party, the social worker should

- Consult with supervisors and colleagues about the best way to manage the situation, and document the consultation
- Consult an attorney who is familiar with state law concerning the duty to warn and/or protect third parties (state laws vary considerably on the obligations of health-care professionals with respect to confidentiality and the duty to protect)
- Consider asking the client to warn the victim (unless the social worker believes this contact would only increase the risk)
- Seek the client's consent for the social worker to warn the potential victim
- Disclose only the minimum amount necessary to protect the potential victim and/or the public
- Encourage the client to agree to a joint session with the potential victim in order to discuss issues surrounding the threat (unless this might increase the risk)
- Encourage the client to surrender any weapons he or she may have

- Increase the frequency of therapeutic sessions and other forms of monitoring
- Be available or have a backup available, at least by telephone
- Refer the client to a psychiatrist if medication might be appropriate and helpful or if a psychiatric evaluation appears to be warranted
- Consider hospitalization, preferably voluntary, if appropriate

Throughout this process social workers should seek relevant consultation from colleagues who have experience in dealing with dangerous clients and should document this consultation, the nature of their own thinking about the case, and the rationale for whatever decision the social worker ultimately makes.

Most important, clients must be informed at the beginning of service that while the therapist ordinarily respects the right to confidentiality, legal limits do exist. As the NASW *Code of Ethics* states:

> Social workers should discuss with clients and other interested parties the nature of confidentiality and limitations of clients' right to confidentiality. Social workers should review with clients circumstances where confidential information may be requested and where disclosure of confidential information may be legally required. This discussion should occur as soon as possible in the social worker-client relationship and as needed throughout the course of the relationship.
>
> (standard 1.07[e])

Social workers should include a brief explanation of confidentiality limits on an information sheet prepared for clients (see NASW *Code of Ethics,* standard 1.07[e]). The form would provide clients with a summary of agency policy concerning disclosure of confidential information: compliance with the law, the circumstances under which the social worker has a duty to warn or protect, reimbursement policies and legal actions that may require disclosure, and emergencies (see the appendix for a sample form). Other items on this information sheet might pertain to service hours, fees, instructions in case of emergency, and the inability to guarantee success in treatment. Clients might be asked to sign a copy of this document, to be inserted in their file, attesting that they read it, understand its content, and were given an opportunity to ask questions. As the NASW *Code of Ethics* states, social workers should also explain confidentiality guidelines to clients; these discussions should be documented.

When a social worker concludes that disclosure is necessary, who should be notified or warned is not always clear. Schutz offers sage advice in these circumstances:

> Generally, it is suggested that the authorities and/or the intended victim should be warned. Warning the authorities makes the most sense when the intended victims are the patient's children, since a warning to the victim is ordinarily useless, and the child protective agency often has broader powers than the police—who might say that they cannot detain the patient (particularly after a failed commitment) because he has not done anything yet. If one decides to warn the victim—who is naturally shocked and terrified by the news that someone intends to kill him—and if nothing occurs, one could be liable for infliction of emotional distress by a negligent diagnosis. One way to reduce this risk might be to include as a part of the warning a statement of professional opinion about the nature and likelihood of the threat; to recommend that the victim contact the police, an attorney, and a mental health professional for assistance to detain (or try to commit) the patient; to inform the victim of his legal rights; and to offer assistance with the stress of such a situation.
>
> (1982:64)

Many attorneys recommend always notifying law enforcement officials, even when the intended victim is warned. From a legal risk management perspective, notifying law enforcement officials shares the responsibility with other professionals.

One pitfall is that social workers' concern about liability could lead them to overreact. That is, to avoid risk social workers might disclose information too quickly or seek civil commitment of individuals who do not in fact require confinement. Such excessive caution can create its own problems. Unnecessary intrusion and violation of clients' rights can trigger legal claims that allege defamation of character, negligent diagnosis, infliction of emotional distress, false imprisonment, invasion of privacy, and malicious prosecution.

In the end social workers must use their judgment about the tension between protecting a client's right to confidentiality and protecting third parties from harm. Explicit, unambiguous guidelines for those decisions cannot be drawn. As M. Lewis notes, "It must . . . be recognized that psychotherapy is an imperfect science. A precise formula for determining when the duty to maintain confidentiality should yield to the duty to warn is, therefore, beyond reach" (1986:614–15). Although court decisions provide some guidance, social workers ultimately must rely on thoughtful judgment based on prudent consultation. After reviewing case law and statutes on the issue, M. Lewis goes on to say,

> The acceptance by many jurisdictions of the duty imposed on psychotherapists to warn or take other reasonable steps for the protection of their patients' potential victims, viewed contemporaneously with an increasing recognition that patients have a right to sue for damages for unauthorized disclosure of confidential information, places mental health professionals in an unenviable predicament. *Tarasoff* and its progeny established that persons harmed by individuals undergoing therapy may sue that patient's psychotherapist for negligent failure to protect them from the patients' dangerous propensities. Case law also makes it clear that mental health professionals have a duty to maintain the confidential nature of their relationships to those to whom they are rendering treatment. A breach of either duty may result in civil liability. The inquiry that arises out of this conflict is whether therapists can uphold a duty of reasonable care with respect to potential victims while continuing to exercise reasonable care toward their patients.
>
> (1986:605–6)

Alcohol and Substance Abuse Treatment

Social workers also need to be well informed about comprehensive restrictions concerning disclosure of confidential information pertaining to alcohol and substance abuse treatment. Strict federal regulations—Confidentiality of Alcohol and Drug Abuse Patient Records—limit social workers' disclosure of confidential information. These regulations broadly protect the confidentiality of the records of substance abuse programs—with respect to the identity, diagnosis, prognosis, or treatment of any client—maintained in connection with any program or activity relating to substance abuse education, prevention, training, treatment, rehabilitation, or research that is conducted, regulated, or directly or indirectly assisted by any federal department or agency. Disclosures are permitted (1) with the written, informed consent of the client; (2) to medical personnel in emergencies; (3) for research, evaluation, and audits; and (4) by court order for good cause (Dickson 1998).[8]

The Patriot Act

The USA Patriot Act was created in response to the attacks of September 11, 2001, and became law less than two months after those attacks. The act gives federal officials greater authority to track and intercept communications, both for law enforcement and foreign intelligence–gathering purposes. It creates new crimes, new penalties, and new procedures for use against domestic and international terrorists. Critics contend some of its provisions go too far and pose a threat to counseling and psychotherapy clients.

Section 215 of the act contains an exception to confidentiality in that it not only requires therapists (and others) to provide FBI agents with books, records, papers, documents, and other items, but it also then prohibits the mental health counselor from disclosing to the client that the FBI sought or obtained the items under the act. This places a clinical social worker in an untenable position in that he is prohibited by law from acting in a client's best interests (informing the client that law enforcement officials have contacted the clinician about the client); in effect the social worker would be functioning as an informant rather than clinician.

The act requires FBI agents to show prior written approval from the FBI director or deputy director and reasonable, factual grounds to prove that the records sought under section 215 are relevant to a terrorism investigation. Officials who request records must assert that they are pertinent to the activities of a suspected terrorist or person in contact with a suspected terrorist. Under the act the recipient of a records request may consult with an attorney and file a challenge to a records request with a Foreign Intelligence Surveillance Court judge.

Student Education Records

Social workers employed in school settings should be familiar with the Family Educational Rights and Privacy Act (FERPA, also known as Buckley) as amended and with its attendant federal regulations. This federal law protects the privacy of student education records and applies to all schools that receive money from the U.S. Department of Education. For example, parents or eligible students have the right to inspect and review the student's education records maintained by the school. Generally schools must have written permission from the parent or eligible student in order to release any information from a student's education record. However, FERPA allows schools to disclose those records, without consent, to certain parties and under specific conditions (for example, to comply with a court order or lawfully issued subpoena, in cases of health and safety emergencies).

More specifically FERPA gives parents certain rights with respect to their children's education records. These rights transfer to the student when she reaches the age of eighteen or attends a school beyond the high school level. Students to whom the rights have transferred are "eligible students." These rights are

- To inspect and review the student's education records maintained by the school. Schools are not required to provide copies of records unless, for reasons such as great distance, it is impossible for parents or eligible students to review the records. Schools may charge a fee for copies.
- To request that a school correct records that parents or eligible students believe to be inaccurate or misleading. If the school decides not to emend the record, the parent or eligible student then has the right to a formal hearing. After the hearing, if the school still decides not to emend the record, the parent or eligible student has the right to place a statement with the record setting forth his view about the contested information.

Generally schools must have written permission from the parent or eligible student in order to release any information from a student's education record. However, FERPA (sec. 99.31) allows schools to disclose those records, without consent, to the following parties or under the following conditions:

School officials with legitimate educational interest
Other schools to which a student is transferring
Specified officials for audit or evaluation purposes
Appropriate parties in connection with financial aid to a student
Organizations conducting certain studies for or on behalf of the school

Accrediting organizations

Compliance with a judicial order or lawfully issued subpoena

Appropriate officials in cases of health and safety emergencies

State and local authorities, within a juvenile justice system, pursuant to specific state law

Schools may disclose, without consent, "directory information" such as a student's name, address, telephone number, date and place of birth, honors and awards, and dates of attendance. However, schools must tell parents and eligible students about directory information and allow parents and eligible students a reasonable amount of time to request that the school not disclose directory information about them. Schools must notify parents and eligible students annually of their rights under FERPA. The actual means of notification (special letter, inclusion in a PTA bulletin, student handbook, or newspaper article) is left to the discretion of each school.

School social workers should take steps to segregate their clinical notes from students' educational records. School administrators and teachers should not have access to social workers' counseling notes.

Deceased Clients

Social workers sometimes receive requests for confidential information about former clients who have died. Surviving family members of a client who committed suicide may seek information to help them understand and cope with their loss, or social workers may be subpoenaed in a legal matter involving a dispute among family members concerning the former client's will. A newspaper reporter or law enforcement official may request information about a deceased client who was somehow involved in a serious crime, or an Internal Revenue Service official may ask for information about a deceased client's lifestyle.

Clients' confidentiality rights do not end in death; thus social workers must take careful steps to protect the confidentiality of deceased clients. As the NASW *Code of Ethics* states, "Social workers should protect the confidentiality of deceased clients" (standard 1.07[r]). Practitioners should not disclose confidential information unless they have obtained proper legal authorization to do so (for example, in the form of a court order or permission from the legal representative of the client's estate).

In one case in which I consulted, an experienced clinical social worker made the mistake of granting an interview to a reporter who was investigating the death of one of the social worker's clients. The social worker specialized in the treatment of sex offenders and inadvertently disclosed confidential information about her deceased client. The state licensing board sanctioned the social worker.

A widely publicized case involved the nationally known therapist Susan Forward, who had been treating Nicole Brown Simpson, the former wife of O. J. Simpson. Forward appeared on several national interview programs and was among the first to disclose Nicole Brown Simpson's history of abuse by O. J. Simpson. The regulatory board in California concluded that Forward's disclosure of confidential information about her deceased client violated professional standards and suspended Forward's license to practice for three months. The board also placed Forward on probation (Madden 1998).[9]

Parents and Guardians

Social workers who provide services to children and adolescents sometimes must make difficult decisions about the disclosure of confidential information. Often these situations occur when minors are engaging in self-destructive behaviors (e.g., high-risk sexual activity, drug abuse, suicidal gestures) or threaten to harm others.

State laws and regulations vary with respect to social workers' obligations in these situations. Social workers should consult local statutes, regulations, and officials to determine the extent to which they are (1) obligated to disclose confidential information to parents and guardians, even without the minor client's consent; (2) permitted—but not obligated—to disclose confidential information to parents or guardians without the minor client's consent; and (3) not permitted to disclose confidential information to parents or guardians without the minor client's consent.

Most states have statutes that explicitly address minors' right to obtain mental health or substance abuse treatment services without notification of parents or parents' consent. Statutory provisions vary considerably among the states; many states have one law governing minors' right to mental health services and another law regarding substance abuse treatment services. For example, some state laws permit minors of a certain age (for example, sixteen) to obtain mental health services without parental notification or consent but permit minors of any age to obtain substance abuse treatment without parental notification or consent. Some state laws permit social workers to provide services to minors without parental notification or consent if the social worker believes that notification of the parents without the minor's consent would be harmful to the minor (for example, if there is evidence that the parents would abuse the child upon learning about the child's substance abuse). Still other state laws permit social workers to provide substance abuse treatment services without parental consent only if two physicians certify that the minor requires addiction services. Given the considerable variation in state laws and that they can change over time, social workers should be sure to consult their state laws as needed.

Family, Couples, and Group Counseling

Social workers who provide services to families, couples, or groups sometimes encounter difficult ethical dilemmas related to confidentiality. For example, members of a family, couple, or group may not respect other clients' confidentiality or will expect the social worker to keep secrets from other family, couple, or group members. According to the NASW *Code of Ethics:*

> When social workers provide counseling services to families, couples, or groups, social workers should seek agreement among the parties involved concerning each individual's right to confidentiality and obligation to preserve the confidentiality of information shared by others. Social workers should inform participants in family, couples, or group counseling that social workers cannot guarantee that all participants will honor such agreements.
>
> (standard 1.07[f])

> Social workers should inform clients involved in family, couples, marital, or group counseling of the social worker's, employer's, and agency's policy concerning the social worker's disclosure of confidential information among the parties involved in the counseling.
>
> (standard 1.07[g])

Many practitioners present clients with forms that explain the importance of confidentiality and request each client's agreement to honor other clients' rights to confidentiality (see appendix).

Before beginning counseling relationships, social workers should ensure that their clients fully understand whether and to what extent their therapeutic communications are privileged under the law, and the rights of each party to access and release the social worker's clinical record. If communications are made in the presence of an unprivileged third party, they may not be privileged, unless the law provides for exemption. Some jurisdictions protect communications made during family or group therapy.

Many social workers who provide counseling to couples are not willing to provide individual counseling to one or both members of the couple, because of the possibility of a conflict of interest and challenges managing the parties' confidential disclosures in individuals' counseling sessions. For example, a husband who receives individual counseling from the couple's therapist may disclose sensitive information in an individual counseling session that he does not want the social worker to share with the husband's spouse (for example, his involvement in an extramarital affair). This places the social worker in a difficult and uncomfortable situation. To avoid such predicaments many social workers who provide couples counseling insist on referring partners to other clinicians for individual counseling.

Disclosure to Outside Agencies

Social workers sometimes receive requests for confidential information from third parties who have some interest in clients' circumstances. Practitioners need to handle these requests carefully, avoiding disclosure without written authorization by the client or other legitimate party.

When clients authorize disclosures to reporters (for example, when a journalist wants to feature a client in a story about how people cope with mental health problems), social workers should discuss with clients in detail the risks that may be involved in permitting their social worker to talk with a reporter (for example, the risks associated with publicity) as well as potential benefits.[10]

Social workers should also be careful when responding to requests for confidential information from law enforcement officials, protective service agencies, and collection agencies. When disclosure is appropriate or required, social workers should limit the disclosure as much as possible. As the NASW *Code of Ethics* states, "In all instances, social workers should disclose the least amount of confidential information necessary to achieve the desired purpose; only information that is directly relevant to the purpose for which the disclosure is made should be revealed" (standard 1.07[c]).

Electronic Records and Communications

A wide range of technological innovations has enabled social workers to transmit confidential information quickly and efficiently, for example, using e-mail and fax machines. Social workers should take a variety of steps to protect clients' confidentiality. According to the NASW *Code of Ethics,*

> Social workers should protect the confidentiality of clients' written and electronic records and other sensitive information. Social workers should take reasonable steps to ensure that clients' records are stored in a secure location and that clients' records are not available to others who are not authorized to have access.
>
> (standard 1.07[l])

> Social workers should take precautions to ensure and maintain the confidentiality of information transmitted to other parties through the use of computers, electronic mail, facsimile machines, telephones and telephone answering machines, and other electronic or computer technology. Disclosure of identifying information should be avoided whenever possible.
>
> (standard 1.07[m])

For example, social workers who use fax machines should obtain clients' informed consent and inform clients about the potential risks involved (i.e., unauthorized individuals may have access to these unprotected communications). Also, social workers should notify the intended recipient by telephone that the fax is being sent and obtain the recipient's agreement to immediately retrieve the document from the fax machine. The document's cover sheet should include a statement alerting recipients to the confidential nature of the communication, along with the sender's telephone number.

Further, practitioners should not leave confidential details in telephone messages intended for their clients if the practitioners are not entirely certain who has access to the telephone messages. As a precaution social workers should talk with clients early in their relationship about where and how to leave messages in a way that safeguards the client's privacy and confidentiality. Clients' preferences should be documented in the clinical record to ensure that all staffers who serve the clients honor their wishes.

Internet communications are also quite risky. E-mail messages can be sent to the wrong party and may not be secure. Social workers should inform clients of their e-mail-related policies. For example, many practitioners have developed what are known as social media policies that inform clients that they are not to use e-mail or social networking sites (such as Facebook) to communicate with social workers about their clinical concerns. A typical social media policy informs clients that social workers cannot guarantee a timely response to e-mail or other electronic messages and that these messages may not be secure. Social workers should discuss their policies with clients at the beginning of their relationship to avoid any misunderstanding (Kolmes 2012).

Social workers must become intimately familiar with the federal regulations that focus explicitly on electronic communications initiated by health-care providers. The Health Insurance Portability and Accountability Act (HIPAA) and its regulations require that personal health information be kept confidential. Failure to comply can result in civil and criminal penalties. Protected health information includes information about a person's health, health care, or payment for health care that identifies a person and is created or received by a covered health-care provider. The term *health* includes mental health and behavioral health. Protected health information may not be disclosed by a covered entity without the informed and voluntary written consent or authorization of the client. Consistent with NASW *Code of Ethics* standards, disclosure of confidential information must be limited to the minimum amount necessary for the purposes of the disclosure, when providers need access to clients' full records; the exception is the transfer of records for treatment. Clients requesting the information must be given a history of disclosures of their protected health information.

To comply with HIPAA regulations, covered health-care providers must designate a privacy official who will develop and implement the privacy policies and procedures of the agency; develop policies and procedures designed to ensure that covered entities are in compliance with the standards and requirements of the regulations; provide privacy training to staff and develop a system of sanctions for employees who violate the agency's policies; meet documentation requirements; and provide written notice of privacy practices in plain English. The notice of privacy practices must include a description of the client's rights, describe anticipated uses and disclosures of information that may be made without authorization (giving at least one example), identify a contact person in the event of a complaint, and inform clients of the right to register a complaint with the secretary of the U.S. Department of Health and Human Services. The agency must post the notice in a visible location, and clients must receive a written copy during their first visit.

Several exceptions under the HIPAA regulations permit disclosure of clients' protected health information without client consent or authorization. Examples include disclosures required by law; disclosures for public health activities (such as reporting diseases, collecting vital statistics); disclosure about victims of abuse, neglect, or domestic violence; disclosures for judicial or administrative proceedings; disclosures for law enforcement purposes; and disclosures to prevent a serious threat to health or safety.

Clinical social workers should be aware that under HIPAA regulations "psychotherapy notes" have special privacy protections. Ordinarily clients must give written consent before a third party can receive psychotherapy notes. The regulations define *psychotherapy notes* as notes recorded (in any medium) by a health-care provider who is a mental health professional documenting or analyzing the contents of conversation during a private counseling session or a group, joint, or family counseling session and that are separated from the rest of the individual's medical record. Excluded from the definition of psychotherapy notes are prescriptions for and monitoring of medication, counseling session start and stop times, modalities and frequencies of treatment furnished, results of clinical tests, and any summary of client diagnosis, functional status, treatment plan, symptoms, prognosis, and progress to date.

The Health Information Technology for Economic and Clinical Health (HITECH) Act, enacted as part of the American Recovery and Reinvestment Act of 2009, was signed into law on February 17, 2009, to promote the adoption and meaningful use of health information technology. Subtitle D of the HITECH Act addresses the privacy and security concerns associated with the electronic transmission of health information, in part through several provisions that strengthen the civil and criminal enforcement of the

HIPAA rules. Section D also implements new rules for the disclosure of patient health information if a breach takes place.

Overall the HITECH Act significantly modifies HIPAA (1996). HITECH expands HIPAA's definition of *business associates* and provides that the HIPAA security standards that apply to health plans and health-care providers will also apply directly to business associates, that is, anyone who must use protected health information, such as billing clerks, as well as the health and mental health professionals with whom social workers collaborate. The HITECH Act also makes the HIPAA privacy provisions applicable to business associates.

Third-Party Payers

Practitioners often receive requests from third-party payers, such as insurance and managed care companies, for information about clients. This information may concern clients' clinical symptoms and profiles, treatment history, and treatment plan. To comply with prevailing ethics standards and federal regulations under HIPAA, social workers should obtain clients' consent or authorization before disclosing such confidential information. Some social workers include wording on the informed-consent or release-of-information form for this purpose that acknowledges that the client understands that the social workers cannot be responsible for protecting confidential information once it is shared with the third-party entity and that the client releases the social worker from any liability connected with a breach of confidentiality by a third-party payer (sometimes called a "hold harmless" clause). According to the NASW *Code of Ethics,* "Social workers should not disclose confidential information to third-party payers unless clients have authorized such disclosure" (standard 1.07[h]).

Transfer or Disposal of Clients' Records

Practitioners who transfer a case record or other confidential material to another agency or colleague should take steps to protect the confidentiality of the information. Further, social workers also should dispose of records (when permitted by relevant regulations, statutes, and standards) in a manner that protects client confidentiality. Confidential paper records should be shredded or otherwise destroyed to prevent access by unauthorized individuals. Electronic records should be properly encrypted and protected from unauthorized access. According to the NASW *Code of Ethics,* "Social workers should transfer or dispose of clients' records in a manner that protects clients' confidentiality and is consistent with state statutes governing records and social work licensure" (standard 1.07[n]).

Client Confidentiality and the Social Worker's Death, Incapacitation, or Employment Termination

Social workers need to prepare for the possibility that they may not be able to continue working with clients because of disability, illness, employment termination, or death. Practitioners should develop procedures to ensure continuity of service and to protect clients' confidential records. This may include arranging for colleagues to assume at least initial responsibility for her cases if the social worker is unable to continue practicing. According to the NASW *Code of Ethics,* "Social workers should take reasonable precautions to protect client confidentiality in the event of the social worker's termination of practice, incapacitation, or death" (standard 1.07[o]). Such steps may include oral or written agreements with colleagues or stipulations that appear in a plan that the practitioner develops with the assistance of a lawyer (for example, designating a personal representative who will manage the social worker's professional affairs). Many experts recommend that social workers prepare a professional will that includes plans for the transfer or disposition of cases if the practitioner dies or becomes incapacitated (Bradley, Hendricks, and Kabell 2012). The will can provide for an executor or trustee who will maintain records for a certain period of time, at the end of which the social worker's practice and records will be sold to a designated colleague for a nominal fee. Such an arrangement can prevent unauthorized people from gaining access to confidential information.

A professional will enables social workers to plan for what happens if they die or become incapacitated. It spells out the steps that colleagues or other parties should take to ensure that clients' needs are met in a timely fashion. This guidance can be particularly helpful when death or incapacitation occurs without forewarning. A comprehensive professional will should address several key issues.

Who will assume responsibility? Social workers need to designate an individual or individuals who will take charge in the event of a social worker's death or incapacitation. This may be a colleague or another trusted party; ideally this designee is a trained professional who is familiar with ethical standards in social work that pertain to client confidentiality and informed consent.

The professional will should include detailed contact information, for example, telephone numbers (land line, mobile, fax), office address, e-mail address. It makes sense to designate one or two backup administrators as well. Social workers should meet with their designee to ensure that that person fully understands the details of the professional will. Practitioners should provide information about the location of office keys and security codes. Administrator-designees should also have information about voice-mail access codes in order to review and respond to clients' messages.

Client records. Social workers should inform their designees about the location of clients' physical records and filing cabinet keys. Social workers who maintain electronic records should ensure that their designees have relevant computer usernames and passwords and information about the names of computer files that hold records. A social worker's administrator-designee should also know how to access the social worker's schedules so that clients who have upcoming appointments can be notified. The professional will can state who will store the records until more permanent arrangements can be made.

Informed consent and client notification. When social workers begin working with clients, they should consider obtaining clients' consent to share their contact information and, if necessary, clinical records with the social worker's designee in the event of an emergency. This can be included in the initial consent to provide services that social workers have clients sign.

Professional wills may identify specific ways that social workers' designees can notify clients of the social worker's incapacitation or death, such as calling each client, placing a notice in the local newspaper, changing the social worker's outgoing voice-mail message to include the announcement, changing the voice-mail message to ask clients to call the social worker's designee for implementing the deceased or incapacitated practitioner's professional will, and sending letters. Which notification approach is most appropriate depends on the nature of the social worker's unique practice and clientele.

Ideally designees who notify clients about the social worker's death or incapacitation should provide clients with information about steps they can take to arrange other services. This may include the names of other providers and their contact information. Whatever forms of notification are considered, social workers and their designees should be mindful of clients' right to privacy and confidentiality. Letters, e-mail messages, and telephone or voice-mail messages that are not carefully handled can inadvertently disclose to third parties that a person is seeing a clinical social worker. This can be particularly problematic, for example, when the client is a domestic violence victim who sought clinical social work services without her partner's knowledge; unintentional disclosure to the abusive partner may exacerbate the client's risk.

Notification of colleagues, insurers, and attorneys. A professional will should identify members of the social worker's peer consultation group to notify in the event of the social worker's death or incapacitation. It should also include information about the social worker's professional malpractice insurer, policy number, and contact information. Further, a professional will should include the name of, and contact information for, an attorney the social worker has used for professional consultation.

Billing information. The social worker's designee will need to know where billing records are located, how to access them (whether paper or electronic records), who prepares and processes the bills (for example, a billing service or office clerical worker), and how pending charges are to be handled.

Expenses. Managing a deceased or incapacitated colleague's affairs can be very time consuming. A professional will ought to specify how the social worker's designee will be compensated. Options include authorizing a customary hourly rate the designee is to be paid, a flat fee, or a token payment. A professional will should include clear instructions about how all expenses are to be paid.

Social workers would do well to have a skilled attorney—particularly one who has expertise in health and mental health law—help prepare and review a draft of the professional will. Once the professional will has been finalized, the social worker should give copies to his attorney and designee. Social workers and their attorneys should decide whether to give the designees access to confidential information such as computer usernames and passwords when the professional will is signed or only upon the social worker's death or incapacitation. Social workers should review and update their professional wills on a regular basis (for example, yearly).

Collection Agencies

It is reasonable for social workers to contact collection agencies when they encounter serious difficulty collecting payment from clients. Before doing so social workers should make every effort to provide clients with sufficient notice and reasonable payment plans (some practitioners wisely inform clients at the beginning of service about how they will handle overdue payments).

When social workers find it necessary to contact collection agencies, they should have strict procedures in place to prevent the inappropriate disclosure of confidential information (for example, clinical information). Information shared with collection agencies should be limited to the client's name, address, telephone number, and the amount of the debt. Social workers should be aware that some state regulations and laws prohibit disclosure of information about clients to collection agencies.

Social workers should keep in mind that bill collection efforts sometimes lead to a licensing board complaint alleging incompetent or harmful treatment. Attorneys typically advise social workers to avoid allowing clients accumulate large bills; when this occurs, social workers become creditors and run the risk of having a conflict of interest and acting in dual roles.

Consultants

Social workers' consultation with colleagues is often reasonable and necessary. To protect clients social workers should obtain their informed consent to share confidential information with consultants when necessary. In addition social workers should share with consultants the least amount of information necessary to achieve the purposes of the consultation. According to the NASW *Code of Ethics,* "Social workers should not disclose identifying information when discussing clients with consultants unless the client has consented to disclosure of confidential information or there is a compelling need for such disclosure" (standard 1.07[q]).

Volunteers and Employees

Social workers should take steps to ensure that volunteers and employees have access only to that confidential information necessary in order to carry out their duties (i.e., they should have access to confidential information on a need-to-know basis). Volunteers and employees should be trained to handle confidential information responsibly. For example, volunteers and paid staff should be trained not to disclose clients' identity and how to avoid inadvertent and unintentional disclosure of confidential information (e.g., responding to a request for confidential information by a police officer or family member, responding to a subpoena, avoiding hallway conversations about clients and leaving confidential information on a desk or displayed on a computer screen). Many agencies ask volunteers and employees to sign formal confidentiality agreements that spell out their duties and responsibilities.

Disclosing Information for Teaching or Training Purposes

Social work educators and trainers often present case material for instructional purposes. In such instances social workers should not disclose any identifying information without clients' informed consent. Clients' names should not be mentioned, and presenters should disguise or alter case-related details to ensure anonymity. Any written case material should be similarly disguised. According to the NASW *Code of Ethics,* "Social workers should not disclose identifying information when discussing clients for teaching or training purposes unless the client has consented to disclosure of confidential information" (standard 1.07[p]).

Social workers who present audio- or video-recorded material should also take careful steps to protect clients. Such material should not be presented unless clients have provided informed consent to the taping itself and to the presentation of the material. With video records it may be possible to protect client confidentiality by recording clients from an angle that limits their visibility or by blurring their distinguishing characteristics (face and voice, especially). According to the NASW *Code of Ethics,* "Social workers should obtain clients' informed consent before audiotaping or videotaping clients or permitting observation of services to clients by a third party" (standard 1.03[f]).

Social workers need to assess clients' ability to make sound judgments about consenting to the disclosure of identifying information or images for teaching or training purposes. Clients who are asked for their consent may feel some pressure, whether intended or not, to accede to their social worker's request. Social workers should be careful to avoid any exploitation or the appearance of exploitation (see NASW *Code of Ethics,* standard 1.06[b]).

Classroom educators should ensure that their students understand their obligation to protect client confidentiality when students are asked to include case material in written assignments or presentations. Educators should discuss with students various ways in which they can disguise case material and avoid disclosing identifying information.

Unauthorized Access

Social workers employed in agency settings must not access confidential client records without authorization. On occasion licensing boards have disciplined social workers when they examined confidential records about people known to them but who were not clients (State of Ohio 2008). Social workers should access confidential records only when they are authorized to do so and on a need-to-know basis.

THE CONCEPT OF PRIVILEGED COMMUNICATION

The *Tarasoff* case and other duty-to-protect cases litigated since *Tarasoff* raise a variety of complex issues concerning the limits of clients' right to privacy, particularly when third parties appear to be at risk. As I noted earlier, privacy and confidentiality are essential ingredients in therapeutic relationships. Nonetheless clients' rights to privacy and confidentiality have limits. For example, social workers now widely accept mandatory reporting laws related to child abuse.

To understand the limits of privacy and confidentiality, social workers must be familiar with the doctrine of privileged communication. The right of privileged communication—which assumes that a professional cannot disclose confidential information without the client's consent—originated in British common law, under which no gentleman could be required to testify against another individual in court. Among professionals the attorney-client relationship was the first to gain the right of privileged communication. Over time other groups of professionals, such as physicians, psychiatrists, psychologists, and clergy, sought legislation to provide them with this right. Social work is one of the most recent professions to actively seek such legislation (Fisher 2013; Madden 2003; Wilson 1978).

Social workers need to understand the distinction between *confidentiality* and *privilege*. *Confidentiality* refers to the professional norm that information shared by or pertaining to clients will not be shared with third parties. *Privilege* refers to the disclosure of confidential information in court or legal proceedings. As Meyer, Landis, and Hays say,

> The terms confidentiality and privilege, though often confused, actually refer to different legal concepts. Confidentiality refers to the broad expectation that what is revealed in a private or "special" relationship based upon trust will not be shared with third parties. Obviously, the kind of information revealed by individuals in therapy fits into this category. Privilege is a narrower concept that concerns the admissibility of information in a court of law, though in practice it really refers to whether courts may legitimately compel revelation of confidential information for the purpose of legal proceedings.
>
> (1988:51–52)

Various groups of professionals have argued that they and their clients or patients need statutory protection from requests to reveal confidential information. As a result many states have enacted legislation that permits practitioners to withhold information shared by a client in confidence. Courts commonly accept four conditions, originally proposed by the jurist John Henry Wigmore, as necessary to the consideration of information as privileged:

- The parties involved in the conversation assumed that it was confidential.
- Confidentiality was an important element in this relationship.
- The community recognizes the importance of this relationship.
- The harm caused by disclosure of the confidential information would outweigh the benefits of disclosure during legal proceedings.

(Wigmore 1961:52)

Regarding the first condition, social workers can reasonably assume that most clients expect that information that they share will be kept confidential. As Hamilton (1951) argued,

It is part of the attributes of a profession that the nature of the confidential relationship assumes significance. In lay intercourse intimate things are told at the teller's own risk. Under authoritative external pressures or prosecution it is assumed that a person is not obliged to incriminate himself, but in law, medicine, and religion it is imperative for successful treatment that the person put himself unreservedly into the hands of his counselor or practitioner or priest. In a general way this is true of social work, and as professional competence has increasingly developed skill in the interviewing process, the client tends to yield himself fully, trusting in the worker's understanding and skill to help him.

(39)

Further, a central tenet of social work practice is that effective casework depends on clients' willingness to trust workers with the most personal details of their lives and that such trust is necessary if this relationship is to be meaningful and productive. In addition the community at large generally accepts the assumption that relations between clients and practitioners are important and valuable, thus satisfying Wigmore's third condition. The fourth condition, that the injury caused by disclosure of confidential information is greater than the benefit gained from disclosure, is ordinarily the most difficult to satisfy and triggers the greatest debate. As the *Washington University Law Quarterly* explains ("Note" 1965):

Against these facts and speculation as to the harm that results from forced disclosure and the frequency with which disclosure occurs, society's interest in the correct disposal of litigation must be balanced. That interest is obviously great, but does not seem to have a constant value, i.e., society as a whole has a greater interest in the correct disposal of a charge of murder than it has in a charge of peace disturbance arising from a marital quarrel. Thus the answer to Wigmore's fourth requirement can be viewed as depending upon the facts of a particular case rather than a predetermined evaluation. For example, the correct disposal of the murder charge probably outweighs any injury that would inure to the social worker–client relation. But the desirability of preserving a marriage of thirty years seems to override the benefit which would be gained by the correct disposal of the charge of peace disturbance.

(quoted in Wilson 1978:114–15)

The most significant court decision with direct bearing on social workers is the landmark case of *Jaffe v. Redmond* (1996), in which the U.S. Supreme Court ruled that the clients of clinical social workers have the right to privileged communication in federal courts (Alexander 1997). In this case a police officer, Mary Lu Redmond, sought counseling from a social worker after the officer killed Ricky Allen, a man involved in a fight. The social worker objected to a court order to disclose notes that she made during counseling sessions with Redmond, arguing that the psychotherapist privilege protected the contents of the conversation. In its decision the U.S. Supreme Court said that "participants [in therapy] must be able to predict with some degree of certainty whether particular discussions will be protected. An uncertain privilege, or one which purports to be certain but results in widely varying applications by the courts, is little better than no privilege at all" (116 S. Ct. at 1932 (1996)). This case is particularly important because it established, for the first time in U.S. legal history, that clinical social worker–client relationships are privileged in federal court proceedings; until the *Jaffe* decision only some state courts recognized social worker–client privilege.

It is important to note that the *client* holds the privilege, not the social worker; the practitioner has a duty to assert the client's privilege and protect relevant information from disclosure. Over the years courts have identified a number of exceptions to the client's right of privileged communication. A number of these exceptions pertain to judicial proceedings, such as when a client introduces in court information that he has received counseling for emotional problems resulting from an automobile accident that has led to a suit for damages or when a social worker's testimony about a client is required so the social worker can defend against a suit filed by the client. Disclosure of privileged information may also be permissible when a client threatens to commit suicide, shares information in the presence of a third person, is a minor and is the subject of a custody dispute, is involved in criminal activity or has been abused or neglected, is impaired and may pose a threat to the public (an actively alcoholic airline pilot or bus driver), has not paid his or her fees and a collection agency is retained, threatens to injure a third party, or has informed the social worker about having committed a serious crime (Fisher 2013; Lakin 1988; VandeCreek, Knapp, and Herzog 1988; Wilson 1978).

Cases in which clients admit or confess to commission of a crime can be particularly troublesome. On the one hand social workers may want to avoid undermining clients' trust by disclosing confidential information. After all, many clients seek out social workers for the express purpose of addressing their guilt feelings and sense of remorse about misdeeds. Practitioners may not want to discourage these constructive efforts. At the same time, however, social workers can understand the legitimate claim by the public that it has a right and need to know who perpetrated serious crimes, particularly those that have not led to an arrest. According to Madden, however, "the general rule is that mental health workers are not required to report past criminal acts of a client. There is no compelling public policy rationale comparable to the protection of public safety in the duty-to-warn cases" (1998:80).[11] Social workers must also recognize that the NASW *Code of Ethics* prohibits disclosure of confidential information when such disclosure would not prevent serious, imminent, and foreseeable harm in the future (for example, when a client tells a social worker that she committed a serious crime years earlier; see standard 1.07[c]). A client's commission of a serious crime years earlier is not likely to provide contemporaneous evidence of serious, imminent, and foreseeable harm.

Although statutes are relatively clear that social workers must disclose information shared by clients concerning child or elder abuse or neglect, they offer less guidance with respect to other crimes committed by clients.[12] In *Missouri v. Beatty* (1989) a psychiatrist's patient admitted during a therapy session that she had robbed a local service station earlier in the day. The psychiatrist placed an anonymous telephone call to the local Crime Stoppers office and, without identifying his patient, reported that the offender had been employed at the restaurant where his patient worked. The Crime Stoppers staff passed this information on to the police, who eventually arrested the patient.

The patient argued in court that her psychiatrist violated her confidentiality rights and that any related evidence should not be admissible. The Missouri Court of Appeals upheld the patient's conviction, ruling that the psychiatrist had not violated the physician-patient privilege because the law creating that privilege applied only to a psychiatrist's in-court testimony ("Psychiatrist's Crime Tip" 1990:1).

In a 1989 California case (*California v. Kevin F.*) a resident at a substance abuse treatment facility confessed to his psychotherapist that six months earlier he had set fire to a friend's home, knowing that people were inside, in an attempt to hide evidence of a theft. A friend of the client's mother and the woman's son were seriously injured. Several months later the psychotherapist referred to the confession in a report to the client's probation officer. The client was eventually charged with arson and placed in a juvenile correctional facility. He appealed his adjudication, arguing that the psychotherapist's disclosure of the confession violated the state's privileged communication statute. The California Court of Appeal ruled, however, that the confession fell under a statutory exception that permitted disclosure when a psychotherapist had reason to believe an individual posed a danger to himself or others ("No Violation of Confidentiality" 1990:4).

In *California v. Cabral* (1993) the California Court of Appeal held that the psychotherapist-patient privilege did not protect a defendant's letter to a therapist in which the patient admitted that he had sexually abused his daughter. The father had written asking to participate in a therapeutic program that the psychologist directed. The psychologist shared the letter with law enforcement officials, and the trial court admitted the letter into evidence. The appeals court held that the letter was not privileged because it did not meet the statutory definition of a confidential communication between "patient and psychotherapist" ("Privilege Did Not Protect" 1993).

Social workers who facilitate group, couples, or family treatment must be especially alert to privileged communication guidelines. Some professionals argue that a client who discloses information to third parties in group, couples, or family treatment forfeits the right to the privilege (because of the client's willingness to share this information with others). Others argue, however, that this sort of disclosure should not invalidate the privilege, and in recent years several states have passed laws that protect the privileged content of group and family therapy sessions (Fisher 2013; Madden 2003). In addition several courts have generally recognized this principle. In *Minnesota v. Andring* (1984), for example, the Minnesota Supreme Court acknowledged that group therapy does involve an expectation of privacy and that the privilege should apply (Meyer, Landis, and Hays 1988). The court ruled on a defendant's attempt to access the records of group therapy sessions. The court concluded that in a group therapy context each client is the therapeutic agent of the other, and the presence of third parties is essential to the unique goals of group therapy. Several years later the California Court of Appeal heard a similar case (*Lovett v. Superior Court* (1988)) brought by a father accused of sexually assaulting his teenage daughter (Madden 1998). The father wanted to question members of a support group in which the daughter participated to help her cope with her traumatic experiences. The court rejected the father's claim that he should have access to group members' testimony.

Also, in *Hulsey v. Stotts* (1994) a federal district court in Oklahoma held that a man who participated in joint counseling with a former girlfriend did not waive the psychotherapist-patient privilege with respect to those sessions. The former girlfriend sought to depose the therapist who conducted the counseling. The court ruled that each member of joint counseling has the right to prevent disclosure by the other: "No division may be made as to where one therapy ends and another's begins" ("Man in Joint Counseling" 1995).

In a 1990 case involving marital therapy (*Cabrera v. Cabrera*), the Connecticut Appellate Court rejected the husband's argument that confidential information shared by the wife with the couple's psychologist was not privileged and should have been disclosed in court. The husband had appealed the outcome of divorce and custody proceedings and wanted to introduce the psychologist's testimony to support his arguments. The husband claimed that the disclosures made by the wife occurred during marital counseling rather than psychological counseling and therefore were not privileged. The appeals court held that the wife's communications were privileged, and, because she had not waived the privilege, the psychologist could not testify about her sessions with the wife or her sessions with the couple. The court concluded that "it would make no sense . . . to divide visits to a psychologist in a case such as this into marital counseling versus psychological counseling and assign privileged status to the latter but not the former" ("Psychologist-Patient Privilege Prevents Counselor" 1991:5).

In contrast in *Redding v. Virginia Mason Medical Center* (1994) the Washington Court of Appeals held that the therapist-patient privilege did *not* protect statements made by one spouse during joint counseling sessions from being disclosed in a later custody dispute between the couple. The court ruled that the records were not privileged because allegations that the wife had a drinking problem, which were discussed in joint sessions, would be significant to a court deciding the custody dispute ("Psychologist-Patient Privilege Did Not Protect Statements" 1994).

In several cases courts have considered allegations that mental health professionals disclosed privileged information inappropriately in custody and divorce proceedings. In *Renzi v. Morrison* (1994) the Illinois Appellate Court held that a psychiatrist inappropriately disclosed confidential information about a patient while testifying for the patient's spouse during a child custody hearing. The psychiatrist evaluated the patient and provided her with counseling services. The psychiatrist then testified at the custody hearing and disclosed information about the patient's psychological test results (which the psychiatrist had shared with the husband); the court awarded temporary custody of the child to the husband. The patient won her suit against the psychiatrist, based on her claim that the psychiatrist's testimony violated her right to privileged communication ("Psychiatrist Who Discloses" 1994). Also, in *Runyon v. Smith* (1999) a New Jersey appeals court ruled that a psychologist breached the client's right to privileged communication by disclosing, without the client's consent, information from a counseling session that led to the client's loss of custody of her children ("Psychologist Breaches . . . Privilege" 2000).13

Social workers should also keep in mind the distinction between formal group therapy and self-help groups. A court may recognize therapist-client privilege with respect to group treatment, where the social worker is functioning in the role of therapist, but not with respect to a self-help group. In a famous New York case members of an Alcoholics Anonymous (AA) group were subpoenaed to testify in a matter involving a group member accused of brutally murdering two people during an alcohol-induced blackout (Madden 1998). The AA group members claimed that they were obligated by the group's rules to avoid disclosure of confidential information shared by group members. The judge in the case rejected the group members' arguments, concluding that a legal privilege did not exist, given that the self-help group was not facilitated by a mental health professional.[14]

Because statutes vary from state to state and because case law sometimes is inconsistent, social workers should consult a lawyer to determine the current status of a particular client's right to privileged communication in their state. Social workers should also keep in mind a key standard in the NASW *Code of Ethics* pertaining to potential conflicts of interest and privileged communication issues when practitioners provide services to two or more people who have a relationship with each other (standard 1.06[d]). In this situation social workers should clarify with all parties (for example, couples, family members) which individuals are considered clients and the nature of social workers' professional obligations to the various individuals who are receiving services. Social workers who anticipate a conflict of interest among these individuals or who anticipate having to perform in potentially conflicting roles (for example, when a social worker is asked to testify in a child custody dispute or divorce proceedings involving clients) should clarify their role with the parties involved and take appropriate action to minimize any conflict of interest (standard 1.06[d]).

Social workers should also be careful to seek clients' permission (or, in the case of minors, the permission of a parent or guardian) or a court order before disclosing privileged information. Otherwise the social worker might be found liable for violating clients' right to privacy and confidentiality. In *Cutter II v. Brownbridge* (1986) a licensed clinical social worker, Robert Brownbridge, prepared a written document concerning the diagnosis and prognosis of his client, Newell Cutter, in response to a request from Cutter's ex-wife. Brownbridge apparently prepared the document in the absence of a subpoena or other court order. Eventually the ex-wife's lawyer filed the document as evidence in a dispute between the Cutters concerning visitation rights involving their children. The husband sued Brownbridge, alleging that he had violated his client's constitutional and common law right to privacy, breached an implied covenant of confidentiality, and intentionally inflicted emotional distress. The California Superior Court, which was upheld on appeal, found that the social worker had "violated his client's right to privacy and confidentiality by voluntarily publishing material concerning his client without first resorting to prior judicial determination" (Austin, Moline, and Williams 1990:70).

Social workers who supervise unlicensed staff should be clear about the extent to which confidential information shared by clients will be treated as privileged; again, legislation and court opinions vary from state to state. For example, in *Missouri v. Edwards* (1996) the Missouri Court of Appeals held that testimony from an unlicensed counselor, who worked under the supervision of a licensed social worker, about conversations with an alleged sexual abuse victim were not privileged under state law ("Testimony . . . Not Privileged" 1996).

Social workers should also pay close attention to the specific contexts in which clients disclose confidential information. The presence of a third party, for example, or a discussion that took place outside a typical counseling session may be significant. For example, in 1998 the Indiana Court of Appeals held that a defendant's admission to child molestation, made in response to a question by his attorney while sitting in his family therapist's office, was not protected by therapist-client privilege (*Kavanaugh v. Indiana* (1998)). The client did not make the comment during a therapy session but rather during a meeting with his attorney, at the therapist's office, to discuss legal issues in the case. Also, the court noted that the defendant made his comment in response to a question from his attorney and that the therapist-client privilege applies only to communications between a therapist and client ("Defendant's Admission to Child Molestation" 1999). Also, a Wisconsin appeals court held that a minor's comments to a psychologist and social worker concerning additional sexual assaults that he had committed were not privileged under state law, because the minor knew that this information could be shared with others outside the treatment setting ("Juvenile's Communications" 2001).

Clearly social workers often are asked or ordered to disclose confidential information in the context of civil or criminal court proceedings. Prominent examples include social workers who are subpoenaed to testify in

- Malpractice cases in which a client has sued another practitioner (for example, a physician). The defendant's lawyer may subpoena the client's social worker to gain testimony about the client's mental status or about comments made during counseling sessions. The defense lawyer may attempt to introduce evidence that the client's allegations merely reflect the client's emotional instability, mental illness, vindictiveness, or irrational tendencies. The defense may also try to show that the client had mental health problems that predated the emotional injury that the client claims were caused by the defendant in the case. Defense lawyers may use a similar strategy in other tort or personal injury cases in which a social worker's client claims to have been injured by the actions of another party (for example, as a result of an automobile or workplace accident).
- Custody disputes in which one parent subpoenas a social worker who has worked with one or both parents, believing that the social worker's

testimony will support the parent's claim (for example, testimony concerning comments made during a counseling session about one parent's allegedly abusive behavior).

- Divorce proceedings in which a social worker is subpoenaed by one spouse who believes that the social worker's testimony about confidential conversations will support claims against the other spouse.
- Criminal cases in which a prosecutor or defense attorney subpoenas a social worker to testify about the defendant's comments during counseling sessions.

RESPONDING TO SUBPOENAS AND COURT ORDERS

Social workers who are subpoenaed may face a special dilemma concerning the disclosure of privileged information. If the social worker practices in a state that grants the right of privileged communication to social workers' clients, avoiding compliance with the subpoena may be easier because the legislature has acknowledged the importance of the privilege. Also, contrary to many social workers' understanding, a legitimate response to a subpoena is to argue that the requested information should not be disclosed or can be obtained from some other source. A subpoena itself does not require a practitioner to disclose information. Instead a subpoena is essentially a request for information, and it may be without merit. As Grossman has said, "If the recipient knew how easy it was to have a subpoena issued; if he knew how readily the subpoena could demand information when there actually was no legal right to command the disclosure of information; if he knew how often an individual releases information that legally he had no right to release because of intimidation—he would view the threat of the subpoena with less fear and greater skepticism" (1978:245). Further, Grossman says, "In private discussions attorneys admit that the harassing tactic of using these writs is as important in court contests as the legal 'right to the truth'" (145). Social workers who are subpoenaed should immediately notify their client and ask the client whether he wants to sign a release-of-information form or contest the subpoena in court.

Resisting disclosure of confidential information is appropriate, particularly if social workers believe that the information is not essential or if they can argue that the information can be obtained from other sources. According to Wilson,

> When data sought by the court can be obtained through some other source, a professional who has been subpoenaed may not have to disclose his confidential data. If the practitioner freely relinquishes his confidential though non-privileged data with little or no objection, the courts may not even check to see if the information can be obtained elsewhere. If the professional resists disclosure, however, the court may investigate to see if it can get the data from some other source.
>
> (1978:138)

Austin, Moline, and Williams (1990:18) and Polowy and Gorenberg (1997) advise that social workers should be aware of various guidelines concerning the service of and response to a subpoena:

- Do not release any information unless you are sure you have been authorized in writing to do so.
- If you do not know whether the privilege has been waived, you must claim the privilege to protect your client's confidentiality.
- Notify your employer (if applicable), so that the employer can notify the malpractice insurer.
- Notify your own malpractice insurer (to determine whether legal representation may be necessary, obtain legal advice about how to respond to the subpoena, and to ensure that the insurer is notified in a timely fashion, in accord with policy provisions that require the insured to notify the insurer of a potential claim).
- Should you employ an assistant or supervise a trainee, it would be wise to claim the privilege to protect confidentiality, even though the court might rule that unlicensed practitioners are not covered by the privilege.
- Determine who served you with the subpoena.
- Determine whether the issuer of the subpoena will pay you a witness fee and cover your travel expenses.
- At a deposition, where there is no judge, you might have your own attorney present or choose to follow the advice and direction of your client's attorney.

- If you feel your information about your client is embarrassing, damaging, or immaterial, you might consider getting written permission to discuss the situation with your client's attorney.
- Unless you are required to produce records only (as with a subpoena duces tecum), and are providing all your client records, you must appear at the location stated in the subpoena.

Social workers can use several strategies to protect clients' confidentiality during legal proceedings (Polowy and Gorenberg 1997). If social workers believe that a subpoena is inappropriate (for example, because it requests information that state law considers privileged), they can arrange for a lawyer (perhaps the client's lawyer) to file a motion to quash the subpoena, which is an attempt to have the court rule that the request contained in the subpoena is inappropriate. A judge may issue a protective order explicitly limiting the disclosure of specific privileged information during the discovery phase of the case (discovery is a pretrial procedure by which one party obtains information—facts and documents, for example—about the other).

In addition social workers, perhaps through a lawyer, may request a review in camera (a review in the judge's chambers) of records or documents that they believe should not be disclosed in open court. The judge can then decide whether the information should be revealed in open court and made a matter of public record. As the NASW *Code of Ethics* states,

> Social workers should protect the confidentiality of clients during legal proceedings to the extent permitted by law. When a court of law or other legally authorized body orders social workers to disclose confidential or privileged information without a client's consent and such disclosure could cause harm to the client, social workers should request that the court withdraw the order or limit the order as narrowly as possible or maintain the records under seal, unavailable for public inspection.
>
> (standard 1.07[j])

Despite a local privileged communication statute and a social worker's attempts to resist a subpoena and disclosure of confidential information, a court could formally order the practitioner to reveal this information. For example, in the 1974 New York State case of *Humphrey v. Norden,* a social worker, whose client was presumably protected by the right of privileged communication, was ordered to testify in a paternity case after the court ruled that "disclosure of evidence relevant to a correct determination of paternity was of greater importance than any injury which might inure to [the] relationship between [the] social worker and his clients if such admission was disclosed" (Wilson 1978:100).

In *Belmont v. California* (1974) a social worker was suspended from her job at the California Department of Social Welfare for willful disobedience of an order to disclose information to the department concerning her clients. The department had requested the information for inclusion in a new computerized database. The social worker, who had provided services to emotionally disturbed clients who were receiving public assistance, refused to share the information and was suspended for five days without pay. The California Court of Appeal ruled that social workers employed in this setting do not have a privilege to refuse to disclose confidential information. The court concluded that "the Department's and the legislature's purpose to make 'maximum use of electronic data processing' in the handling and storage of welfare recipient information, under the facts embraced by appellants' offer of proof, flouted neither the 'right of privacy' nor other Fourth Amendment principle" (R. Cohen 1979:146).

In *In re* Lifschutz (1970) a teacher, Joseph F. Housek, sued John Arabian for damages, alleging that Arabian assaulted him. In a deposition Housek testified that he received counseling services for approximately six months from a psychotherapist, Joseph E. Lifschutz. Lifschutz, however, refused to testify in response to a subpoena, even with respect to whether he had treated Housek. Lifschutz claimed that information about any relationship he has with a client is privileged. Both lower and appellate courts held Lifschutz in contempt because the psychotherapist privilege in California does not apply when clients introduce to the court proceedings their emotional or mental condition (Grossman 1978). Further, the privilege belongs to the client, not the therapist.

The California Supreme Court refused to hear the case, and Lifschutz continued to refuse to testify. Eventually he was jailed for contempt of court. After a hearing on Lifschutz's challenge of the contempt finding, the California Supreme Court ruled that he was indeed obligated to testify. The court concluded that Lifschutz's client waived the privilege by openly testifying that Lifschutz had treated him. The court also rejected Lifschutz's

various arguments concerning, for example, the extent to which his livelihood would be threatened by disclosure of confidential information and
the claim that Lifschutz did not receive equal protection under the clergy-
penitent-litigant act. This case is particularly important because it recognized that no previous cases had applied the patient-litigant exception to the
psychotherapist-client privilege (Austin, Moline, and Williams 1990:47).

A mental health clinician was also found in contempt of court for refusing to disclose confidential information in *Caesar v. Mountanos* (1976).
Dr. George Caesar, a psychiatrist, was providing treatment to Joan Seebach following injuries she allegedly sustained in an automobile accident.
Despite Seebach's willingness to waive in writing the psychotherapist-
patient privilege,

> Caesar refused to answer a number of questions concerning the relation-
> ship between Seebach's emotional condition and the accident. Caesar con-
> tended that disclosure of this confidential information could be harmful
> to Seebach. The U.S. Court of Appeals for the Ninth Circuit affirmed the
> judgment of the federal district court, concluding that there needs to be "a
> proper balance between the conditional right of privacy encompassing the
> psychotherapist-patient relationship and [California's] compelling need to
> ensure the ascertainment of the truth in court proceedings."
>
> (Austin, Moline, and Williams 1990:52–53)

Unique issues can emerge when clients share confidential information
with student interns. Social workers must determine whether their state's
statutes extend the concept of privileged communication to clients seen by
student interns. In *California v. Gomez* (1982) a court concluded that privileged communication pertains only to licensed professionals, not to student interns. This case involved information that John Gomez shared with
two student interns about his intention to kill a man with whom his wife
had become involved. Gomez argued that the trial court erred by allowing
the student interns to testify concerning his comments about wanting to
kill his wife's lover. Gomez claimed that the psychotherapist-patient privilege should apply. Since the *Gomez* decision, however, the California legislature has passed laws that extend the psychotherapist-patient privilege to
some registered interns who are completing their practicum requirements
(Austin, Moline, and Williams 1990:55).

UNINTENTIONAL DISCLOSURE OF
CONFIDENTIAL INFORMATION

Clearly in many instances social workers have to make a deliberate decision about whether to disclose confidential information to third parties. Cases involving the duty to protect, suicide, child abuse, and fee collection, for instance, sometimes call for difficult judgments about the limits of privacy and the need for others to know details of a client's life.

Far more common, however, are unintentional disclosures of confidential information, with no deliberate intent to breach a client's right to privacy. In these instances a social worker typically has simply been absent-minded, careless, or sloppy.

Bev E., a social worker at a local family service agency, had an 11 A.M. appointment to meet with another social worker, Carl F., at a nearby community mental health center. Bev E. and Carl F. were members of a subcommittee of the state NASW chapter charged with planning the chapter's annual meeting. Bev E. and Carl F. agreed to meet in Carl F.'s office to map out details related to the keynote address, workshop topics, scheduling, and so on.

Bev E. arrived at the community mental health center about ten minutes early. She took an elevator to the fourth floor office, walked into the waiting room, and introduced herself to the receptionist. The receptionist told Bev E. that Carl F. would be with her momentarily, offered her a cup of coffee, and invited her to take a seat. Bev E. sat on a nearby chair and began skimming a magazine. Several minutes later one of the center's other social workers walked out of her office and through the waiting room, leaving the agency's suite. The receptionist noticed this other worker and said, "Oh, Mary, Sue Smith called a few minutes ago. She said she won't be able to keep her two-thirty appointment. Apparently she has a child-care problem. She said she'd call back to reschedule."

This reminded Bev E. of her own afternoon schedule. She glanced at the schedule on her electronic tablet and realized she should call a colleague with whom she was planning to meet that afternoon in order to get driving directions. Bev E. pulled out her smartphone to make the call and asked the receptionist whether she could borrow a pen and pad of paper in order to write down the directions. The receptionist said she needed to run down the hall to make a photocopy and invited Bev E. to use the pen and pad on her desk.

Bev E. made her telephone call; as she glanced down at the desk, Bev E. noticed an open case record on which the receptionist was working. To avoid staring at the record Bev E. turned away from the desk, only to find herself staring at a partially typed letter on the receptionist's computer monitor.

At that point Carl F. walked into the waiting room area to greet Bev E. They met in Carl F.'s office to discuss the upcoming NASW conference. After about twenty minutes Carl F.'s telephone rang. He placed his hand over the mouthpiece and asked Bev E. whether she minded if he took the call. He explained that one of his clients was moving to another state and he was transferring the client to a social worker in that state. Bev E. indicated that he should take the call from the social work colleague.

Before long Bev E. heard Carl F. give the caller identifying information about the client's age, family circumstances, treatment history, and presenting problems. During the conversation Bev E. also gazed around the office and eventually noticed several case records sitting on top of Carl F.'s desk, with clients' names exposed on the file labels. As soon as Carl F. hung up the telephone, an exasperated colleague knocked on his door and said he needed to get some advice about the delivery of services to one of the agency's clients, an undocumented immigrant. The visiting social worker mentioned the client's name and circumstances in front of Bev E. Carl F. advised the visiting colleague to fax information about the client's mental health status to the client's attorney. The visiting colleague dialed the wrong fax number, and the confidential material was sent to a local factory, whose fax number was similar to the attorney's, and read by an office worker who recognized the client's name.

After the telephone call Carl F. and Bev E. finished a rough draft of the conference schedule. They walked down the hall to make a photocopy. When Carl F. opened the photocopy machine cover, he found part of a case record that a colleague had left in the machine. While Carl F. made a photocopy of the conference schedule, Bev E. glanced down at the waste basket next to the machine. On top of the pile of discarded paper was a slightly crumpled copy of the face sheet of a client's record. Apparently it had been copied on the wrong size paper and thrown out.

At that point Carl F. asked Bev E. whether she had time for a quick bite to eat at a nearby deli. Bev E. accepted the offer, and the two proceeded to the building's elevator. When they got on the elevator, they were greeted by three other agency workers, who proceeded to animatedly discuss a case in which they were all involved. Bev E. heard one staffer mention the name of a client involved in the case.

Bev E. and Carl F. then walked to the local deli for lunch. They sat at their table and continued to discuss the upcoming conference. Before long, however, Bev E. could not help but overhear the three staff members who had been on the elevator continuing their discussion of the case while seated at a nearby booth.

After lunch Bev E. went on her way, and Carl F. returned to his office. At the end of the day Carl F. gathered two case records that he wanted to work on at home, tidied up his desk, and went to catch the 5:15 P.M. bus. On his way home on the bus Carl F. pulled out a case record. As he reviewed it and made some notes, a passenger seated next to him began reading the exposed material, unbeknown to Carl F.

Carl F. continued working on the case when he got home. When his wife got home, Carl F. left the record on the kitchen table, and he and his wife went out to a dinner meeting, leaving their children with a babysitter. While Carl F. and his wife were out, the hungry babysitter sat down at the kitchen table to have a snack. She began flipping through the case record.

At about 9 that evening a custodian entered Carl F.'s office to empty the trash, straighten the furniture, and dust. As the custodian was dusting Carl F.'s desk, he noticed the name on the case record that Carl F. had left on top of the desk. It was the name of the custodian's second cousin, and the custodian sat down and thumbed through the record.

Although this case example is fiction, I have witnessed every component of the vignette. My guess is that many details will be familiar to readers.

Daily pressures in social work settings can exacerbate inadvertent disclosures of confidential information. In these instances practitioners mean no harm. They do not make deliberate decisions to violate clients' right to privacy. These breaches of confidentiality are mistakes. According to the NASW *Code of Ethics,* "Social workers should not discuss confidential information in any setting unless privacy can be ensured. Social workers should not discuss confidential information in public or semipublic areas such as hallways, waiting rooms, elevators, and restaurants" (standard 1.07[i]).

Social workers can take a number of steps to prevent these mistakes and the liability risks that they involve. An important step is to provide systematic routine training to all agency staffers. Including professional and nonprofessional staff members (for example, secretaries, clerks, cooks for residential programs, and maintenance staff) in a program is especially important because both have access to confidential information. Because of the turnover in social service agencies the training on confidentiality should be offered periodically. This produces knowledgeable staff and enhances protection of clients' and staff members' rights, and it provides some measure of protection to the agency because it can demonstrate its efforts to ensure that staff members understand how to handle confidential information. The same recommendation pertains to private practitioners, of course.

Training on confidentiality should include two major components: written material and verbal communication of information related to clients. Written confidential material can take several forms, including such case record items as intake forms, assessment and diagnostic reports, progress notes, insurance forms, and correspondence. Social workers need to be acquainted with guidelines concerning access to paper and electronic case records by (1) third parties outside the agency (other service providers, insurance companies), (2) staff within the agency, (3) clients, and (4) clients' families, guardians, executors, and/or significant others. In general contents of case records should not be released to parties outside the agency without the client's informed consent (see chapter 3 for a discussion of informed-consent procedures). Although some exceptions are permissible (life-threatening emergencies, for example), clients' informed consent ordinarily is essential. Social workers need to be especially careful when asked for confidential material by close friends or colleagues employed in other agencies who may feel entitled to information because of their unique relationship.

Sharing of information between public agencies can also be a special problem. Staffers at a state public welfare department may feel entitled to case record material located in a state child welfare agency when a particular client is involved with both agencies. Unless the agencies have negotiated a clear memorandum of agreement, releasing confidential information without the client's consent is inappropriate.

Agency-based social workers must also be careful about releasing confidential information to other staff members *within* the organization. Staffers sometimes mistakenly assume that their mere employment in an agency entitles them to information contained in clients' records. Certainly in many cases various staff members in an agency should have access to the record. In a community mental health center, for example, giving a variety of professionals access to confidential material may be appropriate in order to coordinate services.

In some instances, however, access by staff should be limited. On occasion staff members who are not directly involved in a client's care may be curious about a case, as when an agency is providing services to a celebrity or notorious individual. The governing principle should be that only staff members who are involved in the client's case and have a *need to know* the confidential information should have access in order to carry out their duties. Staffers who cannot satisfy the need-to-know criterion should not have access.

Social workers also need to be clear about clients' rights to their own records. Professionals' thinking about this has changed dramatically over time. Once, few practitioners believed clients should be able to examine their own records. Therapists typically viewed records as agency property and for staffers' eyes only. However, social workers and other professionals have come to appreciate why clients may need or want to see their records and that such disclosure can indeed have therapeutic value if handled properly. As Wilson observes,

> Only a few short years ago, the social work profession simply assumed that a record was the private property of the professional or the agency, and that was that. A few therapists occasionally advocated client participation in recording as part of the therapeutic process, and others began using the video-recorded interview as a means of allowing the individual to study how he communicates and to provide feedback regarding the therapist's effectiveness. However, such procedures were considered experimental rather than routine. . . . There will be increasing pressure from consumers (and also as a result of the ethical philosophy of the social work profession) for all settings to be more open in sharing record materials with clients.
>
> (1978:83, 85)

Many agencies and private practitioners have developed policies concerning clients' access to records. Clients may be allowed to have photocopied portions of the record, for instance, or may examine the record while in the presence of a staff person. Such policies often spell out the circumstances in which clients may be denied access, such as when the

practitioner has reason to believe that the client would be harmed emotionally. In these instances an alternative is to release the information to the
client's legal representative. Of course, social workers must be careful not to
share the contents of a client's case record with family members, significant
others, or guardians without proper consent or legal authorization. These
guidelines are reflected in the NASW *Code of Ethics:*

> Social workers should provide clients with reasonable access to records con-
> cerning the clients. Social workers who are concerned that clients' access to
> their records could cause serious misunderstanding or harm to the client
> should provide assistance in interpreting the records and consultation with
> the client regarding the records. Social workers should limit clients' access
> to their records, or portions of their records, only in exceptional circum-
> stances when there is compelling evidence that such access would cause
> serious harm to the client. Both clients' requests and the rationale for with-
> holding some or all of the record should be documented in clients' files.
>
> (standard 1.08[a])

> When providing clients with access to their records, social workers should
> take steps to protect the confidentiality of other individuals identified or
> discussed in such records.
>
> (standard 1.08[b])

Written and electronic information about clients can also be released
quite accidentally, as demonstrated by the case example involving Bev. E.
Both professional and clerical staff members need to be careful not to leave
confidential information on desktops and conference tables to which others may have visual access; provide visual access to computer monitors that
contain confidential information; or leave confidential material in a pho-
tocopier. Also, they should not discard confidential information in a way
that risks exposure (that is, social workers should tear up or shred confidential material before disposing of it, and ensure proper deletion of electronic
records). They need to be sure that passengers on buses, trains, or airplanes
cannot read confidential information over the social worker's shoulder; to
take care not leave confidential information exposed to family members or
visitors at home; to take adequate precautions when disclosing confidential information or when mailing material to a client's home with the social

worker's name and title on the envelope (unless the client says she is not concerned about this form of disclosure). Many social workers and agencies omit the practitioner's or agency's name from envelopes mailed to a client in order to protect the client's right to privacy. Social workers should ensure that their electronic devices—laptops, smartphones, and flash drives—are encrypted and require secure passwords.

Widely available technology such as fax machines also poses special problems. Although the social worker who sends the information may not intend for anyone other than the recipient to read the written communication, fax machines are often located in areas that give others access to the material. Social workers who fax confidential material should be sure that the recipient is available to retrieve the information immediately and should include a confidentiality notice on the cover sheet. This is one example:

> The documents accompanying this facsimile transmission contain confidential information. The information is intended only for the use of the individual(s) or entity(ies) named above. If you are not the intended recipient, you are advised that any disclosure, copying, distribution, or the taking of any action based on the contents of this information is prohibited. If you have received this facsimile in error, please notify us immediately by telephone at the above number to arrange for return of the original documents.

As the case example also illustrated, inappropriate release of confidential information through verbal communication is a common problem. A great deal of confidential information is divulged inadvertently when third parties seated in waiting rooms hear staff members greet clients by name; hear staffers discuss clients in a hallway, in a waiting room or elevator, at a social gathering, or in a restaurant or other public facility; and overhear social workers discuss a case on the telephone. Social workers must also be careful to edit the messages that they leave at a client's workplace and home.

Voice mail can also pose a problem. Although a practitioner may believe that the client or a professional colleague is the only one who will listen to the confidential message, others may have access to the voice mail. According to the NASW *Code of Ethics,* "Social workers should take precautions to ensure and maintain the confidentiality of information transmitted to other parties through the use of computers, electronic mail, facsimile machines, telephones and telephone answering machines, and other electronic or computer technology. Disclosure of identifying information should be avoided whenever possible" (standard 1.07[m]).

Several other circumstances also warrant special attention to confidentiality. In group or marital therapy and family counseling, social workers must be careful to respect clients' wishes concerning the disclosure of confidential information. In several cases social workers have inadvertently divulged confidential information without their clients' consent.

Marriage or couples counseling can pose other problems as well, particularly when one partner contacts the social worker and shares confidential information that he does not want disclosed to his partner. Some social workers permit such confidential disclosures, or secrets, and do their best to respect the confidence. Other social workers prohibit such secrets, usually for therapeutic reasons. This is a complicated professional debate, one that I cannot settle here. Suffice it to say that social workers should always be clear ahead of time how they would handle such circumstances, and they should clearly present their policy on this issue to their clients. Those practitioners who permit such secrets ought to share this policy with clients at the beginning of treatment. Clients can then state whether they are comfortable with the arrangement. Social workers who prohibit secrets should inform clients of this policy (see NASW *Code of Ethics,* standard 1.07[g]).

Even such clear policies do not prevent problems, however. In one case a social worker was providing marriage counseling to a couple. The wife was particularly distressed about the husband's drinking and insisted that he seek treatment. To save the marriage the husband sought alcohol treatment and talked about his progress in sessions with his wife and the social worker.

Several months after treatment began, the social worker was attending a professional conference at a local hotel and encountered the husband outside the hotel bar. The husband was clearly inebriated. The husband pleaded with the social worker not to tell his wife about his drunkenness. The social worker had to decide whether he had an obligation to share this information with the wife, particularly when the husband refused to do so himself. The social worker felt uncomfortable participating in therapy sessions in which he knew the husband was actively deceiving his wife. The social worker also felt he was colluding with the husband and reinforcing the husband's lying and deception. The social worker resolved the matter by agreeing to work with the husband individually for four weeks to help the husband acknowledge his problem to his wife during subsequent joint counseling sessions.

A final problem has to do with statements about confidentiality that appear on agencies' or private practitioners' public relations materials, such as brochures, pamphlets, and client's rights statements. Many agencies provide brochures that briefly describe agency services, hours, staff, and fees. Often they contain statements such as this one, which appears on a family service agency brochure: "All counseling sessions are held in strict confidence." In addition many agencies and practitioners distribute client's rights statements that spell out confidentiality policy among other policies related to civil rights, grievances, medication, fees, and cancellations. The following is a statement that appears on the client's rights statement prepared by a community mental health center:

> Your privacy is very important to us. No one will be told that you are a client at XYZ Agency without your written permission. Your case record is a confidential document and is protected by federal and state laws. It will be accessible only to clinical staff members responsible for your treatment and support personnel as required during normal business hours. During other times, the medical record is secured in a locked room. No information about you will be obtained or given out to anyone, including your family or private doctor, without your written authorization.

After reading the statement on the first agency's brochure and on the second agency's client's rights form, clients might reasonably expect that *everything* they reveal in counseling would be considered confidential. They might be quite surprised to learn of the various exceptions, such as social workers' need to comply with mandatory reporting laws related to child and elder abuse and legal guidelines in cases in which a client threatens to harm third parties (duty-to-protect guidelines). Therefore clarifying the legal limits to clients' right to confidentiality is important. Although spelling out these limits in great detail in these documents may not be appropriate, at the very least the statements should state that such limits exist. I advise adding a phrase along the lines of "All information in your record will be considered confidential *to the extent permitted by law*." At an appropriate time early in the relationship, social workers should spell out, as gently and diplomatically as possible, the nature of these limits (see standard 1.07[e] in the NASW *Code of Ethics*).

In sum, formulating comprehensive policies to prevent inappropriate disclosure of confidential information is important. Such policies should address a variety of topics and issues, including

1. Disclosure of information over the telephone, computer (e-mail and attachments), and fax machine
2. Access to agency facilities and clients by outsiders (for example, to attend meetings or take a tour)
3. Physical safeguarding of paper and electronic records
4. Record retention and destruction
5. Access to client records by staff, clients, significant others, and legal representatives
6. Disclosure of information to outside agencies
7. Audio and video recording of clients
8. Photocopying of confidential information
9. Display of confidential information on computer terminals in public or semipublic areas
10. Discussion of confidential information in waiting rooms, hallways, offices, elevators, and other public and private settings
11. Use of voice mail
12. Statements concerning confidentiality on agency brochures and documents
13. Disclosure of confidential information to the news media and law enforcement officials

In formulating confidentiality policies social workers can find assistance by consulting a variety of documents, including state and federal laws, accreditation standards, union policies, licensing regulations, agency policies, insurance company policies on disclosure, professional literature, and codes of ethics.

Clearly respect for clients' rights to privacy and confidentiality is among the most enduring of social work values. Privacy and confidentiality are essential ingredients in effective social work practice. Practitioners know, however, that various circumstances may warrant or require disclosure of confidential information. In other instances social workers may disclose confidential information unintentionally or inadvertently. Social workers can avoid liability risks by being aware of the various ways in which confidentiality can be breached appropriately and inappropriately.

3

The Delivery of Services

MOST SOCIAL WORKERS ARE COMPETENT professionals who provide sound interventions. But on occasion liability complaints are filed against social workers alleging that their interventions were somehow flawed. Ordinarily these claims allege that the social worker's intervention departed from the standard of care in the profession or violated licensing standards. The claimant, usually a client, former client, or family member of a client, sometimes alleges that the social worker carried out his duties in a negligent or illegal fashion (acts of misfeasance or malfeasance) and sometimes that the social worker failed to carry out his duties (acts of nonfeasance). Whatever the setting and whatever the practice method, social workers need to be concerned about the malpractice and liability risks associated with flawed treatment.

Statistically most malpractice and liability claims and licensing board complaints alleging improper treatment stem from some sort of clinical practice, that is, social work with individuals, families, or treatment groups. Some claims also involve social work administration, usually related to personnel matters. Relatively rarely claims pertain to community organizing and research.[1]

This chapter focuses primarily on risks related to clinical practice. In particular I discuss risks related to the violation of clients' rights; informed consent; assessment and high-risk intervention; boundary issues and dual relationships; undue influence; suicide; commitment proceedings; protective services; defamation of character; digital technology; and social media.

CLIENTS' RIGHTS

Especially since the 1960s, state legislatures, the U.S. Congress, and the courts have recognized an increasing number of client rights. Some of these rights have emerged as a result of litigation (for example, concerning psychiatric patients' right to refuse services), and others are the product of legislative proposals and debates.

To protect clients' rights and minimize risks, social workers employed in agency settings and independent practice should ensure that they have policies and procedures in place (see the appendix for a sample client rights form):

- Confidentiality and privacy. As I discussed at length in chapter 2, clients have a wide range of confidentiality and privacy rights. Social workers should have clearly worded confidentiality policies that describe these rights (and exceptions) and procedures to acquaint clients with these rights. In addition social workers should caution clients about confidentiality risks if clients communicate with social workers using e-mail or messaging options on social networking sites (such as Facebook and LinkedIn). The NASW *Code of Ethics* requires social workers to inform clients of their confidentiality rights and any exceptions, for example, social workers' duty to disclose confidential information without client consent to protect clients or third parties from imminent and serious harm or to comply with a court order (see standard 1.07[e]).
- Release of information. Social workers should have well-established policies and procedures for obtaining a client's (or guardian's) authorization for the release of confidential information.
- Informed consent. As I discuss in detail later in this chapter, social workers should have sound policies and procedures for obtaining a client's consent to release confidential information, acknowledgment of awareness of treatment options, and permission to conduct activities such as video recording and audio recording or observation by a third party of service provision to the client.
- Access to services. Social workers should inform clients routinely of their rights to various services offered by their agency. This is particularly important in settings where clients are held involuntarily, such as prisons, juvenile correctional institutions, psychiatric facilities, and other programs to which clients are remanded by a court.

- Access to records. As I discussed in chapter 2, clients ordinarily have the right to inspect their records. Social workers who are concerned that a client's access to these records could cause serious misunderstanding or harm to the client should provide assistance in interpreting the records and consultation with the client regarding the records. Only in exceptional circumstances—where the evidence is compelling that a client's access to these records would cause serious harm to the client—are social workers permitted to limit clients' access to their records (or portions of their records). Social workers' client rights statement should summarize the nature of clients' rights to see and obtain copies of information in their record. Agencies that hire former clients (for example, addictions programs) should ensure that staffers who were once clients do not inappropriately access records—their own records or records of other clients they knew during their time as clients.
- Service plans. Many social workers seek to include clients in the development of treatment and service plans as a way to empower clients and engage them in the helping process. The client rights statement should explain the ways in which clients have an opportunity to participate in the formulation of service and treatment plans.
- Options for alternative services and referrals. Clients have the right to know whether they can obtain services from other providers. This is consistent with social workers' obligation to respect clients' right to self-determination and to give informed consent before services are provided to them. The client rights statement should explain to clients the options that they have in regard to being referred to, and receiving services from, other agencies and providers.
- The right to refuse services. In general clients have the right to refuse services (recognizing that in some instances clients do not have this right, for example, when a court orders a client to receive services). The client rights statement should inform clients about the extent of their right to refuse available services.
- Termination of services. Social workers should inform clients about the agency's or practitioner's policies concerning the termination of services, for example, the circumstances under which services may or will be terminated, along with relevant criteria and procedures (see chapter 8 for additional detail).
- Grievance procedures. In many settings clients have the right to challenge or appeal decisions with which they disagree and that are related to,

for example, treatment plans, benefits, eligibility for services, and termination of services. The client rights statement should explain to clients the extent to which they have the right to appeal adverse decisions and what the relevant grievance procedures are.

- Evaluation and research. Some agencies involve clients in evaluation or research activities (such as clinical research and program evaluations). The client rights statement should inform clients about policies and procedures designed to protect evaluation and research participants (often known as "protection of human subjects" guidelines). These guidelines should be consistent with widely accepted standards related to informing clients about the purpose of the research and evaluation; foreseeable risks, discomforts, or negative consequences; potential benefits to clients and others; alternatives to participation that might benefit the client; confidentiality or anonymity provisions; compensation; provisions for treatment in the event of harm of injury; and contact people available to respond to questions about the research and evaluation.

One practical suggestion is to provide clients with a written summary or "service contract" that summarizes key features of the social worker's (and agency's) relationship with clients. Typical written agreements summarize the practitioner's areas of expertise; training and education; professional affiliations; privacy, confidentiality, and privileged communication guidelines, as well as clients' rights and responsibilities; boundaries in the professional-client relationship; social media policies (policies related to social networking, digital and electronic services, e-mail and other electronic communications, electronic searches, location-based services, consumer review sites); how to handle emergencies; and fee arrangements, billing procedures, and collection methods. The ideal service contract is written in user-friendly, diplomatic language that is not legalistic in tone.

INFORMED CONSENT

Social workers have always recognized the central importance of a client's consent, whether to services, release of information, medication, or audio/video recording. Because of social workers' long-standing commitment to the principle of client self-determination, informed consent has been a centerpiece of professional practice (S. Bernstein 1960; Keith-Lucas 1963; Perlman 1965; McDermott 1975; Reamer 1987c).

The historical roots of informed consent trace to Plato, who in *Laws* compares the Greek slave-physician who gives orders "in the brusque fashion of a dictator" with the free physician who "takes the patient and his family into confidence . . . [and] does not give prescriptions until he has won the patient's support" (President's Commission 1982:5). The medieval French surgeon Henri de Mondeville also stressed the importance of obtaining a patient's consent and confidence, although he also urged his colleagues to "compel the obedience of his patients" by selectively slanting information provided to them (4–5).

By the late eighteenth century European and American physicians and scientists had begun to develop a tradition that encouraged professionals to share information and decision making with their clients. The first major legal ruling in the United States on informed consent came in the landmark 1914 case of *Schloendorff v. Society of New York Hospital,* in which Benjamin Cardozo, then sitting on the New York Court of Appeals (the state's highest court), set forth his oft-cited opinion concerning an individual's right to self-determination: "Every human being of adult years and sound mind has a right to determine what shall be done with his own body" (Pernick 1982:28–29). To do otherwise, Cardozo argued, is to commit an assault upon the person.

Current informed-consent legislation and guidelines were devised after revelations of medical experiments performed without consent of the subjects in Germany during World War II and in the United States until 1972. The 1957 case of *Salgo v. Stanford University* introduced the phrase "informed consent." The plaintiff, who became a paraplegic following a diagnostic procedure for a circulatory disturbance, alleged that his physician did not properly disclose ahead of time pertinent information regarding risks associated with the treatment.

Although the concept of informed consent has its origins in medicine and health care, it has recently been applied legislatively, judicially, and administratively to a wide range of other client groups. Social workers regularly provide services to such client groups as those with mental illness and cognitive impairment, minors, elderly, hospital patients, prisoners, and research participants. In agencies that provide mental health services, for example, social workers must be familiar with consent requirements related to voluntary and involuntary commitment and the rights of institutionalized and outpatient clients regarding the use of psychotropic medication, restraints, aversive treatment measures, isolation, sterilization, and psycho-surgery (Berg et al. 2001; Schutz 1982).

Social workers in agencies that serve children must keep pace with evolving standards regarding consent of minors. State laws vary consider-ably and are subject to change. Consent issues arise in relation to abortion counseling, contraception, treatment of sexually transmitted diseases, men-tal health services, substance abuse treatment, and foster care. In *Dymek v. Nyquist* (1984), for example, the custodial parent of a nine-year-old boy was his father. But the boy's mother took him to a psychiatrist, who treated him for one year without the father's knowledge and consent. The suit alleged that the psychiatrist knew that the mother was not the custodial parent and that she had not obtained from the court permission for the psychiatrist to treat the boy. The Illinois court found in the father's favor, ruling that the psychiatrist had no authority to provide psychotherapy to the child (Aus-tin, Moline, and Williams 1990:187).

Traditionally minors have not been considered capable of giving informed consent or entering into contracts; the consent of parents or someone standing in loco parentis has typically been required, unless it is a genuine emergency (Berg et al. 2001; Cowles 1976; Rozovsky 1984; White 1994). Especially since the 1970s, however, a number of states have recog-nized the concepts of mature or emancipated minors, which imply that certain minors are in fact capable of providing their own consent in their relationships with professionals. Mature minors are those who are "judi-cially recognized as possessing sufficient understanding and appreciation of the nature and consequences of treatment despite their chronological age" (Rozovsky 1984:240). Emancipated minors are those who have obtained the legal capacity of an adult because they are self-supporting, living on their own, married, or in the armed forces.

States vary considerably in the extent to which they grant minors auton-omy and the right to consent. For example, with respect to abortion ser-vices, substance abuse treatment, dispensing contraceptives, and treatment of sexually transmitted diseases, some states permit professionals to treat minors without obtaining parental consent; some require that parents be notified, that their consent be obtained, or both; some require practitio-ners to make a "good faith" effort to have the minor notify the parents for purposes of obtaining parental consent; and some merely permit agency staff members to notify parents, obtain their consent, or both. State laws also vary in the extent to which parental consent is required to place a child in an inpatient or outpatient mental health program.

Consent issues related to the care of medical patients have received considerable attention, especially regarding the care of hospital patients and their right to die, be informed of medical risks, refuse treatment on religious grounds, consent to experimental treatment, participate in research, and donate organs. Once again states vary considerably in the amount of autonomy that they grant patients and the procedures that health-care staff members are expected to follow when patients request controversial treatment or fail to provide consent. In the famous case of Karen Ann Quinlan (*In re* Quinlan 1976), the Supreme Court of New Jersey required hospital staff to consult with a hospital ethics committee, rather than a court of law, concerning the decision to remove extraordinary treatment. This important court case led to the proliferation of ethics committees in a wide range of health and mental health settings (Hester and Schonfeld 2012). However, in *Superintendent of Belchertown v. Saikewicz* (1977) the Massachusetts Supreme Judicial Court rejected the New Jersey approach, with its reliance on administrative procedures, in favor of court approval of decisions concerning life-prolonging care of incompetent patients.

Debate concerning client consent to participate in research has also received much attention. Discussion has been especially vigorous with respect to clients whose competence to consent is considered questionable or who are considered especially vulnerable. Particular attention has been paid to the right of the mentally ill, elderly, minors, and prisoners to consent to participate in research related to drugs, treatment techniques, and program evaluation (Berg et al. 2001; Rozovsky 1984; White 1994).

Although states and local jurisdictions have different interpretations and applications of informed-consent standards, what constitutes valid consent by clients depends upon prevailing legislation and case law (see the appendix for a sample consent form for the release of confidential information). In general for consent to be considered valid six standards must be met: coercion and undue influence must not have played a role in the client's decision; clients must be capable of providing consent; clients must consent to specific procedures or actions; the forms of consent must be valid; clients must have the right to refuse or withdraw consent; and clients' decisions must be based on adequate information (Berg et al. 2001;

Cowles 1976; President's Commission 1982; Rozovsky 1984; White 1994). The NASW *Code of Ethics* also reflects these concepts:

> Social workers should provide services to clients only in the context of a professional relationship based, when appropriate, on valid informed consent. Social workers should use clear and understandable language to inform clients of the purpose of the services, risks related to the services, limits to services because of the requirements of a third-party payer, relevant costs, reasonable alternatives, clients' right to refuse or withdraw consent, and the time frame covered by the consent. Social workers should provide clients with an opportunity to ask questions.
>
> (standard 1.03[a])

Absence of coercion and undue influence. Social workers frequently maintain some degree of control over the lives of their clients. Access to services, money, time, and attention are but a few of the resources that social workers control. That social workers not take advantage of their positions of authority to coerce a client's consent, subtly or otherwise, is especially important (Giordano 1977; Reamer 1979, 2009). Practitioners who want clients to agree to enter or terminate a program, release information to third parties, participate in a research project, or take medication, for example, need to be aware that clients may be particularly susceptible to influence, which would jeopardize the validity of their consent.

Reif v. Weinberger (1974) illustrates the inappropriate use of coercion. The evidence showed that a number of welfare clients had been coerced into agreeing to sterilization procedures; they had been told that a portion of their welfare benefits would be withheld unless they agreed to the procedures. A federal district judge in Washington, D.C., issued an order prohibiting the use of tax dollars to pay for some sterilizations because of the use of coercion.

Capacity to consent. Although professionals widely agree that only competent clients are capable of giving informed consent, they are in much less agreement about the determination of competence. In its influential 1982 report, *Making Health Care Decisions,* the President's Commission for the Study of Ethical Problems in Medicine and Biomedical and Behavioral Research considered several different informed-consent standards. These included patients' ability to make choices, comprehend factual issues, manipulate information rationally, appreciate their current circumstances, retain information, and "test reality." After its comprehensive review of various perspectives the commission decided that competency is determined by the client's recognition of a set of values and goals, ability to communicate and understand information, and ability to reason and deliberate.

Despite the unsettled debate about how to determine competence, practitioners seem to agree that no one should assume that any particular client group, such as children, the elderly, or people with mental illness or mental retardation, are incompetent, except for those who are unconscious. Rather, clients in some categories—perhaps children or individuals with severe intellectual disability—should be considered to have a greater *probability* of incapacity. Assessments of a client's capacity should at least consist of such measures as a mental status exam (which accounts for a person's orientation to person, place, time, and situation; mood and affect; content of thought; and perception), the ability to comprehend abstract ideas and make reasoned judgments, any history of mental illness that might affect current judgment, and the client's recent and long-term memory. When clients are judged to be incompetent, practitioners should be guided by the principle of substituted, or proxy, judgment (Berg et al. 2001; Buchanan and Brock 1989), in which a surrogate attempts to replicate the decision that the incapacitated person would make if able to make a choice (President's Commission 1982). An important point for social workers to consider is that clients whose competence fluctuates may be capable of giving or withdrawing consent during a lucid phase (Rozovsky 1984:18). According to the NASW *Code of Ethics:*

> In instances when clients lack the capacity to provide informed consent, social workers should protect clients' interests by seeking permission from an appropriate third party, informing clients consistent with the client's level of understanding. In such instances social workers should seek to ensure that the third party acts in a manner consistent with clients' wishes and interests. Social workers should take reasonable steps to enhance such clients' ability to give informed consent.
>
> (standard 1.03[c])

Consent to specific procedures. Social service agencies often have clients sign general consent forms at a first or second appointment or at the time of admission to a residential program. In a number of precedent-setting cases, however, clients have challenged such blanket consent forms in court, claiming that they lacked specificity and failed to authorize interventions introduced subsequently. In *Winfrey v. Citizens & Southern National Bank* (1979), a Georgia woman challenged her physician's authority to perform a complete hysterectomy, based on her consent to an exploratory operation. In *Darrah v. Kite* (1969) the father of a young child challenged a New York neurosurgeon's authority to conduct a ventriculogram on the child when the consent form referred only to "routine brain tests" and a workup. Professionals are thus advised not to assume that general consent forms are valid. Rather, consent forms should include specific details that refer to specific activities or interventions. As Rozovsky has observed, "Reliance on a general consent form may be of questionable merit. Courts have been known to examine the circumstances of a specific case to determine whether the general consent was broad enough to permit the treatment in question" (1984:26).

Social workers and agency staff should also refrain from having clients sign blank consent forms; this is a practice occasionally used to avoid having to contact clients in person for their signatures at a later date. If challenged in court, these consent forms might not be considered valid, given the absence of information related to treatment or intervention when the client signed the form. Having clients sign blank forms clearly violates the spirit of the concept of informed consent.[2]

In addition the language and terminology that appear on consent forms must be understandable to clients, and clients should have ample opportunity to ask questions. Practitioners should avoid as much as possible the use of complex and technical jargon. Clients who do not have good command of English need particular care; social workers should be aware that some clients who are able to speak English reasonably well (expressive language skill) may not be equally capable of understanding the language (receptive language skill). Having access to an interpreter in such instances is important. In addition social workers should be certain that clients who have auditory or visual impairments are provided with the assistance they need in order to provide informed consent. According to the NASW *Code of Ethics,* "In instances when clients are not literate or have difficulty understanding the primary language used in the practice setting, social workers should take steps to ensure clients' comprehension. This may include providing clients with a detailed verbal explanation or arranging for a qualified interpreter or translator whenever possible" (standard 1.03[b]).

Valid forms of consent. Many states authorize several forms of consent. Consent may be written or verbal, although some states require written authorization. In general consent obtained verbally is considered valid, providing that all other criteria for valid consent have been met. In addition consent may be expressed or implied. Expressed consent entails explicit authorization by a client for a specific intervention or activity such as admission to a residential facility or the release of specific information to a third party. Implied consent occurs when consent is inferred from the facts and circumstances surrounding a client's situation. An example is a client who answers questions that are part of an anonymous, mailed, and voluntary client satisfaction survey. A reasonable assumption is that the client has consented to the activity. Another example of implied consent is when a social service agency that serves adolescents informs parents and guardians that agency staffers are administering a client survey and assume that parents and guardians consent to the survey unless they "opt out" or notify the agency that they do not want their child to participate.

Right to refuse or withdraw consent. While developing sound procedures for obtaining valid consent from clients is important for social workers and agencies, practitioners also should plan for the possibility that clients will refuse or withdraw consent. Of course, clients who do so also should be legally and mentally capable of such a decision, and their decisions need to be informed by details shared by practitioners concerning the risks associated with refusing or withdrawing consent. Taking psychotropic medication or being disabled to some degree by mental illness does not by itself provide ground for being denied the right to refuse or withdraw consent. Rather, social workers should judge clients' capacity in terms of their ability to think clearly, grasp details relevant to their condition, understand the extent to which their psychiatric history is likely to affect their current judgment, and understand the extent to which they pose a public health risk. Ordinarily social workers serve their own best interests by having their clients sign a release form absolving social workers, or their agencies, of responsibility for any adverse consequences stemming from a decision not to give consent. If a client refuses to sign such a form, the client's record should include detailed notes describing the client's decision and the negotiation.

Adequate information. Professionals generally agree about the topics that they should cover in discussions with clients before obtaining consent. Commonly cited elements of disclosure include the nature and purpose of the recommended service, treatment, or activity; the advantages and disadvantages of the intervention; substantial, probable, or significant risks to the client, if any; potential effects on the client's family, partner, job, social activities, and other aspects of the client's life; alternatives to the prospective intervention; and anticipated costs to be borne by the client and relatives. This information must be presented to clients in understandable language (taking into consideration clients' learning disabilities, cognitive impairment, literacy, and English comprehension), without coercion or undue influence, and in a manner that encourages clients to ask questions (Berg et al. 2001; President's Commission 1982; Rozovsky 1984; White 1994). Consent forms should also be dated and should include an expiration date. Many social workers' forms state that the consent is valid for ninety or 180 days, unless the client withdraws the consent at an earlier date. Consent forms without an expiration date may be considered invalid if the original signature was obtained long before the form was actually used.

Social workers must also consider that obtaining informed consent entails more than having clients sign a form. Consent is a process that includes the systematic disclosure of information to a client over time, along with an opportunity to discuss with the client the forthcoming treatment and service. As part of this process social workers must be especially sensitive to clients' cultural and ethnic differences related to the meaning of such concepts as self-determination, autonomy, and consent. The President's Commission for the Study of Ethical Problems notes Robert Hahn's observation that, for example, "the individualism central in the doctrine of informed consent is absent in the tradition of Vietnamese thought. Self is not cultivated, but subjugated to cosmic orders. Information, direct communication, and decision may be regarded as arrogant" (1982:55–56). In contrast the commission (1982:56) cites Alan Harwood's suggestion that mainland Puerto Rican Hispanics expect to be engaged in the therapeutic process and have a strong desire for information and for information given without condescension. Social workers must be cognizant of such cultural beliefs and preferences if they are to obtain informed consent effectively and sensitively.

Exceptions to informed consent. In a variety of circumstances professionals may not be required to obtain informed consent before intervention
(Berg et al. 2001; Rozovsky 1984:114–23). These include instances involving emergencies, client waiver, and therapeutic privilege. In genuine emergencies, for example, professionals may be authorized to act without the
client's consent. According to many state statutes and much case law, an
emergency entails a client's being incapacitated and unable to exercise the
mental ability to make an informed decision. Interference with decision-
making ability must be a result of injury or illness, alcohol or drug use, or
any other disability. In addition a need for immediate treatment to preserve a life or health must exist. As Rozovsky has noted, it is important for
practitioners not to assume "that a person who has consumed a moderate
amount of alcohol or drugs or who has a history of psychiatric problems is
automatically incapable of giving consent: the facts and circumstances of
individual cases are essential to such determinations" (1984:89).

Further, many statutes authorize practitioners to treat clients without
their consent in order to protect them or the community from harm.
Cases involving substance abusers, prisoners, and people with sexually
transmitted diseases are examples (President's Commission 1982:195;
Rozovsky 1984: 41–51). As social workers have come to learn, they may be
obligated to disclose information to third parties without clients' consent
if they have evidence that serious injury to others or to the state might
otherwise result. As I explained in chapter 2, the *Tarasoff* case and other
duty-to-protect cases included circumstances in which a mental health
professional was expected to disclose confidential information to third
parties. Instances involving abuse and neglect (involving children, older
adults, and people with disabilities) and the request for social services by a
minor also are relevant.

Both statutes and case law have recognized the right of clients to request
that they not be informed of the nature of risks associated with impending treatment or services (see, for example, *Holt v. Nelson* (1974); *Ferrara v. Galluchio* (1958)). In these instances clients may decide that they
are better off not knowing what the services or treatment will entail and
thus waive their right to give informed consent. Professionals are generally
advised to document such a waiver and to consider having clients sign a
waiver form. The most controversial exception to informed consent concerns the concept of therapeutic privilege. In several statutes involving the

physician-patient relationship, for example, states have permitted practitioners to withhold information if they believe that disclosure would have a substantially adverse effect on a patient's welfare. These statutes allow considerable discretion by professionals and thus have led to extensive debate about the possibility of misuse of the privilege by physicians and other health and mental health professionals. This controversy has been fueled by the growing trend to avoid paternalism and toward full disclosure to patients and clients by the professionals who care for them (Reamer 1983b, 2013a). In general practitioners are cautioned to exercise the exception of therapeutic privilege only in extreme circumstances that can be thoroughly documented. As Schutz wisely notes,

> Once the therapist invokes the therapeutic privilege, he must accept the burden of proof that a full disclosure would have harmed the patient. Otherwise, he faces a potential charge that the incomplete disclosure was abuse of duty. On the other hand, if he does make a full disclosure, he faces the charge that the statements given caused an injury or caused the patient to refuse a treatment and that, as a result, the patient suffered an injury.
>
> (1982:39)

CLINICAL ASSESSMENT AND INTERVENTION

Social workers in direct practice settings—such as family service agencies, community mental health centers, psychiatric hospitals, and private practice—routinely assess clients in an effort to formulate an intervention plan. Particularly in work with individual clients and families, social workers draw on a wide array of assessment and diagnostic frameworks, reflecting different theoretical orientations. Some practitioners may favor psychodynamically oriented assessments and interventions, while others may favor cognitively or behaviorally oriented assessments and interventions. By now most social workers agree that no one theoretical perspective can claim a monopoly. Although practitioners may favor one view or approach over another, many draw on the strengths of various perspectives while keeping in mind their respective limitations and biases.

Whatever the social worker's ideological or theoretical perspective with respect to assessment and intervention frameworks, every social worker must be mindful of a range of malpractice and liability risks. As I discussed in chapter 1, claims alleging malpractice or negligence ordinarily argue that the social worker somehow departed from the standard of care associated with contemporary practice. Courts typically avoid rendering opinions about the relative merits or demerits of one practice approach versus another; so long as a significant minority within the profession embraces an approach, courts tend to be respectful of a professional's right to pursue it. Rather, what matters is whether evidence exists that the practitioner's use and implementation of that approach was somehow flawed or below par (the breach of professional duty) and resulted in injury to the plaintiff (usually the client or the client's legal representative).

Social workers need to be aware of several potential problems related to assessment and intervention, including failure to diagnose or assess properly and incompetent delivery of service.

Well-trained social workers are expected to have the skill to diagnose (a medical term I prefer to avoid) or assess a variety of client problems. Although not every social worker may be skilled in all areas of assessment, most practitioners involved in direct practice are trained to assess common mental health disorders and problems in living (Corcoran and Walsh 2010).

Problems can arise, however, when social workers do not conduct thorough assessments consistent with the standard of care in the profession or make erroneous assumptions based on the data available to them. Imagine a client with symptoms of depression who seeks help from a social worker. During the first interview the client also mentions that she has chronic headaches.

The social worker conducts a cursory assessment and neglects to ask additional questions about the headaches—their intensity, frequency, duration, and so on. As a result the social worker does not recommend that the client consult a physician who is trained to assess the organic causes or correlates of headaches. The client turns out to have a brain tumor, and she sues the social worker, alleging negligence. The client does not expect the social worker to be able to diagnose a brain tumor, of course. She can claim, however, that the social worker should ask detailed questions about somatic complaints and, if appropriate, refer her to a physician.

In *Kogensparger v. Athens Mental Health Center* (1989), an Ohio court held a mental health center liable in failing to consider the possibility that organic problems caused a patient's symptoms, which included behavioral disorders and complaints of abnormal discomfort in his head. Staff members maintained that schizophrenia caused the symptoms, which included consuming excessive amounts of food and water. The patient, who had been hospitalized for more than three years, suffered a grand mal seizure and died one week later. An autopsy disclosed a brain tumor. Experts agreed that the tumor was slow growing and must have been detectable for several years before the patient died; the court ruled that the center's failure to provide appropriate care was the proximate cause of death ("Mental Health Center's Failure" 1992:2).

A number of important legal precedents related to failure to diagnose come from the field of medicine. Most concern problems of misdiagnosis, missed diagnosis (the failure to identify a problem), and improper treatment. Over the years courts have held physicians liable when they have not used a standard and well-accepted diagnostic test (*Narcarato v. Grob* (1970); *Smith v. Yohe* (1963); *Estate of Davies v. Reese* (1977)), interpreted test data incorrectly (*Green v. State* (1975)), and have not responded to a patient's adverse reaction to a diagnostic test (*Dill v. Miles* (1957)). Doctors have also been held liable for the consequences of inaccurate test results, although they can avoid liability if the misdiagnosis does not affect treatment or if the misdiagnosis is followed by correct treatment (R. Cohen 1979; Cohen and Mariano 1982: 150–51).

Other failure-to-diagnose suits have alleged failure to pursue information that seemed relevant and turned out to be essential. In *Merchants National Bank v. United States* (1967), a federal district court in North Dakota found that a psychiatrist was negligent in not pursuing a patient's allegation that her husband had attempted to harm her. Mental health professionals also have been held liable in the failure to forward significant information to another therapist. In *Underwood v. United States* (1966) an air force psychiatrist, who was being transferred off base, did not inform his patient's new psychiatrist of the patient's threats to kill his wife. The new therapist permitted the patient to return to duty and draw a firearm, which he then used to kill his wife. The victim's father won his suit alleging that the psychiatrist's failure to forward the information constituted negligence (Schutz 1982:25–26).

In a Wisconsin case the plaintiff's mother had dated a man and ended the relationship. Subsequently the man entered the woman's home by throwing himself through a window; he was armed with a shotgun. The man tortured the woman and then murdered her in the presence of her children. The man then killed himself. During the month before this happened, the man had received clinical services at two counseling centers. The lawsuit alleged that the counselors were negligent in failing to diagnose the man's homicidal intentions and failing to warn the police or the mother. One counseling center settled the case for $400,000 and the second for $600,000 ("Man Kills Woman" 1994).

Not surprisingly many cases involving failure to diagnose involve allegations that a mental health professional did not exercise sound judgment and that as a result the client or patient suffered an injury. In *Chatman v. Millis* (1975) a psychologist was sued by the ex-husband of a woman who sought to terminate his visitation rights with their two-and-a-half-year-old child by alleging that the husband had sexually molested the boy (R. Cohen 1979). The psychologist interviewed the mother and son but not the father. As a result of the assessment the psychologist concluded that the father's visitation rights should be terminated or, at the very least, that his visits with the child should be supervised. Although the Arkansas Supreme Court ruled that the husband could not sue for negligence suit because he never had a doctor-patient relationship with the psychologist, one justice issued a strong dissenting opinion:

> Defendant was negligent and careless in making such diagnosis by failing to exercise the degree of skill and care, or to possess the degree of knowledge, ordinarily exercised or possessed by other psychological examiners or psychologists engaged in this type of practice . . . in that he failed and neglected to ever interview the plaintiff and in fact did not even know him, failed to administer any diagnostic tests . . . or to use any of the proper methods that psychologists use in exercising ordinary care to protect others from injury or damage; the defendant acted in a manner willfully and wantonly in disregard to the rights of the plaintiff.
>
> (R. Cohen 1979:164)

Courts do not expect absolute precision in professionals' assessments. Judges recognize the inexact nature of assessment. What they do expect is conformity to the profession's standard of care with regard to assessment procedures and criteria. Although the outcome of a case may be tragic and the social worker's assessment may be wrong, the practitioner may not have been negligent. To be considered negligent a diagnosis must be wrong (an error in judgment) *and* determined in a negligent fashion (Schutz 1982:25). An error in judgment is not by itself negligent.

Many failure-to-diagnose cases involve suicide attempts. Typically the plaintiff (ordinarily a client who failed in an attempt to commit suicide and was injured in the process or a family member of a client who committed suicide) alleges that the social worker (or other mental health professional) did not properly diagnose the potential for suicide. In a New Hampshire case the plaintiff was a thirty-one-year-old woman who was admitted to a hospital by two friends who were concerned about her substance abuse and recent suicide attempt. The suit contended that the hospital staff did not properly assess her suicide risk. During the initial assessment a hospital staff member noted recent slash marks on the plaintiff's left wrist but accepted her explanation that the cuts were accidental. The staff had not interviewed the plaintiff's friends and therefore did not know of the recent suicide attempt. Shortly after the plaintiff's admission to the hospital she was found hanging in a bathroom. She suffered permanent anoxic brain damage, although it was unclear whether the damage was entirely the result of the hanging or if she had a preexisting condition that was aggravated by the hanging ("Patient Admitted to Hospital" 1990:2). The case was settled for $175,000.

In 1991 a U.S. District Court found a VA hospital in Tennessee liable for failure to properly assess the risk of suicide. The plaintiff was a thirty-three-year-old veteran who had been diagnosed with chronic paranoid schizophrenia and whose records showed that he drank as much as a fifth of alcohol per day. The man was taken to the VA hospital by ambulance, and the trip ticket stated that the patient had been seeing demons and intended to kill himself. The VA nurse testified during the trial that she had placed the trip ticket on the chart; however, the resident psychiatrist stated that she did not see the trip ticket when she examined the patient later that afternoon. The resident psychiatrist examined the patient, "who was a little nervous but rational," and the patient was sent home. The next morning the patient was found dead from a self-inflicted shotgun wound. The court found that the VA hospital had deviated from the standard of care, either by failing to transmit the ambulance trip ticket or by failing to consider its contents, and that the psychiatrist failed to take an adequate history ("Hospital Liable for Failure to Admit" 1991:4).

Baker v. United States (1964) demonstrates the difference between an inaccurate judgment and negligence. The suit was filed by the wife of Kenneth Baker. Mrs. Baker was guardian for her husband, a psychiatric patient receiving care at the VA Hospital in Iowa City, Iowa. He attempted suicide by leaping into a thirteen-foot-deep window well located on the grounds of the hospital. He was seriously injured, suffering a variety of fractures and complete paralysis of his right side. Mrs. Baker alleged in her suit that the physician who admitted her husband to the hospital failed to properly diagnose his mental illness. According to Mrs. Baker, she had conferred with the acting chief of the neuropsychiatric service at the hospital and had informed him of her husband's suicidal tendencies. She also told the physician that she had found a gun that her husband had hidden several weeks earlier. Mr. Baker was subsequently placed on an open ward; the physician did not think he was a suicide risk.

The U.S. District Court ruled that the admitting physician was not negligent and "exercised the proper standard of care required under the circumstances." In addition, the court concluded, "Diagnosis is not an exact science. Diagnosis with absolute precision and certainty is not possible" (Austin, Moline, and Williams 1990:167).

Similar issues related to professional judgment arose in *Boyer v. Tilzer* (1992). The police took a man into custody and transported him to a Missouri state mental health facility where he was involuntarily admitted for a period not to exceed ninety-six hours. An emergency room report described the patient as combative, hyperreligious, and manic. He was apparently hearing voices, seeing demons, and thinking he was God. A psychiatric resident diagnosed the patient as suffering from alcohol abuse and probable PCP (phencyclidine) psychosis and recommended treatment for substance dependency.

The hospital released the patient after three days. One week later he began having hallucinations and delusions. He stabbed his girlfriend's hand with a knife and fatally stabbed a third party who had come to her assistance. The patient was arrested and diagnosed as having paranoid schizophrenia.

The dead woman's estate sued the psychiatric resident, alleging that the patient had been incorrectly diagnosed and released. The trial court found in favor of the resident, concluding that no proof existed that the resident had acted in bad faith or in a grossly negligent fashion. The estate appealed, and the Missouri appeals court also found no evidence that the psychiatric resident had not performed his duties in good faith and without gross negligence ("Psychiatrist Not Negligent" 1992:1).[3]

In a Virginia case involving a social worker, a twenty-four-year-old mother was admitted to a psychiatric hospital after a suicide attempt involving a gun. About two weeks after the woman's discharge from the hospital, the social worker learned that the gun was back in the woman's house and made a note to "get it out"; however, the record shows that the social worker did not intervene directly. After the woman canceled two consecutive group therapy sessions, the social worker wrote himself a note to "get ahold of Mary right away," but the social worker did not follow through. The woman shot herself in the head as her husband approached the house on the day that he returned from naval duty. The jury awarded the husband and children more than $2 million ("Wife Kills Self" 1995).

NEGLIGENT INTERVENTION

Most social workers provide skilled service to clients that is consistent with prevailing standards in the profession. On occasion social workers are negligent. In these instances their intervention approaches or techniques deviate from the standard of care in the profession. As I noted in chapter 1, many liability judgments against social workers stem from genuine mistakes (speaking about confidential matters too loudly in an agency hallway) or good intentions (disclosing privileged information without a client's consent in order to protect third parties). Other judgments, however, are triggered by professional misconduct, which I address more fully in chapter 4. The emphasis here is on liability risks that pertain to negligent departures from the standard of care.

Social workers' intervention approaches and techniques can be negligent in many ways. In some instances social workers may use techniques for which they have not received proper training, such as biofeedback or hypnosis, or carried them out in some flawed fashion. A social worker who uses such techniques improperly and whose lack of skill causes injury to a client may be found liable for abuse of the psychotherapeutic process (Reid 1999).

Using nontraditional approaches can also trigger liability claims and licensing board complaints. Although social workers should not feel compelled to conform entirely to commonly used techniques endorsed by the majority of colleagues or to completely avoid experimentation, they should be wary of radical departures from common practices in the profession. For example, in one nationally publicized case a Colorado social worker was sentenced to sixteen years in prison in the suffocation death of a ten-year-old girl whom she was treating for an attachment disorder. The social worker was convicted of death resulting from reckless child abuse, for using so-called rebirthing therapy. The therapy included wrapping the child in a flannel blanket, meant to represent the womb; according to the evidence, the child cried when she was not able to breathe and ended up lying in her own vomit and dying of asphyxiation (Nicholson 2001).

In another case a former client sued a Virginia social worker, who was subsequently disciplined by the state board of social work. According to a published report (Barr 1997), the social worker used past-life regression techniques, spiritual guides and masters, and nontherapeutic bodily contact. According to the news story, the social worker also took the client flying in a plane that he had rented and loaned the client money.

In Arizona a psychologist treated a woman for depression, anxiety, and drug and alcohol abuse. The psychologist allegedly used a variety of unorthodox treatment techniques, including channeling, Holotropic Breathwork, shamanic journeying, spirit depossessions, and soul retrievals. The jury awarded the plaintiff $205,000 in compensatory damages and $120,000 in punitive damages ("Psychologist's Unorthodox Treatment" 1995).[4]

A number of malpractice claims filed against clinicians claim that they used "recovered memory" techniques and implanted "false memories" of child or sexual abuse. Although some courts have not been willing to admit into evidence testimony about recovered memories because of debate about their validity, others have. In a prominent California case a jury awarded damages to a father after finding that a psychiatrist and a social worker had implanted false memories of incest in his daughter's mind while treating her for bulimia. Gary Ramona, a former winery executive, was awarded $500,000 (McArdle 1994).[5]

In a Texas case parents alleged that their child's psychiatrist negligently produced recovered memories in the child that led him to claim that his father had sexually abused him. The Texas jury awarded the parents $350,000 ("Psychiatrist Sued" 1995). In another Texas case a woman alleged that her counselor implanted in her memories of satanic ritual abuse and parental incest and was responsible for her multiple personality disorder and alienation from her family. The jury found the counselor 60 percent negligent and the plaintiff 40 percent negligent ("Woman Claims Psychological Counselor" 1995).[6]

In *Hammer v. Rosen* (1960) Alice Hammer and her father sued her psychiatrist, Dr. John Rosen. Rosen had treated Alice Hammer, who had been diagnosed with schizophrenia. The plaintiffs claimed that Rosen beat Alice Hammer during treatment sessions. According to court records, Rosen treated his schizophrenic patients by also acting in a schizophrenic manner at times. Ultimately the New York Court of Appeals, the state's highest court, reversed the lower court decision and found Rosen liable for improper treatment and malpractice (Austin, Moline, and Williams 1990:156–57).

A Michigan case raised similar issues. The plaintiff was a legal secretary who went to St. Joseph Hospital with symptoms of panic disorder and agoraphobia. One defendant was a social worker. The plaintiff alleged that she was discharged to outpatient treatment without being informed of the diagnosis or given an explanation of her condition. She claimed that attempts to treat her condition were limited to comments about less painful methods of suicide and New Age spiritual guidance. The case was settled for $100,000 ("Patient Improperly Treated" 1992:6).

Social workers who use nontraditional or unorthodox intervention approaches must be vigilant in their efforts to adhere to prevailing ethical standards. As Austin, Moline, and Williams urge,

> If you are using techniques that are not commonly practiced, you will need to have a clear rationale that other professionals in your field will accept and support. It is important to consult colleagues when you are using what are considered to be nontraditional approaches to treatment. This is primarily because it is not difficult to prove deviation from average care. Some examples of what may be considered nontraditional therapeutic techniques might include asking clients to undress, striking a client, or giving "far-out" homework assignments.
>
> (1990:155–56)

Social workers should keep in mind several relevant standards from the NASW *Code of Ethics* (2008:8–9, 25) that pertain to the use of novel or experimental treatment approaches and to providing services outside one's areas of expertise and competence (for example, when an agency places a practitioner with insufficient training or expertise in a position in order to address a staffing shortage):

> Social workers should provide services and represent themselves as competent only within the boundaries of their education, training, license, certification, consultation received, supervised experience, or other relevant professional experience.
>
> (standard 1.04[a])

> Social workers should provide services in substantive areas or use intervention techniques or approaches that are new to them only after engaging in appropriate study, training, consultation, and supervision from people who are competent in those interventions or techniques.
>
> (standard 1.04[b])

> When generally recognized standards do not exist with respect to an emerging area of practice, social workers should exercise careful judgment and take responsible steps (including appropriate education, research, training, consultation, and supervision) to ensure the competence of their work and to protect clients from harm.
>
> (standard 1.04[c])

> Social workers should critically examine and keep current with emerging knowledge relevant to social work and fully use evaluation and research evidence in their professional practice.
>
> (standard 5.02[c])

Another potential source of problems is advice giving. If social workers give clients advice that departs from the standard of care—such as advising clients about psychotropic medication doses or the therapeutic benefits of herbal remedies for symptoms of clinical depression—they could be held liable (for example, for practicing medicine without a license). In a Florida case a clinical social worker was disciplined by the licensing board after evidence was presented that the social worker prescribed the medications Pamelor, Klonipin, and Soma to a client (Florida Board 2001). A Wisconsin social worker was also accused of prescribing medications to a client and giving the client sample medications. According to the licensing board, "The client has testified that on at least one occasion during the course of Respondent's therapy, Respondent provided the client with a prescription order for medication, which bore the signature of the psychiatrist associated with Respondent in practice. This prescription had been provided to Respondent, pre-signed in blank, and were then filled out by Respondent, on her own authority, and given to the client to fill at a pharmacy" (Wisconsin Department of Safety 2013).

In a widely publicized case a New Jersey social worker employed at a mental health clinic told the New Jersey State Board of Medical Examiners that social workers were being allowed to order refills of patients' medication prescriptions because of a shortage of psychiatrists. The social worker said that she and other clinic social workers would order prescriptions by telephone, and staff psychiatrists would later sign the prescription forms. She also alleged that social workers occasionally would change patients' medication—including antipsychotic and antidepressant drugs—and modify dosages without consulting a physician. After she blew the whistle, the social worker said, "I knew that [social workers] prescribing medications was wrong, and I was surprised something like this could be going on, but I was really getting involved in my [psychotherapy] cases and I enjoyed the group I was leading, so I thought I would try to change things from within" ("Member Blows Whistle" 1990:11).

The state board investigated and reprimanded the clinic's consulting psychiatrist, finding that she had inadequately supervised patients who were on prescription drugs. She admitted no wrongdoing but faced $8,000 in penalties. An independent consultant was to monitor the clinic for two years.

In addition social workers and the agencies for which they work can be sued for mistreating clients, for example, in the form of verbal or emotional abuse. Consider what happened in a Washington, D.C., case. The plaintiff was a thirty-six-year-old attorney who participated in a five-day program that included lectures, "guided fantasies," and experimental psychological exercises. He experienced psychotic symptoms (hallucinations) during the training, along with hyperactivity and sleep deprivation. He was hospitalized for five days, discharged, and about three months later was readmitted to the hospital, where he was then treated for about three more months. The attorney had no previous history of mental illness. He sued, claiming intentional infliction of emotional distress, negligence, and fraud (in the form of an introductory session that he alleged was misleading). The District of Columbia jury found in favor of the defendant with respect to intentional infliction of emotional distress but found in favor of the plaintiff with regard to the allegations of negligence and fraud. The plaintiff was awarded $297,387 ("Attorney Suffers Psychotic Breakdown" 1991:1).

In another case the plaintiff sued sponsors of what were known as EST seminars, which were popular in the 1970s and 1980s. These seminars, created by Werner Erhard, were designed for people who sought personal transformation and included controversial treatment techniques. The plaintiff alleged that the treatment caused several psychological problems and a suicide attempt. The plaintiff, who had a history of abuse and psychological difficulties, was recovering from an automobile accident and was depressed because of her injuries. She claimed that during the sessions the trainer and other participants told her that the automobile accident was really her fault and that she chose to be in the accident. The plaintiff claimed that the sponsors should have had a procedure to screen out individuals who were in treatment elsewhere. The Utah case was settled for $50,000 ("Woman Claims Psychological Problems" 1992:6).

Of course, many lawsuits alleging negligent intervention are not successful. In *Hess v. Frank* (1975) a New York patient sued his psychiatrist, claiming that the doctor used abusive language and that such language caused anguish and serious injury to the patient. The plaintiff sought $100,000 in damages and $20,000 previously paid to the psychiatrist for treatment but lost the case (R. Cohen 1979:164).

BOUNDARY ISSUES AND DUAL RELATIONSHIPS

Especially since the 1980s, social workers have developed an increasingly mature grasp of a wide range of boundary and dual relationship issues (Congress 1999; Jayaratne, Croxton, and Mattison 1997; Kagle and Giebelhausen 1994; Reamer 2012a; Strom-Gottfried 1999). Boundary issues arise when social workers encounter actual or potential conflicts between their professional duties and their social, sexual, religious, or business relationships (St. Germain 1993, 1996). Some dual relationships are clearly unethical (for example, engaging in a sexual relationship with one's client); however, other dual relationships may be unavoidable (for example, when practitioners work and live in small rural communities) and require careful management. According to the NASW *Code of Ethics,*

> Social workers should not engage in dual or multiple relationships with clients or former clients in which there is a risk of exploitation or potential harm to the client. In instances when dual or multiple relationships are unavoidable, social workers should take steps to protect clients and are responsible for setting clear, appropriate, and culturally sensitive boundaries. (Dual or multiple relationships occur when social workers relate to clients in more than one relationship, whether professional, social, or business. Dual or multiple relationships can occur simultaneously or consecutively.)
>
> (standard 1.06[c])

Social workers should be alert to a number of boundary issues that arise in practice and that can be a central issue in malpractice claims and licensing board complaints (Celenza 2007; Syme 2003; Reamer 2001a, 2012a; Zur 2007):

• Sexual relationships with current and former clients. A significant portion of dual relationships entered into by social workers involve sexual contact (although the evidence suggests that only a small percentage of practitioners engage in such conduct). The consensus among social workers is that sexual relationships with current clients are unethical (NASW *Code of Ethics* standard 1.09[a]). In general sexual relationships with former clients also are unethical. According to the NASW *Code of Ethics,* "If social workers engage in conduct contrary to this prohibition or claim that an exception to this prohibition is warranted because of extraordinary circumstances, it is social workers—not their clients—who assume the full burden of demonstrating that the former client has not been exploited, coerced, or manipulated, intentionally or unintentionally" (2008:13).

• Counseling of former sexual partners. Moving from an intimate sexual relationship to a professional-client relationship (for example, when a social worker's former lover seeks the social worker's professional advice or services) can be detrimental to the client. Former lovers who become clients are likely to find it difficult to shift from the role of an egalitarian partner in an intimate relationship to a party who, to some degree, is in a dependent or subordinate position. According to the NASW *Code of Ethics,* "Social workers should not provide clinical services to individuals with whom they have had a prior sexual relationship. Providing clinical services to a former sexual partner has the potential to be harmful to the individual and is likely to make it difficult for the social worker and individual to maintain appropriate professional boundaries" (standard 1.09[d]).

• Sexual relationships with clients' relatives or acquaintances. Current ethical standards also prohibit sexual activities or sexual contact with clients' relatives or other individuals with whom a client maintains a close personal relationship, particularly when risk of exploitation or potential harm to the client exists. According to the NASW *Code of Ethics,* "Sexual activity or sexual contact with clients' relatives or other individuals with whom clients maintain a personal relationship has the potential to be harmful to the client and may make it difficult for the social worker and client to maintain appropriate professional boundaries" (standard 1.09[b]).

• Sexual relationships with supervisees, trainees, students, and colleagues. Social workers must also avoid sexual relationships with staff members whom they supervise and other individuals (such as trainees and students) over whom they exercise some form of authority. The power differential in these relationships exposes supervisees, trainees, and students to potential exploitation and harm (see NASW *Code of Ethics,* 2008:17, 19, standards 2.07[a][b], 3.01[c], 3.02[d]).

• Physical contact with clients. Social workers must be careful to distinguish between appropriate and inappropriate physical contact. Briefly holding the hand of a distressed client or a brief good-bye hug at the end of a long-term clinical relationship may be appropriate. Sustained physical contact is not. According to the NASW *Code of Ethics,* "Social workers should not engage in physical contact with clients when there is a possibility of psychological harm to the client as a result of the contact (such as cradling or caressing clients). Social workers who engage in appropriate physical contact with clients are responsible for setting clear, appropriate, and culturally sensitive boundaries that govern such physical contact" (standard 1.10). Social workers should be mindful of clients' religious, cultural, and ethnicity norms pertaining to physical contact. For example, some religions and cultures prohibit physical contact—including handshakes—between unmarried individuals of the opposite sex.

• Friendships with current and former clients. Friendships that develop between social workers and their clients sometimes arise out of genuine affection; in some instances, however, friendships reflect social workers' own emotional needs, personal crises, and personal issues. Social workers must be alert to the ways in which friendships with current clients are unethical and the ways in which friendships with former clients may constitute inappropriate dual relationships. As with sexual relationships, friendships with clients have the potential to harm clients and interfere with their ability to benefit from social work services. Social workers should be aware that digital contact with clients and former clients on social networking sites (such as Facebook) may be viewed as evidence of a friendship.

• Encounters with clients in public settings. Social workers often encounter clients in public settings, such as stores, festivals, or receptions at social events. This is especially likely in rural and other small communities such as military bases. Social workers should discuss this possibility with clients in advance, focusing on constructive, ethical ways of handling these encounters. Such proactive measures can help clients and practitioners avoid awkwardness and misunderstanding about the nature of their relationship.

• Attendance at clients' social, religious, or life-cycle events. Social workers hold many and varied opinions concerning their attendance at these events (such as weddings, graduations, and funerals). Some social workers believe that such attendance can be therapeutically beneficial and supportive; they argue that refusal to attend may damage the clinical relationship and lead to clients' feeling betrayed. Social workers' understanding of clients' religious and cultural norms around attendance at such events may influence their judgment. In contrast many social workers worry about the potential for blurred boundaries when practitioners attend social, religious, or life-cycle events. Social workers should address the issue explicitly and establish clear guidelines, taking into consideration current ethical standards concerning dual relationships and the potential for ethics complaints and litigation. Social workers who face such decisions would be wise to seek and document consultation, thereby demonstrating their good-faith effort to manage the boundaries responsibly.

• Gifts from clients. Challenging boundary issues sometimes emerge when clients offer gifts or special favors to social workers. Some gifts (such as a plate of homemade cookies at holiday time) may be completely innocent and harmless; others may be loaded with clinical meaning and may be a precursor to an inappropriate dual relationship. Social workers should develop guidelines to distinguish between circumstances in which they may accept modest, token gifts from clients and circumstances in which accepting gifts is inappropriate. It is also helpful to develop procedures to help social workers respond skillfully and sensitively to clients who offer gifts.

• Gifts to clients. In most instances it is unethical for social workers to give clients gifts because of the implication of an inappropriate dual relationship. Some practitioners and agencies have acknowledged unique exceptions, for example, when clients in an independent living program invite agency staff to see their new apartment. In these instances social workers should develop clear guidelines to minimize harm (for example, ensuring that the client understands that the modest gift is from the agency rather than an individual staff member).[7]

• Favors for clients. A variety of circumstances may tempt social workers, for altruistic reasons, to offer clients favors (for example, giving a stranded client a ride, lending money to a destitute client, giving a vulnerable client one's home telephone number). Although such gestures may be completely innocent and relatively innocuous, social workers should be aware of the ways in which their altruistic instincts may generate boundary issues. In some instances clients may interpret such gestures as an indication of the social worker's interest in a nonprofessional relationship.

• The delivery of services in a client's home. Social workers who provide services in clients' homes (for example, in home-health programs or home-based crisis intervention programs) must be particularly alert to potentially problematic boundary issues. Providing services in such nonoffice, informal, and relatively intimate settings may confuse clients and practitioners about the nature of the professional-client relationship. Social workers must be prepared to respond appropriately to family members' invitations to join them for meals, family outings, and other social events.

• Financial conflicts of interest. Introducing financial transactions into the professional-client relationship (for example, when social workers invest in a client's new business venture or borrow money from an affluent client) is likely to distract both practitioners and clients from the social services agenda with which they began their work, compromise clients' interests, and introduce conflicts of interest (where the social worker's judgment and behavior are affected by the financial considerations). Entering into a business relationship with a client is clearly unethical. In addition social workers should not take advantage of their relationships with clients to advance their own financial interests. (In one case in which I consulted, a social worker provided clinical services to terminally ill clients with AIDS. On the weekends the social worker moonlighted as an antiques dealer. Through her work with terminally ill clients, the social worker learned of antiques that would become available at estate sales after the clients' deaths. The social worker understood that she had to be very disciplined about not taking advantage of this information.) Also, staff, administrators, and board members should not enter into financial relationships with their agencies or other organizations in a manner that would constitute a conflict of interest (for example, having a personal financial stake in the agency's property, investments, or business transactions). Agencies should have clear policies about staff members' employment in other settings (for example, whether clinical staff at a community mental health center can establish their own part-time private practice) and delivery of services to former clients when staff terminate their employment (for example, when clients choose to transfer their care to their practitioners' new employment setting).[8]

• Delivery of services to two or more people who have a relationship with each other (such as couples or family members). As I discussed briefly in chapter 2 with respect to confidentiality issues, social workers often provide services to two or more people who have a relationship with each other, typically in the context of family, marital, or couples counseling. In these situations social workers should clarify with all the parties involved which individuals will be considered clients and the nature of the social worker's professional obligations to the various individuals who are receiving services. Social workers who anticipate a conflict of interest among the individuals receiving services or who anticipate having to perform in potentially conflicting roles (for example, when a social worker is asked to testify in a child custody dispute or divorce proceedings involving clients) should clarify their role with the parties involved and take appropriate action to minimize any conflict of interest.

• Barter with clients for goods and services. Social workers hold many opinions about the use of barter. Many believe that barter is appropriate in limited circumstances when they can demonstrate that such arrangements are an accepted practice among professionals in the local community, considered essential for the provision of services, negotiated without coercion, and entered into at the client's initiative and with the client's informed consent (see NASW *Code of Ethics* standard 1.13[b]). Others argue that barter is fraught with risk, particularly when defects in the bartered goods or services lead to conflict in, and consequently undermine, the professional-client relationship. According to the NASW *Code of Ethics,* "Social workers who accept goods or services from clients as payment for professional services assume the full burden of demonstrating that this arrangement will not be detrimental to the client or the professional relationship" (standard 1.13[b]).

• Management of relationships with clients in small or rural communities. As I noted earlier, the likelihood of unanticipated boundary issues and dual relationships increases in geographically small communities, especially in rural areas. Social workers in these communities often report how challenging it is to separate their professional and personal lives. Clients may be the proprietors of local businesses that social workers must patronize or may end up being social workers' service providers in other contexts (for example, when a client is the only fourth-grade teacher in town and the social worker's child is enrolled in that class). Social workers in these circumstances must be vigilant in their efforts to protect clients, by taking into consideration such factors as the practitioners' own comfort level and confidence in their ability to manage the overlapping relationships; clients' opinions about and perceptions of the boundary issues and their ability to handle them; and the type and severity of the clients' presenting problems. Similar issues can arise in small cultural, ethnic, and religious communities, for example, when a religiously observant social worker employed by a family service agency is actively involved in her religious community and provides services to some members of that community, or a lesbian clinical social worker is actively involved in her local lesbian community and receives requests for services from members of that community.

• Self-disclosure to clients. Social workers' self-disclosure to clients is a complex topic. Social workers generally agree that relatively limited and superficial self-disclosure, handled judiciously, may be appropriate and therapeutically helpful. Social workers also recognize that self-disclosure can harm clients, particularly when the self-disclosure occurs primarily to meet the social worker's emotional needs. For example, social workers in recovery from substance abuse face unique challenges when they encounter clients at recovery meetings (such as Alcoholics or Narcotics Anonymous).

• Collegial relationships with a former client. On occasion, social workers may encounter former clients who have become professional colleagues (for example, former clients who decide to enter the social work field as a result of their personal experiences). In these situations social workers should discuss with their former clients any problematic boundary issues and ways of dealing with them. In some instances professional relationships with a former client may not be harmful or risky and may require no special accommodations; in other instances, however, the intensity and complexity of the former professional-client relationship may make a collegial relationship difficult and challenging. In these situations social workers may need to make special arrangements (such as resign from a professional task force on which both parties serve).

• Hiring former clients. Some social service programs, such as community mental health centers and substance abuse treatment programs, consider hiring former clients or consumers. This practice usually stems from professionals' belief that, because of their personal experiences, former clients may provide unique and valuable empathy and services to current clients. Many also view hiring former clients as a way to empower these individuals, promote client growth, and provide current clients with valuable role models. Social workers need to carefully consider the ethical and clinical implications of this practice. In addition to a range of potential benefits, hiring former clients poses several risks. Hiring former clients may complicate relationships between practitioners and the former clients who are now agency employees and who must relate to their former service providers as colleagues or employment supervisors. Unique challenges may arise if a former client who is now a staff member needs to reenter treatment and become a client again. Also, former clients who were not hired may feel resentful and hurt. Further, hiring former clients may introduce complex issues related to former clients' access to confidential agency records.

MANAGING BOUNDARY RISKS

Effective risk management concerning dual relationships and boundary issues should provide both conceptual guidance and practical steps that enhance protections of all parties involved. The following is a decision-making model, based on several available frameworks (Corey and Herlihy 1997; Epstein 1994; Gottlieb 1995; Reamer 2000b, 2001a, 2012a), that

practitioners can use when they encounter potential or actual dual relationships and boundary issues:

1. Attempt to set unambiguous boundaries at the beginning of all professional relationships.
2. Evaluate potential dual relationships and boundary issues by considering (a) the amount of power the practitioner holds over the client,
(b) the duration of the relationship, (c) the clarity of conditions surrounding planned or actual termination, (d) the client's clinical profile, and
(e) prevailing ethical standards. How much power does the social worker
have over the client? How likely is it that the client will return for additional services? In clinical relationships to what extent do the client's clinical needs, issues, vulnerabilities, and symptoms increase the risk that the
client will be harmed? To what extent does the dual relationship breach
prevailing ethical standards? Especially risky are relationships that entail
considerable practitioner power (such as a parole officer or a practitioner
who provides court-ordered services), are long lasting, do not involve clear-
cut termination, involve clinical issues that render clients vulnerable, and
are not consistent with relevant ethical standards.
3. Based on these criteria, consider whether a dual relationship in any
form, including digital and online contact, is warranted or justifiable.
Recognize that gradations exist between the extreme options of a full-
fledged dual relationship and no dual relationship. For example, a social
worker may decide that attending a client's graduation ceremony at a substance abuse treatment program is permissible and important therapeutically but that attending the postceremony party at the client's home is
not. A practitioner may decide to disclose to a particular client that he is
a new parent without disclosing intimate details concerning his struggle
with infertility. A social worker may accept e-mail messages from clients
to reschedule appointments but not engage in online conversations that
include clinical or personal content. A grant administrator may collaborate on a joint project with a private agency in which her husband is
employed but recuse herself from all decisions at her agency concerning
funding of her husband's program.
4. Pay special attention to potentially conflicting roles in the relationship,
or what Kitchener (1988) calls "role incompatibility." For instance, a clini-

cal social worker should not agree to counsel her secretary or have a Face-book relationship with a former client. An administrator should not su-pervise her spouse. Of course, sometimes social workers do not agree about the extent of role incompatibility, which entails divergent expectations and power differentials; among the best examples is the debate among social workers about whether practitioners in recovery should attend Alcoholics Anonymous or Narcotics Anonymous meetings at which a client is present and whether community-based mental health programs should hire former clients as staff members.

5. Whenever there is any degree of doubt about dual relationships or boundary issues, consult thoughtful, principled, and trusted colleagues. It is important to consult with colleagues who understand one's work, par-ticularly in relation to services provided, clientele served, and relevant ethi-cal standards.

6. Discuss the relevant issues with all the parties involved, especially cli-ents. Clients should be actively and deliberately involved in these decisions, in part as a sign of respect and in part to promote informed consent. Fully inform clients of any potential risks.

7. Work under supervision whenever boundary issues are complex and the related risk is high.

8. If necessary and feasible, refer the client to another professional in order to minimize risk and prevent harm.

9. Document key aspects of the decision-making process, for example, col-leagues consulted, documents reviewed (codes of ethics, agency policies, statutes, regulations, relevant literature), and discussions with clients.

UNDUE INFLUENCE

On occasion liability problems arise in the delivery of social work services because of the phenomenon of undue influence. Undue influence occurs when social workers use their authority improperly to pressure, persuade, or sway a client to engage in an activity that may not be in the client's best interest or that may pose a conflict of interest. Undue influence may take several forms. Examples include persuading an elderly client to include the social worker in his will, influencing a minor in a way that is contrary to her parents' wishes, and convincing a client to include the social worker, during treatment, in a lucrative investment or business partnership. Gifis offers the legal definition of undue influence:

> It is established by excessive importunity, superiority of will or mind, the relationship of the parties (e.g., priest and penitent or caretaker and senior citizen) or by any other means constraining the donor or testator [one who makes and executes a testament or will] to do what he is unable to refuse. . . . The elements of undue influence are susceptibility of testator/donor to such influence, the exertion of improper influence, and submission to the domination of the influencing party.
>
> (1991:508)

According to the NASW *Code of Ethics,* "Social workers should not take unfair advantage of any professional relationship or exploit others to further their personal, religious, political, or business interests" (standard 1.06[b]). This issue arose in an Alabama case in which the licensing board revoked the license of a public health social worker who was found guilty of soliciting significant funds from a client as payment for not reporting information to Medicaid that would cause the client to lose his coverage (Alabama State Board 2003).

A lower court case from New York, *Geis v. Landau* (1983), illustrates how subtle issues involving undue influence can be (Austin, Moline, and Williams 1990:224–25). Dr. Jon Geis, a clinical psychologist, had provided counseling services to Betsy Landau for approximately eight years. During this period Landau was going through a divorce and explained to Geis that she was having difficulty paying his fees. When the therapy terminated, Landau had an outstanding bill of $8,000. Geis sued Landau for the unpaid fees. In her defense Landau contended that Geis, who allowed her fees to build up unpaid, failed to discuss with her the problem that she was "getting in over her head." At one point Geis wrote Landau a note stating "not to worry about the bill"; according to testimony, Geis had confidence that Landau would eventually pay the bill. According to court records, Geis also stated that he had decided that referring Landau to a low-cost mental health clinic would be unwise. According to the court, Geis "made a unilateral decision that only he could help the defendant." The judge ruled that Geis had exercised excessive power over his client, who was dependent upon him for resolution to her problems.

The judge stated that he had doubts that no other alternative (low-cost clinic) was available to Landau to assist her with further treatment. The judge stated that his decision to grant judgment to the defendant (Landau) did not mean that a therapist can never "extend credit to a patient," but, when a therapist knows that the client has no means by which to pay the account, such credit is not considered fair (Austin, Moline, and Williams 1990:225).

In 1979 the *New York Times* reported a highly unusual case involving a social worker who exerted undue influence. A social worker in New York City was convicted of killing his sixty-eight-year-old client after stealing a substantial sum of money from her by persuading the woman to withdraw more than $13,000 from a bank and then throwing the woman's weighted body into the East River. He was sentenced to a minimum of twenty-five years in prison (Besharov 1985:180).

Undue influence can be difficult to prove, as illustrated by the classic case of *Patterson v. Jensen* (1945). Although this Wisconsin case involves a physician rather than a social worker, it contains many issues broached in undue influence cases. Mary Faulks named her personal physician, a Dr. Patterson, as the primary beneficiary in her will. In addition to serving as her physician, Patterson had borrowed money from Faulks to buy a house. Faulks had also given Patterson money for an airplane hangar, partial payment on an airplane, and a family vacation. In response to one gift Patterson promised Faulks that he would attend to her medical needs for the rest of her life. The man whom Faulks and her husband had raised as a young boy, Will Jensen, objected to the relationship between his guardian and Patterson. He argued that it was not in her best interest and that she was "susceptible to undue influence." The court ruled that Faulks was not impaired when she had her last will drafted and that it had no clear evidence that Patterson influenced the contents of the will or became the primary beneficiary as a result of undue influence. The court concluded that influence that resulted from kindness and affection was not undue "if no imposition or fraud be practiced, even though it induced the testator (Mrs. Faulks) to make an unequal and unjust disposition" (quoted in Austin, Moline, and Williams 1990:223–23).

Lawsuits against social service professionals alleging undue influence are rare. Nonetheless social worker–client relationships certainly pose the potential for the exercise of undue influence.

SUICIDE

Many cases alleging improper assessment and intervention involve suicide. As I discussed earlier, a distressingly large number of liability cases allege that a mental health professional did not adequately assess for suicide risk and therefore did not take proper precautions to prevent a suicide. In a federal court case the plaintiff's husband was admitted to a hospital after showing signs of depression and slitting his wrists. The man was released about two-and-a-half weeks later after receiving medication and psychotherapy. Several months later the man was admitted to a VA hospital after buying a shotgun with the intention of killing himself. The hospital staff made no attempt to obtain the patient's earlier records or contact the physicians who had treated him. In addition staff members did not take a complete history at the time of admission and did not conduct a thorough interview with the patient's family about his history. The patient then attempted suicide for the third time, unsuccessfully, by jumping in front of a truck while out of the hospital on a weekend pass. Two months after his admission to the VA hospital the patient walked out of the facility and committed suicide by throwing himself under the wheels of a bus directly in front of the hospital and on the hospital grounds. The VA hospital was found liable, and the plaintiff was awarded $570,841 ("$570,841 Judgment Returned" 1991:3).

In another case raising similar issues, a patient sued a psychiatric facility, two psychiatrists, two psychiatric nurses, and a psychiatric social worker in Massachusetts. The plaintiff, a nineteen-year-old patient who jumped from the sixth floor of a psychiatric facility, alleged that the defendants did not properly diagnose his suicidal ideation and did not take precautions to prevent a suicide attempt. Before his suicide attempt he had a one-year history of psychiatric illness and previous psychiatric hospitalization. He had hallucinations, delusions, and symptoms of depression. A note by a nurse reported that the patient had said that he had given his body to Satan. Three days after his admission the patient was released on a pass to attend a psychiatric group therapy session on the sixth floor of the building. After the therapy session the patient was left momentarily unattended. He walked to an open atrium foyer and jumped. He suffered severe injuries, including hip and leg fractures, brain damage, and loss of an eye, kidney, and spleen. The jury found the defendants 85 percent negligent and the plaintiff 15 percent contributively negligent; the plaintiff ultimately settled for $3 million during the damages phase of the trial ("Psychiatrists Liable" 1991:1).

As I discuss more thoroughly in chapter 5, in still other cases plaintiffs allege that social service staff members did not provide adequate supervision of a suicidal client. As Meyer, Landis, and Hays conclude,

> While the law generally does not hold anyone responsible for the acts of another, there are exceptions. One of these is the responsibility of therapists to prevent suicide and other self-destructive behavior by their clients. The duty of therapists to exercise adequate care and skill in diagnosing suicidality is well-established (see *Meier v. Ross General Hospital*, 1968). When the risk of self-injurious behavior is identified an additional duty to take adequate precautions arises (*Abille v. United States*, 1980; *Pisel v. Stamford Hospital*, 1980). When psychotherapists fail to meet these responsibilities, they may be held liable for injuries that result.
>
> Not every completed suicide or gesture is cause for liability—only those which could reasonably have been prevented. Demonstrating negligence requires proof that the patient should have been identified as suicidal based on widely recognized criteria used by most other therapists of the same training.
>
> (1988:38)

As Meyer, Landis, and Hays suggest, *Meier v. Ross General Hospital* (1968) sets an important precedent in litigation involving suicide. The widow and children of the patient, Kurt Meier, brought a wrongful death suit against the California hospital and Dr. James Stubblebine, director of the psychiatric unit, after Meier committed suicide while a patient in the hospital. The family had brought Meier to the hospital after he had attempted suicide by cutting his wrists. The hospital had what it described as an "open door" policy for its psychiatric patients in order to provide a homelike atmosphere. The patients were free to move about the hospital and even to leave if they so wished. Staff members recognized that this open door policy lessened security and exposed potentially suicidal patients to greater risk, but they believed that ultimately the enhanced freedom of movement improved the prospects for rehabilitation (R. Cohen 1979:106–7).

Approximately one week after Meier slashed his wrists, he committed suicide by jumping head first from an open window in his second-floor room. The trial court found in favor of the hospital and psychiatrist.

On appeal to the California Supreme Court, however, the decision was reversed, and the court ordered a new trial. The state supreme court opinion contains important language concerning professionals' responsibility when they perceive a risk of suicide:

> If those charged with the care and treatment of a mentally disturbed patient know of facts from which they could reasonably conclude that the patient would be likely to harm himself in the absence of preclusive measures, then they must use reasonable care under the circumstances to prevent such harm [*Wood v. Samaritan Institution* (1945)]. Given this duty and the fact that defendants placed decedent, following an attempted suicide, in a second floor room with a fully openable window, the jury could find from the fact of decedent's plunge through this window that defendants more probably than not breached the duty of care owed to decedent. Even in the absence of expert testimony which describes the probability that the death or injury resulted from negligence, the jury may competently decide that defendant more probably than not breached his duty of care when the evidence supports a conclusion that the cause of the accident (here, the openable window) was not inextricably connected with the course of treatment involving the exercise of medical judgment beyond the common knowledge of laymen.
>
> (Cohen and Mariano 1982:156)

Similar reasoning appears in *Sayes v. Pilgrim Manor* (1988). This case involved a police officer who was injured when he dived into the water in an effort to rescue an emotionally disturbed nursing home patient who was attempting suicide by wading toward deep water. In his suit against the nursing home the police officer alleged that his injury was caused by its negligent care of the woman. The Louisiana Court of Appeal ultimately held that the nursing home was negligent in allowing the woman to leave the facility unattended. In its ruling the appellate court made three main points:

> First, the nursing home's voluntary acceptance of the resident, after her release from a state mental hospital, with full knowledge of her mental and physical disorders, obligated it to take extra care and precautionary measures to assure that she would not injure herself or others.

Second, the nursing home had allowed the resident complete freedom to leave the home's premises, despite the fact that she had been rehospitalized on four occasions due to her violent and/or destructive outbursts.

Third, immediately preceding the suicide attempt, the resident had exhibited behavior that should have placed the nursing home on notice that she was likely to engage in violent, combative and destructive behavior. These warning signs were ignored.

("Nursing Home Liable" 1990:1)

As is often the case, courts do not expect mental health professionals to have the ability to always predict accurately whether a client is likely to commit suicide. Rather, what is required is competent assessment, consistent with the standard of care in the profession and a good faith effort to protect the client from harm.[9]

Porter v. Maunnangi (1988) illustrates this reasoning concerning good faith effort. The mother of a former state hospital patient filed a wrongful death suit alleging that psychiatrists at the hospital to which her son had been involuntarily committed did not diagnose his suicidal condition and did not provide adequate psychiatric treatment for him. The hospital won the suit because Missouri law provided that licensed physicians cannot be civilly liable so long as their decisions are made "in good faith and without gross negligence" ("Psychiatrists Not Liable" 1989:2). The plaintiffs had not alleged that the psychiatrists had acted in bad faith or were grossly negligent.

A number of suicide cases allege that staff in a psychiatric facility did not remove from a client's possession, or supplied patients with, dangerous objects—particularly those that could facilitate suicide. A 1989 Minnesota case is prototypical. A forty-two-year-old man appeared at a hospital emergency room and reported that he was fantasizing about killing his parents, his family, and himself. He had been depressed because his employer had transferred him to another city. He agreed to be admitted to the locked psychiatric unit of the hospital, where his room was checked every thirty minutes. The nurse who interviewed him shortly after admission removed his safety razor, nail clippers, and cologne bottle. She did not, however, take away a thirty-inch leather shoulder strap that could be detached from his personal luggage. At that point the nurse decided the man should be placed on suicide precautions with fifteen-minute room checks. During the evening after he was admitted, staff members noted that the patient was pacing the room, wringing his hands, clenching his fists, holding his head, and sighing. A nurse also observed the man hunched over and rigid. Staff members administered Haldol and left the man alone. Ten minutes later staff members found the patient hanging by his luggage strap.

A wrongful death suit alleged that hospital staff did not take reasonable precautions to prevent suicide. The man's family argued that the staff should have removed the luggage strap and the patient should have been placed on constant observation or in a room where self-destructive behavior would be minimized or eliminated. The hospital argued that belts and straps are less lethal than sharp objects and to take the former away might antagonize patients and interfere with the patient-staff relationship. The jury awarded $940,000 to the plaintiffs ("Hospital Liable for Failure to Prevent Suicide" 1990:2).

A 1989 Georgia case raises similar issues. A forty-nine-year-old nurse with a history of severe psychiatric problems, for which she had been hospitalized several times, had been admitted to a drug and alcohol abuse treatment hospital. For several weeks before her admission the patient had experienced hallucinations and had attempted suicide. She also stopped taking the medication that had been prescribed for her. Her family took her to the drug and alcohol abuse treatment hospital, where she was placed in a single room. According to testimony, the patient was not treated for depression, despite signs of depression. About one week after she was admitted, the hospital staff provided the patient with a hair dryer, which had a long extension cord that the patient used to commit suicide. The family sued the hospital, claiming that the staff did not properly diagnose and monitor the patient and that staffers had provided the extension cord. The jury awarded the plaintiff $750,000 ("Hospital Liable for Suicide" 1990).

A 1991 case against a psychiatric hospital also involved allegations that the hospital should not have permitted a suicidal patient access to a dangerous object, but the defense was rather novel. The plaintiff's twenty-seven-year-old son, who had a history of schizophrenia, was admitted to the hospital for psychiatric treatment for suicidal ideations. About six months after admission the patient committed suicide by hanging himself with fishing line that his treating psychiatrist had permitted him to keep in his room. The hospital denied any negligence, claiming that because the patient was an outdoorsman, the fishing line was therapeutic. The Texas case was settled for $320,000 ("Schizophrenic Patient Hangs Self" 1991:6).10

Madden summarizes current thinking about liability risks associated with suicide:

> There is no general duty to protect a client from self-harm. In fact, some mental health professionals have argued for a right of individuals to commit suicide (Knuth 1979). Even for those who take the self-determination position, the legal analysis rests on whether the reasonable actions of the professional could have prevented the harm.
>
> When a client is evaluated as needing protection due to age or mental disability, the duty to intervene so as to prevent the harm is implicated most strongly. The legal issues that therapists face are related to the quality and thoroughness of the evaluation as well as the degree of control the worker maintained over the client. Just as in duty-to-protect cases, the therapist duty is greater when the client is in a controlled, residential, or institutional setting than when he or she is in an outpatient clinic.
>
> (1998:76)

To prevent malpractice and liability claims related to suicide, social workers should take a number of precautions and preventative steps (Austin, Moline, and Williams 1990; Meyer, Landis, and Hays 1988; Schutz 1982; Worchel and Gearing 2010):

- Social workers should be familiar with their agency's manual containing policies and guidelines for dealing with suicidal clients. Agencies that do not have a manual containing such policies and guidelines should develop one.
- Social workers in private practice should obtain regular peer supervision that reviews guidelines and policies for dealing with suicidal clients.
- Early in the therapeutic relationship social workers should obtain information from clients about significant others who should be contacted in case of emergency. Clients should also be asked to sign a written consent form, giving their social worker permission to contact these individuals, should the social worker determine that the client is or may be suicidal. In general clients should be informed when the social worker contacts significant others about the client's risk of suicide.

- Social workers should use a formal assessment form to assess the likelihood or probability of suicide. The assessment should obtain information related to the client's treatment history and history of suicidal thoughts and/or attempts. The social worker can explain that completion of the intake form is standard procedure for every new client. This may help to avoid situations in which clients conclude that the social worker is worried that the client is suicidal. (For examples of criteria to consider in a suicide assessment, see Meyer, Landis, and Hays 1988:278–79; Schutz 1982:68–72; Worchel and Gearing 2010).
- Social workers should document in writing in the case record all their observations, impressions, and courses of action related to suicide risk.
- Social workers dealing with minors should consider having each minor and parent sign a written contract specifying the procedures to be followed if the social worker believes the client is suicidal.
- Social workers should obtain proper consultation when faced with a client who is or may be suicidal. Documenting the consultation sought and received is important.
- Social workers must be careful to ensure that suicidal clients with whom they have terminated treatment have access to competent care (see the discussion of abandonment in chapter 8).
- When the risk of suicide is high, social workers are obligated to take proper steps to control the client, as in seeking emergency treatment or hospitalization. The social worker should thoroughly document these efforts.
- Social workers should be familiar with local statutes concerning their duty to protect and duty to warn when a client is or may be suicidal.
- Social workers should explain and clarify their availability to clients and how to handle emergencies and absences during the practitioner's vacations or illness.

Social workers should follow widely accepted guidelines for managing a suicidal client. The following, for example, is adapted from Schutz (1982:72–73):

1. Elicit from the client, if possible and credible, a promise that he will control his impulses or will call the therapist or a local emergency number (many social workers draw up a "suicide contract" with suicidal clients).

2. Make sure that any weapons in the client's possession are placed in the hands of a third party.

3. Increase the frequency of treatment sessions.

4. Contact significant others in the client's social network (with consent) and ask them to assist in supporting the client between sessions or in joint sessions.

5. Use a call-in system between sessions to monitor the client's stability.

6. Obtain psychiatric consultation in regard to the possibility of using medication as an adjunct to treatment. Bear in mind, however, that antidepressants may initially increase the risk because the seriously depressed client may become sufficiently energized to make an attempt. Also, a client may hoard the medication to collect a lethal dose.

7. Consider taking steps to have the client hospitalized, preferably voluntarily but, if necessary, involuntarily.

INVOLUNTARY CIVIL COMMITMENT

Clinical social workers are sometimes involved in civil commitment decisions. Although they may not be authorized to sign the commitment papers, social workers are often consulted and relied on for information related to commitment proceedings. Cases involving potential suicide often lead in this direction.

The stakes in these cases are high. Hospitalization, whether voluntary or involuntary, can be traumatic. It restricts the clients' freedom, and they may experience significant emotional distress. Clients also could be abused in the process (Pinals and Mossman 2012).

A substantial number of lawsuits in the mental health field are responses to attempts to commit clients to psychiatric facilities (see, for example, "Woman Evicted and Taken to Hospital" 1993; "Court Reinstates False Imprisonment Suit" 1993; "Teenager Claims No Probable Cause" 1994; "Woman Falsely Imprisoned" 2001; *Lee v. Alexander* (1992)). Some suits allege that a mental health professional failed to conduct a proper, thorough assessment and that the commitment therefore was inappropriate. This may constitute false imprisonment, which arises from the "nonconsensual, improper, or unlawful restraint or confinement of one person by another for any period of time" (Cohen and Mariano 1982:380). As Meyer, Landis, and Hays assert,

> Following the Supreme Court's decision in *Addington v. Texas* (1979), the burden of proof is on the petitioner and the state, who must demonstrate by "clear and convincing evidence" that the detainee meets the statutory criteria for commitment. This level of proof is a compromise between mere "preponderance" of the evidence, used in other civil matters, and "beyond a reasonable doubt," the standard in criminal proceedings, and reflects a balance of the need to protect individual rights against the presumably well-intentioned intervention by the state. The court determined that language in the Constitution requires significant due process protections, but not as much as in criminal matters.
>
> (1988:117)

Other cases allege that a mental health professional made an error in judgment about the client's mental health and vulnerability or relied on hearsay evidence. In *Kleber v. Stevens* (1964) the plaintiff claimed that a psychiatrist's commitment papers were improper because they were based on hearsay. The New York trial court awarded the plaintiff $20,000 in damages.

In addition some suits allege that the mental health professionals involved did not confine a client in the least restrictive alternative. In the classic case of *Lake v. Cameron* (1966), Catherine Lake challenged her confinement at St. Elizabeths Hospital in Washington, D.C. (Austin, Moline, and Williams 1990:199). A police officer had found her wandering the streets and took her to Washington General Hospital. Twelve days later Lake filed a writ of verbal habeas corpus in U.S. District Court; a judge concluded that she was "of unsound mind" and authorized her transfer to St. Elizabeths Hospital. Staff concluded that Lake was a danger to herself and in need of care and supervision that her family was not able to provide.

At the district court commitment hearing and the habeas corpus hearing, Lake testified that she was competent to be free. At the U.S. Court of Appeals hearing Lake also stated that, consistent with the newly enacted District of Columbia Hospitalization of the Mentally Ill Act, she would be willing to consider a less restrictive alternative to the psychiatric institution. The court ultimately concluded that "the government, while seeking to provide some sort of custodial care, could not compel Mrs. Lake to accept its help at the price of her freedom. She had a right to be treated with the least restrictive alternative" (Austin, Moline, and Williams 1990:201).[11]

Several important cases also demonstrate that hospitalized clients are entitled to treatment while detained. In *O'Connor v. Donaldson* (1975) the plaintiff, Kenneth Donaldson, then forty-nine, was civilly committed to the Florida State Hospital in Chattahoochee with a diagnosis of paranoid schizophrenia (Austin, Moline, and Williams 1990:203). He was confined to the hospital against his will for fifteen years. On several occasions during his hospitalization, Donaldson unsuccessfully petitioned state and federal courts for his release, claiming that he did not pose a threat of danger, was not mentally ill, and that the hospital was not providing him with treatment.

In 1971, when he was sixty-four, Donaldson filed suit again in U.S. District Court, alleging that the hospital's superintendent and staff had deprived him of his constitutional right to liberty. Evidence presented during the trial demonstrated that Donaldson received primarily custodial care rather than treatment. The jury found in favor of Donaldson. The U.S. Supreme Court stated that "regardless of the grounds for involuntary civil commitment, a person confined against his will at a state mental institution has 'a constitutional right to receive such individual treatment as will give him a reasonable opportunity to be cured or to improve his mental condition'" (Austin, Moline, and Williams 1990:206).[12]

Psychiatric patients also have a right to *refuse* treatment in some circumstances, particularly when coerced treatment violates their First Amendment rights to freedom of religion and speech or their Eighth Amendment rights to protection from cruel and unusual punishment. *Rennie v. Klein* (1978) addressed the right to refuse treatment. Rennie, who had been hospitalized on twelve previous occasions, had refused to take medication ordered by his psychiatrist. A federal district court in New Jersey ruled that involuntary psychiatric patients *may* have the right to refuse medication or other forms of treatment in the absence of an emergency, consistent with the constitutional right to privacy. In addition, the court ruled, due process must be followed in order to coerce medication. To overrule the patient's refusal, an objective independent party should consider four factors: the patient's capacity to decide on his particular treatment; the patient's physical threat to other patients and staff; whether any less restrictive treatment exists; and the risk of permanent side-effects from the proposed treatment. The court ultimately overruled Rennie's refusal, based on these four criteria. Nonetheless this decision has been influential in right-to-refuse-treatment cases (Meyer, Landis, and Hays 1988:134; Saks 2002).

Finally, some lawsuits contend that mental health staff members did not adequately monitor a client's progress and condition. In *Whitree v. State* (1968) a patient who had been hospitalized in a state institution for fourteen years alleged that he had been falsely imprisoned. A lower court in New York found in his favor, noting in particular the infrequent examinations of the patient and the lack of depth of the examinations that were conducted. The court also concluded that "the lack of psychiatric care was the primary reason for the inordinate length of this incarceration, with the concomitant side effects of physical injury, moral degradation, and mental anguish" (R. Cohen 1979:139). The plaintiff was awarded $300,000 in damages.

As Austin, Moline, and Williams (1990:207–8) suggest,

- Before seeking involuntary commitment, social workers should inform clients of their rights regarding detainment.
- Social workers should develop a good working relationship with a psychiatrist whom they can consult when necessary.
- Treatment plans should respect clients' right to be treated with the least restrictive alternative. Social workers should be familiar with available resources, both institutional and noninstitutional, the restrictions that they impose, and their therapeutic value.
- Social workers should ensure that hospitalized clients are receiving proper treatment in addition to appropriate custodial care. They should also be familiar with clients' right to refuse treatment.
- Social workers should monitor the care that clients are receiving in residential settings to which they have been admitted.
- Social workers should ensure that clients' progress is reviewed and updated regularly.
- Social workers should be familiar with local statutes concerning criteria for commitment (see Meyer, Landis, and Hays 1988: 125–31, for example) and commitment procedures. Social workers should be particularly familiar with the role that they are permitted to assume in commitment proceedings.

As Meyer, Landis, and Hays state with respect to practitioners' involvement in commitment proceedings,

> Psychotherapists can serve as petitioners; in fact, in many states they may bypass some of the paperwork involved and arrange for the person to be taken to the hospital simply by calling the authorities. For example, if a client disclosed an intent to commit suicide, a licensed therapist can generally ask the police to take him or her to an inpatient facility immediately, leaving the paperwork for later. Practicing therapists should acquaint themselves with the pragmatics of commitment procedures in their communities *before* a crisis arises. Magistrates and clerks of court are usually very cooperative in explaining the relevant laws and procedures and may "walk through" a petition to illustrate the entire process. Therapists should understand whom to call to arrange a mental health warrant, the criteria that apply in their jurisdiction, how and where to complete the necessary paperwork, and the location of the community evaluation center. Further, they should be able to explain all of the above to members of the community.
>
> (1988:120)

PROTECTIVE SERVICES

Many social workers face protective service issues during their careers. The most obvious circumstances are those encountered by child welfare professionals who have day-to-day contact with child abuse and neglect cases. Practitioners also have a good understanding of protective service issues involving other special populations, such as older adults and people with disabilities.

Even those social workers who are not employed directly in protective service positions are bound to have at least some indirect encounter with protective service issues at some point in their career. Clinical social workers in a community mental health center, family service agency, juvenile correctional facility, school, hospital, day treatment program, rehabilitation program, addictions treatment center, senior center, or in private practice are, like many other professionals, mandated reporters. Every state now has a statute obligating mandated reporters to notify local protective service officials when they suspect abuse or neglect of a child, and most have comparable statutes pertaining to suspected abuse or neglect of older adults and people with disabilities. Social workers are mandated reporters in all states. States typically mandate reporting of suspected physical abuse, physical neglect, sexual abuse, emotional maltreatment, and institutional maltreatment. The terms used in states' statutes vary but usually include language such as *physical battering, physical endangerment, physical neglect, medical neglect, sexual abuse, sexual exploitation, emotional abuse, developmental neglect, emotional neglect, improper supervision, educational neglect, abandonment,* and *institutional maltreatment* (Besharov 1985; DePanfilis and Salus 2003).

Not surprisingly cases involving mandatory reporting and protective services are highly charged. Allegations of the strongest and most provocative kind are often leveled by and against family members and partners. Otherwise-trusted professionals are obligated to report suspected abuse or neglect against a client's wishes. Reports of abuse and neglect may also be used as a weapon in child custody disputes.

One understandable consequence of false allegations, harassment, and so on is that the accused will hire a lawyer and sue mandated reporters and protective service workers. As a result social workers need to be particularly knowledgeable about and sensitive to related liability and malpractice risks.

Social workers need to be aware of four broad areas of risk: reporting of abuse and/or neglect, inadequately protecting a child, violating parental and caregiver rights, and inadequate foster care services (Besharov 1985; DePanfilis and Salus 2003).

Reporting of Abuse and/or Neglect

With respect to reporting of abuse and/or neglect, a common claim is failure to report. Since 1964 all states have passed laws that require the reporting of suspected child abuse and neglect. The list of mandated reporters varies from state to state (as do definitions of what constitutes reportable abuse and neglect); however, social workers (and teachers and most medical professionals) are mandated reporters in all states. Despite this clear mandate, the evidence suggests that human service workers, including social workers, sometimes fail to notify authorities of abused and neglected individuals whom they encounter (Besharov 1985:24; DePanfilis and Salus 2003; Lloyd 2001; U.S. National Center on Child Abuse 1981).

In addition to criminal penalties that may be imposed for failing to report suspected abuse or neglect, social workers risk civil penalties and lawsuits. A suit brought in Arizona accused a social worker of failing to report, even though she had urged the mother of the child to report to the police an allegation involving molestation. The social worker believed that she had complied with state law by urging the mother to report what happened and that reporting it against the client's wishes might harm the client and jeopardize the therapeutic relationship. Although the charges were eventually dropped because the state's haphazard record-keeping system could not be relied on to prove that a report was not made immediately, the case makes clear the real possibility of criminal liability if a mandated reporter fails to make a report (Besharov 1985:28–29).

A number of important civil suits allege negligence, stemming from failure to report, on the part of mandated reporters. Thirty-nine adolescent boys who were residents in a group home in the state of Washington sued independent therapists who were retained to provide mental health counseling. The plaintiffs claimed that the therapists failed to report sexual and physical abuse occurring in the group home. The case was settled for $8 million ("Therapists Fail to Notify" 2001). In 1970 a California father sued the police, two hospitals, and individual doctors, claiming that no one notified child protective services about a child with severe injuries consistent with abuse. The five-month-old had been taken to the hospital on several occasions with such injuries as a fractured skull, contusions, blood blisters on his penis, marked swelling and discoloration of the left arm and fingertips, burned fingers, puncture wounds and strangulation marks, and welts. The infant's father, who was separated from the mother, sued the defendants, claiming that the hospital did not report and that the lack of report was the cause of the infant's permanent brain damage. The California case was settled out of court for $600,000 (Besharov 1985:32–33).[13]

Wrongful reporting can also expose social workers to liability risks. All states grant immunity from civil and criminal liability to people who report. Almost all states require that professionals report suspected abuse and neglect *in good faith* if they are to be granted immunity from liability (Besharov 1985:39; DePanfilis and Salus 2003). Hence "bad faith" reporting may expose social workers to liability. In a California case, for example, a father and daughter sued a psychologist who, the plaintiffs alleged, reported to authorities in bad faith that the father had molested the daughter. As a result of the reports the father was unable to see his daughter for more than eighteen months. The jury awarded the plaintiffs $1.9 million ("Treating Therapist Falsely Reports" 1997). A 1980 suit against a Virginia physician accused the doctor of maliciously reporting a child who had various bruised knots on his body. The doctor berated the parents on two occasions for their treatment of the child and allegedly made "unnecessarily irresponsible and defamatory" remarks toward the parents. It was eventually demonstrated, however, that the bruising was the result of the child's hemophilia. The case was settled for $5,000 (Besharov 1985:41).

In contrast the mental health counselor sued in *Lux v. Hansen* (1989) for filing a report of child abuse was not found liable, even though her conclusion that the child had been sexually abused by her father was erroneous. The U.S. Court of Appeals for the Eighth Circuit concluded that the counselor had reason to suspect child abuse, in light of comments made by the child, and that under the qualified immunity doctrine, "liability may be found only if a defendant's conduct reflects bad faith or violates clearly established statutory or constitutional rights" ("Counselor Who Suspected Child Abuse" 1990:4).

Similar issues emerged in *Vineyard v. Craft* (1992), in which a Texas appellate court held that a father could not sue a psychotherapist for harm to the family relationship after the therapist erroneously concluded that the father had sexually abused the child and reported the suspicion to the child protection agency ("Psychotherapist May Not Be Sued" 1992:4). The court held that the risk of harm to the family's interests that may result from an erroneous child abuse report was outweighed by the public's interest in protecting children by obtaining professionals' opinions when sexual abuse is suspected.[14]

Controversy surrounding reports of abuse and neglect can sometimes trigger what are known as adverse employment action lawsuits. An example would be a suit filed by a worker in a residential program who claims that actions she took to report institutional abuse resulted in some form of disciplinary action against her by agency administrators. Besharov presents a compelling case summary of this phenomenon:

> I was fired from my position as the only social worker at [a center for the treatment of cerebral palsy] because I was advocating for a child who attended the center. The child, an eleven year old who was fully ambulatory,

was tied into a wheelchair from 9 to 3 each day for the past three years in order to prevent his acting out [with] self abusive behavior. A helmet was placed on his head and tied to the back of the wheelchair and his upper arms were tied behind him. No motion was possible. In addition, he was heavily sedated. On the basis of my previous, extensive work with handicapped children, examination of the reports in the child's file and discussions with my colleagues at the agency, I believed that the child had, in addition, been misdiagnosed as severely retarded and was in the wrong program at the Center. After trying, without success, for four months to convince the Center administration, the psychologist and the doctors to untie the boy, to reevaluate him and to plan a proper educational program for him, I contacted the Chairman of the Board of Trustees of our agency and asked him to intervene. Three weeks after contacting him, the child's situation was unchanged and I then notified [the state agency that had placed the child and the state agency responsible for investigating reports of child abuse].

I did not seek support from the child's parents because staff members had reported that the child was tied and kept in a closet at home. I had met the mother and believed that she could not, at that time, be helpful to the child.

I then gave information to the [state agency] and was immediately suspended from my job. I received my salary for 55 days and was then fired, with a dismissal letter containing false statements that will totally damage my professional reputation as a social worker. I asked for an evaluation of my work at the agency the day I was fired and was refused. I also utilized all of the grievance procedures that were available to me according to the agency's written Personnel Policies, but my efforts were ignored.

(1985:43–44)

The social worker accepted a $5,000 settlement after realizing that she might end up paying her lawyer far more than any additional payment she might receive.

Inadequately Protecting a Child

Social workers are frequently in a position to investigate reports of abuse and neglect and then arrange, provide, or monitor substitute care for children who have been abused or neglected. Such care may be provided in foster care, group homes, or other residential settings. This daunting task overwhelms many public and private child welfare agencies. In many programs budgets and resources cannot keep pace with ever-growing caseloads (DePanfilis and Salus 2003; Pecora et al. 2009).

One unfortunate correlate of strained programs and social workers is litigation related to protective service professionals' failure to accept a report for investigation. *Mammo v. Arizona* (1983) is a classic example. In this case the father of an infant filed a wrongful death suit against the Arizona Department of Economic Security; he alleged that the department had failed to carry out its duty to accept and investigate reports. The infant died as a result of an apparent homicide. Both the police and the father—the noncustodial parent—had contact with the department, conveying their concern about the possibility of child abuse. During two weekends the father had observed bruises on the bodies of the infant's two older siblings. After the father spoke with an intake unit supervisor in the department's child protective services division, the department took no action except to recommend that the father retain an attorney to contest the mother's custody of the children. The jury awarded the father $1 million in damages, although the trial judge reduced the award to $300,000 (the judge believed the award was excessive) (Besharov 1985:58–59).

Jensen v. Conrad (1984) illustrates a lawsuit alleging lack of proper investigation of a report. The county department of social services attempted to contact a woman named Clark after the principal of her child's school alerted the department to the possibility of child abuse. After numerous attempts to contact Clark by letters, telephone calls, and home visits, the department classified the case as unfounded and closed the investigation. About two months later the child's younger brother was killed by Clark's boyfriend, who was subsequently tried and convicted of murder.

Once protective service staff members are concerned about a child's safety, they have a responsibility to place a child in protective custody. They may be liable if they do not take proper steps to protect the child. In a case reported by Besharov, a Louisville, Kentucky, child protection worker and the worker's supervisor were charged with official misconduct in the death of a three-year-old child. A physician attending the child was also indicted. The allegation was that the various professionals failed to take appropriate steps to protect the child by placing the child in protective custody. All charges were dismissed but only because the judge concluded, "It offends my sense of fairness that these three people were chosen [for prosecution] when everyone else who came into contact with the child could have been charged as well" (Besharov 1985:66).

Issues related to allegations of inadequate protection of a child were central to the landmark case of *DeShaney v. Winnebago County* (1989). In this case the U.S. Supreme Court ruled that the Winnebago County (Wisconsin) Department of Social Services and several of its social work staff members could not be held liable for damages in not protecting a child who had been severely abused by his father. *DeShaney* raised a number of important constitutional issues, primarily related to the Fourteenth Amendment, which forbids the state or its agents from depriving individuals of their right to life, liberty, or property without due process of law. In 1987 the U.S. Court of Appeals for the Seventh Circuit held in this case that "the state's failure to protect people from private violence, or other mishaps not attributable to the conduct of its employees, is not a deprivation of constitutionally protected property or liberty" (*DeShaney*, 812 F.2d at 301). That is, a state's failure to protect an individual against a private act of violence does not constitute a violation of the due process clause.

Social workers can also incur liability risks in returning at-risk children to dangerous foster parents and in providing inadequate case monitoring. Practitioners must be careful to ensure that children are returned home only when the evidence is substantial that the parents no longer pose a danger. Social workers must also be sure to monitor children's progress carefully. In a 1980 case in Iowa, for example, the noncustodial father claimed that the department of social services was negligent in the monitoring of his thirty-four-month-old daughter's safety after he reported his suspicion of abuse. Although the staff had decided to leave the child in the home and provide supportive services, no follow-up visit to the family was made. The mother's lover later killed the child. The case was settled for $82,500 (Besharov 1985:70).

Violating Parental Rights

Child protective service workers must be careful not to violate parents' rights during investigations and must be sure to provide social services after reports of abuse or neglect. Because of the volatility of family emotions surrounding allegations of abuse and neglect, social workers must be particularly alert to any violations of parents' rights.

An investigation can be unnecessarily intrusive if the social worker's investigative methods are excessive, harassing, or constitute an unreasonable invasion of privacy. In a Virginia Beach case, for example, a father who was investigated sued two workers and the agency, alleging that the workers harassed him, threatened him with prosecution, and publicized false remarks about him to third parties. The case was settled for $4,000 (Besharov 1985:79).

Of course, investigations of abuse and neglect sometimes result in the removal of children from the home. Often these placements are in the children's best interest, and the parents do not contest the decision. On other occasions, however, parents vehemently object to the children's removal. In some cases parents sue, alleging wrongful removal (DePanfilis and Salus 2003). Besharov cites a 1984 Minnesota case that illustrates this phenomenon. Parents sued Hennepin County, alleging that the child protection agency unjustly removed their child from the home. The court found that the parents had made a "sufficient showing that fact questions exist concerning whether defendants' actions were reasonable and in good faith" (Besharov 1985:94).

Inadequate Foster Care Services

Once children are placed in foster care, social workers have a responsibility to ensure the safety and overall quality of this substitute care. Sometimes children are placed with abusive foster parents (DePanfilis and Salus 2003; Pecora et al. 2009). A number of court cases document this tragic phenomenon (Besharov 1985:111–15).

Of course, foster children can also pose a risk to foster parents (Besharov 1985; DePanfilis and Salus 2003; Pecora et al. 2009). Lawsuits against social workers and child welfare agencies have alleged that foster children have killed a foster parent (*Snyder v. Mouser* (1971); *Kreuger v. Louise Wise Services,* cited in Besharov 1985:109); damaged or destroyed property (*Seavy v. State* (1966)), and infected a foster parent with a serious virus (*Vaughn v. North Carolina* (1979)). Clearly social workers must do their best to identify risks that foster children may pose and either inform potential foster parents of the risk or seek alternative placements.

Once children are placed in foster care, social workers may be held accountable if they do not provide proper treatment services to the children and in some cases their parents. Although relatively few lawsuits make these allegations, some do. In *Little v. Utah* (1983), for example, the state agency was found liable after an autistic child died; the court found that the agency had failed to adequately train the girl's foster parents and other substitute caretakers, make timely evaluations of her condition, provide appropriate safety equipment (such as headgear), and arrange for proper supervision. In *Cameron v. Montgomery County* (1979), one claim of the plaintiff, a foster child, was that the child welfare agency had prevented parental supervision and failed to provide services to the mother that might have helped the child return home. The federal district court case was settled for $5,000 (Besharov 1985:120).

DEFAMATION OF CHARACTER

Social workers involved in protective services have to be particularly careful to avoid defamation of parents' character. Practitioners must avoid unwarranted characterizations of parents—whether oral or written—that might be considered defamatory. But social workers in all settings must be careful about defamation. According to the NASW *Code of Ethics,* "Social workers should not use derogatory language in their written or verbal communications to or about clients. Social workers should use accurate and respectful language in all communications to and about clients" (standard 1.12).

Defamation occurs as a result of "the publication of anything injurious to the good name or reputation of another, or which tends to bring him into disrepute" (Gifis 1991:124). Defamation can take two forms: libel and slander. Libel occurs when the publication is in written form (Price, Duodu, and Cain 2009). Slander occurs when the publication occurs in oral form. More specifically social workers can be liable for defamation if they say or write something that is untrue, they knew or should have known to be untrue, and caused some injury to the plaintiff. The social worker's defense against an allegation of defamation is that the statement was true, the client signed a valid consent form authorizing the release of information, or the social worker had a legal responsibility to disclose the information, for example, to comply with a mandatory reporting law (Schutz 1982:10).

In the well-known Utah case of *Berry v. Moench* (1958), Berry sued Dr. Moench, a psychiatrist, because he wrote a letter that Berry alleged included false and derogatory information about him. Berry had been Moench's patient seven years before. Moench had written a letter to a Dr. Hellewell concerning Berry's emotional stability and background. Berry was engaged to the daughter of former patients of Hellewell, who had requested the letter from Moench. In his letter to Hellewell, Moench made the following comments about Berry:

> He was treated here in 1949 as an emergency. Our diagnosis was Manic [*sic*] depressive depression in a psychopathic personality. . . . The patient was attempting to go through school on the G.I. bill. . . . Instead of attending class he would spend most of the days and nights playing cards for money. . . . During his care here, he purchased a brand new Packard, without even money to buy gasoline. . . . He was in constant trouble with the authorities during the war. . . . He did not do well in school and never did really support his wife and children. . . . My suggestion to the infatuated girl would be to run as fast and as far as she possibly could in any direction away from him.
>
> (Austin, Moline, and Williams 1990:91)

Moench acknowledged that much of the information contained in the letter was based on information obtained from Berry's ex-wife, his referring doctor, and Berry's former sister-in-law. The court ruled that Moench had committed libel.

Social workers involved in protective services must be especially aware of defamation issues. In the Virginia case involving the child with hemophilia, for example, the physician accused of wrongful reporting of child abuse also was accused of making "unnecessarily irresponsible and defamatory" remarks toward the parents (Besharov 1985:41). Similar allegations were made in the Virginia Beach case, discussed earlier in relation to unnecessarily intrusive investigations. In this case the plaintiff alleged that the workers "maliciously and falsely addressed remarks to third persons, the substance of which were [*sic*] that the plaintiff was an alcoholic; that the plaintiff was mentally unstable and was a 'very sick man'; that he was guilty of child molestation; that they were going to take his child or children away from him; and that he would be prosecuted criminally" (Besharov 1985:79).[15]

DIGITAL TECHNOLOGY AND SOCIAL MEDIA

Widespread use of digital technology—including online counseling, social networking sites, text and instant messaging, and e-mail—has created unprecedented risk management challenges, particularly with respect to self-disclosure, privacy, confidentiality, and practitioner availability (Gutheil and Simon 2005; Reamer 2013b). As Zur notes,

> The technological explosion toward the end of the 20th century, with its widespread use of cell phones, e-mails, and more recently, Instant Messaging (IM), chat rooms, video teleconferencing (VTC), text messaging, blogging, and photo-cell technology, has changed the way that billions of people communicate, make purchases, gather information, learn, meet, socialize, date, and form and sustain intimate relationships. Like global, national, and cultural boundaries, therapeutic boundaries are rapidly changing as a result. . . .
>
> Telehealth and online therapy practices challenge boundaries both around and within the therapeutic relationship. Telehealth or online therapy transcends the physical boundaries of the office as phone or Internet-based therapies take place in the elusive setting we often refer to as cyberspace. Nevertheless, telehealth is subject to exactly the same federal and state regulations, codes of ethics, and professional guidelines that define the fiduciary relationship in face-to-face and office-based therapy.
>
> (2007:133, 136)

Social workers must recognize that considerable controversy surrounds the appropriate use of online interventions, social media, and electronic communications. Some practitioners are enthusiastic supporters of these technologies as therapeutic tools. Others are harsh critics or skeptics, arguing that heavy reliance on online interventions and social media compromises the quality of social work services and could endanger clients who are clinically vulnerable and who would be better served by in-person care.

Social workers who consider engaging with clients electronically would do well to develop comprehensive policies and guidelines that address relevant risks. For example, discussing these issues with clients at the beginning of the working relationship can help avoid boundary confusion and misunderstanding. Kolmes (2013) offers a useful template that addresses policies concerning practitioners' use of diverse digital and related technology, such as online counseling, social networking sites, e-mail, text messages, and search engines. Social workers are quickly discovering that a social media policy reflecting current ethical standards can simultaneously protect clients and practitioners.

Online Counseling

The Internet now features hundreds of online counseling services (Barak at al. 2008; Midkiff and Wyatt 2008; Santhiveeran 2009). People who struggle with depression, addiction, marital and relationship conflict, anxiety, eating disorders, grief, and other mental health and behavioral challenges can use electronic search engines to locate clinical social workers who offer counseling services using live online chat. Clients can pay for online chat services with a credit card.

Live online chat is an example of what computer experts call *synchronous* communication, meaning it occurs simultaneously in real time. This contrasts with *asynchronous* communication, where communication is not synchronized or occurring simultaneously (for example, when a client sends a social worker an e-mail message regarding a clinical issue and waits for a response).

Telephone Counseling

Some social workers provide local and long-distance counseling services entirely by telephone to clients they never meet in person. After providing a counselor with a user name and credit card information, clients receive telephone counseling. These may be regularly scheduled or crisis calls.

Videocounseling

An increasing number of social workers offer clients live distance-counseling using webcams, pan-tilt zoom cameras, monitors, and such services as Skype or encrypted videoconferencing services. Some clinicians offer videocounseling services to clients they never meet in person. Other clinicians may supplement their face-to-face counseling with videocounseling, for example, when a client who is ordinarily seen face to face is going to be out of town for an extended period and feels the need for clinical sessions.

Cybertherapy

Some clinicians offer individual and group counseling services to clients by using a three-dimensional (3-D) virtual world in which clients and practitioners interact with each other visually by using avatars rather than real-life photos or live images. An avatar is a digitally generated graphic image, or caricature, that clients and social workers use to represent themselves in a virtual world that appears on their computer screen. Clients and social workers join an online therapy community, create their avatars, and electronically enter a virtual therapy room for individual or group counseling. Many providers use software known as Second Life, a massive multiplayer universe set in a 3-D virtual world.

Self-guided Web-based Interventions

Social workers now have access to a wide variety of online interventions designed to help people who struggle with diverse mental health and behavioral issues, such as alcoholism. For example, users complete online questionnaires concerning their drinking use, patterns, and habits and then receive electronic feedback and resources that can help them decide whether to change their alcohol use.

Some websites are designed for mental health professionals who provide services to adolescents. Recognizing that, given their preoccupation with digital technology, many adolescents find online services more appealing than in-office services, some practitioners use well-known therapeutic principles, such as solution-focused therapy, to help adolescents address challenges in their lives, sometimes in the form of online therapeutic games.

Electronic Social Networks

Social networking sites, such as Facebook and LinkedIn, are now pervasive in both clients' and social workers' lives. Some clinicians believe that maintaining online relationships with clients on social networking sites can be a therapeutic tool (Barak and Grohol 2011; Graffeo and La Barbera 2009); they claim that informal contact with clients on social networking sites humanizes the relationship and makes practitioners more accessible.

An innovative example helping people in crisis through online social networking is a collaborative service from the Substance Abuse and Mental Health Services Administration (part of the U.S. Department of Health and Human Services) and the National Suicide Prevention Lifeline that uses Facebook. The service enables Facebook users to use either the Report Suicidal Content link or other report links found throughout the site to alert Facebook administrators to a suicidal comment posted by a friend. The person who posted the suicidal comment will then immediately receive an e-mail from Facebook encouraging her to call the National Suicide Prevention Lifeline or to click on a link to begin a confidential chat session with a crisis worker (Substance Abuse and Mental Health Services 2011).

E-mail

Multiple websites offer people the opportunity to receive mental health services by exchanging e-mail messages with clinical social workers. Typically these practitioners invite users to e-mail a therapy-related question for a flat fee and guarantee a response within twenty-four to forty-eight hours. Some practitioners offer clients monthly e-mail packages that include a set number of e-mail exchanges (for example, six to eight). Other practitioners choose to exchange occasional clinically relevant e-mails with clients as an extension of their office-based services (Finn 2006; Gutheil and Simon 2005; Peterson and Beck 2003).

Text Messages

Some practitioners have chosen to exchange text messages with clients informally, for example, when clients wish to cancel or reschedule an appointment or provide the social worker with a brief update during a crisis (Barak and Grohol 2011). Other practitioners and some social service programs have incorporated text messaging as a formal component of their intervention model. For example, staffers in some programs that serve adolescent clients have concluded that they should follow the long-standing social work axiom "start where the client is" and engage adolescents by using text messaging because that is many adolescents' communication medium of choice (Whittaker et al. 2012).

Risk Management Challenges

A number of compelling risks are emerging as social workers make increasing use of a wide range of digital and other electronic technology (Abbott, Klein, and Ciechomski 2008; Barnett 2005). Key issues include practitioner competence, client privacy and confidentiality, informed consent, conflicts of interest, boundaries and dual relationships, consultation and client referral, termination and interruption of services, and documentation.

Practitioner competence. Social workers have a duty to meet minimum standards of competence when providing services to clients, particularly when clinicians use novel and emerging intervention protocols. Thus social workers who choose to use digital and other electronic forms of technology to serve clients should review pertinent research and practice literature and become familiar with rapidly emerging ethical standards.

Client privacy and confidentiality. For decades social workers have understood their obligation to protect client privacy and confidentiality and to be familiar with exceptions (for example, when mandatory reporting laws concerning abuse and neglect require disclosure of information without client consent or when laws or court orders require disclosure without client consent to protect a third party from harm). However, the rapid emergence of digital technology and other electronic media to deliver services has added a new layer of challenging privacy and confidentiality issues. For example, social workers who deliver services using e-mail, avatars, live chat, and videocounseling must be sure to use sophisticated encryption technology to prevent confidentiality breaches (hacking) by unauthorized parties and comply with the strict guidelines of the Health Insurance Portability and Accountability Act (HIPAA). Currently available encryption technology protects client confidentiality quite effectively and is HIPAA compliant; in fact such encryption offers significantly more protection than do traditional paper documents (Hu, Chen, and Hou 2010).

That said, encryption is more challenging with some forms of technology than others. With regard to Skype, for example, NASW attorneys reviewed relevant research and legal guidelines and concluded that "assuring that clients' confidential communications via Skype will be adequately protected is a difficult and uncertain task" (Morgan and Polowy 2011). Social workers are wise not to assume that Internet sites and electronic tools they use are necessarily encrypted; the ethical burden is on the social worker to ensure trustworthy encryption.

Informed consent. In recent years social workers and other health-care providers have been held to increasingly demanding standards for informed consent standards (Berg et al. 2001). The recent advent of distance-counseling and other social services delivered electronically has enhanced social workers' ethical duty to ensure that clients fully understand the nature of these services and their potential benefits and risks. This can be difficult when social workers never meet their clients in person or have the opportunity to speak with clients about informed consent. Special challenges arise when minors contact social workers and request electronic services, particularly when social workers offer free services and do not require credit card information; state laws vary considerably regarding minors' right to obtain mental health services without parental consent (Madden 2003).

Although state and federal laws and regulations vary in their interpretations and applications of informed consent standards, in general professionals agree that the following standards must be met for consent to be considered valid:

1. Coercion and undue influence must not have played a role in the client's decision. Practitioners who provide online and other distance or remote services must ensure that clients do not feel pressured to grant consent.

2. A client must be mentally capable of providing consent. Clearly some clients (for example, young children and individuals who suffer from serious mental illness or dementia) are unable to comprehend the consent procedure. Other clients, however, may be only temporarily unable to consent, such as individuals who are under the influence of alcohol or other drugs at the time consent is sought or who experience transient psychotic symptoms. In general social workers should assess clients' ability to reason and make informed choices, comprehend relevant facts and retain this information, appreciate current circumstances, and communicate wishes. Such assessment can be especially challenging when social workers interact with clients only electronically, do not meet with them in person, and may have difficulty confirming clients' identity and age.

3. Online consent forms and procedures must be valid. Social workers sometimes present clients with general broadly worded consent forms that may violate clients' right to be informed and may be considered invalid if challenged in a court of law (Recupero and Rainey 2005).

Conflicts of interest. Historically social workers have understood their duty to avoid conflicts of interest that may harm clients. For example, social workers who work full time in an agency setting should not refer clients to their own part-time online private practice for additional services.

Novel forms of distance-counseling may introduce conflicts of interest that were previously unknown in social work. For example, some videocounseling sites offer free services to social workers and their clients; the sponsors pay for the development and maintenance of the websites by selling advertisements that include on-screen links to various products and services. Clients may believe that their social workers endorse these products and services.

Boundaries and dual relationships. Social workers' use of digital technology has introduced new and complicated boundary issues. For example, social workers face several challenges involving their use of social networking sites such as Facebook. First, many social workers receive requests— either delivered electronically or in person—from current and former clients asking to be social networking "friends" or contacts. Electronic contact with clients and former clients on social networking sites can lead to boundary confusion and compromise clients' privacy and confidentiality. Clients who have access to social workers' social networking sites may learn a great deal of personal information about their social worker (such as information about the social worker's family and relationships, political views, social activities, and religion), which may introduce complex transference and countertransference issues in the professional-client relationship. Some social workers have managed this risk by creating two distinct Facebook sites, one for professional use (known as a Facebook page) and one for personal use (Facebook profile).

Clients' postings on social networking sites may lead to inadvertent or harmful disclosure of private and confidential details. In addition social workers who choose not to accept a client's "friend" request on a social networking site may inadvertently cause the client to feel a deep sense of rejection.

Consultation and client referral. Social workers who provide online and electronic services to clients they never meet in person must take assertive steps to ensure that clients are familiar with the information they would need to locate and access emergency, counseling, case management, and other supportive services. In addition ethically competent social workers are assertive about collaborating with clients' other service providers and facilitating ancillary services when needed. This may be difficult or impossible to do when social workers never meet their clients in person, do not live in the same community, and do not have professional relationships with clients' other service providers. The result may be inadequate coordination of services and incomplete or inaccurate clinical assessments, particularly when clients are at risk of harming themselves or others.

Termination or interruption of services. Social workers who provide online and electronic services also face unique risks related to what lawyers refer to as abandonment. Abandonment occurs when a social worker–client relationship is terminated or interrupted and the social worker fails to make reasonable arrangements for the continuation of services, when needed. Online and electronic services could be terminated for a variety of reasons. Clients may terminate services abruptly, disappear, or otherwise fail to respond to a social worker's e-mail, text messages, or telephone messages. Social workers may terminate or interrupt services, perhaps inadvertently, because of computer or other electronic equipment failure or because a social worker fails to respond to a client's e-mail, text, or telephone message in a timely fashion.

Documentation. There are compelling reasons for social workers to document clinically relevant information electronically; in principle properly encrypted electronic records are more secure than traditional paper records. Yet social workers' use of online and other electronic services has posed unprecedented documentation challenges. Social workers must develop strict protocols to ensure that clinically relevant e-mail, text, social networking (for example, Facebook), and telephone exchanges are documented properly in case records. These are new expectations that are not reflected in social work's long-standing literature on documentation guidelines (Sidell 2011).

It is not surprising that social workers' use of online and other electronic tools to provide services includes potential benefits and risks. Clients who struggle with anxiety or extreme shyness, for example, may prefer to engage with a social worker remotely, at least initially. Also, clients who are severely disabled physically or who live great distances from social workers' offices may benefit from receiving services electronically that they would otherwise have great difficulty accessing. In addition people who feel the need for help during nonworking hours or whose work schedules do not align conveniently with social workers' office hours can access services remotely any hour of the day or night. And people who are in crisis typically can access assistance by telephone or Internet almost immediately, often at a cost that is lower than fees for in-person services. Denying services to people in need simply because social workers are not comfortable with reputable digital and electronic technology is not consistent with social workers' ethical obligation to meet the needs of vulnerable people (NASW 2008).

However, online and other distance services also come with considerable risks (Barak and Grohol 2011). Social workers fully understand how important visual and nonverbal cues are when providing clinical services; it is easy to miss these cues entirely when services are provided only online and by telephone. The risk of misunderstandings may increase when social workers and clients are not together in person. Also, some clients, such as those who struggle with severe and persistent mental illness, may not be well served by clinical services delivered by social workers they never meet in person. Further, there is always the possibility, although perhaps not the probability, of technology failure and confidentiality breaches that could harm clients.

In addition clients who e-mail or text social workers may not have realistic expectations of a reasonable turnaround time for responses, and this may lead to misunderstandings and conflict in the social worker–client relationship. Social workers who provide digital and telephone counseling services across state lines run the risk of violating licensing laws that require social workers to be licensed in the state in which the client resides (McAdams and Wyatt 2010; NASW and ASWB 2005). Finally, social workers who provide services using digital and other electronic technology run the risk of encountering identity fraud perpetrated by clients they never meet in person. According to the NASW and ASWB (2005) standards on social workers' use of technology, "Social workers who use electronic means to provide services shall . . . make efforts to verify client identity and contact information" (10).

Zur encourages practitioners to make the following disclosure to clients regarding the use of digital and other technology to serve and communicate with clients:

> It is very important to be aware that computers, e-mail, and cell phone communication can be relatively easily accessed by unauthorized people and hence can compromise the privacy and confidentiality of such communication. E-mails, in particular, are vulnerable to such unauthorized access because servers have unlimited and direct access to all e-mails that

go through them. Additionally, Dr. XX's e-mails are not encrypted. Dr. XX's computers are equipped and regularly updated with a firewall, virus protection, and a password. He also backs up all confidential information from his computers on CDs on a regular basis. The CDs are stored securely offsite. Please notify Dr. XX if you decide to avoid or limit in any way the use of any or all communication devices such as e-mail, cell phone, or faxes. Unless Dr. XX hears from you otherwise, he will continue to communicate with you via e-mail when necessary or appropriate. Please do not use e-mail or faxes for emergencies. Although Dr. XX checks phone messages frequently during the day when he is in town, he does not always check his e-mails daily.

(2007:141)

Zur also offers a series of practical guidelines to prevent problems when using technology to provide clinical services:

1. Identify the client and obtain basic information such as full name, address, age, gender, phone, fax, emergency contacts, and so on.
2. Provide clients with a clear informed consent form detailing the limitations of telehealth [the delivery of health-related services using telecommunication technology, such as e-mail, social media, videoconferencing, telephone], in general, and confidentiality and privacy, in particular.
3. Inform the clients of potential limitations of telehealth when it comes to crisis intervention and dealing with dangerous situations.
4. Practice within your limits of clinical and technological competence.
5. Have a crisis intervention plan in place, including ways to reach local emergency services and make referrals to local psychotherapists, psychiatrists, and psychiatric hospitals in the client's vicinity.
6. Provide thorough screening when considering which clients may not be suited to this kind of medium.
7. Have a clear agreement with regard to what is being charged, how it is being charged, and the rates and method of payment.
8. Do not render medical or psychiatric advice by giving a diagnosis or proposing a course of treatment except to those with whom you have established professional psychotherapeutic relationships.
9. Follow your state laws, your licensing board rules, and your state and national professional association guidelines, and practice within the standard of care.

10. Screen clients for technical and clinical suitability for telehealth.

11. Telehealth is one of the fastest growing fields in medicine. Update yourself on the latest research on telehealth.

(2007:144–45)

Social workers who provide clinical services electronically using online counseling, cybertherapy, e-mail, and telephone should develop clear guidelines that draw on emerging ethical standards. For example, the International Society for Mental Health Online, American Distance Counseling Association, and Association for Counseling and Therapy Online have developed useful ethics standards. In addition literature is beginning to emerge that addresses boundary and other ethical issues associated with online counseling (Jones and Stokes 2009; Kraus, Stricker, and Speyer 2011; Reamer 2012c; Zur 2007). Social workers must be scrupulous about the ways in which they claim expertise. Practitioners should avoid any misrepresentation of their qualifications or ability to help people who seek assistance. According to the NASW *Code of Ethics,* "Social workers should ensure that their representations to clients, agencies, and the public of professional qualifications, credentials, education, competence, affiliations, services provided, or results to be achieved are accurate. Social workers should claim only those relevant professional credentials they actually possess and take steps to correct any inaccuracies or misrepresentations of their credentials by others" (standard 4.06[c]).

4

Impaired Social Workers

SOME LIABILITY CLAIMS AND LICENSING board complaints against social workers are the result of honest mistakes. Careless oversight, such as forgetting to get a client to complete a consent form before releasing confidential information to another agency, or failing to protect an electronic record, can lead to a lawsuit or licensing board complaint. Other complaints may result from well-intentioned, deliberate decisions, as when a social worker decides to breach a client's privacy in order to protect a third party from harm. However, many complaints result from incompetent practice by a relatively small percentage of social workers who are impaired.

George M., MSW, was the director of clinical services at Family Services Associates, Inc., a local family service agency. He had been clinical director for six years, after serving as a caseworker and family counselor at the agency for five years. George M. had also worked for three years as a mental health coordinator at a local community mental health center. George M. was in the process of divorcing his wife, which caused him a great deal of stress and seriously impaired his judgment.

In addition to supervising clinical staff, George M. usually carried three or four cases of his own. One involved a twenty-six-year-old woman who sought counseling for anxiety symptoms and problems with self-esteem. George M. conducted the initial intake interview and decided to handle the case himself. He and his client spent several weeks fruitfully exploring a number of family-of-origin issues that concerned the client.

During the eighth week of treatment the client mentioned that she wanted to talk about an event that occurred when she was seventeen, when her older brother sexually molested her. In her judgment a considerable portion of her present-day anxiety could be traced to that event and subsequent sexual contact with her brother. George M. and his client spent several weeks exploring these issues.

At the end of the twelfth session the client began crying, following some discussion about the sexual assault. George M. got up from his chair and embraced the client, as he had during several other therapy sessions when the client was distraught. He also began to kiss her. The client did not resist George M.'s caresses and kisses. George M. then said that he thought he could be helpful to his client by showing her what unconditional, sincere lovemaking was like. He dimmed the lights in his office and made love to his client.

George M. and his client continued to have sexual contact for about two months, at which point the relationship became strained. The client began treatment with a new social worker in a different agency. The client disclosed to the new social worker that she and George M. had been sexually involved during their professional relationship. After considerable discussion with her client, the social worker encouraged her to file an ethics complaint against George M. and to consult an attorney about suing him. The client filed a lawsuit against George M. and a complaint with his licensing board. The licensing board conducted a formal investigation and concluded that George M. was too impaired to practice social work. The board revoked his license.

THE NATURE OF IMPAIRMENT

In the 1970s and 1980s various professions began to pay increased attention to the problem of impaired practitioners (Reamer 1992a). In 1972, for example, the Council on Mental Health of the American Medical Association released a statement that said that physicians have an ethical responsibility to recognize and report impairment among colleagues. In 1976 a group of attorneys recovering from alcoholism started Lawyers Concerned for Lawyers to address chemical dependence in the profession, and in 1980 a group of recovering psychologists inaugurated a similar group, Psychologists Helping Psychologists (Coombs 2000; Kilburg, Nathan, and Thoreson 1986; Knutsen 1977; Laliotis and Grayson 1985; McCrady 1989). In 1981 the American Psychological Association held its first open forum on impairment at its annual meeting (Stadler et al. 1988).

Social work's first national acknowledgment of the problem of impaired practitioners came in 1979, when the NASW released a public policy statement on alcoholism and alcohol-related problems (NASW 1987a). By 1980 a small nationwide support group for chemically dependent practitioners, Social Workers Helping Social Workers, had formed following a gathering of fifty recovering social workers (by 1987, however, it had only sixty-five members; see NASW 1987a and Stoesen 2002). In 1982 NASW established the Occupational Social Work Task Force and charged it with developing a "consistent professional approach for distressed NASW members" (NASW 1987a:7). In 1984 the NASW Delegate Assembly issued a resolution on impairment, and in 1987 NASW published the *Impaired Social Worker Program Resource Book,* prepared by the NASW Commission on Employment and Economic Support, to help practitioners design programs for impaired social workers. The introduction to the resource book states:

> Social workers, like other professionals, have within their ranks those who, because of substance abuse, chemical dependency, mental illness or stress, are unable to function effectively in their jobs. These are the impaired social workers. . . . The problem of impairment is compounded by the fact that the professionals who suffer from the effect of mental illness, stress or substance abuse are like anyone else; they are often the worst judges of their behavior, the last to recognize their problems and the least motivated to seek help. Not only are they able to hide or avoid confronting their behavior, they are often abetted by colleagues who find it difficult to accept that a professional could let his or her problem get out of hand.
>
> (1987a:6)

In addition, in 1995 NASW produced a brochure, "Chapter Guide for Colleague Assistance or Impaired Social Workers," that notes that "a social worker whose personal problems interfere with his or her professional judgment or performance has an ethical responsibility to his or her clients to seek help for the problem. But social workers, like our clients, are sometimes blind to increasingly destructive patterns of behavior" (Stoesen 2002:3).

Organized efforts to address impaired workers began in the late 1930s and early 1940s after Alcoholics Anonymous was formed and because of the need to retain a sound workforce during World War II. These early occupational alcoholism programs eventually led, in the early 1970s, to the emergence of employee assistance programs (EAPs), which are designed to address a broad range of problems experienced by workers.

More recently strategies for dealing with professionals whose work is affected by problems such as substance abuse, mental illness, and emotional stress have become more prevalent and visible. Professional associations and informal groups of practitioners are convening to examine the extent of impairment among colleagues and to organize efforts to address the problem (Bissell and Haberman 1984; Coombs 2000; Prochaska and Norcross 1983; Reamer 2012a; Zur 2007).

Ironically, however, in contrast to a number of other helping professions, the social work literature contains little discussion of impaired professionals (Bissell, Fewell, and Jones 1980; Fausel 1988; Reamer 1992a, 2012a). A comprehensive review of the literature suggests that although a number of other professions have begun extensive discussions in journals and books of the problem of impaired practitioners—discussions that are a major means of educating members and preventing malpractice and liability claims—social work has not. Despite the occasional discussion in the social work literature of specific forms of impairment among practitioners—most notably alcoholism—there is a paucity of discussion of the general problem of impairment (U.S. Department of Health and Human Services 1989; Reamer 2012a). At this point in its history social work knows little about the prevalence of impairment within its ranks, and the profession's efforts to address the problem and prevent liability claims are nascent at best (Berliner 1989; Reamer 1992a, 1992b, 2012a; Siebert 2006; Strom-Gottfried 1999).

EXTENT OF IMPAIRMENT

Both the seriousness of impairment among social workers and the forms it takes vary. Impairment may involve failure to provide competent care or violation of the ethical standards of the profession. It may also take such forms as providing flawed or inferior psychotherapy to a client, sexual involvement with a client, or failure to carry out professional duties as a result of substance abuse or mental illness. Lamb, Presser, et al. (1987) provide a comprehensive definition of impairment among professionals:

> Interference in professional functioning that is reflected in one or more of the following ways: (a) an inability and/or unwillingness to acquire and integrate professional standards into one's repertoire of professional behavior; (b) an inability to acquire professional skills in order to reach an acceptable level of competency; and (c) an inability to control personal stress, psychological dysfunction, and/or excessive emotional reactions that interfere with professional functioning.
>
> (598)

No precise estimates of the extent of impairment among social workers are available. No one has conducted comprehensive surveys. Only rough estimates (at best) of the extent of the problem have been made. For example, in the foreword to the *Impaired Social Worker Resource Book,* published by the NASW Commission on Employment and Economic Support (1987a), Ruth Antoniades, who chaired the commission, states, "Social workers have the same problems as most working groups. Up to 5 to 7 percent of our membership may have a problem with substance abuse. Another 10 to 15 percent may be going through personal transitions in their relationships, marriage, family, or their work life" (4). The report goes on to conclude, however, that "there is little reliable information on the extent of impairment among social workers" (6). A 1992 survey sponsored by the NASW Indiana Chapter found that of impairments reported among social workers, 26 percent were alcohol or drug related. Results of a survey of NASW members in New York City found that 43 percent of respondents reported knowing a colleague with a drinking or drug abuse problem (Stoesen 2002).

Given the distressing absence of empirical data on social workers, it is not possible to estimate precisely the prevalence of impairment within the profession. Therefore social workers must look primarily to what is known about impairment in professions that are allied with social work, such as psychology and psychiatry. Of course, prevalence rates for social workers cannot be inferred on the basis of data from these professions. However, despite some important differences in their mission, methods, and organizational context, practitioners in these professions offer a number of similar services and face similar forms of occupational stress and strain.

Prevalence studies conducted among psychologists, for example, suggest a significant degree of distress within that profession. In a study of 749 psychologists, Guy, Poelstra, and Stark (1989) found that 74.3 percent reported "personal distress" during the previous three years, and 36.7 percent of this group believed that their distress decreased the quality of care that they provided to clients. Pope, Tabachnick, and Keith-Spiegel reported that 62.2 percent of the members of Division 29 (Psychotherapy) of the American Psychological Association admitted to "working when too distressed to be effective" (1987:993). In their survey of 167 licensed psychologists Wood et al. (1985) found that nearly one-third (32.3 percent) reported experiencing depression or burnout to an extent that interfered with their work. Wood et al. also found that a significant portion of their sample reported being aware of colleagues whose work was seriously affected by drug or alcohol use, sexual overtures toward clients, or depression and burnout. In addition evidence exists that psychologists and psychiatrists commit suicide at a rate five to six times higher than that for the general population (Farber 1983, cited in Millon, Millon, and Antoni 1986).

In the one published prevalence study that included social workers, Deutsch (1985) found that more than half of her sample of social workers, psychologists, and master's-level counselors reported significant problems with depression. Nearly four-fifths (82 percent) reported problems with relationships, approximately one-tenth (11 percent) reported substance abuse problems, and 2 percent reported suicide attempts. Bissell and Haberman (1984:65) report that 24 percent of a sample of fifty alcoholic social workers whom they surveyed reported overt suicide attempts, a rate higher than that reported by dentists, attorneys, and physicians in the Bissell and Haberman sample of alcoholics.

In a comprehensive review of a series of empirical studies focused specifically on sexual contact between therapists and clients, Pope (1988) concluded that the aggregate average of reported sexual contact is 8.3 percent by male therapists and 1.7 percent by female therapists. Pope reported that one study (Gechtman and Bouhoutsos 1985) found that 3.8 percent of male social workers admitted to sexual contact with clients.

Not all sexual abuse engaged in by social workers involves clients. A compelling example of this appeared in the *Providence (Rhode Island) Journal-Bulletin:*

> A social worker who at one time counseled abused children was sentenced yesterday to serve 20 years in prison for sexually assaulting two minors.
>
> Lawrence F. Coleman, 41, of 1540 Douglas Ave., North Providence was sentenced by Judge John F. Sheehan. The judge imposed a 30-year sentence but suspended 10 years.
>
> The victims, who are now adults, were not in any counseling program with Coleman.
>
> One of the victims addressed the court before sentencing. Her voice choked with emotion, she said that the sexual assaults had devastated her and given her low self-esteem. . . .
>
> In January Coleman was arraigned on 10 counts of first degree sexual assault before Superior Court Judge John P. Bourcier. He was freed on $100,000 surety bail. In March he pleaded guilty before Judge Sheehan, who kept bail at the same amount.
>
> Coleman earned a degree in clinical psychology from Rhode Island College in 1981 and another in social work from Boston University in 1984.
>
> He worked as a counselor at a health center in Greenville, counseling children who were victims of physical and sexual abuse.
>
> (Crombie 1989:B3)

CAUSES OF IMPAIRMENT

Several studies report a variety of forms and sources of impairment among mental health professionals. Guy, Poelstra, and Stark (1989) and Thoreson, Miller, and Krauskopf (1989) found clinicians reported diverse sources of stress reported in their lives, including their jobs, the illness or death of family members, marital or relationship problems, financial problems, midlife crises, personal physical or mental illness, legal problems, and substance abuse.

Lamb, Presser, et al. (1987) argue that professional education itself can produce unique forms of stress and impairment, primarily as a result of the close clinical supervision to which students are typically subjected, the disruption in their personal lives that is often caused by the demands of schoolwork and internships, and the pressures of their academic programs. These authors found that the most common sources of impairment are personality disorders, depression and other emotional problems, marital problems, and physical illness. It is interesting that those surveyed rarely cited academic problems and alcohol or drug abuse as sources of impairment.

This review of research suggests that distress among clinicians generally falls into two categories: environmental stress, which is a function of employment conditions (actual working conditions and the broader culture's lack of support for the human services mission), or professional training and personal stress, caused by problems with marriage, relationships, emotional and physical health, and finances. Of course, these two types of stress are often interrelated.

With respect to psychotherapists in particular, Wood et al. (1985) note that professionals encounter special problems from the extension of their therapeutic role into the nonwork aspects of their lives (such as relationships with friends and family members), the absence of reciprocity in relationships with clients (therapists are "always giving"), the frequently slow and erratic nature of the therapeutic process, and personal issues that are raised as a result of their work with clients. As Kilburg, Kaslow, and VandenBos conclude,

> [The] stresses of daily life—family responsibilities, death of family members and friends, other severe losses, illnesses, financial difficulties, crises of all kinds—quite naturally place mental health professionals, like other people, under pressure. However, by virtue of their training and place in society, such professionals face unique stresses. And although they have been trained extensively in how to deal with the emotional and behavioral crises of others, few are trained in how to deal with the stresses they themselves will face. . . . Mental health professionals are expected by everyone, including themselves, to be paragons. The fact that they may be unable to fill that role makes them a prime target for disillusionment, distress, and burnout. When this reaction occurs, the individual's ability to function as a professional may become impaired.
>
> (1988:723)

A recurring theme in cases involving practitioner impairment is the problem of professional boundaries (Reamer 2012a). Particularly in cases involving sexual involvement with clients, practitioners typically display confusion about what constitutes appropriate boundaries between themselves and their clients and about the need to clearly delineate the practitioner's and client's involvement in each other's lives (Landers 1992). The combination of a needy social worker and needy client can be disastrous. In these instances both parties are more likely to be confused about, or will simply ignore warning signs and risks related to, inappropriate involvement that may take the form of sexual contact, socializing, or business involvement unrelated to treatment. These dual relationships have generated a wide range of ethical problems and liability risks. As A. Brodsky notes,

> A sexual intimacy between patient and therapist is one example of a dual relationship. Dual relationships involve more than one purpose of relating. A therapy relationship is meant to be exclusive and unidimensional. The therapist is the expert, the patient the consumer of that expertise. Once a patient accepts an individual as a therapist, that individual cannot, without undue influence, relate to that patient in any other role. Relating to the patient as an employer, business partner, lover, spouse, relative, professor, or student would contaminate the therapeutic goal. The contamination is much more intense in a psychotherapy relationship than it would be in the relationship between a client and a professional in any other field—for example, between a client and an internist, a dentist, a lawyer, or an accountant.
>
> (1986:155)

The problems of confused boundaries and dual relationships were readily apparent in a case on which I consulted. In this case a thirty-seven-year-old woman with a history of childhood sexual abuse sought counseling from a clinical social worker. They worked together for a number of months. Over time, however, the social worker and the client began spending time together outside counseling sessions. Ultimately the client sued the social worker, alleging that the social worker's improper maintenance of boundaries was injurious. In addition the state attorney general's office filed an action in administrative court seeking to revoke the social worker's license. Evidence presented in the suit and in depositions filed in the case suggested that the social worker and client shared a motel room while the social worker attended a professional conference, the social worker provided the client with a number of gifts and wrote affectionate and intimate notes to the client, they dined together in the social worker's home, they had inappropriate physical contact, the social worker disclosed personal details of her own life to the client, and together they viewed a videotape while both were on the social worker's bed in the social worker's home. In her defense the social worker argued that all the actions that she took in the case were for "therapeutic purposes."

Social workers who violate sexual boundaries sometimes target particularly vulnerable clients. In a Michigan case a clinical social worker who provided services to individuals with serious brain injuries became sexually involved with multiple clients. These severely compromised clients testified that the social worker, who was sentenced to prison following his conviction in criminal court, groomed them over time in his effort to develop sexual relationships with them (Martelle 2009).

In recent years the two problems of sexual contact between social service professionals and clients and of substance abuse among social service professionals have begun to receive particular attention. These two phenomena have figured prominently in a significant number of liability and malpractice claims against social workers.

SEXUAL ABUSE OF CLIENTS

A significant percentage of liability claims and licensing board complaints against social workers involve allegations of sexual contact between practitioner and client (Bullis 1995; Reamer 2012a; Strom-Gottfried 1999). Clearly this is a serious problem, one that is not unique to social work. Other therapeutic professions and disciplines (for example, psychiatry, psychology, counseling) face comparable problems (Celenza 2007; Simon 1995, 1999; Syme 2003; Zur 2007).

All the available data suggest that the vast majority of cases involving sexual contact between professionals and clients involve a male practitioner and female client (A. Brodsky 1986; Celenza 2007; Pope 1988; Simon 1999; Syme 2003; Zur 2007). Gartrell et al. (1986, cited in Meyer, Landis, and Hays 1988:23) report in their nationwide survey of psychiatrists that 6.4 percent of respondents acknowledged sexual contact with their own patients; 90 percent of the offenders were male.

A relatively small number of cases involve sexual contact between a female practitioner and male client and between practitioner and client of the same gender. However, as A. Brodsky suggests in her discussion of offending psychologists, typically

> the following characteristics constitute a prototype of the therapist being sued: The therapist is male, middle aged, involved in unsatisfactory relationships in his own life, perhaps in the process of going through a divorce. His patient caseload is primarily female. He becomes involved with more than one patient sexually, those selected being on the average 16 years younger than he is. He confides his personal life to the patient, implying to her that he needs her, and he spends therapy sessions soliciting her help with his personal problems. The therapist is a lonely man, and even if he works in a group practice, he is somewhat isolated professionally, not sharing in close consultation with his peers. He may have a good reputation in the psychological or psychiatric community, having been in practice for many years. He tends to take cases through referral only. He is not necessarily physically attractive, but there is an aura of power or charisma about him. His lovemaking often leaves much to be desired, but he is quite convincing to the patient that it is he above all others with whom she needs to be making love.
>
> (1986:157–58)

A. Brodsky (1986) also describes other sexually abusive therapists, including those who tend to be inexperienced and in love with one particular client, and therapists with a personality disorder (typically antisocial personality disorder) who manipulate clients into believing that they—the therapists—should be trusted and that they have the clients' best interest at heart.

The case of *Walker v. Parzen* (1983) typifies the sexual abuse of a client by a therapist. According to court records, Dr. Parzen, a psychiatrist, had sex with Walker during a two-and-a-half year period, all the while charging her an hourly rate per session. The plaintiff eventually divorced her husband, lost her rights under California community property law, and lost custody of her two children. Parzen had also prescribed excessive medication for Walker, who claimed that she had tried to commit suicide more than a dozen times by using pills obtained from Parzen or his office, according to court records. Parzen ultimately referred Walker to another physician, referring to her as a "borderline psychotic." The jury awarded the client $4.63 million in damages (Reaves 1986:175).

Another representative case involved a social worker who developed a sexual relationship with a woman he had seen in both individual and group therapy. The social worker was treating the client for bipolar disorder and substance abuse. The client eventually attempted suicide and claimed that the clinic that employed the social worker was negligent in hiring, training, and supervising the social worker ("Woman Has Sexual Relationship" 1999).

Many licensing board cases involve allegations of sexual misconduct with current clients. For example, in a Wisconsin licensing board case, a social worker's recorded telephone conversations documented a sexual relationship with a client who visited the social worker's home (Wisconsin Department of Safety 2012). The Alabama licensing board revoked the license of a social worker who became involved sexually with a client (Alabama State Board 2006). In a New Jersey case the licensing board disciplined a social worker who was convicted of having sexual contact with a "mentally disabled" client (New Jersey State Board 2000).

A number of licensing board cases involve allegations that social workers entered into sexual relationships with former clients. For example, in a Louisiana case a social worker who provided substance abuse counseling services became sexually involved with a former client (Louisiana State Board 2013c). In a Maryland case the licensing board disciplined a clinical social worker who admitted having a sexual relationship with a former client who was being treated for posttraumatic stress disorder and adjustment disorder. The record indicates that the social worker invited the client and members of the client's family to the social worker's home and that the social worker had visited the client at the client's workplace (Maryland Board 2012).

A handful of therapists who have been sued have tried to defend their sexual contact with clients by offering two arguments that strain credibility (Schutz 1982:34–35). The first is that the sexual contact was an essential and legitimate component of therapy. The therapist typically claims that he was merely trying to be helpful to the client. The defense offered by a Dr. Cooper in a 1972 California case is illustrative:

> Dr. Cooper is a firm believer in the fact that the body has a tremendous significance and influence on our actions; and the awareness of one's body is one of the keys to personal health; mental health; and his techniques may be considered new, revolutionary, and even bizarre perhaps to some people. But none of us knows the potential of the human body in relation to the human mind, and to explore that and make a person whole is Dr. Cooper's dedicated professional goal.
>
> (Schutz 1982:34–35)

A second defense is that the sexual relationship was conducted independently of the therapeutic relationship. In these instances the defendant-therapist usually argues that he and the client were able to separate their sexual involvement from their professional relationship. As Schutz suggests, however, this argument "has not been a very successful defense, since courts are reluctant to accept such a compartmentalized view of human relationships. A therapist attempting to prove the legitimacy of sexual relations between himself and a patient by establishing that two coterminous-in-time but utterly parallel relations existed has a difficult task" (1982:35). It is important to note that the NASW *Code of Ethics* states explicitly that "social workers should under no circumstances engage in sexual activities or sexual contact with current clients, whether such contact is consensual or forced" (2008:13).

Listed here is a mere sample and diverse cross section of a large number of court cases and disciplinary hearings involving allegations of sexual misconduct:

- A psychiatrist hospitalized a thirty-year-old housewife and had sexual contact with her in the hospital and subsequently during office visits. A psychologist involved in the case was accused of encouraging the woman to have sexual relations with the psychiatrist. The psychiatrist did not deny the sexual contact but claimed that he was in love with the plaintiff. The psychologist argued that she did not encourage their relationship. The Pennsylvania case was settled for $275,000 ("Psychologist Encourages" 1989:2).

- The patient of a psychiatrist claimed that they had sexual relations in the psychiatrist's office. The plaintiff alleged that the psychiatrist told her that they could not have a sexual relationship if she was his patient and that the psychiatrist orchestrated a phony termination process. Under the doctrine of comparative negligence the jury found the defendant 82 percent liable and the plaintiff 18 percent liable. The Colorado jury awarded the plaintiff $218,000 ("Psychiatric Patient Has Sexual Relationship" 1989:4).
- A fifty-five-year-old housewife claimed that she and her psychiatrist had a sexual relationship for thirteen years during office visits. The psychiatrist admitted the sexual relations but claimed that the relationship had been consensual. The plaintiff was awarded $3 million in the Oregon case ("Psychiatrist Has Sex" 1989:6).
- A troubled wife sought counseling from a marriage therapist. The husband also attended three sessions. When the husband mentioned suicide during one session, the therapist suggested that he should go ahead and kill himself, the suit claimed. Ten months after the wife moved from the area, the therapist contacted her and convinced her to meet with him again, according to the suit. They began to have sexual relations. Both the wife and husband sued, the latter claiming loss of consortium, professional malpractice, outrageous conduct, and reckless infliction of emotional distress. The wife settled for $375,000 during trial. The California jury awarded the husband $1.85 million in compensatory damages and $1.53 million in punitive damages. After the verdict the parties settled for $850,000 ("Marriage Therapist Has Affair" 1990:3).
- A woman sought counseling from a psychologist regarding the effects of childhood sexual abuse by her father. The woman sued the psychologist, alleging that within weeks after treatment began the psychologist had her sitting near his feet, then on his lap, and then began stroking her hair and back. According to the suit, shortly thereafter the two were involved in sexual relations. The suit claimed that as a result the woman would not be able to hold a meaningful job, was unable to maintain a normal relationship with men, attempted to commit suicide, and would require treatment for the rest of her life. The New York case was settled for $2.6 million in 1990 ("Patient Sexually Abused" 1990:3).
- A woman sought counseling from a counselor, a lesbian, to address issues related to a sexual problem that she was having with her female roommate and occasional lover. The client believed that the counselor's own sexual

orientation would help her deal with the issues. During the course of treatment the client invited the counselor to have dinner with her and three other women. The counselor and client became sexually involved while the counselor was still providing the woman with counseling services. The California Board of Behavioral Science Examiners found that the counselor was grossly negligent and revoked her license ("Counselor Begins Sexual Relationship" 1991:1).

- A fifteen-year-old was admitted to a residential treatment center for substance abuse counseling. One month before the youngster's discharge, he and his father learned that the boy's counselor was having an affair with the boy's mother. The Texas jury awarded $3.34 million, including $3 million in punitive damages ("Drug Treatment Counselor" 1992:3).[1]

A number of lawsuits and licensing board complaints involve clients' claims that they were harmed by sexual relationships that began *after* the termination of the professional-client relationship. In *Heinmiller v. Department of Health* (1995) the Washington Supreme Court affirmed sanctions against a social worker who engaged in a sexual relationship with a client the day after the formal professional-client relationship had ended. In a California case a therapist acknowledged a sexual relationship with her client but argued that it occurred after termination of the professional-client relationship. The case was settled for $220,000 ("Female Therapist" 2000). In an Illinois case a psychiatrist claimed that he ended the patient's therapy, with her full agreement, and did not begin his sexual relationship with her until the following year. The Illinois Appellate Court affirmed a six-month license suspension (see *Pundy v. Illinois Department of Professional Regulation* (1991) and "Psychiatrist's License Suspended" (1993)). In another licensing board case, *Elliott v. North Carolina Psychology Board* (1997), the North Carolina Court of Appeals affirmed the suspension of a psychologist's license because he had a sexual relationship with two former clients shortly after terminating the professional-client relationship and because he had dated two other former clients ("Court Affirms Suspension" 1997).[2]

In some cases involving allegations of sexual contact, courts have ruled that a counselor was not negligent because the client did not have a "trust relationship" with the counselor. In *Sisson v. Seneca Mental Health* (1991), for example, the West Virginia courts found that because an outpatient at a mental health facility had met the counselor only once in his professional capacity at the hospital, their subsequent relationship had been outside the context of therapy sessions ("No 'Trust Relationship'" 1991:4).

Several authors believe that clinicians who engage in sexual misconduct can be categorized conceptually (Reamer 2012a). Twemlow and Gabbard (1989) characterize therapists who fall in love with clients—a particular subgroup of clinicians who become sexually involved with clients—as lovesick therapists. Lovesickness includes several key elements: emotional dependence; intrusive thinking—the therapist thinks about the client almost constantly; physical sensations like buoyancy or pounding pulse; a sense of incompleteness, of feeling less than whole when away from the client; an awareness of the social proscription of such love, which seems to intensify the couple's longing for each other; and an altered state of consciousness that fosters impaired judgment on the part of the therapist when in the presence of the loved one.

According to Schoener (1995), he and his colleagues base their widely cited classification scheme—which includes a broader range of offending therapists—on empirical evidence gathered from psychological and psychiatric examinations of sexually exploitative therapists. These clinical clusters (the italicized terminology is Schoener's) include:

1. *Psychotic and severe borderline disorders.* While few in number, these practitioners have difficulties with boundaries because of problems with both impulse control and thinking. They are often aware of current ethical standards but have difficulty adhering to them because of their poor reality testing and judgment.
   1a. *Manic disorders.* Most typically this applies to practitioners diagnosed with mania who go off medication and become quite impulsive.
2. *Sociopaths and severe narcissistic personality disorders.* These are self-centered exploiters who cross various boundaries when it suits them. They tend to be calculating and deliberate in their abuse of their clients (Olarte 1997). They often manipulate the treatment by "blurring the professional boundaries with inappropriate personal disclosure that enhances and idealizes transference, and by manipulating the length or the time of the sessions to facilitate the development of a sexual relationship with the client. . . . If caught, they might express remorse and agree to rehabilitation to protect themselves or their professional standing, but they will show minimal or no character change through treatment" (Olarte 1997:205).

3. *Impulse control disorders.* This includes practitioners with a wide range of paraphilias (sexual disorders in which unusual fantasies or bizarre acts are necessary for sexual arousal) and other impulse control disorders. These professionals often have other impulse control problems in other areas of their lives. They are typically aware of current ethical standards, but these do not serve as a deterrent. These practitioners often fail to acknowledge the harm that their behavior does to their victims and show little remorse.

4. *Chronic neurotic and isolated.* These practitioners are emotionally needy on a chronic basis and meet many needs through their relationships with clients. They may suffer from long-standing problems with depression, low self-esteem, social isolation, and lack of confidence. At times these practitioners disclose personal information to clients inappropriately. Typically they deny engaging in misconduct or justify the unethical behavior as their therapeutic technique designed to enhance their suffering client's self-esteem. They may also blame the client's claims on the client's pathology. Such practitioners are often repeat offenders.

5. *Situational offenders.* These therapists are generally healthy with a good practice history and free of boundary violations, but a situational breakdown in judgment or control has occurred in response to some life crisis or loss. These practitioners are generally aware of current ethical standards. According to Olarte, "Their sexual contact with a client is usually an isolated or limited incident. Frequently at the time of the boundary violation, these therapists are suffering from personal or situational stresses that foster a slow erosion of their professional boundaries. They most often show remorse for their unethical behavior, frequently stop such violations on their own, or seek consultation with peers" (1997:204).

6. *Naive.* These therapists are not pathological but have difficulty understanding, and operating within, professional boundaries because they suffer from deficits in social judgment. Their difficulties stem in part from their lack of knowledge of current ethical standards and their confusion about the need to separate personal and professional relationships.

In contrast to this framework Simon offers a typology that includes somewhat different clinical dimensions. Simon places vulnerable therapists in five categories:

- *Character disordered.* Therapists diagnosed with symptoms of borderline, narcissistic, or antisocial personality disorder.

- *Sexually disordered.* Therapists diagnosed with frotteurism (recurrent intense sexual urges and sexually arousing fantasies in regard to a nonconsenting person), pedophilia, or sexual sadism.
- *Incompetent.* Therapists who are poorly trained or have persistent boundary blind spots.
- *Impaired.* Therapists who have serious problems with alcohol, drugs, or mental illness.
- *Situational reactors.* Therapists who are experiencing marital discord, loss of important relationships, or a professional crisis.

(1999:35)

Based on his extensive experience with vulnerable and offending therapists, Simon (1999) argues that boundary violations are often progressive and follow a sequence, or "natural history," that leads ultimately to a therapist-client sexual relationship. Although the sequence is not always this linear, the general pattern is common. The sequence unfolds as follows:

- The therapist's neutrality gradually erodes. The therapist begins to take special interest in the client's issues and life circumstances.
- Boundary violations begin between the chair and the door. As the client is leaving the office, and both client and worker are standing, the therapist and client may discuss personal issues that are not part of the more formal therapeutic conversation.
- Therapy becomes socialized. More time is spent discussing nontherapy issues.
- The therapist discloses confidential information about other clients. The therapist begins to confide in the client, communicating to the client that she is special.
- Therapist self-disclosure begins. The therapist shares information about his own life, perhaps concerning marital or relationship problems.
- Physical contact begins (for example, touching, hugs, kisses). Casual physical gestures convey to the client that the therapist has warm and affectionate feelings toward her.
- The therapist gains control over the client. The client begins to feel more and more dependent on the therapist, and the therapist exerts more and more influence in the client's life.
- Extratherapeutic contacts occur. The therapist and client may meet for lunch or for a drink.

- Therapy sessions are longer. The therapist extends the customary fifty-minute session because of the special relationship.
- Therapy sessions are rescheduled for the end of the day. To avoid conflict with other clients' appointments, the therapist arranges to see the client as the day's final appointment.
- The therapist stops billing the client. The emerging intimacy makes it difficult for the therapist to charge the client for the time they spend together.
- Dating begins. The therapist and client begin to schedule times when they can be together socially.
- Therapist-client sex occurs.

Celenza (2007:11, 29–38) studied a sample of therapists who engaged in sexual misconduct and found a number of common precursors related primarily to the therapist's personality, life circumstances, past history, and the transference-countertransference dynamics of this particular therapist-client pair. More specifically Calenza found that clinicians who manifest the following traits are more likely to engage in sexual misconduct:

- Long-standing narcissistic vulnerability. Therapists reported a lifelong struggle with a sense of unworthiness, inadequacy, or outright feelings of failure.
- Grandiose (covert) rescue fantasies. Therapists presented a mild-mannered, self-effacing, and humble exterior that hid underlying (and unchallenged) beliefs in powers of rescue and omnipotence.
- Intolerance of negative transference. Often as a result of fragile self-esteem, some therapists have difficulty tolerating and exploring disappointments, frustrations, and criticisms that the client may have about the services she or he is receiving.
- Childhood history of emotional deprivation and sexualized overstimulation. Some therapists reported sexualization of their relationship with a primary caregiver (usually the mother), often in the form of overstimulation of the child in a sexualized manner rather than outright sexual abuse.
- Family history of covert and sanctioned boundary transgressions. Some therapists' families showed evidence of high moralism accompanied by hypocrisy, for example, in the form of marital infidelity or fraudulent financial activity.
- Unresolved anger toward authority figures. Some therapists appeared to engage in sexual misconduct as a way to rebel against the authority of their

profession and as a result of an underlying desire to break the rules, perhaps because of anger toward an authoritarian parent.

- Restricted awareness of fantasy (especially hostile/aggressive). Many therapists, especially those who felt intense guilt and remorse, were unable to admit to or access hateful or desirous wishes except in conventional or muted ways. These therapists had difficulty perceiving aggression in themselves or others.
- Transformation of countertransference hate to countertransference love. Some therapists had difficulty tolerating their own aggression and perceiving themselves as depriving clients or not nurturing them. These therapists harbored the unrealistic belief that they should love and help every client.

PRACTITIONER SUBSTANCE ABUSE

Most studies related to substance abuse among social service professionals focus on alcohol. Relatively little research has been conducted on other drug use among practitioners. Here is an illustrative case example:

Miss Jones was the clinical supervisor for an off-site social work follow-up counseling service of a large public hospital. She was 61 years old, and she had recurring mild back pain resulting from a herniated disk, a problem that could be managed without surgery through diet control, exercise, and correct posture. She had worked for the agency for approximately 8 years, serving for the last 2 as supervisor of the off-site outpatient counseling and guidance service. She supervised a clinical staff of four social workers, one psychologist, and three counselors, all of whom were between 25 and 45 years old. Miss Jones had gradually become the agency's resident "alcohol expert" because she had been sent to a number of seminars and workshops on alcohol-related problems during the last 5 years.

Some months after Miss Jones had transferred to the off-site office, individual staff members began to note an apparent deterioration in her work performance. She became less available for supervision of and consultation with staff members, less systematic in the review of cases, and erratic in keeping supervision appointments, and she began to end supervision sessions abruptly after only 10 to 15 minutes. Moreover, clinical staff also was beginning to hear complaints from clients who had direct clinical contact with

Miss Jones. Furthermore, Miss Jones's administrative functioning seemed to be deteriorating; she seemed unable to produce needed administrative reports, was erratic and inconsistent in administrative decision making, and was unable to systematically follow through on administrative details.

Concurrently, her co-workers noted an apparent change in personality and behavior. She seemed to have withdrawn and become aloof. She spent less time informally chatting with staff, and she stopped sharing lunch hours with her co-workers. Her absences from work increased, and it became more and more frequent that she would arrive at work late or leave work early because of "not feeling up to par." Clinical and clerical staff began to note a pattern of Miss Jones's having alcohol on her breath during the afternoon and to appear more frequently to be behaviorally "under the influence of alcohol."

Initially individual staff members commented in private to Miss Jones about one or another concern about her behavior. Her response to such comments or expressions of concern was defensive. She attributed all of her present difficulty to her "back problems," subtly suggested a lack of empathy on the part of the given staff member, and intimated that the staff member's "concern" was placing more pressure on her. . . .

After administrative staff found liquor bottles in her desk and filing cabinets, the program director placed Miss Jones on indefinite administrative leave with the option that if she sought "appropriate help" (still undefined) and adequately demonstrated a return to "normal functioning," she could return to her previous position. Miss Jones decided to seek voluntary hospitalization in a facility specializing in the treatment of stress disorders. While in the facility, she ultimately decided to seek early retirement for "health reasons."

(VandenBos and Duthie 1986:224–26)

Estimates of the prevalence of alcoholism among professionals vary. Many are based on data from treatment groups or impressions from practitioners' clinical experience. A precise way to measure the incidence of substance abuse among professionals does not exist. The more thorough, detailed estimates suggest that roughly 5 to 6 percent of professionals are alcoholic, with a somewhat higher incidence among men and lower incidence among women (Thoreson and Skorina 1986:85–87).

Professionals, like the general public, manifest various signs of impairment because of alcohol use. Freudenberger (1986) claims to have found a recognizable pattern among many alcoholic professionals:

I have worked with at least 60 impaired professionals, psychologists, social workers, dentists, physicians, and attorneys during the past ten years and have found certain personality characteristics to be common. For the most part, impaired professionals are between 30 and 55 years of age. This is in essential agreement with Farber and Heifetz (1981) who suggested that "suicides of physicians, when they happen, are most likely to occur in the 35–54 age group" (p. 296). Early childhood impoverishment is another common characteristic. This is in agreement with Vaillant, Brighton, and McArthur (1970), who pointed to the "lack of consistent support and concern from their parents" in his study of drug-using physicians.

Most, if not all, of the patients I worked with led consistently unhealthy lifestyles. They tended to be masochistic, to have low self-images, and to be self-destructive in their personal and professional lives. Eighteen of the 60 had been married more than one time, 10 were bachelors, and the remainder were separated or divorced. Those who were married had frequent extramarital affairs. They all worked excessively long hours and, as Pearson and Strecker (1960) suggested, "had poor organizational habits . . . seldom took vacations, lunch hours and had few outside interests" (p. 916).

Their masochism made them prone to their patients [sic] beyond their own personal limits. All tended to be perfectionists and were usually never pleased with their work. "I know I can be better, I'm not good enough, I could have done more" are frequently heard refrains. They tended to conduct their lives, both at home and in the office, in such a way that they found little, if any, relief from their chores. They had a desperate need to be needed and rationalized taking drugs as doing something for themselves. . . . They rationalized, denied, and overcompensated to an excessive degree.

While expressing a sense of dedication and commitment, they denied that abusing drugs or alcohol or sexually abusing clients might eventually lead to their destruction. As a group they were risk takers with their own as well as their patients' lives.

(137–38)

As with other forms of impairment, little is known about the prevalence of alcoholism among social workers. Although various estimates have been made of the incidence of substance abuse among social workers—generally about 5 to 15 percent (see estimates contained in NASW 1987a:4, 6)—no one really knows how widespread the problem is. As Bissell and Haberman (1984) conclude after surveying fifty alcoholic social workers, along with other professionals, "An attempt to review the literature on all aspects of impairment in social workers revealed very little. Except for a 1980 study conducted by one of us, the studies mentioned above, and a brief description of social workers included in a hospital EAP, nothing could be located on the subject of alcoholism in this group" (153).

A number of social work licensing boards have disciplined practitioners who abused substances. For example, the Iowa licensing board suspended the license of a social worker based on evidence of significant substance abuse–related impairment (Iowa Board of Social Work 2013). A Texas social worker was disciplined by the licensing board based on evidence that she used substances at work (Texas Department of State Health Service 2013). The Arkansas licensing board disciplined a social worker based on evidence that she provided "social work services while under the influence of alcohol, other mind-altering or mood-altering drugs" (Arkansas Social Work Licensing Board 2013). In an Alabama case the licensing board disciplined a social worker who admitted to "habituation to drugs or to habit forming drugs that impair the ability to perform social work duties" (Alabama State Board 1999).

RESPONSE TO IMPAIRMENT

To minimize liability and malpractice risks social workers must devise ways to prevent impairment and respond to impaired colleagues. Little is known about the extent to which impaired social workers and other professionals voluntarily seek help for their problems. A comprehensive search of the literature produced few empirical studies of impaired practitioners' efforts to seek help. Guy, Poelstra, and Stark (1989) found that 70 percent of the distressed clinical psychologists whom they surveyed sought some form of therapeutic assistance. One-fourth (26.6 percent) entered individual psychotherapy, and 10.7 percent entered family therapy. A small portion of this group participated in self-help groups (3.4 percent) or was hospitalized (2.2 percent). Some were placed on medication (4.1 percent). Exactly 10 percent of this group temporarily terminated their professional practice.

These findings contrast with those of Wood et al. (1985), who found that only 55.2 percent of clinicians who reported problems that interfered with their work (substance abuse, sexual overtures toward clients, depression, and burnout) sought help. Two-fifths (42 percent) of all those surveyed, including impaired and unimpaired professionals, reported having offered help to impaired colleagues at some time or having referred them to therapists. Only 7.9 percent of the sample said they had reported an impaired colleague to a local regulatory body. Approximately two-fifths (40.2 percent) were aware of instances in which they believed no action was taken to help an impaired colleague.

We can draw several hypotheses concerning impaired professionals' reluctance to seek help and the reluctance of their colleagues to confront them about their problems. Until recently professionals were hesitant to acknowledge impairment within their ranks because they feared how practitioners would react to confrontation and how such confrontation might affect the future relationships of colleagues who must work together (Bernard and Jara 1986; McCrady 1989; Wood et al. 1985). VandenBos and Duthie present the problem succinctly:

> The fact that more than half of us have not confronted distressed colleagues even when we have recognized and acknowledged (at least to ourselves) the existence of their problems is, in part, a reflection of the difficulty in achieving a balance between concerned intervention and intrusiveness. As professionals, we value our own right to practice without interference, as long as we function within the boundaries of our professional expertise, meet professional standards for the provision of services, and behave in an ethical manner. We generally consider such expectations when we consider approaching a distressed colleague. Deciding when and how our concern about the well-being of a colleague (and our ethical obligation) supersedes his or her right to personal privacy and professional autonomy is a ticklish matter.
>
> (1986:212)

Thoreson et al. (1983) also argue that impaired professionals sometimes find it difficult to seek help because of their mythical belief in their infinite power and invulnerability. Because many psychotherapists are in private practice, the reduced opportunity for colleagues to observe their unethical or inept practice exacerbates the problem.

In a valuable study by Deutsch (1985) a diverse group of therapists (including social workers) who admitted to personal problems gave a variety of reasons for not seeking professional help, including believing that an acceptable therapist was not available, seeking help from family members or friends, fearing exposure and the disclosure of confidential information, concern about the amount of effort required and about the cost, having a spouse who was unwilling to participate in treatment, failing to admit the seriousness of the problem, believing they should be able to work their problems out themselves, and believing that therapy would not help.

Rehabilitation of mental health professionals who have been sexually involved with clients is particularly daunting. One-time offenders who made an isolated mistake with an individual client can often be helped through therapy and education. However, the rehabilitative prospects for chronic offenders and professionals with personality disorders, such as antisocial personality disorder, are often grim. As A. Brodsky (1986) concludes, "The therapist whose motives were less than honorable, who had intimacies with several patients, and who, in the case of men, is chronically problematic in relationships with women outside of therapy is probably not easily rehabilitated. In some cases of personality disorder, it is questionable whether or not retraining of the therapist is possible" (164).

As I mentioned earlier, in recent years several organized efforts have been made to identify and address the problems of impaired professionals. The consensus is growing that a model strategy for addressing impairment among professionals should include several components (Reamer 2012a; Schoener and Gonsiorek 1988; Sonnenstuhl 1989; VandenBos and Duthie 1986). First, adequate means for identifying impaired practitioners are needed. Professionals must be willing to assume some responsibility for acknowledging impairment among colleagues. And, as Lamb, Presser, et al. (1987) note, it certainly would help to develop reasonably objective measures of what constitutes incompetent skills, impaired professional functioning, and failure to live up to professional standards.

Second, a social worker's initial identification and documentation of a colleague's impairment should be followed by exploration of the causes and by what Sonnenstuhl (1989) describes as "constructive confrontation."

Third, once a social worker decides to confront the impaired colleague, the social worker must decide whether to help the impaired colleague identify ways to seek help voluntarily or to refer the colleague to a supervisor or local regulatory body (such as a licensing board).

Assuming the data are sufficient to support a rehabilitation plan, the impaired practitioner's colleague, supervisor, or local regulatory body should make specific recommendations. The possibilities include close supervision, personal psychotherapy, and treatment for substance abuse. In some cases a licensing board may need to impose some type of sanction such as censure, probation, limitations on the professional's social work practice (for example, concerning clientele that can be served), or loss of license. Whatever action is taken should be monitored and evaluated. Here is an illustration of effective intervention with an impaired professional:

Mr. Brown was the director of a community-based county work release/ rehabilitation program in a medium-sized town. He was 34 years old. Mr. Brown was noted for his friendliness, his openness with colleagues and community leaders, his dedication to making the program work for the community and those enrolled, and his well-balanced approach in solving problems and in instructing others about how best to approach the participants in the program. Due to a cut in state funding to be made available to the county, the county board of administration found it necessary to reallocate funds for the next year's budget in such a way that several programs, including the program directed by Mr. Brown, would have to be redefined or possibly even eliminated. Mr. Brown prepared extensive documentation on the success of his program and presented it to the board, making an impassioned plea for its continuation. The board began its deliberations.

Although not directly involved in the decision-making process, Mr. Brown was well known to many of the board members and, as the board's deliberations progressed, some board members formed factions representing a range of opinions about what should happen to the program and shared information on the board's day-to-day deliberations, which were marked by continual changes in opinions, with Mr. Brown. As a result, over a period of six months, Mr. Brown became progressively more frustrated, uncertain, and stressed about the eventual outcome.

Mr. Brown's co-workers began to notice him gradually withdrawing from those around him. Rather than having his lunch in the cafeteria with his colleagues, he began to eat alone in his office, declaring that he was too busy to do otherwise, and he participated less and less in the ordinary social activity of the staff. He also began to limit "business" contact with his colleagues and members of the community to meetings that were as brief as possible. Several of his co-workers as individuals expressed concern about these changes to him. Mr. Brown's explanation was that the uncertainty about the outcome of the board's deliberations was creating a great deal of pressure on him and, as a result, it was difficult for him to concentrate, and he had to focus more intensely on getting his work done.

Others also noted the changes in Mr. Brown. In particular, these changes were noted by an industrial/organizational psychologist working for a large company, which had participated in the work release program for many years, and who considered Mr. Brown to be both a colleague and a friend. His colleague asked Mr. Brown to conduct a training session for several new employees on the staff on how to work effectively with participants in the work release program. On the day following the session, she called Mr. Brown and asked to meet with him in order to share feedback on the session, and they set a meeting time. During the meeting, she expressed concern about the changes she had noted in Mr. Brown's behavior both personally and professionally and her feeling that those changes seemed to represent a pattern of behavior indicating depression. She went on to say that it was apparent that the depression was not being attended to by Mr. Brown.

As an example of what had caused her to be concerned, she pointed out that during the training session Mr. Brown, who was ordinarily a patient, flexible individual, had responded to members of the group with anger and hostility when they challenged or even questioned elements of his presentation and when they expressed disagreement with his interpretations of material. She noted that this was very inconsistent with his usual behavior. At the same time, she mentioned in passing that she had overheard comments by others—including co-workers and community members—regarding his apparent inaccessibility, both professionally and emotionally. She suggested that Mr. Brown's attempts to control and cope with his distress were not being fully effective and that she and his co-workers wanted to offer whatever support they could. At the same time, she suggested that Mr. Brown might consider entering therapy. Initially, Mr. Brown reacted defensively and angrily. He expressed his feeling that his colleague was intruding. However, after continued discussion, it became apparent to him that her

concern was genuine and that she expressed the shared caring and frustration of herself, his coworkers, and others. The effect of her simultaneously
confrontational and supporting approach was to break through Mr. Brown's
defensiveness and denial. He began to identify and acknowledge other indi-
cations of depressive symptomatology. He also mentioned that his rumina-
tion about possible "political outcomes" and his withdrawal from others was
further complicating the situation for him. Following this confrontation, he
went into short-term therapy and his depression was quickly resolved—Mr.
Brown again became his friendly, open, effective self.

(VandenBos and Duthie 1986:227–29)

Relatively little research has focused on the effectiveness of efforts to
rehabilitate impaired professionals (Sonnenstuhl 1989; Trice and Beyer
1984). Moreover the few published empirical evaluations—which report
mixed results for various treatment programs—focus primarily on impaired
physicians (Herrington et al. 1982; Morse et al. 1984; Pearson 1982; Shore
1982). Studies typically report only whether the practitioner is still alive,
still licensed, or in practice. Many investigations have serious methodologi-
cal flaws or limitations. Few studies compare the outcome of efforts to treat
impaired professionals with control groups or even other patient groups,
and follow-up periods tend to be relatively short (Bissell and Haberman
1984). The results of the handful of outcome studies on the treatment of
impaired professionals are as follows:

- Goby, Bradley, and Bespalec (1979, cited in Bissell and Haberman 1984:104)
  report on their follow-up survey of forty-three alcoholic physician-patients
  treated over a ten-year period at Lutheran General Hospital in Illinois.
  One was in prison, and seven had died (one committed suicide, one died of
  lung cancer, three died drinking excessively, and two died from unknown
  causes). Nineteen of the forty-three (44 percent) had been abstinent since
  discharge from the program; nine reported some drinking but were abstinent
  for a full year or more at the time of the survey. Only eight did not report a
  significant decrease in alcohol consumption. Most of the physicians reported
  good physical and emotional health and were working.
- Kliner, Spicer, and Barnett (1980, cited in Bissell and Haberman 1984:104)
  reported on results of a mail survey of fifty-seven alcoholic physicians treated
  at the Hazelden Foundation in Minnesota one year after discharge. Fifty-one

of the fifty-seven reported abstinence since discharge, five reported serious difficulty with continued drinking, and one reported continued drinking but no related problems. The respondents also reported improvements in self-image, health, professional performance, and personal adjustment.

- Morse et al. (1984, cited in Bissell and Haberman 1984:104) reported on outcomes for fifty-three alcoholic physicians who had been treated for at least two weeks at the Mayo Clinic. One to five years after discharge, 83 percent of the physicians reported complete abstinence or having been in relapse for no more than one week—and as abstinent when surveyed—compared to 62 percent of a nonphysician "general group" of patients. Eighty-nine percent of the physicians resumed their practice.
- Herrington et al. (1982) reported on a study of forty alcoholic physicians and dentists treated in an impaired-physician program in Milwaukee, Wisconsin. The treatment included a thirty-day inpatient program, Alcoholic and/or Narcotics Anonymous, and follow-up. Seven physicians dropped out of treatment early. Of the thirty physicians and three dentists who remained in treatment, twenty-two reported abstinence since discharge and six reported only a single relapse. The majority continued to practice.
- Pearson (1982) reported on the treatment of 250 physicians over a thirty-six-year period. Slightly more than one-third (36 percent) had a history of substance abuse, about one-fifth (18 percent) were diagnosed with psychotic symptoms or affective disorders, and slightly more than one-fourth (28 percent) manifested neurotic or situational problems. Of the 160 who received actual treatment, 42 percent were classified as recovered or much improved, 22 percent as slightly improved, and 36 percent as worse or unimproved.
- Shore (1982) reported on a study of twenty-seven alcoholic or drug-addicted physicians treated in Oregon under state board supervision. The Oregon Board of Medical Examiners had placed all on professional probation. Data suggested that twenty-two of the twenty-seven improved, with fourteen reporting no relapse. Seventy-nine percent returned to practice, but during an average 3.6 years on probation, 53 percent had relapses.

RISK MANAGEMENT STRATEGY

Social workers can take various steps to protect clients and to minimize the likelihood of lawsuits and ethics complaints associated with boundary problems and impairment. With specific respect to sexual misconduct,

Simon highlights five basic principles underlying constructive boundary guidelines:

1. Rule of abstinence: Practitioners should strive, above all else, to avoid sexual involvement with clients and to resist acting on sexual attraction toward clients.

2. Duty of neutrality: Practitioners should seek to relate to clients as neutrally as possible. Neutrality entails the absence of favoritism, preferential consideration, and special treatment.

3. Client autonomy and self-determination: Practitioners should respect clients' right to self-determination, which means avoiding any manipulative behaviors or behaviors that might promote clients' dependence or constitute "undue influence."

4. Fiduciary relationship: Fiduciary relationships are based on trust. Clients must be able to trust their therapists and to assume that their therapists would not engage in manipulative, exploitative, or seductive behaviors for self-interested purposes.

5. Respect for human dignity: Practitioners must maintain deep-seated respect for their clients, act only in a caring and compassionate manner, and avoid engaging in destructive behaviors.

(1999:32)

More concretely practitioners should adhere to a number of guidelines to protect clients and minimize risks associated with sexual attraction (Calfee 1997; Celenza 2007; Reamer 2012a; Simon 1999; Syme 2003; Zur 2007):

Maintain relative therapist neutrality (the absence of favoritism).
Foster psychological separateness of the client.
Protect client confidentiality.
Obtain informed consent for treatments and procedures.
Interact with clients verbally.
Ensure no previous, current, or future personal relationship with the client.
Minimize physical contact.
Preserve relative anonymity of the therapist.
Establish a stable fee policy.
Provide a consistent, private, and professional setting for treatment.
Define the time and length of the treatment session.

Beyond these broad guidelines, social workers should pay special attention to clients' unique clinical issues that may complicate boundary phenomena. For example, if a therapist senses that a client is feeling attracted to him, the therapist might avoid scheduling the client at times when no one else is in the office suite. As Gutheil and Gabbard (1993) observe, "From a risk-management standpoint, a patient in the midst of an intense erotic transference to the therapist might best be seen, when possible, during high-traffic times when other people (e.g., secretaries, receptionists, and even other patients) are around" (191). Therapists in solo private practice must be especially careful because of professional isolation and the absence of institutional or collegial oversight and restraints (Simon 1995).

Further, therapists who sense potential boundary issues involving sexual attraction should avoid out-of-the-office contact with clients. A common example includes counseling sessions conducted during lunch in a restaurant:

> This event appears to be a common way station along the path of increasing boundary crossings culminating in sexual misconduct. Although clinicians often advance the claim that therapy is going on, so, inevitably, is much purely social behavior; it does not *look* like therapy, at least to a jury. Lunch sessions are not uncommonly followed by sessions during dinner, then just dinners, then other dating behavior, eventually including intercourse.
>
> (Gutheil and Gabbard 1993:192)

Boundary violations can also arise from seemingly innocent gestures, such as offering a stranded client a ride home after a counseling session. Clinically relevant discussion may continue during the ride and while the therapist and client are parked in front of the client's home. Conducting sensitive discussion in the context of the therapist's personal space can lead to boundary ambiguity, confusion, and, ultimately, violation: "From a fact finder's viewpoint, many exciting things happen in cars, but therapy is usually not one of them" (Gutheil and Gabbard 1993:192).

One must consider these guidelines in relation to different treatment approaches and ideologies. Some treatment techniques assume that therapists will spend time with clients outside the office. As Gutheil and Gabbard (1993) note,

> It would not be a boundary violation for a behaviorist, under certain circumstances, to accompany a patient in a car, to an elevator, to an airplane, or even to a public restroom (in the treatment of paruresis, the fear of urinating in a public restroom) as part of the treatment plan for a particular phobia. The existence of a body of professional literature, a clinical rationale, and risk-benefit documentation will be useful in protecting the clinician in such a situation from misconstruction of the therapeutic efforts.
>
> (192)

Simon (1995) urges practitioners to conduct an "instant spot check" to identify whether the therapist has committed, or is at risk of committing, a boundary violation. Using this approach, the first question to ask is whether the treatment is for the benefit of the therapist or for the sake of the client's therapy. Second, is the treatment part of a series of progressive steps in the direction of boundary violations (for example, inviting the client to have lunch after a counseling session in order to continue discussion of compelling clinical issues)? Simon argues that an affirmative answer to either question should put the therapist on notice to desist immediately and take corrective action.

THE CHALLENGE FOR SOCIAL WORK

In his oft-cited address to the National Conference of Charities and Correction, Flexner (1915) asked, "Is social work a profession?" At the time Flexner noted that one essential attribute of a profession is its tendency toward self-regulation. Greenwood (1957) made a similar observation in his classic essay on the professions.

Over the years social work has certainly strengthened its regulatory functions. Social work licensing boards often act responsibly and vigorously to sanction social workers engaged in misconduct.

However, for a profession to be truly self-regulating it cannot rely entirely on the efforts of dissatisfied or abused clients to file ethics complaints or lawsuits against impaired practitioners. For a variety of reasons clients often are reluctant to get involved in the formal adjudication process. Therefore members of the professions must be vigilant in their efforts to confront the incompetence, unprofessional conduct, and unethical activities of their colleagues. The profession must provide active yet constructive monitoring of its members; sophisticated and sensitively administered support and rehabilitation services; and, when necessary, adjudication procedures that adhere to accepted principles of due process. All these activities should also help reduce the risk of liability and malpractice claims' being filed against social workers.

As a profession social work has not paid sufficient attention to the problems of impaired practitioners. Unlike a number of other professions, such as medicine, law, and psychology, social work's literature contains little on the subject. Empirical research on the prevalence of impairment in the profession also is distressingly sparse. Moreover most states do not have ambitious efforts to identify and respond to impaired social workers.

To the profession's credit, however, in 1992 the president of NASW created the Code of Ethics Review Task Force (which I chaired); it proposed adding new principles to the *Code of Ethics* on the subject of impairment. The approved additions became effective in 1994 and were revised slightly for the current code:

> Social workers should not allow their own personal problems, psychosocial distress, legal problems, substance abuse, or mental health difficulties to interfere with their professional judgment and performance or to jeopardize the best interests of people for whom they have a professional responsibility.
>
> (standard 4.05[a])

> Social workers whose personal problems, psychosocial distress, legal problems, substance abuse, or mental health difficulties interfere with professional judgment and performance should immediately seek consultation and take appropriate remedial action by seeking professional help, making adjustments in workload, terminating practice, or taking any other steps necessary to protect clients and others.
>
> (standard 4.05[b])

Social workers who have direct knowledge of a social work colleague's impairment that is due to personal problems, psychosocial distress, substance abuse, or mental health difficulties and that interferes with practice effectiveness should consult with that colleague when feasible and assist the colleague in taking remedial action.

(standard 2.09[a])

Social workers who believe that a social work colleague's impairment interferes with practice effectiveness and that the colleague has not taken adequate steps to address the impairment should take action through appropriate channels established by employers, agencies, NASW, licensing and regulatory bodies, and other professional organizations.

(standard 2.09[b])

One can only speculate about why social work generally has paid less attention than other professions to the problem of impaired practitioners. It is difficult to know whether the magnitude of the problem is smaller in social work than in other professions (and hence attracts less attention), whether denial of impairment in social work is greater than in other professions, whether social workers have a higher threshold of tolerance for impairment in general, or whether social workers simply write and publish less than members of other professions. Whatever the explanation, social work, like every profession, unquestionably has its share of impaired practitioners (albeit a relatively small percentage of the profession) and needs to strengthen its efforts to respond to them.

Toward this end social work must actively pursue a number of goals. First, social work must embark on a program of empirical research designed to produce valid and reliable measures of impairment, its prevalence in the profession, and its consequences. For social work to mount an ambitious effort to address impairment, it must have an adequate database on the extent of the problem. Surveys of social workers and agency administrators need to be conducted to establish a baseline against which to measure changes in levels of impairment over time.

In addition the profession must strengthen its efforts to identify impaired practitioners and to respond to them in a meaningful way. Social workers, like many other professionals, may be reluctant to confront impaired colleagues. This reluctance is understandable. Nonetheless it is incumbent on the profession to confront incompetence and unethical behavior and to offer humane assistance. Attention should be paid to social workers in solo private practice, as well as those who work in group settings where the opportunity to observe impairment may be greater.

NASW—at the national level and through its state chapters—must take the lead in strengthening efforts to identify and assist impaired members. Local licensing boards should also address this challenge.

Social workers must expand education about the problem of impaired social workers. Relatively few social workers have been trained to identify and confront impairment. The profession's organizations and associations must begin to conduct workshops and in-service training on the subject to acquaint social workers with current information about the forms that impairment can take, the signs to look for, and ways to confront the problem.

Social work students, especially, need to be introduced to the subject. The emphasis should be on prevention through acquainting prospective practitioners with warning signs to look for in their own and colleagues' lives and with potential remedies, including therapy, time management, stress management, and career planning. Such training, which is being introduced in social work education programs with somewhat greater frequency, should be part of an aggressive effort to expand education about professional ethics in social work (Joseph 1989; Reamer 1990, 2001c, 2013a; Reamer and Abramson 1982).

Social workers should develop comprehensive and accessible collegial assistance programs to assist impaired practitioners. Although some cases of impairment must be dealt with through formal adjudication procedures by licensing boards, many cases can be handled primarily by arranging therapeutic or rehabilitative services for distressed workers. Impaired social workers should have access to competent service providers who are trained to understand professionals' special concerns and needs. For instance, state chapters of NASW can enter into agreements with local EAPs to which impaired members can be referred (NASW 1987a).

As social workers intensify their focus on impairment in the profession, they must be careful to avoid reductionist explanations of the problems that colleagues experience. Although emphasizing psychotherapeutic and other rehabilitative efforts in instances that call for them (including chemical dependence or mental illness) is certainly appropriate, social workers must not lose sight of the environmental stresses that often lead to such disabilities. Distress experienced by social workers often is the result of unique challenges in the profession for which the resources are inadequate. Social workers who work day by day with clients who are subjected to poverty, hunger, homelessness, child abuse, crime, mental illness, and so forth are prime candidates for stress and burnout. Inadequate funding, thin political support, and public criticism of social workers' efforts often combine to produce low morale and high stress (Jayaratne and Chess 1984; Johnson and Stone 1986; Koeske and Koeske 1989; Siebert 2006). In addition to responding to the private troubles of impaired colleagues, social workers must confront the public issues and environmental flaws that can produce impairment. Those who confront impairment among colleagues must avoid blaming the victim, just as they resist doing so with their own clients.

Social work is a grand and noble profession with a grand and noble mission. Its tradition is addressing the problems of individuals and the environmental stresses that surround them. The same tradition must be extended to impaired colleagues. This form of self-regulation is a hallmark of a profession and is especially important in one that exercises considerable influence over the lives of others.

5

Supervision

THE CONCEPT AND PRACTICE OF supervision have always been central in social work. Practitioners' training typically includes considerable attention to theory and skills related to supervision (Campbell 2006; Caspi and Reid 2002; Kadushin 1992; Miller 1987; Munson 2001; Shulman 2008; Tsui 2005; Wonnacott 2012). Over the years the social work literature has addressed a variety of issues related to supervision, including the administrative and clinical responsibilities of the supervisor, the challenge in moving from practitioner to supervisor, and the importance of leadership qualities in supervision.

Not surprisingly lawsuits and licensing board complaints sometimes name social workers who have supervisory responsibilities. Although supervisors may not have been directly involved in the event or circumstances immediately surrounding the case, they may be found responsible, at least in part.

Liability claims and licensing board complaints related to supervision tend to be of two types. The first includes cases involving client supervision, that is, instances in which social workers are alleged to have failed in their duty to properly supervise clients. The second includes cases involving staff supervision. These cases usually allege that a social worker failed to properly supervise a staff member who was negligent or who committed some act of misfeasance, malfeasance, or nonfeasance.

CLIENT SUPERVISION

Howard C., BSW, was a social worker in a residential facility for adolescents with major mental illness and behavioral challenges. He had worked at the facility for three years; during that time he had worked as a child-care worker and, most recently, a unit supervisor. In his position as unit supervisor Howard C. supervised three child-care workers on his shift and also had responsibility for helping to supervise the youngsters on the unit. Most youths on the unit had been admitted with such symptoms as severe depression, violent behavior, self-mutilation, hallucinations and delusions, and attempted suicide.

On one particular Thursday morning only two child-care workers and Howard C. were on the unit. The third child-care worker had called in sick. As a result Howard C. was expected to put his administrative duties aside and assume the responsibilities of the third child-care worker. That is, Howard C. was to be physically present on the unit instead of spending much of his time in the corner office where the unit supervisors shared a desk.

Howard C. began the shift on the unit. The residents were engaged in various activities. Several were involved in counseling sessions, some were being tutored on their schoolwork, and others were working on their journal entries. The youths for whom Howard C. was primarily responsible were relaxing, watching television.

Howard C. decided to use this time to finish up some paperwork that each unit supervisor was expected to complete (incident reports). He told the youths for whom he was responsible that he would be in his office. After about twenty minutes two youths began to argue about the television station that they were watching. They could not agree on what show to watch and began screaming at each other. One youth picked up a chair and hit the other over the head with it. The youth who was assaulted fell to the floor unconscious. He was rushed to the hospital with a serious brain injury.

The youth suffered permanent brain damage. His parents sued Howard C. and the program, alleging that supervision of residents was inadequate and that Howard C. in particular failed to carry out his supervisory responsibilities as the program's policies called for.

The social service field is filled with cases in which individual practitioners and their agencies have been sued because of alleged failure to supervise clients adequately. Ordinarily the plaintiff alleges that staff did not monitor clients' activities closely enough or that the staff-client ratio was inadequate for proper supervision. As cases cited in this chapter will show, these lawsuits often describe instances in which clients attempted suicide, assaulted one another or staff, or were injured when restrained by staff, actions that plaintiffs allege proper supervision could have prevented (chapter 3 also addresses issues related to supervision of suicidal clients).

In Iowa the parents of a resident of a hospital for people with mental retardation filed suit alleging that staff members should be held responsible for injuries to their son during an assault at the hospital. The man was bitten by his roommate at least fourteen times and suffered a broken jaw, broken foot, and various cuts and bruises. Some inflictions of injuries were not witnessed by staff or occurred under circumstances in which staff members could not protect the injured resident. The judge found that the staff should have separated the roommates four months earlier. A court awarded the plaintiffs $146,000 ("Resident at Hospital" 1989:4).

After a patient raped a fourteen-year-old girl, a suit brought on her behalf claimed that the Colorado hospital and a doctor failed to supervise the patient who attacked her. She had been admitted to a psychiatric facility after attempting suicide. The suit claimed that the girl was not adequately protected while at the facility, that a sixteen-year-old male patient sneaked into her room and assaulted her. Upon her admission the staff had been concerned that she might attempt suicide and placed her on a fifteen-minute watch schedule. On the night of the assault, however, staff was not watching the girl because, staff claimed, her condition had improved. Her attorney contended that she was in a facility in which she was supposed to feel safe and that she would never feel safe again. A jury awarded her damages of $24,218 ("Psychiatric Patient Raped" 1989:4).

A case against a Florida hospital raised similar issues; the plaintiff, a psychiatric patient, alleged that another patient raped her and that the hospital was negligent when that patient gained access to her room. The court awarded the plaintiff $35,000 ("Patient Raped" 1989:6).[1]

In contrast in the 1989 case of *Hothem v. Fallsview Psychiatric Hospital* the Ohio courts did not find the hospital negligent in an assault on one patient by another. One patient was admitted to the hospital for treatment of organic delusional syndrome. The second patient was admitted several days later with a diagnosis of paranoid schizophrenia. The second patient accused the first patient of communicating with the devil, threatened to kill her, and then assaulted her. The courts found, however, that the hospital did not have reason to anticipate the second patient's actions and was not negligent in its supervision of him ("Hospital Not Negligent" 1992:3). Similarly a Texas appeals court affirmed that a state school and its staff were not liable for injuries that a resident with mental retardation incurred when attacked by another school resident. The appeals court found sufficient evidence to support the jury's conclusion that the staff had followed the violent resident's treatment plan and that staff followed proper procedure when the violent resident's behavior was out of control (*Parker v. Miller* (1993) and "School and Staff Not Liable" 1994:3).

Many cases involve allegations that staff members failed to properly supervise clients in residential facilities who attempted suicide. A state of Washington case against a physician and a hospital involved a forty-year-old woman who was admitted to the hospital for psychiatric treatment and who was allowed to make telephone calls in an interview room with an unscreened window. This occurred one day after admission. The patient claimed that she had a panic reaction and attempted to escape from the hospital through the window. She suffered fractured vertebrae, neurogenic bowel and bladder dysfunction, and head and foot injuries. The patient claimed that being left alone in a room with an unscreened window constituted negligence on the part of the staff. The defendants argued that the woman showed no suicidal ideation and that the family had failed to provide a complete psychiatric history. The case was settled for $150,000 ("Patient Jumps" 1989:2).

The circumstances in another case against a hospital are also commonplace. In this Texas case parents took their daughter to the hospital after she told them that she was going to commit suicide. The parents told hospital staff that their daughter had tried to commit suicide previously by hanging herself while a patient at another hospital. Shortly after her parents left, the daughter walked out of her room, left the building, climbed to the top of a nearby parking garage, and jumped to her death. The plaintiffs argued that hospital staff members should be adjudged negligent in failing to supervise or control a patient whom the staff had been told was suicidal. The case was settled for $290,000 ("Suicidal Patient" 1990:3). Other cases that present similar allegations of improper supervision and suicides committed by hospitalized patients include *McNamara v. Honeyman* (1989) and *Bramlette v. Charter-Medical-Columbia* (1990).[2]

Some cases also involve allegations that staff at a secure residential setting did not properly supervise clients who as a result escaped and then attempted suicide. In a case brought against the Commonwealth of Virginia and its mental health agency, the plaintiff, a woman diagnosed with schizophrenia, claimed that she was not supervised adequately after she was committed involuntarily to an inpatient mental health facility. The woman attempted to escape four times during the last three days of her two-week hospitalization. On the fourth attempt she walked onto a busy highway and into the path of an oncoming car. The plaintiff suffered compound fractures of both legs and permanent nerve injury. A jury awarded her $115,000 ("Mental Patient Escapes" 1990:3).

In some instances courts may find social service staff and agencies liable when clients injure themselves accidentally. A woman's family sued the hospital after the thirty-nine-year-old homemaker and mother died; the Minnesota suit claimed that she was not adequately supervised and monitored. The woman had been admitted to a locked psychiatric ward with a diagnosis of schizoaffective disorder. During lunch a nurse and an orderly supervised the woman and nine other patients. The woman stuffed large amounts of food in her mouth; the nurse offered to cut the woman's food, but the woman refused. The woman ate all the food on her plate. She subsequently choked on her food and died shortly thereafter. The jury awarded $613,695 to her family ("Psychiatric Patient Not Properly Monitored" 1990:4).[3]

STAFF SUPERVISION

Sue S., MSW, was the clinical director at North County Mental Health Services, Inc., a local community mental health center. Sue S. was responsible for supervising five clinical social workers on the center's staff. One of her supervisees was Scott M., MSW.

Scott M.'s caseload was diverse, including people recently discharged from a nearby state psychiatric hospital and clients referred by the local school district. Scott M. was working with a ten-year-old boy who had been referred by the local grade school. The boy had been having a number of problems in school, including several instances of fire setting and self-mutilation. Scott M. had been working with the boy for about three months. Scott M. also had extensive contact with the boy's family. Scott M. and Sue S. spent considerable time during supervision discussing this clinically complex case.

One afternoon the principal of the boy's school, who had initially referred the case to the mental health center, called Scott M. and asked him how the boy and his family were doing. The principal asked whether Scott M. could summarize the boy's progress and forward it to her. The next week Scott M. prepared a case summary, which included details of the boy's allegation that his father had sexually abused him.

During a subsequent conversation with the school principal, the father learned that Scott M. had disclosed this information to the school without his consent. The father sued Scott M. and his supervisor, Sue S., alleging that they had breached his right to privacy with respect to sharing the information with the school. The father specifically alleged that Sue S. had failed to properly perform her supervisory duties in that she did not ensure that his consent had been obtained before disseminating Scott M.'s report to the school principal.

Large numbers of social workers supervise staff. A clinical director in a family service agency may supervise caseworkers and counselors. A unit supervisor in a residential treatment facility may supervise mental health or child-care workers. An assistant director of a public welfare agency may supervise administrative staff. In each setting supervisors must carry out a variety of tasks, which may include monitoring workers' activities, providing feedback about workers' performance, conducting personnel evaluations, and teaching.

Social work supervision has historical roots in the nineteenth-century Charity Organization Society, when a master exercised control over the tasks and activities of an apprentice. The staffs of the Charity Organization Society's agencies provided what was essentially oversight for the large numbers of people (then called visitors) who aided people in need.

However, most references to supervision in the social work literature have appeared since 1920. Between 1920 and 1945 *Family and Social Casework* published roughly thirty-five articles devoted to supervision (Kadushin 1976:14). The first half-century of social work also saw several germinal publications on the subject, including Virginia Robinson's *Supervision in Social Case Work* (1936) and *The Dynamics of Supervision Under Functional Controls* (1949), Bertha Reynolds's *Learning and Teaching in the Practice of Social Work* (1942), and Charlotte Towle's discussion of supervision in *Common Human Needs* (1945) and in *The Learner in Education for the Professions* (1954). This solid intellectual foundation helped pave the way for a steady progression of scholarly discussions of supervision. As Miller suggests, "Supervision has remained

the principal method—with the individual conference as its keystone—
by which knowledge and skill are transmitted from the experienced to
the inexperienced, from the trained to the untrained, and in professional education, from the teacher and field instructor to the student"
(1987:749).

Over time a variety of norms, related primarily to the content and
implementation of supervision, have emerged in social work supervision
(Campbell 2006; Kadushin 1976, 1992; Miller 1987; Munson 2001; Shulman 2008; Tsui 2005; Wonnacott 2012). Although variation exists, the
literature provides considerable conceptual guidance related to the goals,
functions, tasks, and styles of supervision.

Social work's literature on supervision has focused almost exclusively
on pedagogical and technical aspects of supervision (Reamer 1989b;
Shulman 2008), particularly issues related to professional accountability
(Slavin 1982; Tsui 2005), role strain involved in shifting from practitioner
to supervisor (Patti 1983; Wonnacott 2012), administrative and managerial tasks of the supervisor (Kadushin 1976; Shulman 2008), leadership in
supervision (Campbell 2006; Austin 1981), the quasi-psychotherapeutic
function of supervision (Munson 1983, 2001; Shulman 2008; Tsui 2005),
and the relationship between organizational dynamics and supervision
(Miller 1987; Shulman 2008). The literature also has addressed broad ethical issues related to the match of supervisors and supervisees, contracting,
informing clients of supervisors' involvement, evaluation of supervisees,
and providing feedback to supervisees (B. Cohen 1987; Levy 1973; Shulman
2008; Tsui 2005).

Although literature on supervision has matured considerably over the
years, relatively little addresses malpractice and liability risks associated
with supervision (Reamer 1993b; Shulman 2008). In fact some risks are
unique. Many supervisors, I have found, do not fully understand the ways
in which they may be held responsible for the actions or inactions of the
staff that they supervise.

Although many malpractice claims allege mistreatment of a client by
a practitioner, a number of claims also implicate the practitioner's supervisor. Such claims typically cite the legal doctrine of *respondeat superior,*
which means "let the master respond." According to respondeat superior,
supervisors are responsible for the actions or inactions of their supervisees

that occur during the course of employment and over which the supervisor has some measure of control (R. Cohen 1979). As Gifis notes,

> This doctrine is invoked when there is a master-servant relationship between two parties. The "respondeat superior" doctrine stands for the proposition that when an employer, dubbed "master," is acting through the facility of an employee or agent, dubbed "servant," and tort liability is incurred during the course of this agency due to some fault of the agent, then the employer or master must accept the responsibility. Implicit in this is the common law notion that a duty rests upon every person to conduct his or her affairs so as not to injure another, whether or not in managing the affairs he or she employs agents or servants.
>
> (1991:416–17)

Although the doctrine of respondeat superior creates liability on the part of the supervisor for the actions or inactions of supervisees, the supervisee also may be held liable. Thus respondeat superior simply provides a client-plaintiff with an additional party to sue. If both supervisor and supervisee are negligent or responsible for the plaintiff's injuries, the finding may be one of joint liability. In these instances the court may divide responsibility for damages between the parties on a percentage basis. For example, if client sued a caseworker and supervisor because the caseworker released confidential information to a third party without the client's consent, and evidence shows that the supervisor had not addressed the issue of consent properly in supervision, the finding could be of joint liability with, say, the supervisor held 35 percent responsible and the caseworker 65 percent responsible. If the court awarded the plaintiff $120,000 in damages, the supervisor would be responsible for $42,000 and the caseworker for $78,000.

Of course, the agency's insurance company might cover both sets of damages and related legal expenses, although this is not always the case. In some instances the agency's insurer may want to distance itself from both the supervisor and the supervisee, or the insurer may want to defend only the supervisor by arguing that the supervisee was grossly negligent (having acted outside the scope of her employment duties) and therefore may argue that the supervisor is not responsible for the supervisee's actions. Given that supervisor and supervisee can become adversaries in such proceedings, *all* employees should carry their own individual malpractice and liability coverage. Relying only on an agency's group policy can be risky.

In principle supervisors can be found liable under the theory of vicarious liability, even if the supervisor adequately fulfilled his supervisory duties. Failing to provide proper supervision (for example, by not meeting with a supervisee regularly, addressing relevant issues, or delegating supervision to another party) may be a separate cause of legal action.

Areas of potential liability for social work supervisors are numerous, including failure to provide information necessary for supervisees to obtain clients' consent; to catch supervisees' errors in all phases of client contact, such as an inappropriate disclosure of confidential information; to protect third parties; to prevent defamation of character; to detect or stop a negligent treatment plan or treatment carried beyond its effectiveness; to determine that a specialist is needed for treatment of a particular client; to meet regularly with the supervisee; to review and approve the supervisee's decisions; and to provide adequate coverage in the supervisee's absence. In addition supervisors can be held liable if a supervisee is involved sexually with a client or exerts undue influence on the client or if the client's record is inadequate and the supervisor does not seek to improve it (Besharov 1985:166–67; Cohen and Mariano 1982; Edwards, Edwards, and Wells 2012; Hogan 1979; Woody 1997).

Social work supervisors must also avoid inappropriate dual relationships with supervisees. In one case on which I consulted, a residential treatment program was sued by a former client who claimed she was mistreated by agency staffers. The client also filed licensing board complaints against senior staffers. The complaints alleged that the program staffers disciplined the former client and terminated services unethically. During my consultation I discovered that the agency director and clinical director had developed an intimate relationship. The former client alleged that this dual relationship compromised the quality of the agency director's supervision of the clinical director. The dual relationship significantly weakened the defense attorney's ability to defend the case. In another case the Louisiana licensing board disciplined a social work supervisor who engaged in physical and sexual contact with a supervisee (Louisiana State Board 2013a).

SUPERVISION CASE LAW

One particularly complex liability claim on which I consulted raises various issues about a social worker's responsibility—and liability—in the actions of a counselor she had hired to work in her group private practice. Some years earlier the social worker and her colleague had started a private practice. A number of their cases involved children with eating disorders. The partners decided to hire a former nurse to provide assessments and evaluations of children. The woman was also enrolled in a masters-level degree program in counseling at a local state university.

The group practice became involved in a case in which one member of the practice saw the child and the former nurse saw the mother. In time the former nurse began providing counseling services to the mother, although this was before the former nurse had received her counseling degree and before she was licensed as a counselor. In her deposition the former nurse acknowledged that at this time she had a "therapist-patient" relationship with the mother.

The mother and her husband sued, alleging that the former nurse was negligent in that she failed to properly handle boundaries between herself and the mother and that the mother was seriously injured as a result. The suit alleged, for example, that the former nurse employed the mother in the former nurse's side business, which was completely unrelated to counseling. In addition the suit claimed that the former nurse and the client-mother had taken care of each other's children during their professional relationship and on one occasion had traveled out of state together.

The mother claimed in her lawsuit that the former nurse had mishandled the professional-client relationship and that this caused her great psychological damage, resulting in her hospitalization and lengthy psychiatric treatment. The husband claimed that his relationship with his wife was severely damaged as a result of the former nurse's actions.

Also named in the suit were the social worker who had started the practice and had hired the former nurse and the social worker's business partner. The claim alleged that the social worker was liable in several respects. First, the plaintiffs claimed that the social worker knew or should have known that the former nurse was providing counseling services without the requisite formal training or credentials, in the form of a graduate degree and license. Second, the plaintiffs alleged that under the doctrine of respondeat superior, or vicarious liability, the social worker's supervision of the case was not adequate. The plaintiffs argued that the social worker was aware that the client-mother was suicidal and in need of competent skilled care by a trained professional and that the social worker should have arranged for someone with considerably more expertise than the former nurse to care for the mother-client. A claim filed against the social worker's partner made similar allegations. According to the lawsuit,

> Defendant breached applicable psychological and counseling principles in the following nonexclusive particulars:
>
> (A) Violating boundary standards between therapist and patient;
>
> (B) Failing to utilize appropriate therapeutic and counseling skills.
>
> (C) Failing to properly diagnose and treat plaintiff;
>
> (D) Engaging in unethical duality violations;
>
> (E) Interfering with plaintiff's relationship with her husband, children and other friends;
>
> (F) Inducing, causing or allowing plaintiff to become exceedingly reliant and dependent upon defendant;
>
> (G) Encouraging, soliciting and inducing plaintiff to participate in defendant's independent . . . business while defendant was plaintiff's therapist;
>
> (H) Borrowing money from plaintiff to operate defendant's independent . . . business;
>
> (I) Causing, inducing and allowing an excessively social and personal relationship to develop and continue while still serving as plaintiff's therapist;
>
> (J) Otherwise breaching ethical and professional standards of conduct with regard to her relationship with plaintiff.
>
> As a result of the aforestated medical negligence of defendant, plaintiff has suffered severe psychiatric disorders including severe depression, panic, mental anguish, inconvenience, humiliation, disruption of marital relationship, suicidal tendencies, rage, helplessness and a severe deterioration of her mental and emotional well being. . . .
>
> Upon information and belief, plaintiff shows that [the social worker and her partner] were defendant's direct supervisors charged with responsibility for supervising, directing and overseeing the quality of counseling provided by defendant to plaintiff.

Upon information and belief, plaintiff shows that [the social worker and her partner] either knew or should have known of the aforestated medical negligence, conflict of interest and ethical breaches by defendant.

Plaintiffs further show that [the social worker and her partner] breached their independent duty to plaintiffs by failing to properly supervise, guide, direct and oversee the counseling and therapy provided by defendant to plaintiff and further in failing to respond appropriately to the multiple acts of medical negligence on the part of defendant set forth hereinabove.

Plaintiffs further show that [the group private practice, as a corporate entity], as the employer of defendant, is directly responsible to plaintiffs for all damages resulting from the aforestated medical negligence of defendant under the doctrine of *respondeat superior* or, alternatively, under the doctrine of actual or apparent authority.

The social worker's partner and the social worker settled the case out of court. The social worker was vulnerable because she knew that the former nurse had not completed her training to be a counselor and was not licensed. Moreover the suit alleged that although the social worker knew of the client's severe symptoms, including suicidal ideation, she did not become more closely involved in the client's treatment and made no referral.

Other cases also raise a variety of important issues related to supervisor liability. In some instances clients have sued the practitioner, the supervisor, and the employing agency. In some of these cases the court found only one defendant liable, although a judge or jury commonly establishes joint liability.

The court cases that I have described thus far have addressed three sets of circumstances. Their outcomes suggest that social work supervisors may be legally responsible for actions of supervisees who ordinarily are directly under their supervision, actions of supervisees who ordinarily are not under the social worker's direct supervision, and the delegation of responsibility by the social worker to a paraprofessional or unlicensed assistant.

For example, in *Rule v. Chessman* (1957) a surgeon who taught medical residents at a hospital was sued when a resident he had supervised and advised during surgery left a sponge in a patient's abdomen (R. Cohen 1979:181). The Kansas Supreme Court found the supervisor and supervisee jointly liable in the errors of the supervisee, who was under the direct supervision of the surgeon.

In *Cohen v. State* (1976) a widow sued after her husband committed suicide the same day that he was released from a voluntary inpatient stay in the psychiatric department of Downstate Medical Center in New York. Alan Cohen had been diagnosed as having paranoid schizophrenia and had been hospitalized for four months. The suit alleged that his medical care, particularly that related to the decision to release Cohen, was not properly supervised, despite the involvement of several physicians. At issue was "whether or not a qualified psychiatrist was actively supervising the care of the decedent" (Austin, Moline, and Williams 1990:232).[4]

In some instances the agency itself may be found vicariously liable. In a Michigan case, for example, a social worker entered into a sexual relationship with a client who was being treated for bipolar disorder and alcoholism. A court awarded damages of $123,500 against the social worker and the agency; the finding against the agency was based on the concept of respondeat superior ("Social Worker Engages in Sexual Relationship" 1999:2). In *Samuels v. Southern Baptist Hospital* (1992) a Louisiana court found that a hospital was liable after a nursing assistant sexually assaulted a sixteen-year-old psychiatric patient ("Hospital Liable for Employee's Sexual Assault" 1992:6). In Colorado a court found that a drug and alcohol rehabilitation center was partially liable after a female client became involved in a sexual relationship with the center's assistant director within a month after the client left the program.

The woman sued, alleging that the center and its executive director were aware that the assistant director had been involved in another similar relationship but did not reprimand him or take steps to prevent a recurrence. The award to the plaintiff included $42,175 from the center and its executive director on the negligent supervision claim ("Official of Alcohol Center" 1990:5).

An Alaska court made a similar finding in *Doe v. Samaritan Counseling Center* (1990). According to the plaintiff, a pastoral counselor at a counseling center made sexual advances toward her during two counseling sessions and had sexual contact with her after treatment ended. The Alaska Supreme Court ruled that under the doctrine of respondeat superior the agency may be held liable for the therapist's sexual contact with the client ("Employer May Be Held Liable" 1990:1).[5]

An important issue in many of these cases is whether the workers' actions fall within the scope of their employment. If they do, the employer and/

or supervisor may be found liable. In *Birkner v. Salt Lake County* (1989), for example, the Utah Supreme Court ruled that a mental health facility could *not* be held liable in an employee's sexual misconduct with a client. The plaintiff claimed that a social worker had a sexual relationship with her during treatment. The trial court found that the social worker was negligent. However, the state Supreme Court reversed the trial court's ruling on the issue of respondeat superior and vicarious liability, concluding that the social worker's actions did not fall within the scope of his employment. The appellate court noted that neither the plaintiff nor the social worker viewed their sexual contact as part of the therapeutic relationship, that these actions are not the type of activities that a therapist is hired to perform, and that the actions did not further the employer's interests ("Employer Not Vicariously Liable" 1989:1).[6]

A practitioner who temporarily depends to some extent on assistance by another agency employee or colleague can also incur liability, even if the assistant is not ordinarily under the direct supervision of the practitioner. In *Minogue v. Rutland Hospital* (1956) a nurse who was assisting an obstetrician was considered a "borrowed servant" of the obstetrician. The Vermont obstetrician was found liable after the nurse pressed on the rib of a woman during childbirth, thereby causing a fracture (R. Cohen 1979:181). Courts made similar determinations in *Yorsten v. Pennell* (1959) and *Norton v. Argonaut Insurance Co.* (1962). In *Yorsten* a patient claimed a resident supervised by the surgeon had made an error. The resident had removed a nail from a worker's leg and prescribed penicillin. Earlier, however, a fourth-year medical student had taken the patient's history and noted that the patient was allergic to penicillin. The patient had a severe allergic reaction to the penicillin. A Pennsylvania court found that the surgeon was liable for damages (R. Cohen 1979:181).

In *Norton* a nurse injected in a patient medication that the physician had intended to be administered orally. The physician, however, did not note in the patient's chart that the medication was to be administered orally. As a result the patient received about five times the intended dosage and died. A Louisiana court found the physician liable in the nurse's actions (R. Cohen 1979:181).

These rulings have implications for social workers who provide treatment in an agency as outside consultants and who occasionally might rely on the assistance of an agency employee not ordinarily under their direct supervision. For example, a social work consultant who oversees a behavioral treatment program in an agency and uses agency employees to help implement the behavioral regimen would be in this category.[7]

However, in *Marvulli v. Elshire* (1973) a California court found that the supervisor, a physician, was not liable in the actions of an assistant, an anesthesiologist. The court reasoned that because the anesthesiologist had been selected in the normal course of events from among available, qualified, reputable, and competent anesthesiologists, the surgeon had no control over his performance. (The case against the anesthesiologist was settled out of court.) The ruling in *Marvulli* suggests that careful and diligent screening of assistants by social workers may prevent findings of liability. If a social worker takes on an assistant or supervisee without adequately checking that person's training, license status, and references, and the supervisee is incompetent, the supervisor may be liable under what is known as the tort of negligent entrustment (Schutz 1982:50).

A number of cases involving supervisory liability concern the delegation of responsibility or specific duties to paraprofessionals and unlicensed supervisees. A number of popular clinical social work interventions—for example, biofeedback, group treatment, and peer support—may involve the use of unlicensed assistants. As a psychiatrist commented after he had been involved in four malpractice suits alleging negligence on the part of supervisees,

> I never saw three of these plaintiffs, nor did I talk to the families. In the other case I saw the plaintiff patient only for 1/2 hour. My associates and partners were not negligent in these cases, but the plaintiff thought so.
>
> The point is that as a senior partner I was considered responsible for the actions of my associates, even though I had never seen the patients. This is an important point to be remembered by every senior physician.
>
> The senior officer in every organization is legally responsible for every act of his juniors, both omission and commission.
>
> (G. Robinson 1962:780)

Laws are vague about how much responsibility professionals can legally delegate to unlicensed assistants. Clearly, however, these laws do not permit mental health professionals to delegate all their responsibilities to an unlicensed person. In addition the assistant or supervisee must be competent to perform the delegated duties (R. Cohen 1979; Woody 1997).

Particular problems can arise when an unlicensed employee of a professional is functioning in a way that leads reasonable people to mistake the employee for a licensed professional. This practice is referred to as "lending out a license," and the professional may be held liable and subject to disciplinary action. Many states consider an assistant to a licensed professional to be legally an extension of the professional (R. Cohen 1979:237; Woody 1997).

Another major source of risk involves situations in which psychiatrists sign a form attesting to the supervision of a social worker, when such supervision never occurred—for example, in order to qualify for reimbursement from an insurance company. In a New Jersey case a psychiatrist signed a social worker's written statement that a client was not dangerous, although the psychiatrist had never interviewed the client. The client subsequently killed his wife and children (Schutz 1982:50). Of course, a supervisee could simply fail to share with the supervisor all the case-related details required for competent supervision. In principle, however, the supervisor may be at risk.

SUPERVISION OF VOLUNTEERS

Social workers in human service agencies that serve people who are in crisis, homeless, disabled, victims of domestic violence, or vulnerable in other ways often recruit, train, and supervise volunteers. Volunteers may provide emergency assistance, crisis intervention services, home-based care, and various other supportive services.

Social workers who supervise volunteers face two kinds of risks. First, volunteers may be injured on the job and sue their supervisor and other agency administrators. This could occur, for example, if a volunteer is attacked by an unstable client. Second, agency clients may allege that they were harmed by volunteers; clients who claim they were harmed by volunteers may allege that volunteers' supervisors failed to provide proper training and supervision.

Volunteers are vitally important to the mission of many human service agencies. However, many volunteers, while well meaning, have not received formal education or training related to social work and relevant ethical standards. Unlike social workers, a typical volunteer has not spent years studying standards and related nuances concerning the complexities of, for instance, client confidentiality and its exceptions, minor clients' right to privacy and to receive services without parental notification or consent, boundaries and dual relationships, and conflicts of interest. In principle volunteers may expose the agency to risk if they breach confidential information without proper authorization (perhaps to a police detective who appears at the agency and asks the volunteer whether a particular suspect has been there recently, or to the volunteer's family members who happen to know a particular client), befriend a client inappropriately (in person or online), or accept gifts or social invitations from clients in a way that constitutes a boundary violation.

Volunteers enjoy individual protection under the federal Volunteer Protection Act of 1997. Generally speaking, this act provides immunity from tort claims that might be filed against the volunteers of nonprofit organizations, where the claim alleges that the volunteer carelessly injured another party in the course of helping the agency. (A tort is a wrongful act or an infringement of a right, other than under contract, leading to legal liability.) It is important to emphasize that the act does not provide immunity to the nonprofit agency itself; agency supervisors and administrators can be sued under the doctrine of respondeat superior.

Before federal legislation was passed, under the law of most states a volunteer who negligently hurt someone would be personally liable. Now the Volunteer Protection Act preempts all such laws, and the volunteer is immune from suit, which may increase the likelihood that people will offer to volunteer for nonprofit agencies. The law applies only to uncompensated volunteers who help nonprofits.

The act provides qualified immunity and protects the volunteer only against claims of negligence and not against claims of gross negligence, willful or criminal misconduct, reckless misconduct, or conscious and flagrant indifference to the rights or safety of the individual harmed by the volunteer. Nonprofit agencies can purchase insurance to protect themselves in the event of a lawsuit alleging that a volunteer was negligent and to compensate parties harmed by volunteers. More specifically, the act states that

> no volunteer of a nonprofit organization or governmental entity shall be liable for harm caused by an act or omission of the volunteer on behalf of the organization or entity if—
>
> (1) the volunteer was acting within the scope of the volunteer's responsibilities in the nonprofit organization or governmental entity at the time of the act or omission;

(2) if appropriate or required, the volunteer was properly licensed, certified, or authorized by the appropriate authorities for the activities or practice in the State in which the harm occurred, where the activities were or practice was undertaken within the scope of the volunteer's responsibilities in the nonprofit organization or governmental entity;

(3) the harm was not caused by willful or criminal misconduct, gross negligence, reckless misconduct, or a conscious, flagrant indifference to the rights or safety of the individual harmed by the volunteer; and

(4) the harm was not caused by the volunteer operating a motor vehicle, vessel, aircraft, or other vehicle for which the State requires the operator or the owner of the vehicle, craft, or vessel to—

(A) possess an operator's license; or

(B) maintain insurance.

To protect clients and reduce risk, social workers and agency administrators should design and offer comprehensive training to volunteers regarding relevant standards of care and ethical guidelines pertaining specifically to the nonprofit agency's mission, clientele, and services. The training curriculum should ensure that volunteers have the knowledge and skills to carry out their duties and have mastered relevant ethical guidelines, especially related to client privacy and confidentiality, informed consent, boundaries and dual relationships, and conflicts of interest. Social workers and agency administrators should mandate and document volunteers' attendance.

LIABILITY AND SOCIAL WORK EDUCATION

Special liability concerns arise with respect to field supervision of social work interns. Traditionally social work faculty based at colleges and universities and the staffs of agencies in which students carry out their field placements share some responsibility for student supervision. However, little consensus exists about which parties have primary liability if a student causes some form of harm during the field placement. Although the doctrine of respondeat superior probably would apply in liability cases involving students, the extent to which the field supervisor and the college or university would be regarded as supervisors is not clear (Reamer 2012b).

In a Pennsylvania case surviving relatives of a man who committed suicide sued a mental health center. The client had admitted himself voluntarily to a psychiatric unit after he swallowed a large number of drugs from the family's medicine cabinet. The client was discharged to an outpatient clinic and was treated by a social work student who allegedly did not review the client's psychiatric history or arrange for any treatment by a psychiatrist. The client killed himself in his own home. The lawsuit alleged that a psychiatrist rather than a relatively untrained social work student should have treated the client. A jury awarded the family $317,500 ("Negligent Care of Mental Patient" 2001:2).

In an effort to address a number of liability issues associated with student internships, Gelman and Wardell (1988) surveyed deans and directors of accredited social work education programs. The respondents confirmed the authors' suspicion that many issues related to supervisory liability are unresolved. Deans and directors cited a number of special liability concerns that they face. Some agencies, for example, require the student or university to purchase personal liability insurance before permitting a student to begin placement. Some students also are required to sign a waiver that holds the agency harmless against all claims brought by a client. Other agencies do not permit students to drive agency vehicles, insist that an agency staff member be present during all sessions with clients, and restrict students' access to agency files and records.

Social work educators and field education supervisors in social work education programs should be familiar with several standards in the NASW *Code of Ethics* (2008) that pertain to field instructors' relationships with students (earlier editions of the code did not address this issue). First, supervisors should be careful not to supervise outside their area of expertise and should provide instruction and supervision based on the most current information and knowledge available in the profession (standard 3.02[a]). Second, field instructors should evaluate students' performance in a manner that is fair and respectful, avoiding capricious grades (standard 3.02[b]), and should take reasonable steps to ensure that clients are routinely informed when services are being provided by students (standard 3.02[c]). Finally, "social workers who function as educators or field instructors for students should not engage in any dual or multiple relationships with students in which there is a risk of exploitation or potential harm to the student. Social work educators and field instructors are responsible for setting clear, appropriate, and culturally sensitive boundaries" (standard 3.02[d]).

PREVENTING SUPERVISORY LIABILITY

Case law on supervisory liability suggests that social workers can take various preventative measures. In particular a good working relationship between the supervisor and supervisee is essential. If they collaborate closely and constructively, they can avoid many problems. As Cohen and DeBetz observe,

> Under ordinary circumstances, supervisory success stands or falls on the quality of the relationship between the participants. The most carefully prepared didactic presentation of material will fall on deaf ears if the learner is alienated from the teacher. Conversely, the least hint of theory or casual reference to the literature may suffice to motivate the inspired trainee to independently research and creatively expand on his teacher's ideas. Therefore the *responsive mutuality,* the sensitivity and respect shared by the supervisor and the supervised, is perhaps the most potent tool in the supervisory repertoire.
>
> (1977:55)

Social work supervisors must give special attention to the frequency and scheduling of supervision. As R. Cohen (1979) notes, although no available case law suggests specific guidelines or an explicit standard of care, it seems reasonable to assume that setting up a pro forma supervision session once a week or once a month, without sufficient structure or rigor, risks legal liability. In fact Cohen and Mariano (1982:315) argue that norms in the mental health professions are inadequate, especially with respect to supervision of psychotherapists in training:

> It would seem to the present authors that this standard [pro forma supervision provided once a week or once a month] upon which the profession has expressed approval by its silence, is too low. If some harm or injury befalls the patient of the student psychotherapist because the supervisor improperly failed to take into account the specific and unique needs of the patient and the supervisee, then it would seem that the doctrine of *respondeat superior* would be applicable.
>
> (1982:315)

Supervisors should not assume that such routinely scheduled sessions comprise adequate supervision in all cases, although such supervision may suffice for nearly all supervisees. Rather supervisors must anticipate the possibility of cases with extenuating circumstances that may require more frequent and lengthier supervision than is customary. In short, provisions need to be made for extraordinary supervision. Supervisees should be monitored closely, and if a referral to another professional or agency is necessary, the referring social worker should ensure that the person or agency is licensed properly and able to respond effectively to the client's needs (see chapter 6 for further discussion of liability issues related to consultation and referral). Social workers who are part of a treatment team—for example, in a residential treatment center—also should pay close attention to the actions of their colleagues because they could be held liable in the negligence of another team member.

Special mention should be made of social workers in solo private practice because they face a special challenge with respect to supervision. Solo private practitioners do not always have easy access to regular, sustained supervision. Some solo private practitioners contract for supervision with a respected colleague or mentor and/or participate in peer supervision or peer consultation groups. Once again, although neither case law nor statute spells out the standard of care with regard to these forms of supervision and consultation, established norms demand some form of supervision or consultation, whether it is peer or otherwise, for solo practitioners. A private practitioner who is sued for negligence and found to be completely without any form of supervision or consultation may be vulnerable. The form of supervision also is important. If a supervisor relies only on brief cursory conversations with a supervisee, the supervisor may be at risk in failing to obtain detailed information from a supervisee. Relying on sparse case summaries or case record material, for example, may not be sufficient, even if this is supplemented by a brief verbal report. As Kadushin (1976) notes in his classic discussion of supervision issues,

> The traditional, and current, heavy dependence on record material and verbal reports for information regarding workers' performance necessitates some evaluation of these sources. Studies by social workers (Armstrong, Huffman, and Spain 1959; Wilkie 1963) as well as other professionals (Covner 1943; Froehlich 1958; Muslin et al. 1967) indicate that case records present a selective and often distorted view of worker performance. Comparison of process recordings with tape recordings of

the same contacts indicated that workers failed to hear and remember significant, recurrent patterns of interaction. Workers do not perceive and
report important failings in their approach to the client. This omission
is not necessarily intentional falsification of the record in order to make
the worker look good, although that does happen. It is, rather, the result
of selective perception in the service of the ego's attempt to maintain
self-esteem. Forty years ago Elon Moore (1934) wrote an article entitled
"How Accurate Are Case Records?" The question, which he answered
negatively, is still pertinent today. Supervision based on the written record
supplemented by the verbal report is supervision based on "retrospective
reconstructions which are subject to serious distortions" on the part of the
supervisee (Ward 1962, p. 1128).

(414)

Consequently Kadushin (1976) and others (Shulman 2008) urge
supervising social workers to supplement case records with direct observation, videotapes, and perhaps supervision during an interview by using a
one-way mirror and transmitter (being sure, of course, to obtain clients'
consent). Although each method has its limitations, it is feasible in many
circumstances. As Kadushin suggests, "Valid evaluation requires that we
know what the worker actually did, not what he thinks he did or what he
says he did" (1976:415).

Of course, one function of supervision is to provide the supervisor
with information on which to base personnel or performance evaluations. The process of personnel or performance evaluation also raises
several risk management and liability issues. Staff members who receive
negative evaluations—and who are disciplined, demoted, released, or
simply not promoted as a result—may sue the supervisor and agency,
challenging the employment action, alleging defamation of character,
and so on. This is another reason for the supervisor to carefully document the nature of all supervision provided and the information upon
which the supervisor based the personnel evaluation. As the NASW
Code of Ethics says, "Social workers who provide supervision should
evaluate supervisees' performance in a manner that is fair and respectful"
(standard 3.01[d]).

In addition supervisors must understand the extent of supervisees'
right of access to their personnel records. Most social work settings now

recognize staff members' right to review the contents of their personnel files, although this was not always the case. As Wilson observes,

> Employee access to personnel records has become the standard in personnel practice. In addition, the Federal Privacy Act's definition of an "individual" and of a "record" makes it quite clear that employees in federal programs have the same right of access to their files as do consumers of services. This includes the right to have copies made and submit corrections and additions to the record. Other governmental programs have adopted a similar policy, as have most educational systems and many private businesses.
>
> (1978:183)

What this means is that supervisors should be careful about the content, wording, and language used in performance evaluations (indeed supervisors should be careful even if for some reason staff members do *not* have access to their evaluations). Presumably all employees are concerned about how their work is evaluated, and they often view performance evaluations with hypersensitivity. Supervisors must be careful to avoid language and terminology that are defamatory, derisive, or otherwise inappropriate.

Although exhortations about preventative measures related to supervision of staff are appropriate, given the increasing likelihood of liability suits against social work supervisors, it is important to recognize that many social workers already are so overwhelmed with responsibility that adding the additional burden of closer and more frequent supervision may be difficult. This goes for the supervisor as well as the supervisee. Therefore agency administrators must acknowledge the importance of enhanced supervision and provide the necessary resources and staff assistance to make it feasible.

Social work agencies should also conduct training sessions with line staff. These sessions should include a discussion and review of issues related to professional ethics and liability, along with a review of relevant federal, state, and local statutes. In particular training should cover the concepts of professional liability and malpractice, licensing board standards, clients' right to confidentiality and the prevention of inappropriate disclosure, the limits of clients' right to confidentiality, the concept of privileged communication, improper treatment, high-risk interventions, the impaired practitioner, defamation of character, consultation with and referral to specialists, documentation, and fraud and deception. Training also should cover such topics as emergency assistance and suicide prevention, proper supervision of clients in residential and nonresidential settings, informed-consent procedures, guidelines for terminating intervention, boundaries and dual relationships, interaction with clients who are acting out, and practitioners' use of digital and online technology. Agency administrators and supervisors need to be able to document that they provided staff with this training if someone files suit alleging negligence on the part of the agency as a result of the actions of a staff member.

Clinical supervisors should consider developing a written understanding that clarifies the nature of supervision and the relationship between the supervisor and supervisee. According to the NASW (1994), Reamer (2013a), and Shulman (2008), key elements include:

- Supervisory context: where supervision will be conducted, by whom, with what frequency, using what methods, for what duration
- Learning plan: goals and objectives of supervision
- Format and schedule: type of supervision (for example, face-to-face supervision, telephone or Internet supervision; video recording, audio recording, or written records; individual or group supervision) and length, frequency, and duration of supervision
- Accountability: requirements related to the use of supervision for personnel evaluation, licensure, third-party payment
- Documentation and recording: format for documentation by the supervisor (e.g., date of contact, progress toward learning goals, specific recommendations) and supervisee (e.g., date of contact, questions and issues brought to supervisor's attention, supervisor's recommendations, follow-up plans); clarification of details to be documented in clients' record (e.g., the client's knowledge that supervision is taking place, the nature of information shared with supervisor, verification that the client has the name, address, and telephone number of the supervisor or other responsible contact person)
- Conflict resolution: procedures for resolving disagreements about issues addressed in supervision
- Compensation: details concerning the ways in which the supervisor will be compensated for her services

- Client notification: plans for notifying clients about the nature and purposes of supervision obtained by the clients' clinician
- Duration and termination: details concerning the time frame for the supervision agreement and the process for termination of supervision

In summary, social workers should be aware of a number of specific liability and licensing board risks related to supervision (see Austin, Moline, and Williams 1990:235; Campbell 2006; NASW 1994; Shulman 2008; Schutz 1982:48–49; Tsui 2005; Wonnacott 2012; Wilson 1978):

- Failure to provide information necessary for the workers to obtain an informed consent or to provide an adequate disclosure to a client
- Failure to catch an error
- Negligent or incorrect misdiagnosis that a client poses a danger to others or himself or has a serious mental illness
- A treatment plan that is negligent or treatment carried out beyond its effectiveness, and the supervisor is responsible for the error or does not detect it
- Failure to determine that a new worker needs to be assigned, treatment terminated, or specialists consulted
- Workers who are involved socially or sexually with clients or exert undue influence on the client
- A client's record that does not contain adequate information about the care that the client has received, and the supervisor does not review the record and require its improvement
- Supervision that is negligent because the supervisor does not meet regularly with the supervisee, review the presented material, or elicit the information necessary to adequately supervise the case
- Workers who are negligent in caring for clients—for example, who did not adequately supervise a suicidal client, who released a dangerous client prematurely, or who failed to provide coverage when unavailable—and supervisors who failed to review and approve these decisions
- Failure to assess the competence of supervisees as to what clienteles and types of cases they can handle
- Supervision of so many supervisees that competent supervision is impossible
- Failure to summarize, record, or otherwise document what occurs in supervision

- Involvement in a dual relationship with a supervisee (see NASW *Code of Ethics* standards 3.01[b][c])
- Failure to give detailed written and verbal evaluations to supervisees
- Failure to review supervisees' records for accuracy and completeness
- Signing of insurance or other forms for cases that supervisors have not supervised
- Failure to provide consistent, regularly scheduled supervision to supervisees
- Use of defamatory or otherwise inappropriate language in performance evaluations of supervisees

Clearly supervision is essential to effective social work practice. Since the earliest days of social work, professionals have recognized that competent supervision is necessary in order to transmit the profession's values and methods and to monitor the performance of supervisees. No competent professional questions the appropriateness of at least some form of supervision.

Understandably social work literature has focused primarily on the technical aspects of social work supervision or what some consider the art of supervision (Campbell 2006; Kadushin 1992; Miller 1987; Munson 2001; Shulman 2008; Tsui 2005; Wonnacott 2012). Modern circumstances, however, require social workers to broaden their perspective and learn about a range of legal and liability risks related to supervision.

Risks related to social work supervision continue to emerge. Although some risks are patently clear—namely those related to the inappropriate delegation of professional responsibility to untrained staff and the failure to provide regular supervisory sessions to supervisees—other risks, such as the assumption of liability by fieldwork agencies and colleges and universities, still need to be clarified. Therefore social workers must enhance their understanding of liability issues and seek clarification of ambiguous circumstances that arise in supervision. In the end the best interests of clients depend on the success of these efforts.

6

Consultation, Referral, Documentation, and Records

SOCIAL WORKERS OFTEN CONSULT WITH colleagues about their work with clients. Colleagues can provide valuable insights and suggestions, especially with respect to complex and challenging clinical and ethical circumstances.

Social workers should understand the differences between supervision and consultation. Supervision typically entails a chain of command, such that the supervisor has some responsibility over the supervisee and the supervisee is accountable to the supervisor. Supervisees are often expected to accept a supervisor's advice, although consultees are not necessarily expected to accept a consultant's advice. Consultation is often much more collegial in nature. According to the NASW (1994), consultation and supervision are differentiated in four ways:

- Consultation involves a relationship voluntarily entered into by both parties wherein the consultant offers her best advice, which the consultee can either accept or reject.
- Although adherence to ethical standards characterizes the consultation relationship, no legal statutes regulate the relationship.
- The authority of the consultant is his expertise; legal responsibility for the clinical (or other) service remains with the consultee.
- Because of the limitations in authority and the voluntary nature of the consultation relationship, consultation does not meet the requirements of many credentialing bodies or insurance companies.

Peer consultation is only one form of consultation in social work. As seasoned practitioners know well, social workers have many other occasions when they need to obtain consultation from colleagues—both social workers and other professionals—who have special expertise that may be required in work with individuals, families, groups, communities, or organizations. This is particularly true when a social worker lacks specialized training and knowledge related to a particular phenomenon, such as substance abuse, eating disorders, or domestic violence.

Clearly social workers are wrong to attempt to provide forms of treatment and intervention outside their range of skill. Although social workers typically receive broad-based education and are rather versatile, for a practitioner to claim specialized skill in an area for which she has little knowledge and training would be unethical. As the NASW *Code of Ethics* states, "Social workers should seek the advice and counsel of colleagues whenever such consultation is in the best interests of clients" (standard 2.05[a]). If a client presents a particular problem that is beyond the social worker's skill range, he should seek consultation or make a referral. Failure to do so risks liability. In some instances it is appropriate for the social worker to continue working with the client, with consultation necessary for only some specific aspect of the case. In other instances, however, it may not be appropriate for the social worker to continue handling the case at all; instead the social worker should refer the client to another practitioner who has the specialized education and knowledge required for competent intervention.

CONSULTATION IN SOCIAL WORK

The nature of consultation in social work has changed over time (Harkness 2008; Kadushin 1977; Rieman 1992; Sears, Rudisill, and Mason-Sears 2006; Shulman 1987, 2008). Consultation was not formally recognized as an important component in social work practice until after World War II. Not until recent years, however, has the profession had substantial literature on consultation. For example, only two entries on consultation appeared in the *Social Service Review* between 1927 and 1966, and the concept was not indexed in the *Social Work Yearbook* until the fifteenth edition (the *Encyclopedia of Social Work*), published in 1965 (Kadushin 1977).

The earliest forms of consultation in social work, particularly in the 1950s, involved social workers as consultees, often to psychiatrists, who typically provided case consultation and education about psychiatric phenomena. Common practice was, and still is, for family service agencies to have a "psychiatric consultant" to consult in individual cases. In 1955 and 1957 the annual meetings of the American Orthopsychiatric Association hosted special workshops on psychiatric consultation to social service agencies (Kadushin 1977).

More recently social workers have broadened their use of consultation to include a wide range of professionals (Harkness 2008; Sears, Rudisill, and Mason-Sears 2006; Shulman 2008). Practitioners in protective service agencies may consult lawyers to interpret case law related to the removal of children from a home. Social workers in a battered women's shelter may consult a specialist in the area of eating disorders. Social workers who use digital and other electronic technology to serve clients may consult colleagues with specialized expertise to ensure compliance with clinical and ethical standards. Social workers in private practice may consult other social workers who have particular expertise in posttraumatic stress disorder. Social work administrators may seek consultation in relation to program evaluation or needs assessments.

Kadushin provides a useful definition of *consultation:*

Consultation is regarded as an interactional helping process—a series of sequential steps taken to achieve some objective through an interpersonal relationship. One participant in the transaction has greater expertise, greater knowledge, greater skill in the performance of some particular specialized function, and this person is designated *consultant.* The *consultee,* generally a professional, has encountered a problem in relation to his job which requires the knowledge, skill, and expertise of the consultant for its solution or amelioration. Consultation is thus distinguished from other interpersonal interactional processes involving the giving and taking of help, such as casework, counseling, psychotherapy, by virtue of the fact that its problem-solving focus is related to some difficulties encountered in performing job-related functions and by virtue of the fact that the identity of the consultee is generally restricted to someone engaged in implementing professional roles.

(1977:25–26)

Consultation in social work can produce two major liability risks. The first involves situations in which a social worker should seek consultation but fails to and a client is harmed as a result. The argument in such cases is that the social worker breached the standard of care by failing to seek appropriate consultation, an act of omission or nonfeasance.

Maryann B., MSW, was a caseworker at the Woodholme Family Service Agency. She specialized in couples and marriage counseling.

Maryann B. began working with a young married couple who were having some difficulty managing the behavior of their four-year-old son. Maryann B. spent considerable time helping the couple to use simple behavioral techniques, such as positive reinforcement and extinction, to manage their son's behavior. In addition Maryann B. helped the couple explore several sources of tension and conflict in their marriage.

After several months in treatment the husband in the couple disclosed that about eight years earlier he had been diagnosed as having multiple personality disorder. He told Maryann B. that he feared that some of his symptoms were reappearing.

Maryann B. continued working with the couple, although she did not seek consultation related to dissociative disorders. She believed that she had sufficient knowledge and skill to be able to work with her client, although he began complaining more and more about what he believed to be symptoms of the disorder.

About ten weeks after his first complaints about the multiple personality disorder symptoms, the husband stabbed his wife. The couple had gotten into a heated argument about disciplining their son. According to the wife, during the stabbing the husband spoke in a foreign accent and claimed that his name was different from the one he ordinarily used.

The wife sued the social worker, claiming that she failed to seek appropriate consultation related to the treatment of multiple personality disorders and dissociative disorders. The suit claimed that had the social worker sought proper consultation, the husband would not have assaulted his wife.

Case law illustrates the liability risks when a professional does not refer a client to a specialist for consultation. A Texas man claimed that his wife's death was the result of a lack of referral for consultation. The woman's regular physician was treating the twenty-four-year-old for depression. The physician prescribed medication for several months without referring her to a psychiatrist or psychologist for consultation and the possibility of treatment.

After the depressive symptoms worsened, the physician referred the woman to a psychiatrist and psychologist in the same clinic. The woman committed suicide after two visits to the clinic psychiatrist. The woman's husband alleged that the physician who did not refer his wife to a psychiatrist for timely consultation was negligent. The court awarded the woman's family $460,000 ("Physician Fails" 1992:2).[1]

Social workers can also incur liability risks when they fail to consult an organization for advice. This may occur when, for instance, a social worker does not consult with, or report to, the local public child protection agency in a case in which child abuse is suspected. As I noted in chapter 3, social workers and other mandated reporters do not report suspected abuse and neglect in a distressingly large percentage of cases. Often the mandated reporters are confident that they can handle the situation without the public agency's involvement, do not have confidence in the protection agency staff, and/or do not want to jeopardize their therapeutic relationship with their clients. The legal risk, however, is that the mandated reporter could be held liable in failing to consult with a specialist—the protection agency—(in addition to being subjected to whatever statutory criminal or civil penalties may exist), along with otherwise failing to adhere to standards of care regarding mandated reporting.

Social workers should select their consultants carefully to ensure that the experts have the requisite education, training, license, knowledge, and expertise to be truly helpful. This is a form of due diligence. Social workers should not rely on consultants who do not have the credentials and demonstrated expertise pertaining to the issue at hand. According to the NASW *Code of Ethics,* "Social workers should keep themselves informed about colleagues' areas of expertise and competencies. Social workers should seek consultation only from colleagues who have demonstrated knowledge, expertise, and competence related to the subject of the consultation" (standard 2.05[b]).

Social workers should especially seek consultation when their work with a particular client seems to be stalled or going nowhere. Clients who are frustrated with the progress, or lack of progress, that they are making in treatment may be particularly prone to sue. As Schutz notes,

> When therapy reaches a prolonged impasse, the therapist ought to consider consulting another therapist and possibly transferring the patient. Apart from

the clinical and ethical considerations, his failure to seek another opinion might have legal ramifications in the establishment of proximate cause in the event of a suit. While therapists are not guarantors of cure or improvement, extensive treatment without results could legally be considered to have injured the patient; in specific [*sic*], the injury would be the loss of money and time, and the preclusion of other treatments that might have been more successful. To justify a prolonged holding action at a plateau, the therapist would have to show that this was maintaining a condition against a significant and likely deterioration. Consultation at this point would establish the reasonableness of one's approach and help establish criteria for when to terminate one's efforts to treat a patient.

(1982:47)

Social workers need to be particularly alert to the need for medical consultation. Consider the case of a social worker who was working with a client who claimed to have chronic low self-esteem. For months the social worker and client focused on family-of-origin issues and issues related to the client's intimate relationships as an adult. On occasion the client would also complain that she was having a hard time remembering things, such as friends' and colleagues' names, appointments she had made, and so on. Periodically the client would complain of incapacitating headaches.

Several months after the client began complaining of headaches, she blacked out while shopping at a local mall. The client was rushed to the hospital, where she was diagnosed with a brain tumor. Surgery removed the tumor, but the client suffered some moderate brain damage.

Shortly after surgery one of the client's doctors told her that had she been seen by a physician one or two months earlier, there was a good chance they could have treated the tumor without surgery. Once the client completely recovered from her surgery, she was angry that the social worker had not referred her to a physician for a medical exam. The client shared her frustration with her sister, who suggested the client talk to an attorney about a negligence suit.

Social workers cannot be expected to be knowledgeable about organic and other medical problems that clients may have. They are, however, obligated to be alert to the need for medical consultation. As Meyer, Landis, and Hays observe in their discussion of liability risks faced by psychologists, "The standard has generally been that others in the same discipline

would seek the help of a specialist in the same circumstances" (1988:50–51).
In addition these authors state,

> Failure to refer is a type of negligence if it leads to some injury to the client.
> For example, a client consulting a psychologist who describes a recent blow
> to the head followed by recurrent headaches, personality changes, and dif-
> ficulty with memory and concentration, may have sustained a neurologic
> injury. Alternatively he may be displaying a conversion syndrome. The psy-
> chologist would be expected to ascertain whether a neurologist or other
> physician was involved in the case, and either consult with that person or
> make an appropriate referral to help in the diagnostic process. If the psy-
> chologist proceeded on the assumption that no organic damage was pres-
> ent, he could be held liable for negligently failing to refer the patient to a
> practitioner capable of treating his problem.
>
> (50)

The second liability problem related to consultation has to do with the
consultation itself. In these cases typically the claim is that the consultation
that a social worker *provided* was somehow flawed or negligent and that
the consultation, or advice stemming from it, caused some injury. This may
occur, for example, if consultants provide training, advice, or guidance on a
topic outside their area of expertise.

Barbara C., MSW, was a social worker in private practice. Her practice
was devoted primarily to the treatment of eating disorders.

One afternoon Barbara C. received a telephone call from a social worker
employed at a small local private school. The social worker told Barbara C.
that a student, a fourteen-year-old girl, seemed to have an eating disorder.
The student had been losing weight, not eating at lunch time, exercising
excessively, and had been found in the lavatory inducing her own vomiting.

The school social worker, who did not have much experience treating
eating disorders, asked Barbara C. to consult on the case. Barbara C. agreed
and met with the social worker and two of the student's teachers. For the
next two months the school social worker and Barbara C. met weekly to
discuss the case and to review the school social worker's intervention.

Over time it became clear that the student was also mutilating herself.
She was sticking needles in her arm and cutting her wrists. The social work
consultant advised the school social worker to ignore the self-mutilation so

as not to reinforce it. The mutilation, however, got worse and worse. About three weeks after the mutilation became apparent, the student slashed her wrists and committed suicide.

The student's parents sued the school, the school's social worker, and the social work consultant, claiming that they failed to provide proper treatment to their daughter. In particular the plaintiffs argued that the social work consultant provided advice outside her area of expertise. Although the plaintiffs acknowledged that the social work consultant had considerable expertise related to eating disorders, an area in which the social work consultant had received extensive training, they challenged her ability to give advice related to self-mutilation, an area in which the social work consultant had received no formal training.

When social workers seek consultation they should be sure to protect clients' confidential information. Social workers should not assume that consultants should have access to client-related confidential information. Ideally social workers should obtain clients' informed consent before disclosing confidential information to consultants. In addition social workers should limit their disclosure of confidential information as much as possible. As the NASW *Code of Ethics* states, "When consulting with colleagues about clients, social workers should disclose the least amount of information necessary to achieve the purposes of the consultation" (standard 2.05[c]).

Not all liability risks related to consultation involve case consultation. Social workers can also encounter problems when they provide consultation to agencies and programs. For example, social workers who have little skill related to program evaluations should not present themselves as experts. A program that relies on the social worker's claim of skill in this area may be injured if the social worker conducts a poorly designed study or evaluation, which may ultimately hurt the program's chances for funding. Clearly social workers should provide consultation only with respect to those subjects and skill areas for which they can demonstrate competence and expertise.

REFERRAL IN SOCIAL WORK

In some cases social workers find that they do not have sufficient expertise to continue working with a particular client. While it makes sense in some instances for a social worker to continue working with a client while seeking consultation on a particular aspect of the client's treatment (for example, a social worker who is trained to intervene in a client's depression but needs consultation regarding the client's eating disorder), in other instances social workers may need to consider referring the entire case to a professional colleague. According to the NASW *Code of Ethics*, "Social workers should refer clients to other professionals when the other professionals' specialized knowledge or expertise is needed to serve clients fully or when social workers believe that they are not being effective or making reasonable progress with clients and that additional service is required" (standard 2.06[a]).

In such cases social workers have an obligation to exercise due care in the process that they use to refer clients to colleagues. Social workers should not make referrals to others indiscriminately or where there is a conflict of interest (for example, when social workers refer clients to close friends or relatives for reasons other than the friends' or relatives' expertise). Instead social workers should be diligent in their efforts to refer clients to colleagues with solid reputations, who have proper credentials, and in whom they have confidence. Otherwise a social worker may risk a claim of negligent referral, that is, a referral that was not made using standard procedures. An article about a mental health professional in the *Providence (Rhode Island) Journal-Bulletin* illustrates this risk:

> A Providence psychiatrist has been disciplined for referring a patient to an unqualified counselor.
>
> The state Board of Medical Licensure and Discipline last month imposed, but stayed, a three-month suspension on Dr. Lee H. Goldstein, an osteopathic physician [and psychiatrist] at 15 Benefit St. The board also fined him $1,500.
>
> Dr. Milton W. Hamolsky, the board's administrator, said that a stayed suspension is like probation. The board, he said, believed that Goldstein's infraction was not serious enough to prohibit him from practicing, but it did warrant a more rigorous penalty than a reprimand.
>
> According to the disciplinary board, a patient saw Goldstein for weekly psychotherapy sessions for 15 months but terminated therapy and complained to the board when Goldstein referred her to an unlicensed counselor. The board considers it unprofessional conduct for a psychiatrist to refer a patient to someone who is not licensed or certified to provide mental health care.

Hamolsky said there was no evidence that Goldstein had a pattern of making inappropriate referrals.

("State Disciplines Psychiatrist" 1992:B3)

A Utah case dealt with similar issues related to referral to an unqualified service provider. The defendant was a counselor who had worked with a woman and her sons (the plaintiffs). During the counseling the defendant referred the plaintiffs to a colleague for additional counseling. The colleague was described as the defendant's associate. The associate, however, did not have specialized training that would qualify him as a counselor. The plaintiffs claimed that the associate's counseling was incompetent, that it caused confusion, bewilderment, anger, and frustration, and that his services were worthless and counterproductive. The defendant settled the suit for an undisclosed sum ("Psychological Counselor Refers Patients" 1991:6).

In an Arizona case a husband and wife claimed that a psychologist was negligent in referring them to a master's-level therapist. The therapist began by seeing the couple together and then provided clinical services to them individually. The therapist eventually entered into a personal relationship with the wife. The couple sued, claiming that when the wife sought to end her relationship with the therapist, the therapist entered her home without permission while the husband was away and verbally assaulted her while she was in the shower. Although the referring psychologist denied liability, a confidential settlement was reached ("Therapist Begins Personal Relationship" 1994:4).[2]

R. Cohen also comments on the legal ramifications that can arise from a negligent referral: "If a referral is indicated, the professional has a duty to select an appropriate professional or institution for the patient. Barring any extraordinary circumstances, the professional making the referral will not incur any liability for the acts of the person or institution that he refers the patient to, provided that the person or institution is duly licensed and equipped to meet the patient's needs" (1979:239). In *Stovall v. Harms* (1974) a Kansas physician—a general practitioner—referred one of his patients to a psychiatrist. The patient was subsequently involved in an automobile accident and alleged that the accident was the result of medication prescribed by his psychiatrist. The plaintiff sued the general practitioner for the injuries sustained in the accident. The general practitioner was not found liable, however, because the plaintiff had not demonstrated that the doctor had been negligent in selecting the psychiatrist. The psychiatrist was qualified, and the general practitioner had no control over the care provided to the patient by the psychiatrist (R. Cohen 1979:184).

Social workers who refer clients to another professional should not expect to be compensated merely for the referral. This would constitute a conflict of interest. According to the NASW *Code of Ethics,* "Social workers are prohibited from giving or receiving payment for a referral when no professional service is provided by the referring social worker" (standard 2.06[c]).

Social workers can also be found liable for *failing* to refer clients to specialists when needed (an example of an act of omission, or nonfeasance). In a Florida case the plaintiffs alleged that a man's health-care provider was negligent in failing to refer him to a psychiatrist and recommend hospitalization—the man committed suicide ("Failure to Refer to Psychiatrist" 1995:6).

SOCIAL WORK DOCUMENTATION AND RECORDS

Social workers who consult with other professionals about a client or refer a client to another professional must provide careful documentation of the consultation/referral in the case record. I have been involved in a number of cases over the years in which social workers were conscientious about obtaining consultation and making referrals. Some social workers have encountered problems, however, because they failed to document the consultation and referrals in the case record. When clients alleged that these social workers neglected to obtain proper consultation or make an appropriate referral, the social workers were unable to produce evidence or sufficient documentation. Lawyers sometimes offer the axioms, "If it isn't recorded, it didn't happen," and "Work not written is work not done."

In fact in one case (*Whitree v. State of New York* (1968)) a court determined that an inadequate record was negligent in itself because such a record does not provide guidance for adequate care in the absence of the professional and contributes nothing useful to the client's treatment history, which could affect a client's subsequent care. Victor Whitree, forty-six, was arrested in New York City on a charge of stabbing another man. Whitree was placed on probation and subsequently ordered to Bellevue Hospital for a psychiatric examination. He was then placed in maximum security confinement for more than four years and kept in a locked cell except for exercise and visits to the bathroom. Whitree eventually sued the state for wrongful confinement and for injuries he sustained as a result of his hospitalization and as a result of various attacks and beatings by patients and guards.

In addition to commenting on the negligence that it determined was involved in Whitree's care, the court found that "the hospital record . . . maintained by the State for claimant was about as inadequate a record as [the judge had] ever examined" and that the "record did not conform to the standards in the community . . . the inadequacies in this record mili- tated against proper and competent psychiatric and ordinary medical care." Further, the lower court concluded, "To the extent that a hospital record develops information for subsequent treatment, it contributed to the inad- equate treatment this claimant received." Whitree was awarded $300,000 in damages for the negligence and false imprisonment (Austin, Moline, and Williams 1990:30).

A much larger issue of liability risks relates to documentation, record- ing, and note taking. Social workers who fail to document properly expose themselves to considerable risk. For example, the Texas licensing board recently disciplined several social workers for "failure to keep accurate records" (Texas Department of State Health Service 2013). The Arkan- sas board recently disciplined a social worker for "failing to keep proper records and documentation of services" (Arkansas Social Work Licensing Board 2013). The Louisiana licensing board disciplined a hospice social worker who documented services to clients that she never provided (Loui- siana State Board 2013b).

Recording is one of those skills that social workers learn early in their careers and is among the oldest social work skills, as illustrated by the 1920 publication of Sheffield's *The Social Case History: Its Construction and Con- tent*. In this landmark work Sheffield described the narrative record as "a body of personal information conserved with a view to the three ends of social case work; namely (1) the immediate purpose of furthering effective treatment of individual clients, (2) the ultimate purpose of general social betterment, and (3) the incidental purpose of establishing the caseworker herself in critical thinking" (Kagle 1987:463). Other critically important works include Hamilton's *Social Case Recording* (1936) and *Principles of Social Case Recording* (1946).

Typically undergraduate and graduate social work education programs include content on recording and documentation. Proficient documentation enhances the quality of services provided to clients. Records identify, describe, and assess clients' situations; define the purpose of service; document service goals, plans, activities, and progress; and evaluate the effect of service (Kagle and Kopels 2008; Wilson 1980). Recording also demonstrates the social worker's thoughtful attention to detail.

In addition recording enhances continuity of care. Carefully written notes help social workers recall relevant detail during intervention and can facilitate coordination of services and supervision among staff members within an agency. Recording also helps to ensure quality care if a client's primary social worker becomes unavailable because of sickness, vacation, or departure from the agency. According to the NASW *Code of Ethics,* "Social workers should include sufficient and timely documentation in records to facilitate the delivery of services and to ensure continuity of services provided to clients in the future" (standard 3.04[b]).

Of course, competent recording is not only good practice. Recording also provides some measure of protection against negligence claims and licensing board complaints. As Kagle states, "By keeping accurate, relevant, and timely records, social workers do more than just describe, explain, and support the services they provide. They also discharge their ethical and legal responsibility to be accountable. This accountability extends beyond the individual agency (and the organizations that fund and accredit it) to the profession as a whole, the community, and, ultimately, the client" (1987:463).

Discussions of social work documentation are no longer limited to clinicians who need to record their interactions with clients to facilitate the delivery of services. The profession has come to recognize the usefulness of documentation for risk management purposes in supervision, management, and administration. Documentation in social work—whether it concerns clinical, supervisory, management, or administrative duties— now serves several primary functions: (1) assessment and planning; (2) service delivery; (3) continuity and coordination of services; (4) supervision; (5) service evaluation; and (6) accountability to clients, insurers, agencies, other providers, courts, and utilization review bodies (Kagle and Kopels 2008; Luepker and Norton 2002; Reamer 2005; Sidell 2011).

Assessment and Planning

In clinical contexts clear and comprehensive documentation of all case-related facts and circumstances is essential. Careful and thoughtful information collection ensures that social workers have an adequate foundation for their clinical reasoning and intervention plans. In addition the data provide a reliable source of measuring performance and outcomes. Incomplete records may lead to inadequate planning and intervention, critical judgment errors, and poor outcomes for clients.

Service Delivery

Comprehensive records are necessary for competent delivery of clinical, community-based, and agency-based services and interventions. Thorough documentation provides a solid foundation for practitioners' efforts to design and deliver high-quality services, whether they involve clinical intervention, efforts to organize community residents to address neighborhood problems, supervision, or agency administrators' management and evaluation of personnel and programs.

Continuity and Coordination of Services

Similarly documentation facilitates professional and interdisciplinary collaboration and coordination of services. For example, social workers employed in hospital, school, and correctional settings often need to share their observations and coordinate services with professionals in other disciplines, such as doctors, nurses, counselors, teachers, and administrators. In clinical settings documentation ensures that staff members have up-to-date information about clients' needs. Administrative records facilitate coordination among supervisors, managers, and administrators in programs and agencies.

Supervision

Under the legal doctrines of vicarious liability and respondeat superior ("let the master respond"), supervisors, as well as administrators and agencies, can be held liable for the errors and omissions of their staff if there is evidence of flawed supervision (Madden 2003; Reamer 2004, 2005). Thus it behooves social work supervisors to carefully document the supervision they provide (NASW 1994). Further, supervisees should be certain to document supervision they have received.

Service Evaluation

In addition to facilitating clinical evaluation in individual cases (so-called single-case or N = 1 designs), records also provide essential data for broader program evaluations (Dudley 2009). Measured outcomes and program effectiveness are central to social work. At their core lie data and information recorded throughout the case management process. Social workers must strive to continually strengthen their documentation and record-keeping practices to maintain the integrity of their programs.

Accountability

Client requests, insurance contracts, interagency collaboration, litigation, licensing board and ethics committee oversight, and utilization review bodies periodically require social workers to include fine-grained details about the services they provide, the meetings they attend, the supervision they offer, and the consultation they obtain. These new demands clearly illustrate the importance of documentation for accountability purposes.

EVOLUTION OF SOCIAL WORK STANDARDS

When social work's pioneers began writing about case recording in the early twentieth century, they could not have imagined the remarkable expansion of documentation functions and requirements that would emerge during the next century. Today's social workers are held to vastly different ethical and legal standards that have serious implications for clinical and community practice, supervision, management, and administration.

Social work's earliest national ethics standards made no mention of documentation. Neither the first NASW ethics code, adopted in 1960, nor the revised code, adopted in 1979, included guidelines concerning documentation. The current code, however, includes the first explicit documentation standards (Reamer 2006). These ambitious additions to the code reflect increased cognizance during the mid-1990s of the ethical implications of competent documentation.

The primary focus of the earliest standards centered on social workers' ethical duty to document the services they provide, clients' right to view their records, and social workers' duty to protect clients' records from unauthorized access or use (Reamer 2006). The current code formally promulgates social workers' ethical duty to accurately document the services they provide and to protect private information contained in records, thus establishing national standards enforced by NASW ethics committees and by state licensing boards that choose to adopt NASW ethics guidelines. Specifically the measures state:

> (a) Social workers should take reasonable steps to ensure that documentation in records is accurate and reflects the services provided.
>
> (b) Social workers should include sufficient and timely documentation in records to facilitate the delivery of services and to ensure continuity of services provided to clients in the future.
>
> (c) Social workers' documentation should protect clients' privacy to the extent that is possible and appropriate and should include only information that is directly relevant to the delivery of services.
>
> (standard 3.04)

Two additional standards in the NASW *Code of Ethics* formally established clients' right to access their own records and social workers' duty to protect the confidentiality of other parties referred to in the record. Specifically:

> (a) Social workers should provide clients with reasonable access to records concerning the clients. Social workers who are concerned that clients' access to their records could cause serious misunderstanding or harm to the client should provide assistance in interpreting the records and consultation with the client regarding the records. Social workers should limit clients' access to their records, or portions of their records, only in exceptional circumstances when there is compelling evidence that such access would cause serious harm to the client. Both clients' requests and the rationale for withholding some or all of the record should be documented in clients' files.

(b) When providing clients with access to their records, social workers should take steps to protect the confidentiality of other individuals identified or discussed in such records.

(standard 1.08)

Finally, two more standards set forth practitioners' ethical duty to store records in a way that protects clients' confidentiality and makes the records available following the termination of services.

(1) Social workers should protect the confidentiality of clients' written and electronic records and other sensitive information. Social workers should take reasonable steps to ensure that clients' records are stored in a secure location and that clients' records are not available to others who are not authorized to have access.

(standard 1.07)

(d) Social workers should store records following the termination of services to ensure reasonable future access. Records should be maintained for the number of years required by state statutes or relevant contracts.

(standard 3.04)

RISK MANAGEMENT STANDARDS AND GUIDELINES

In addition to promulgating new ethics standards related to documentation, social workers have also recently developed elaborate risk management standards designed to enhance the delivery of services to clients and protect practitioners in case they have to defend themselves against ethics complaints (filed with state licensing boards or NASW) or lawsuits that allege professional negligence (Barker and Branson 2000; Madden 2003). This section provides a summary of these guidelines, based on extant literature, prominent court decisions, and my experience as chair of an NASW chapter committee on inquiry and as an expert witness in many court cases throughout the United States in which social workers have been plaintiffs or defendants.

Risk management guidelines related to documentation and case recording can be placed into conceptually distinct categories: (1) the content of documentation, (2) language and terminology, (3) credibility, and (4) access to records and documents.

Content of Documentation

Too much content, too little content, or the wrong content can harm clients and expose practitioners to considerable risk of liability. The days when social workers could proclaim, "I just don't keep detailed notes" are long gone. As Berner (1998), a lawyer and social worker, observes with respect to documentation in clinical settings:

> Because the practice of clinical record-keeping is of such long standing, and because courts in particular understand that the reason for clinical documentation is, in fact, not for the convenience of attorneys and judges, but to further the goal of good patient care, "everyone" expects that clinicians will keep records. "Everyone" means your patients, your professional society's ethics board, your professional discipline's licensing board, the newspapers, the general public, and perhaps most relevant for us . . . the courts. Courts know what everyone else knows, and courts expect clinicians to keep records documenting their work.
>
> (60–61)

To ensure appropriate content in documentation, social workers should consider several issues. A primary function of documentation is to serve and protect all parties. The content, however, must tread a careful line, striking a balance between too much and too little information. In a crisis situation social workers need to observe some precautions when recording case information. Furthermore they should follow specific guidelines for documenting services to families and couples, and the extent to which individual members may be privy to that information.

Serve and protect. Practitioners' first rule of thumb when documenting cases should be to include sufficient detail to facilitate the delivery of services and protect themselves in the event of an ethics complaint or lawsuit. In clinical settings such details involve social histories, assessments, and treatment plans; informed consent procedures; contacts with clients (type, date, and time); contacts with third parties; consultation with other professionals; decisions made and services provided; critical incidents; instructions, recommendations, advice, and referrals to specialists; failed and canceled appointments; previous or current psychological, psychiatric, and medical evaluations; information concerning fees, charges, and payments;

termination of services; final assessment; and other relevant documents (Moline, Williams, and Austin 1998; Reamer 2001a).

Social work supervisors should document the date, time, and content of supervision sessions, including specific recommendations, critical incidents, and consultations. Social work managers and administrators should document key discussions, consultations, and meetings that address ethical and legal issues. For example, they should note the steps taken to determine whether to disclose confidential information without a client's consent to protect a third party from harm, address an employee's impairment or unethical conduct, or develop conflict-of-interest guidelines for agency personnel (Barsky and Gould 2002; Luepker and Norton 2002). David Gould (1998), a veteran malpractice attorney who has defended several mental health practitioners, writes:

> These types of cases, like almost all medical negligence cases, are won or lost by what is contained, or not contained, in the medical record. It has been my experience that mental health notes, particularly in the outpatient setting, are, more often than not, deficient. . . . Inadequate notes leave the clinician at the mercy of a plaintiff's attorney, especially when he is asked years later to recall an event that is poorly documented, if at all.
>
> (345)

Strike a balance. Documenting too much or too little can be perilous (Berner 1998). For example, in clinical settings too little detail about a client's suicidal ideation may compromise the quality of services provided by an on-call colleague who reviews incomplete or vague entries in the client's chart. Furthermore social workers who do not include sufficient detail concerning the steps they took to address a client's crisis are likely to have difficulty defending their actions in the event of an ethics complaint or negligence lawsuit (Bergstresser 1998).

Too much detail—a client's fantasies or involvement in a crime committed many years earlier, for instance—could be used against the client if that client's spouse subpoenas the record as part of a child custody dispute. Admittedly distinguishing between too much and too little detail can be difficult. It requires experience and reasoned decision making. Social workers should strive for a reasonable balance, considering what information is clinically essential to properly assess clients' needs; plan, coordinate, deliver, supervise, and evaluate services; and be accountable to clients, insurers, agencies, other providers, courts, and utilization review bodies.

Avoid overdocumentation in a crisis. Social workers also need to strive for balance during crises, avoiding the temptation to overdocument. Including excessive detail in a case record in the context of a crisis can be a red flag when records are reviewed during an ethics hearing or litigation (Bergstresser 1998; Simon 1998). A social worker's claim that he handled the matter in a manner that is consistent with prevailing standards in the profession may be challenged in the face of inordinate detail in the case record. Such detail may in fact suggest that the case was handled in an extraordinary or unusual way. As Berner asserts, it is far more important in a clinical crisis to "write smarter, not longer. . . . Writing smarter means being succinct" (1998:54).

Use caution with personal notes. Clinical social workers, supervisors, managers, and administrators sometimes maintain separate personal notes to keep track of details that do not belong in an official agency record. As I discussed earlier, social workers sometimes assume—mistakenly—that such personal notes will always be treated as confidential and that adversarial parties cannot gain access to them, for example, in a malpractice lawsuit. In fact in most court jurisdictions lawyers can subpoena social workers' personal notes during legal proceedings (Polowy and Gorenberg 1997). Thus social workers who maintain personal notes assume some risk. Information in personal notes could be used against a client. For example, information contained in the notes may become central during divorce, termination of parental rights, or child custody proceedings. Personal notes can also be used against the social work supervisor, manager, or administrator who documents potentially embarrassing details concerning interstaff relationships. Social workers who maintain personal notes should word entries without an expectation of privacy and with the assumption that someday the notes may be reviewed by third parties whose interests may be adversarial (Moline, Williams, and Austin 1998).

Some years ago the American Psychiatric Association drafted the Model Law on Confidentiality of Health and Social Service Information in an effort to protect practitioners' personal notes:

> a. A service provider is not required to but may, to the extent he or she determines it necessary and appropriate, keep personal notes regarding a client wherein he or she may record:

(i) sensitive information disclosed to him or her in confidence by other persons on condition that such information would never be disclosed to the client or other persons excepting, at most, other service providers; and

(ii) sensitive information disclosed to him or her by the client which would be injurious to the client's relationships to other persons;

(iii) the service provider's speculations, impressions, hunches and reminders. No authorization to disclose confidential information shall be effective with respect to such personal notes of a service provider except on authorization to disclose the same to another service provider occupying a professional service relationship with the client by reason where of it would serve the client's interests for him to have the personal notes and whereby he is bound to observe confidentiality.

Upon receipt of such personal notes by such other service provider, they shall be deemed to be his personal notes except to the extent that he transfers information from such notes to regular health and social service records pertaining to the client.

b. The keeping of such personal notes shall not relieve a service provider from any obligation to record and maintain in an official record information pertaining to such matters as diagnosis, treatment, progress and all other information required in an individualized treatment plan.

(Wilson 1978:51)

This language is clearly reflected in the subsequently enacted Illinois Mental Health and Developmental Disabilities Confidentiality Act of 1981 (and subsequent amendments), one of the most explicit codified statements on the subject of personal notes.[3] The act addresses the issue of personal notes by stating that the client's record "does not include the therapist's notes, if such notes are kept in the therapist's sole possession for his own personal use and are not disclosed to any other person, except the therapist's supervisor, consulting therapist or attorney. If at any time such notes are disclosed, they shall be considered part of the . . . record." The act goes on to say that the therapist's personal notes may include "information disclosed to the therapist in confidence by other persons on condition that such information would never be disclosed to the recipient or other persons; information disclosed to the therapist by the recipient which would be injurious to the recipient's relationship to other persons; and the therapist's speculations, impressions, hunches, and reminders." In fact in

1998 the Illinois Appellate Court held that a psychiatrist's personal notes were protected from discovery in a malpractice claim against him (see *In re Estate of Bagus* (1998)).

Although the support for such personal notes may provide social workers with some comfort, they must realize that outside Illinois a lawyer *could* subpoena such notes, along with formal agency or private practice records (subpoena duces tecum). Lawyers have in fact subpoenaed such items as appointment books, scraps of paper, calendars, and any other documents on which the practitioner may have written notes related to the matter at hand. Also, most states do not distinguish between professional and personal notes. According to Madden:

> Many therapists wonder about the legality of keeping two sets of records, the official record, and a second file including personal notes, hypotheses, subjective comments, or other information not directly relevant to the reason for treatment. Although a few states do allow separate working notes (see, e.g., Illinois Mental Health and Developmental Disabilities Confidentiality Act, 1996), this practice is generally discouraged. Except where protected by statute, personal notes are subject to a subpoena and lawyers routinely include reference to personal notes when requesting client records. These subjective or speculative notes may contain information that can be used to undercut the conclusions in the formal file. If case notes are carefully written, there should be no reason to keep a separate set of notes.
> (31–32)

Be cautious in documenting services provided to families and couples. Clinical social workers who counsel families and couples are often in an untenable position: If they maintain a single record for the family and couple, they risk exposing confidential information in the event the record is subpoenaed. Maintaining separate records for all parties, on the other hand, is cumbersome and inconsistent with social workers' belief that the family or couple as a whole is the client. According to Barker and Branson:

> There are advantages and disadvantages to whichever choice this worker, or any worker, makes. The only virtue in having separate files—but it is a significant one—is in the event that members of the client-group have major disputes. When their disputes lead to legal action, one client or another

may seek the worker's files. An individual may be able legally to have access
to his or her own records, but what about when the information is inter-
twined with that of another person, especially another person who is now
an opponent in a lawsuit? If the files are written separately, then every person can claim access only to their own files, and the worker's position is
much less uncomfortable.

(2000:154–55)

Some social workers compromise by maintaining separate records for
sensitive information that must be protected and joint files for more routine assessments and summaries of services provided. For example, a social
worker who provides an individual counseling session to one member of a
couple, as a supplement to counseling the couple, can create a separate file
for that client in which private issues, such as a report of struggles with sexual orientation, family violence, infidelity, or substance abuse, are recorded.
In the couple's joint file the social worker would record their having sought
marital counseling to address "relationship issues." Maintaining separate
records in these circumstances may help the social worker protect each client in the event that a dispute arises—a child custody dispute or divorce,
for example (Barsky and Gould 2002; Moline, Williams, and Austin 1998;
Reamer 2006. In such circumstances social workers should consult standards in the NASW *Code of Ethics* concerning conflicts of interest that can
arise when they "provide services to two or more people who have a rela-
tionship with each other" (standard 1.06[d|). The social worker has a duty
to explain at the outset her role during the case and to anticipate and minimize potential conflicts of interest.

Do not air agency dirty laundry. Details concerning understaffed programs, conflicts among staffers, or personal opinions about the competence
of a colleague do not belong in a client's record. Documentation of personnel and staffing problems should appear in administrative files. Including
such detail in clients' records may expose agencies to considerable risk in
the event of a negligence lawsuit.

Furthermore line social workers, supervisors, managers, and administrators who become involved in disputes among staff members—a disagreement about an agency policy or administrative order, for example—should
not include documentation about the dispute in clients' records. When
there is reason to create a paper trail, relevant opinions, decisions, and

actions can be documented in administrative memoranda or logs. Put simply, evidence of jousting among staff should not appear in clients' records (Berner 1998).

Language and Terminology

Wording in documentation is just as important as the substance of the content. Loose and casual language and terminology can be catastrophic to the social worker, the supervisor, and the agency. Social workers must choose their words carefully, taking care to be clear, to fully support conclusions drawn, to avoid defamatory language, and to write knowing there is always an audience.

Writing with clarity. Practitioners should use clear, specific, unambiguous, and precise wording. Lack of clarity, specificity, and precision provides considerable opportunity for adversarial parties to raise doubts about social workers' claims, observations, and interpretations. In addition these shortcomings in a report may confuse colleagues who are depending on the notes to provide follow-up services to clients (Reamer 2005; Simon 1998). Conversely clear, specific, unambiguous, and precise wording enhances the delivery of services and strengthens social workers' ability to explain and defend previous decisions and actions.

In addition to using precise wording, social workers should avoid the use of professional jargon, slang, or abbreviations that may be misunderstood. For example, the abbreviation DD could mean dual diagnosis or developmental disability. BPD could mean bipolar disorder or borderline personality disorder. SA could mean substance abuse or sexual assault. Such ambiguity could prove disastrous if the abbreviations are misinterpreted by a colleague or debated in an ethics hearing, licensing board inquiry, or litigation.

Drawing conclusions. Documenting conclusions with terms or phrases such as "the client was confused" or "the unit social worker behaved aggressively toward the client" without including supporting details is risky. Today's practitioner therefore needs to always include details that support a conclusion or assertion. Summary statements about the mental health status or behavior of a client, employee, or colleague should always be supported with sufficient specific information. Terms such as *hostile, under the influence,* or *incompetent* should always be reinforced and followed by the phrase "as evidenced by," with appropriate details included (Bergstresser 1998; Berner 1998).

Avoiding defamatory language. Practitioners should also take steps to avoid using language that might constitute libel or slander, the two forms of defamation of character (Moline, Williams, and Austin 1998; Reamer 2006). Libel (the written form of defamation) and slander (the oral form of defamation) occur when social workers write or say something about a client, colleague, or third party that is not true, the social worker knew to be untrue or should have known was untrue, and harmed the individual who was the subject of the written or oral communication. Examples include untrue statements alleging mental illness, substance abuse, incompetence, or inappropriate behavior.

Writing for an audience. Social workers should expect managed care authorities, utilization review personnel, and third-party payers to review documents and records. Poorly worded and inadequate documentation may affect payment for services to clients. Also, social workers should protect clients' privacy when they share records with such outside parties (see NASW *Code of Ethics* standard 1.07[h]).

Credibility

When disputes arise concerning the appropriateness of social workers' actions—whether they conducted adequate assessments of clients, maintained proper boundaries, terminated services appropriately, obtained needed consultation, or provided proper supervision, for example—case records and administrative files provide essential evidence. Without thorough documentation social workers may have difficulty defending their actions. Thoroughness, however, is not sufficient. Even thorough documentation needs to be credible, and the credibility of social workers' documentation can be enhanced or compromised in several ways. Time is of the essence when documenting cases, but practitioners must take care not to jump the gun and record events that are only anticipated. Likewise the writing in documentation must always be professional. Finally, when a mistake is made, a credible social worker will be forthright and honest.

Documenting in a timely fashion. Few social workers relish the task of documentation, whether for clinical, supervisory, management, or administrative purposes. Careful documentation takes time and often looms as an onerous task—a necessary evil associated with professional life. As a result social workers sometimes put off documenting their decisions and actions. Delayed documentation can compromise the credibility of social workers' claims about what the notes reflect (Berner 1998; Moline, Williams, and Austin 1998; Simon 1998). Adversarial parties, especially opposing legal counsel, can use evidence of delayed documentation to challenge the credibility of social workers' testimony. According to Barsky and Gould:

> The timing of note taking can have great legal significance. Ideally, notes should be made contemporaneously with the events being recorded (i.e., during a session with a client, immediately following, or within 24 hours). Evidentiary rules assume that information recorded contemporaneously with the events is more likely to be accurate. Behavioral science research supports the fact that notes contemporaneously taken are more accurate than those recorded at a later time, even if it is later the same day.
>
> (2002:135)

Avoiding prognostic documentation. In an effort to save time and expedite documentation, social workers occasionally record notes in advance of an intervention or event. Sometimes, however, the planned interventions or events do not occur or they unfold differently than expected. The prematurely recorded notes would therefore not accurately reflect what happened and thus would undermine the social worker's credibility (Barsky and Gould 2002; Berner 1998).

Striving for professional prose. Social workers do not always pay close attention to the legibility or grammatical correctness of their documentation. Colleagues may have difficulty understanding, or may misinterpret, illegible entries and may miss important cues that are essential for proper intervention, supervision, management, or administration. Therefore it is imperative that social workers print or write entries legibly and use proper grammar when recording case information. Copies of social workers' documentation typically become tangible evidence and exhibits during ethics hearings, licensing board inquiries, and courtroom proceedings. Peer-review or regulatory bodies, lawyers, expert witnesses, judges, and jurors may see photocopies or overhead projections of case records. Illegible entries and a pattern of grammatical and spelling errors are a professional embarrassment to the practitioner and the agency represented. Such inattention to detail severely weakens credibility (Barsky and Gould 2002; Moline, Williams, and Austin 1998; Simon 1998). Worse, it could also result in the provision of misleading information.[4]

Acknowledging errors. To err is human, and every social worker is capable of inadvertently inserting incorrect facts in, and omitting important facts from, case documentation. Ethics committee members, licensing boards, lawyers, and judges recognize that any professional can make occasional errors.

To avoid undermining their credibility, social workers should never attempt to cover up or camouflage their errors (Barsky and Gould 2002). Such efforts can backfire. For example, opposing lawyers can access documents before social workers attempt to conceal the errors. Social workers who alter records in anticipation of legal proceedings, or after legal proceedings have been initiated, therefore assume great risk and public humiliation if the inconsistencies are brought to light. As Barsky and Gould observe, "If a clinician is aware of an impending legal process or has been subpoenaed, doctoring or destroying documents can result in such charges as contempt of court or obstruction of justice, malpractice suits, and professional disciplinary actions" (2002:145). Instead social workers should always acknowledge their errors, making clear that the new entry occurred after the error was discovered. In clinical settings that use paper records, practitioners should enter a new note that acknowledges and corrects the error or draw a thin line through the error and insert the correction, along with the social worker's initials, the date, and the word *error.* Social workers should ensure that errors in electronic records are acknowledged forthrightly and corrected. Clyde Bergstresser, a seasoned malpractice attorney, emphasizes:

> Do not change or lose your records. Do not make "additions" or "corrections" to clarify what you meant. You would be amazed at how many people cannot resist the temptation to make sure that in hindsight the records say what was meant. When you get caught, your credibility will be destroyed, and it is very likely you will be caught. Copies of "lost" records have a habit of cropping up when you least expect it. Document experts are now very sophisticated in their ability to determine from writing patterns whether an entry was made all in one sitting, even from a copy.
>
> (1998:342)

Access to Records and Documents

Social workers generally assume that case records and documents will remain confidential. In reality a truly confidential case record does not exist. An extraordinarily wide array of laws, regulations, contracts, and court rules require or permit disclosure of otherwise confidential documents.

Furthermore social workers need to be cognizant of security risks associated with the widespread use of computers to store confidential records and documents. Thus social workers should be familiar with the various circumstances under which records and documents may be disclosed. Practitioners need to know how to respond to subpoenas, be familiar with applicable state and federal laws and regulations, and secure documentation for future access.

Know how to respond to a subpoena. Perhaps the most frequent trigger for the disclosure of documents is the subpoena. A subpoena duces tecum requires a party who is in control of relevant documents to bring them to a deposition or court hearing. Social workers should not confuse subpoenas to appear with documents with an order to disclose the documents' contents. Subpoenas and court orders are entirely different phenomena. In fact the NASW *Code of Ethics* obligates social workers to take steps to protect the confidentiality of relevant documents during legal proceedings:

> Social workers should protect the confidentiality of clients during legal proceedings to the extent permitted by law. When a court of law or other legally authorized body orders social workers to disclose confidential or privileged information without a client's consent and such disclosure could cause harm to the client, social workers should request that the court withdraw the order or limit the order as narrowly as possible or maintain the records under seal, unavailable for public inspection.

> (standard 1.07[j])

Social workers should not release any confidential information contained in documents unless they are sure they are authorized to do so—based on client consent or in response to a court order, for example (Polowy and Gorenberg 1997).

Know relevant statutes and regulations. Many federal and state statutes and regulations govern the handling of confidential documents (Dickson 1998). For example, the federal Health Insurance Portability and

Accountability Act, or HIPAA, and its regulations address the protection of personal health-related information. Clinical social workers should be especially familiar with explicit HIPAA provisions that are unique to psychotherapy notes. The regulations define these specifically as notes recorded in any medium by a health-care provider who is a mental health professional documenting or analyzing the contents of conversation during a private counseling session or a group, joint, or family counseling session, and that are separated from the rest of the individual's medical record. Further, the Health Information Technology for Economic and Clinical Health Act provides the Department of Health and Human Services with the authority to establish programs to improve health-care quality, safety, and efficiency through the promotion of health information technology, including electronic health records and private and secure electronic health information exchange (the American Recovery and Reinvestment Act of 2009).

Other key federal regulations govern the handling of confidential documents related to privacy of personally identifiable information about individuals that is maintained in systems of records by federal agencies (Privacy Act of 1974 as amended), alcohol and substance abuse treatment (Confidentiality of Alcohol and Drug Abuse Patient Records) and school records (the Family Educational Rights and Privacy Act, or FERPA). States also have specific laws and regulations governing the release of confidential documents contained in health, mental health, school, and child welfare records (Dickson 1998). The Patriot Act authorizes federal agents to access social workers' documents in conjunction with an authorized investigation of international terrorism—and we've all been learning just how all-encompassing such investigations can be.

Secure records. Social workers should store records (clinical, personnel, supervisory, and administrative) in secure locations to prevent unauthorized access (Barsky and Gould 2002). When using electronic media, practitioners should exercise caution to ensure that this information cannot be accessed by unauthorized parties (see NASW *Code of Ethics* standards 1.07[l],[m]). Social workers should consult relevant federal and state statutes, regulations, codes of ethics, and contracts (for example, insurance company and managed care contracts) to determine the length of time that documents should be retained. If and when records are destroyed or disposed of, care must be taken so that the disposal still protects client confidentiality (Barsky and Gould 2002; NASW 2008).

Social workers should keep a number of criteria in mind with respect to recording and case notes (Austin, Moline, and Williams 1990:25–44; Reamer 2001a; Schutz 1982:51–52; Wilson 1978:31–55, 83–97). In particular the social worker should record

- Informed-consent procedures and enclose in the file signed consent forms for release of information and treatment.
- All contacts made with third parties (such as family members, acquaintances, and other professionals), whether in person or by telephone. The record should include a brief description of the contacts and any significant events surrounding them.
- Any consultation with other professionals, including the date that the client was referred to another professional for services.
- A complete social history, assessment, and treatment plan, stating the client's problems, the reason for requesting service, objectives and relevant timetable, intervention strategy, planned number and duration of contacts, assessment and evaluation of progress, termination plan, and reasons for termination.
- A brief description of the social worker's reasoning for all decisions made during the course of intervention.
- Any instructions, recommendations, and advice provided to the client, including referral to and suggestions to seek consultation from a specialist.
- A description of all clinically relevant contacts with the client, including type of contact (e.g., in person versus telephone, email or text message; individual, family, couples, group) and dates and times of contacts. The record also should include notation of failed or canceled appointments and any previous or current psychological, psychiatric, or medical evaluations relevant to the social worker's intervention.

In addition social workers should not keep process (narrative) recordings in a case record, even temporarily. According to Madden, "One exception to the discouragement of unofficial notes involves process recording or other written notes made for the purposes of supervision or education/ training. In these documents, therapists and students should be careful not to include any identifying information about the client and to maintain these notes in a separate location from the client's official file" (1998:32). The record also should not contain information regarding a client's political, religious, or other personal views unless this detail is directly relevant to the intervention. Intimate, gossipy, and other personal details that are not directly germane to intervention should be omitted, as should any information that could in any way be used against the client in a court of law.

State statutes, federal regulations, and insurance company contracts may specify a retention period for records. The American Psychological Association's *Specialty Guidelines for Delivery of Services* suggests that when no statutes address the time period for retaining notes, practitioners should retain full records for three years and either the full record or a summary of the record for twelve more years; practitioners should dispose of no record until fifteen years after completion of service (Austin, Moline, and Williams 1990:38–39). In contrast counseling psychology's guidelines suggest that the full record be maintained for at least fourteen years after completion of planned services or after the date of last contact with the client, whichever is later; that the counselor maintain at least a summary for an additional three years, if not the full record; and that the practitioner may dispose of the record no sooner than seven years after the completion of planned services or after the date of last contact, whichever is later (Austin, Moline, and Williams 1990:38–39). Case records pertaining to minors ordinarily should be kept longer because the statute of limitations may not begin to run until the child reaches the age of majority. According to the NASW *Code of Ethics,* "Social workers should store records following the termination of services to ensure reasonable future access. Records should be maintained for the number of years required by state statutes or relevant contracts" (standard 3.04[d]).

As I discussed in chapter 2, social workers would also be wise to prepare a will that includes plans for the transfer or disposition of cases in the event of death or incapacitation. Experts suggest providing for an executor or trustee to maintain records for a period of thirty days, at the end of which the social worker's practice and all records may be sold to a designated colleague (often for a nominal fee of $1).

Because of the potential problems involved in recording and note taking, some professionals have proposed doing away with records entirely. As Wilson observes, "A serious suggestion has been made, and is being carried out in some social work settings, that there simply be no records at all. Advocates of this tactic prefer that all old files be destroyed and no new recording be done on social-work activity" (1978:48). Some argue that the absence of records would be particularly helpful when practitioners are subpoenaed to court, where in principle therapists could claim that they do not fully remember what happened in the case. Most professionals agree, however, that the elimination of records would create more problems, legal and otherwise, than it would solve. Also, the NASW *Code of Ethics* requires social workers to maintain records for the number of years required by state statutes or relevant contracts (standards 3.04[b] and [d]). Watson states the position well in his comments about the use of records in psychoanalysis:

> In relation to legal matters, they [records] have two purposes: (1) to refresh our memory about what we are doing for a patient in order that we may maintain our own working contact with a patient accurately. . . . (2) In the event the therapist is called to account legally for work with his patient, records add substantially to what lawyers call his *credibility*. Mere absence of records will not keep one from being subpoenaed. There are evidentiary dangers in saying that you do not remember things about a patient whom you have treated. . . . [A] good cross-examining lawyer would then tax the analyst's narcissism rigorously as he began to explore the implications of nonmemory about the case. That could cause the therapist considerable embarrassment when he found himself in the position of saying he treats patients but does not remember anything about them. In other words, one should not fool oneself into believing that the problem of testimony will be solved by "not having any records." Neither will it be possible to readily convince the judge that he should pay attention to your notions of relevance, when you cannot demonstrate what you did through some kind of record. In short, if you jeopardize your credibility with the judge by playing games about memory, it is very likely he will pay no attention to you when you attempt to argue that certain matters are irrelevant and also damaging to your patient, so far as privilege is concerned. Therefore, such a tactic would be basically foolish and self-defeating.
>
> (1972, quoted in Wilson 1978:53)

Although the vast majority of social workers agree that keeping good case notes is important, some do not do so. In chapter 5, for example, I described a case involving a social worker who was a partner in a private practice and was sued under the doctrine of respondeat superior in connection with mistakes alleged to have been made by a former nurse whom the social worker had hired. In that case the plaintiff alleged that the former nurse, who was originally hired to conduct eating disorder assessments and evaluations of children, provided incompetent counseling services to her before the former nurse had completed her formal education in a counseling program and before she was licensed as a counselor. The plaintiff also claimed that the social worker should be held liable both because the former nurse provided the counseling and in relation to the monitoring and intervention in the case by the social worker, which the suit claimed was inadequate. The specific allegations included claims that the former nurse promoted the client's dependency on her; involved the client in her side business, which was completely unrelated to counseling; traveled out of state with the client; and otherwise was involved in inappropriate dual relationships with the client. The client and her husband sued, claiming that she had been manifesting serious symptoms, including depression and suicidal ideation.

One key issue involved in the case, which was settled before trial, concerned the claim that during the intervention neither the former nurse nor the social worker maintained notes about the case. When the plaintiff's attorney deposed the former nurse, the following dialogue took place, beginning with the lawyer:

Q: What kinds of clients do you tend to see?

A: What do you mean?

Q: Do you specialize in certain kinds of problem areas?

A: No, not really. I see lots of different kinds of clients.

Q: Do you have case notes on all of your clients?

A: Some yes, some no.

Q: What about [the plaintiff]? Why didn't you keep notes in this case?

A: You have to understand that this is a very complicated case. There were two other clinicians involved, plus lots of other service providers outside of our own agency. This wasn't my case primarily, so I didn't feel the need to keep detailed notes. There were so many others involved, it just didn't seem necessary. I was usually in touch with the other counselors. So I just didn't think there was a problem.

Q: Well, frankly, I am confused about this. I am trying to imagine what it must be like to keep track of so many clients. I can't imagine keeping it all in my head. What if I get a call from a client I haven't seen in some time? How am I supposed to remember all those details? It seems to me that any professional who provides services to clients—or patients—ought to keep careful notes to keep track of all the details of the case. Suppose you get sick or have to go away in an emergency? What happens if some colleague of yours needs to know what's happening in the case? Don't you think you have a responsibility here?

A: I guess we see these things differently. I've been operating this way for years. I think I have the ability to remember the important things that are going on in my clients' lives. I guess it's possible that I'd forget something, but I've never considered it a problem. In this particular case I was in pretty close touch with my colleagues involved with [the plaintiff]. Whenever I felt the need for some consultation I would contact one of my colleagues here. That happened a lot. Maybe it would have been a good idea to write all this stuff down, but I didn't. I just didn't think I needed to.

The next week the social worker (the partner in the private practice who had hired the former nurse), who was being sued under the doctrine of respondeat superior, was also deposed, and here too the plaintiff's lawyer pursued the subject of recording and note taking:

Q: Let me ask you this question, Ms. [mentions the social worker's name]. Do you ordinarily keep detailed case notes?

A: It depends, but usually not.

Q: What do you think about that?

A: What do you mean?

Q: I mean, do you think that's standard procedure in social work?

A: Look, I don't really know what standard procedure is in general. I know what I do and what I think is acceptable. I've never kept detailed case notes on every client.

Q: You've always practiced this way?

A: Yes, since day one. I've never felt the need to handle my practice any differently.

Q: Is this what you were taught to do when you went to school to become a social worker?

A: Not really. It's never been a problem before.

Q: Well, I'm not really concerned about problems before now. I want to know whether there was a problem in this case.

A: I guess we have a different view of this.

Q: Is it ever necessary for you to keep case notes?

A: Only if there's something highly unusual.

Q: Highly unusual?

A: Like a suicidal client—something like that.

Sometimes social workers whose records are subpoenaed are tempted to alter the record in order to fill in any gaps or to correct errors. In some instances social workers have actually destroyed all or a portion of a record in order to cover up some error. This is a serious mistake. In addition to engaging in deception (see chapter 7), the social worker may be held liable because of the altered or destroyed record. As R. Cohen notes, "Some professionals foolishly attempt to 'tighten up' or alter the records so that the records will show them in a better light in court. What these professionals do not know is that the plaintiff's attorney may have somehow gotten to the records and copied them long before the letter advising [the defendant] of the litigation was sent. In such a case, the 'doctored' records will then reflect quite poorly on the health professional" (1979:275). In addition, destroying case notes is a felony in some states (Austin, Moline, and Williams 1990:34). Many experts argue that any material in the records is going to be less incriminating than evidence that a practitioner altered or destroyed a record.

Issues pertaining to altered records arose in the Florida case that I discussed earlier that involved a health-care provider who was sued after a patient committed suicide; the suit alleged that the health-care provider had failed to refer the man to a psychiatrist and had failed to recommend hospitalization ("Failure to Refer to Psychiatrist" 1995:6). In that case the primary health-care provider had referred the client to a psychologist, who had treated him. The psychologist's chart indicated that he had recommended referral of the client to a psychiatrist and for hospitalization. The plaintiff challenged the authenticity of the psychologist's record and a document analyst concluded that the disputed entries had been made at least several weeks *after* the man committed suicide.

Understand clients' right to access their own records. As I discussed earlier, clients generally have a right to examine their own records. Social workers who are concerned that clients' access to their records could cause serious misunderstanding or harm to the client should provide assistance in interpreting the records and consultation with the client regarding the records. Social workers should limit clients' access to their records, or portions of their records, only in exceptional circumstances when compelling evidence exists that such access would cause serious harm to the client. In a Texas case the state licensing board disciplined a social worker "related to failure to respond to, and provide information to a patient regarding a request for patient records" (Texas Department of State Health Service 2013).

7

Deception and Fraud

WHEN I CONDUCTED A WORKSHOP in a large midwestern city on ethics and liability issues in social work, a participant approached during a break to ask me a question. She explained that she was a social worker in solo private practice in a nearby suburban community. She complained that insurance companies often will not approve psychotherapy for "adjustment disorders," which occur when people have difficulty coping with stress and trauma. She explained that because her livelihood depended on third-party payment, she felt compelled to camouflage her treatment of adjustment disorders by changing the coding for clients' diagnoses to those for which insurance companies will authorize therapy (for example, major depressive episode, generalized anxiety disorder, acute stress disorder). The social worker asked whether I thought she could, as a result, "get in trouble."

A variety of circumstances in social work provide opportunities for some form of deception or fraud—that is, a deliberate attempt by a social worker to give a false impression to a client, colleague, insurance provider, employer, or some other party. The potential problem is sufficiently serious to warrant its own standard (4.04) in the NASW *Code of Ethics:* "Social workers should not participate in, condone, or be associated with dishonesty, fraud, or deception."

Fraud—which often, but not always, involves financial transactions—is typically considered an intentional tort, as Schutz suggests in his discussion of legal liability in psychotherapy:

Fraud is the intentional or negligent, implied, or direct perversion of truth for the purpose of inducing another, who relies on such misrepresentation, to part with something valuable belonging to him or to surrender a legal right. If one misrepresents the risks or benefits of therapy for one's own benefit and not the patient's, so as to induce him to undergo treatment and pay the fee, this is fraud. Telling a patient that sexual intercourse is therapy may be seen as a perversion of the truth so as to get the patient to part with something of value. Hence, this would be seen as fraud.

(1982:12)

Social workers who engage in deception and fraud do so for various reasons and with various motives. Some social workers—a small percentage—are simply dishonest and attempt to take advantage of others for reasons of greed, malice, or self-protection. Other social workers engage in deceit and fraud for what appear to be more altruistic reasons, that is, to be as helpful as they can be to their clients and agencies.

SELF-INTERESTED DECEPTION AND FRAUD

The vast majority of social workers enter the profession with remarkably pure motives. For a variety of reasons they are moved to help vulnerable people. Some social workers have been influenced by an admired mentor and some by family values. Some enter social work as a result of their own personal trauma or experience as a client. Whatever the reasons, most social workers are attracted to the profession for noble purposes—to assist people who are experiencing serious problems in living that are related to poverty, mental illness, substance abuse, child or elder abuse, family conflict or violence, physical disability or illness, and so on.

However, some social workers enter the profession with ignoble motives or develop them along the way. Consider this prominent example of social workers who were convicted in federal court and sentenced to prison for engaging in health care fraud:

THREE SENTENCED FOR SCHEME TO DEFRAUD MEDICARE

BATON ROUGE, LA—United States Attorney Donald J. Cazayoux, Jr. announced that U.S. District Judge Brian Jackson sentenced Alton Bates, 62, an attorney in Baton Rouge, Louisiana, to thirty-four months in prison, to pay restitution of $1,063,873 to Medicare, to forfeit the gross proceeds of his scheme to defraud Medicare, and to three years supervised release after imprisonment. Judge Jackson also sentenced co-defendants Robert Ivory Levy, 59, and Juanita Anderson Hilton, age 42, both of whom are residents of Baton Rouge and were Licensed Clinical Social Workers. Levy was sentenced to fifteen months imprisonment, ordered to pay restitution of $120,946.89 to Medicare, and to three years supervised release after imprisonment. Anderson Hilton was sentenced to three years probation with a condition that she serve six months in a local halfway house and repay $89,450 to Medicare. . . .

Alton Bates, Robert Levy, and Juanita Anderson Hilton schemed to defraud the Medicare program by submitting false and fraudulent claims for psychotherapy services that were not provided. In total, the three defendants' participation in this scheme involved more than 7,700 false claims seeking Medicare payments totaling $3,052,838. Due to the scheme, Medicare program paid more than $1,000,000 to Above and Beyond, LLC, the Baton Rouge company which the defendants operated between 2003 and 2005.

("Three Sentenced" 2011)

State licensing boards have also disciplined social workers who have engaged in fraud, especially financial fraud. The Ohio board revoked the license of a social worker who pleaded guilty in federal court to embezzlement and theft of federal funds in connection with her position as director of a social service program (State of Ohio 1996). In another case New Jersey suspended the license of a social worker who was convicted of Medicaid fraud when, in his position as executive director of a behavioral health program, he billed for therapy services that were never provided (New Jersey State Board 2004).

In most fraud cases evidence shows that financial greed and self-interest led to the misconduct. In other cases no direct financial motive is involved, for example, when social workers fraudulently declare to licensing boards that they have completed mandated continuing education courses. The Iowa licensing board disciplined a social worker who, when she submitted her application for license renewal, stated that she had completed required continuing education, when she had not (Board of Social Work 2012). In another case Alabama revoked the license of a social worker who submitted fraudulent forms to the board indicating she had received clinical social work supervision (Alabama State Board 2009). In Maryland the state board suspended the license of a social worker who, while working as a therapist at a mental health clinic, forged the signature of a client's guardian on a treatment plan (Maryland State Board 2013).

As I discussed in chapter 4, a number of impaired social workers, particularly those who sexually abuse clients, may use their power, status, and authority as professionals to seek opportunities to meet their own needs by exploiting clients. Social workers who have addictions—whether to gambling or substances such as alcohol or other drugs—may use their professional positions to extort or steal money from impressionable or incompetent clients or use deceit and undue influence to persuade clients to enter into agreements primarily designed to benefit the social worker.

Paul S., BSW, was a caseworker at Elder Services of Boone County. He had been employed at the agency as a case coordinator for five years. Paul S. provided case management services for a caseload of twenty-five clients. Most of his clients needed assistance with home health care, homemaker services, crisis management, grief counseling, and income maintenance and insurance benefits. Several clients had been declared incompetent. Most, however, were able to participate in the management of their affairs.

One of his clients was a seventy-six-year-old man, John M. John M. had been a client of the agency for three years, and Paul S. had gotten to know him quite well during that time. In fact the two men had become so close that John M. often referred to Paul S. as the "son I always wanted."

John M. was living in a congregate housing development where he had a small private apartment and shared kitchen facilities with six other residents. Before his retirement at age seventy, he had been a highly successful furniture manufacturer. He had developed a large furniture factory, ultimately employing about three hundred people. When he sold the business, John M. became a wealthy man.

Recently John M. was diagnosed with liver cancer. Paul S. spent quite a bit of time with him, reminiscing about John M.'s life and talking about his impending death. Clearly John M. was dying and becoming more and more confused. The psychiatric consultant said that John M. would probably need to be placed on psychotropic medication to help him with his confusion.

At about this time Paul S., the social worker, was having serious financial problems. A couple of years earlier he had taken his brother-in-law's advice and, without his wife's knowledge, had invested most of their savings in the options market. Within a year, however, he had lost nearly everything. Paul S. had two children in private school and was feeling guilty and desperate about the money that he had lost.

During one conversation with John M., Paul S. said that he was worried about one of his daughters who, Paul S. lied, was gravely ill and disabled. Over three days Paul S., who had become quite important to John M., convinced John M. to rewrite his will to include Paul S. as a beneficiary.

Not all cases of this sort, in which unscrupulous social workers use undue influence and deceit to benefit themselves, involve incompetent or close-to-incompetent clients. In many cases clients are competent but vulnerable and impressionable. A social worker providing psychotherapy to a client who originally sought counseling for a serious self-esteem problem may find a ripe opportunity to convince the client to include the social worker as a partner in her thriving business. The social worker may deceitfully convince the client that nothing about this relationship is inappropriate. Or, a social worker who has serious financial problems may use fraud to convince an impressionable client to invest in a legitimate-sounding limited partnership that in actuality is a Ponzi scheme (a swindle in which an initial investment provides a quick return paid out of funds from new investors).

Other forms of self-interested deceit and fraud are more straightforward. One more common form involves clinical social workers—albeit a relatively small percentage—who submit fraudulent information on claim forms to third-party payers and insurance companies. Insurance companies may be billed for counseling sessions that did not occur. Or, social workers may collude with a psychiatrist who for a fee signs forms attesting to the client's diagnosis and treatment when the psychiatrist was virtually uninvolved in the case and had no contact with the client. In one widely publicized signing-off case a social worker in private practice spent a weekend in jail after pleading guilty in an insurance fraud case. She was also ordered to perform 720 hours of community service (NASW 1987b:1).

In the discussion of respondeat superior and problems related to staff supervision in chapter 5, I described a case involving a social worker who was a partner in a private practice and who was accused of improper supervision of an employee, a former nurse who was providing counseling services. Another aspect of that case involved allegations that a physician was

signing insurance claim forms attesting to his involvement in the social
worker's cases when in fact his involvement was minimal. The formal lawsuit included the following allegations, among others:

> Plaintiffs further show that [the private practice] submitted numerous
> charges to plaintiffs' insurer which were signed by Dr. A. [identity deleted
> by author].
>
> Plaintiffs further show that said insurance claim forms suggest and imply
> that the therapy listed thereon was provided by Dr. A.
>
> Plaintiffs show that Dr. A. provided no such services to plaintiff.

As the following excerpt shows, the plaintiffs' attorney pursued this
issue aggressively during the deposition conducted with the social worker
defendant:

Q: I'm rather confused by what I see here on the forms. These numbers here, is
that a diagnostic code for the insurance company? Is that what you have to put
down to get reimbursed by the insurance company?

A: Yes, that's what the number's for. That was Dr. A.'s diagnosis.

Q: Dr. A. gave a diagnosis in this case?

A: Yes. He's my consulting psychiatrist, and he gives the diagnoses in the cases we
discuss.

Q: So he's the one that came up with this diagnostic category? Dr. A.'s the one who
said you should put this number down?

A: Sort of. We came up with the number during our discussion.

Q: Is it safe for me to assume that Dr. A. examined the client?

A: No.

Q: No what? What do you mean?

A: I mean Dr. A. never saw the client.

Q: Is that typical?

A: Typical of what?

Q: For Dr. A. to sign the form without examining the client?

A: Are you asking whether he does this all the time?

Q: I'm asking whether he usually does this with your clients.

A: Yes, it's routine practice with us. As far as I know this is pretty common. Are we
really that different?

Q: I'm just trying to figure out how you handled these procedures. You're saying that this is what usually happened?

A: That's right.

Q: So when Dr. A. signed these forms he was saying, in effect, that in his professional judgment, based on his medical and psychiatric background, that this is the right diagnosis?

A: Yes.

Q: And was he saying that this person needed psychotherapy?

A: Yes.

Q: But how could he know this if he never met the client?

A: Well, Dr. A. would often attend our agency staff meetings, so he would learn what was going on in different cases. He knew a lot about what was happening with clients.

Q: Do you see a problem here, with this arrangement?

A: What do you mean?

Q: I mean I'm puzzled about this arrangement where you had a psychiatrist signing a form about what a particular client needs, his or her psychiatric and therapy needs, but this psychiatrist never actually saw the client.

A: This is pretty common.

Q: That doesn't mean it's right or acceptable, does it?

A: No.

Allegations of improper billing also arose in *Suslovich v. New York* (1991). In this case a psychologist's license was suspended after the clinician submitted insurance reimbursement forms for ten client sessions, although the client attended only five ("Psychologist Did Not Maintain" 1992:6).

Another serious problem concerns social workers' designation of diagnostic codes on insurance or other third-party payer claim forms (Kirk 2005). Many third-party payers rely on the American Psychiatric Association's *Diagnostic and Statistical Manual* classifications. Most claim forms require the social worker to list one or more diagnostic codes to qualify for reimbursement. Some diagnostic classifications, however, are not reimbursable, and as a result some social workers use bogus—but reimbursable—diagnostic codes on claims forms.

An important study by Kirk and Kutchins documented the extent of this form of deception and fraud among social workers. These authors set out to investigate the extent of deliberate misdiagnosis by clinical social workers:

> Such acts are legal and ethical transgressions involving deceit, fraud, or abuse. Charges made for services not provided, money collected for services to fictitious patients, or patients encouraged to remain in treatment longer than necessary are examples of intentional inaccuracy. These activities are more likely to be reported by journalists than by the professionals who may abhor such practices but believe that they occur too rarely to be consequential. Very little has been written about these kinds of legal and ethical misdeeds in the mental health field.
>
> (1988:226)

Kirk and Kutchins surveyed a random sample that included 10 percent of the individuals listed in the National Association of Social Workers' *Register of Clinical Social Workers.* At the time of their survey the *Register* included the names of more than eight thousand experienced clinical social workers. These practitioners held master's degrees, had at least two years of experience, and were members of the Academy of Certified Social Workers or were licensed by their respective states at an equivalent level. Respondents completed a lengthy questionnaire that focused on their attitudes and opinions about psychiatric diagnosis, actual diagnostic practices that they had observed in their professional work, the frequency of and reasons for their use of the *Diagnostic and Statistical Manual,* and their professional background. Open-ended comments were also invited.

The respondents were clearly familiar with the *Diagnostic and Statistical Manual.* One-fourth of the sample reported daily use of the *DSM,* and another quarter reported using the book at least once a week. Thirty percent of the sample reported using the *DSM* several times each month.

To explore the incidence of misdiagnosis Kirk and Kutchins presented the social workers with a list of various diagnostic practices. Respondents were then asked to report the extent to which they had observed these practices.

Respondents said that in many instances clinicians use a more serious diagnosis than is warranted by the client's clinical profile. About three-fifths of the sample (59 percent) reported that they report significant clinical diagnoses (the major mental disorders) to insurance companies, although they are not warranted clinically. Nearly three-fourths of the sample (72 percent) reported being aware of cases in which more-serious-than-warranted diagnoses were used to qualify for reimbursement. About one-fourth of the sample reported that this practice occurs frequently. Eighty-six percent of the social workers reported being aware of instances of listing diagnoses for individuals, although the focus of treatment was on the family (again, many third-party payers do not reimburse for family treatment). More than 80 percent indicated that third-party payer requirements often influence diagnosis. Kirk and Kutchins finally conclude that "these data suggest that deliberate misdiagnosis occurs frequently in the mental health professions. If it is as widespread as these respondents suggest, it is puzzling that it has been almost unrecognized in the literature on diagnostic errors" (1988:231).

The temptation of course is to argue that deliberate overdiagnosis is done primarily to benefit clients. That is, clients may not receive needed services unless their social workers can qualify for reimbursement. Hence deliberate overdiagnosis is a form of beneficent lying. The problem is sufficiently serious, however, that the current version of the NASW *Code of Ethics* includes a standard (3.05) that addresses this issue: "Social workers should establish and maintain billing practices that accurately reflect the nature and extent of services provided and that identify who provided the service in the practice setting" (2008:20). As Kirk and Kutchins appropriately conclude, in many cases the social worker's self-interest may be a driving force behind fraudulent billing:

> The manifest function of underdiagnosis is to protect clients; with overdiagnosis, the accurate diagnosis is replaced by a deliberately inaccurate one in order to deceive others. In particular, misdiagnosis is used so that the therapist's services will qualify for third-party reimbursement. Here the rationale is also nonclinical, but the argument that the therapist is acting only for the client's benefit is strained. The rationale that it is being done so that the client can obtain needed service is colored by the obvious self-interest of the therapist. Agencies, both public and private, also benefit when they obtain reimbursement as a result of such diagnostic practices.
>
> (1988:232)

Social workers who market or advertise their services also need to be particularly careful to avoid deception and fraud. According to the NASW

Code of Ethics, "Social workers should ensure that their representations to clients, agencies, and the public of professional qualifications, credentials, education, competence, affiliations, services provided, or results to be achieved are accurate. Social workers should claim only those relevant professional credentials they actually possess and take steps to correct any inaccuracies or misrepresentations of their credentials by others" (standard 4.06[c]).

In one prominent case the director of a Massachusetts hospital-based social service department resigned after evidence emerged that she falsified her social work credentials on her resume (Ballou 2007). As the *Boston Globe* reports:

> The state Department of Public Health has launched a sweeping review of how it verifies the licenses of employees at public hospitals following the resignation of the director of social services at the state-operated Lemuel Shattuck Hospital in Jamaica Plain over allegations that she falsified her academic credentials and licenses. . . .
>
> Sarah Pawa, who ran a department of seven people at a hospital geared toward the indigent and mentally ill, resigned last week after her superiors received an anonymous letter alleging that Pawa had lied on her resume.
>
> Pawa—hired on June 20, 2002—listed a doctorate in education and a master's degree in social work from Boston University on the resume she gave hospital officials when she applied for the job. BU officials confirmed for the *Globe* this week that she holds no degree from their school, though she did attend classes.
>
> Pawa, 44, also said on her resume that she was a practicing psychologist and clinical social worker. She said in a letter that accompanied her resume that she treated patients with "significant addiction issues and trauma history" in private practice. State licensing officials said this week that she has never held either license in Massachusetts.

Although most social workers provide fair and accurate descriptions of their services and expertise, some social workers who advertise intentionally or unintentionally misrepresent their programs, effectiveness, qualifications, education, or skills. Examples include advertising or other publicity material that essentially promises effective treatment; falsely portrays the social worker's training, credentials, or expertise (see *Corgan v. Muehling* (1991)); or promises services the social worker does not intend to provide.

In a widely publicized case the president of a Louisiana correspondence school, LaSalle University, which granted unaccredited degrees in social work, admitted that he conspired to commit fraud by misleading prospective students and telling them that the school was accredited by a fictitious organization, the Council on Post-Secondary Christian Education ("Issuer of Degrees" 1997).

Allegations of fraud related to marketing arose in a Washington, D.C., case that I discussed in chapter 3. This case involved an attorney who sued an educational–psychological training program for injuries that he claimed he sustained while participating in a five-day program of lectures, guided fantasies, and experiential psychological exercises. In addition to claiming intentional infliction of emotional distress, his suit alleged that the program engaged in fraud through its representations of the nature of the program. The jury awarded him $297,387 after finding the program liable for negligence and fraud ("Attorney Suffers Psychotic Breakdown" 1991:1).

Social workers must also avoid deception and fraud when applying for liability insurance, employment, a license, or some other form of certification. In *Gares v. New Mexico* (1990), for example, the state Board of Psychologist Examiners revoked a practitioner's certificate because of fraud and deception in applying for certification, and the psychologist appealed the court order affirming revocation of his license. The state certification board had revoked his license after finding that his certification application had involved a statement indicating that he had not engaged "in any activities which misrepresented his professional qualifications, affiliation, or purposes or those of the institutions with which he was associated." The clinician had been sexually involved with three female clients during the course of treatment and had represented to the clients that such sex was a component of their therapy ("Psychologist's License" 1991:6).

Falsification of records and official documents takes other forms as well. One involves staff members who falsify records to cover their tracks, so to speak. In these cases social workers typically alter or falsify records to create the impression that they provided services or supervision that they never actually provided or that they obtained informed consent when they had not done so. In some cases social workers falsify records to camouflage a genuine mistake. In other instances, however, no mistake was made. Rather the social worker knowingly and intentionally failed to provide the service or supervision, for instance, and simply falsified or altered the record to cover up the negligence.

In a dramatic case a social worker was sentenced to prison after a criminal court judge found that she had committed record-keeping fraud. According to court records, the social worker directed the day-to-day operations of a Philadelphia-funded social service agency. A child with cerebral palsy who was served by the agency died. The agency had been hired to provide in-home services to families at risk of abuse or neglect. As the *Philadelphia Inquirer* reports:

> Authorities said that after [fourteen-year-old Danieal] Kelly died, [Michal] Kamuvaka, who is known as "Dr. K" and who has a doctorate from the University of Pennsylvania, orchestrated a fraud to backdate and falsify records in an attempt to fool city auditors into thinking that the agency [MultiEthnic Behavioral Health Inc.] had been making visits to children, including Kelly, that never occurred.
>
> When the feds began investigating, prosecutors said Kamuvaka convinced one former MultiEthnic co-worker to lie to federal agents and schemed to obstruct the federal grand jury's investigation by withholding and shredding agency records related to Kelly and dumping them into a trash bin.
>
> Before imposing sentence, Dalzell said Kamuvaka's stewardship of Multi-Ethnic was so "lackadaisical" that it was "just a matter of time" before one of the children under its care would die.
>
> The judge also said that Kamuvaka and Manamela had engaged in an "orgy of document fabrication" and that neither defendant appreciated the "full import" of the crimes.
>
> (Hinkelman 2010).

Several years ago I conducted in-depth training for a group of experienced social workers employed in a public child welfare agency. Most were involved in protective services, although some had responsibility for special needs adoptions and juveniles who had been committed to the state training school. The training focused primarily on ethical and liability issues that arise in child welfare settings. During the discussion that addressed deception and fraud in child welfare, one social worker, a supervisor, shared the following experience:

I sure am glad you brought up this topic. I've been stewing about this for months and haven't really discussed it with anyone. I think I need to bring it up now. Perhaps my colleagues can help me figure out how to handle this problem I've had with one of my caseworkers.

One of my caseworkers is supposed to spend most of his time conducting follow-up home visits to families whose children have been returned to them from temporary foster placement. The typical situation involves a child who has been placed in foster care because of alleged or substantiated abuse or neglect. Often, of course, when allegations are unfounded or a family has participated in treatment and received various services, the child is returned.

As a condition of the child's return home, the family must agree to announced and unannounced visits from one of our caseworkers. During the child's return home a caseworker may visit as many as five times per week.

One of my caseworkers was out of work because of a death in his family, and because we were short-staffed I took over his caseload. I went to visit the Green family, which included a five-month-old girl and her mother. The infant had been returned to her mother from foster care about three months earlier. The child was placed initially because of evidence of neglect (failure to thrive).

I visited the family and had the impression that things were going reasonably well. During the visit I asked Ms. Green whether she was finding my caseworker's recent visits at all helpful. Ms. Green gave me a puzzled look and indicated that she hadn't seen the caseworker in about seven weeks. I tried to keep my composure and tried not to show my dismay.

When I got back to my car I carefully reviewed the record and discovered that the caseworker had made entries indicating that he had been making regular home visits to the Green family during the recent seven-week period.

When the caseworker returned to work, I confronted him with my discovery. He confessed that he had not in fact made the recent home visits, despite the entries in the record. With considerable trepidation he confessed that he had a serious alcohol problem and had not been functioning well at all.

What do you folks think I should do?

One can only begin to imagine the liability risks involved here. If the child were neglected or abused during the period when the agency was supposed to have been making home visits, the agency quite likely would be vulnerable. The noncustodial father, for example, might sue the agency, alleging failure to supervise properly and to protect the child (see chapter 3). The casework supervisor might also have been vulnerable under the doctrine of respondeat superior.

Sometimes social workers may believe that they are being pressured to alter records to protect their employing organization as well as themselves. Consider this case involving a social worker who was employed at a public psychiatric hospital. According to the social worker, who sued the hospital for wrongful termination of her employment, the director of social work asked her and several members of the social work staff to amend records if necessary before a site visit from a national accreditation organization. According to the suit, the director of social work had sent a memo to staff members instructing each person to review a random sample of a colleague's case records to ensure that they included all appropriate information, such as assessment information, treatment plans, progress notes, and discharge plans. The suit alleged that the memo reiterated instructions that the director had given at an earlier staff meeting. According to the plaintiff, the director of social work instructed each staff member to review the case records and to add any missing information, although the social workers would be reviewing cases for which they had not been responsible. The memo included the following text:

> As you know [the accreditation organization] will be here this Thur./Fri.—so we must be caught up and on target with our work.
>
> I will be reviewing every active chart in the hospital, paying particular attention to MTP's [master treatment plans] (being individualized) and documentation of discharge planning notes.
>
> Please re-check your charts and make any additions/deletions changes necessary. The purpose of this is not a witch hunt, but for us all to be ready for the survey!
>
> In addition, for QA [quality assurance], each of you will need to do 10 charts before Thur.
>
> [mentions a social worker's name]—any 10 from 4W
>
> [a second social worker's name]—any 10 from 2W
>
> [a third social worker's name]—I will get with you—if you have time—5 charts from 3W.

I will cover 3W and 5th floor. For this month's QA, do not just note probs [problems], but where you can—actually make the changes on the chart.

This does not mean changing dates, etc. It means if the MTP does not have individualized strategies, then add them. If a signature is needed on the plan, go get it!!

If there are no DC [discharge] planning notes, review the chart and add a final soc-services DC note.

Any questions, see me. Realize that these are things we SHOULD ALREADY HAVE BEEN DOING. Thank you.

The social worker plaintiff claimed that the memo constituted a directive to the staff to alter the records, if necessary, to cover up any omissions. She said that the director did not instruct the staff to indicate that the record had been amended and claimed that he wanted staff to participate in his attempt to deceive the accreditation team. Her view was that making entries in records of cases on which they had not worked was unconscionable and that this was what the director was asking staff to do.

The social worker–plaintiff claimed that she was forced to resign her position because of her refusal to participate in the director's plan. She alleged that she was given an ultimatum to either quit her job or be fired. In the lawsuit she alleged that she lost wages, her career was interrupted, and she experienced serious mental anguish as a result of the incident and her employment termination.

The director of social work defended his actions and the statements in his memo. The director claimed that aspects of the social worker's job performance were unacceptable and that on one occasion the worker had violated patients' privacy rights. What follows is an excerpt from the director's deposition, conducted by the social worker's attorney (I have excerpted a significant portion of this deposition to illustrate the fine detail that is often examined during this aspect of legal proceedings, usually called pretrial discovery):

Q: . . . Can you tell me what happened that led to her [the plaintiff's] termination then in September?

A: On September 20th we were having a group Social Service meeting. We had invited—there were two Social Work interns—I'm not sure if it was their first day, but possibly the first day they had ever seen or been in [the hospital]—and they were invited to also attend the meeting. And we had a survey approaching, I think with [the accreditation organization], I'm not sure if it was—yeah, it was [the accreditation organization].

Q: That's the national psychiatric hospital group you referred to at the beginning?

A: You know what that is.

Q: Okay.

A: And in that meeting, what I—I told each of the employees to make—part of QA—back to QA—is an ongoing, where you check your active charts to make sure that treatment plans accurately reflect the services that are being provided. So, I encouraged all of the Social Workers to continue to do that.

Q: So, in other words, keep your charts up to snuff?

A: Well, what that would mean would be: if a patient was receiving medication. And where you see that would be in the Process Notes and the Progress Notes. If a nurse administered the meds it's documented. If a patient gets activities therapy, it's documented. If nursing encourages and gets a patient's feelings, she'll document it. And if the Master Treatment Plan does not document those procedures and services that are being performed, then we have an inaccurate record.

Q: And that was the Social Worker's responsibility?

A: Correct.

Q: To make sure that the Master Treatment Plan reflected what was actually happening?

A: Correct.

Q: Okay.

A: I instructed them on their active charts to make sure and do that. And I also told each of them to pull ten charts of discharged patients and to review the Progress Notes and compare it to the treatment plan to see if there were any procedures that had been done which were not documented on the treatment plan, which would be an inaccurate chart. And if they were documented, the Progress Notes, to add those procedures on to the treatment plan, to document what was actually being done.

Q: Was this like the usual treatment, a QA, if they didn't do their own or did they do other people's?

A: This was like when they were doing other people's; ten random charts.

Q: So, this was on patients they had never seen?

A: Correct.

Q: Now, [what] was usual procedure on QA?

A: I would usually get feedback from QA on exactly those same issues routinely, and they would routinely do that on the active charts.

Q: So, they would routinely do it on the active charts which are their own, or other people's?

A: Their own.

Q: Okay. And this was different in that these were not their own?

A: They would routinely give feedback on those exact issues whether it was an active record or closed charts which were not their own.

Q: But in this case, they're going to the medical records you've described, picking out random charts, and they are to see whether the Progress Notes and treatment notes matched, and if they don't, they're to add them—

A: Not if they match.

Q: Not if they match?

A: See, if there is—to see if there's documentation of services or procedures received in the Progress Notes that that is also documented on the Master Treatment Plan.

Q: Okay. But these were patients who had closed charts?

A: Correct. Actually, it wasn't a closed chart, really, until they did that, because it was inaccurate record.

Q: But, routinely, it was the job of the Social Worker who worked with that patient to do this, not people who had never seen them?

A: Routinely, on the active charts the Social Workers would do that and they would routinely give me feedback on those same issues on closed charts . . .

Q: Why was this time, on the 20th of September, any different than what had been done in the past? Why did you ask them to do this?

A: I probably should have done that all along. Because what was leaving was— they would give me the feedback—I was leaving inaccurate records. I was leaving a treatment plan which didn't accurately reflect what actually happened to the patients. So in retrospect, I probably should have had them do it all of the time.

Q: Go back in and fix up closed charts?

A: No, go back in and make sure the treatment plan reflects accurately the procedures that are actually performed as documented in the Progress Notes.

Q: On open charts?

A: No, on closed charts.

Q: Okay. So, your view is you should have been doctoring closed charts all of the time?

A: No, no, that's not what I said. My view is, if a closed chart—in the Progress Notes, the patient receives antidepressant medication every day and if the Master Treatment Plan, which is supposed to be a summary of all of the services that are being provided, and the patient's responses to it, doesn't document that they are receiving antidepressant medication, it's an inaccurate chart.

Q: Right. But these are supposed to be contemporaneous records, correct?

A: I'm not sure what you mean.

Q: These things are supposed to be documented at the time the patient's in the hospital, not after the chart's gone to the record room?

A: The chart—it's preferable if as—it is preferable if the chart, on an ongoing basis, accurately reflects what is being performed. That is preferable, if the plan reflects that.

Q: Was this your idea or did someone suggest you do this?

A: This was my idea.

Q: No one suggested it to you?

A: Initially, it was my idea . . .

Q: Now these are closed charts?

A: Correct . . .

Q: And you wanted them to go through the record and add summaries or individual strategies—which you've described as if they were receiving medication or activity—and they were to add them?

A: If there was documentation that they were receiving them.

Q: Okay. How, physically, were they supposed to do that in the record? This is all handwritten?

A: Correct.

Q: And they were just to stick it in where it belonged?

A: To put in under—if it was a medical intervention that was being done and it was documented in the Progress Notes, to add it in the appropriate place on the Master Treatment Plan.

Q: Would anyone looking at this have known that it was added later?

A: I'm not sure.

Q: So, it's possible that there was nothing to say it was or wasn't added later where it was done?

A: I am not sure.

Q: You did some of them didn't you?

A: Yes.

Q: Was there any way, on the ones you did, to tell—for anyone to tell that they were added at a later time then [*sic*] when the chart was closed?

A: Probably not . . .

The social worker who sued was not successful. The lower court dismissed the case, and the social worker lost her subsequent appeal to the state's supreme court, which ruled that there was insufficient evidence that the social work director's instructions to his staff were inappropriate.

In general, if a practitioner finds that accurate details were inadvertently omitted, a possibility in every social worker's professional life, the information can be added, but the record should clearly show that the entry was made subsequently. The social worker should sign and date the change to show that it is an emendment. It is hard to imagine any circumstance in which it would be appropriate for social workers to fill in gaps or make other entries in records for cases on which they did not work.

A troubling form of deceit and fraud that I have encountered concerns social work administrators who produce false accounts of expenditures and other allocations of agency resources. Social work administrators often need to juggle budget categories in order to enhance productivity, access to services, and effectiveness. It is one of the enduring challenges of administrative positions.

However, social work administrators occasionally have been too creative with their budgets, sometimes for self-serving reasons, and end up being deceitful or fraudulent to cover their tracks. The anecdote that follows describes a set of circumstances that I encountered in a community action program.

Joanne M., MSW, was the executive director of a community action program that served a county of 120,000. The agency's services included a meal site for the elderly, heating and fuel assistance, emergency housing assistance, a variety of concrete services for low-income women and their children, and a teen parenting program.

Joanne M. had been director of the program for six years. She was well regarded in the community and by her board of directors. Several staff members, however, were critical of Joanne M.'s administrative style and leadership.

The community agency program depended on federal funds and an annual grant from the state public welfare department to provide casework services to women with young children who were clients of the state welfare program. The funds were used to pay the salaries of three caseworkers and overhead involved in the delivery of services.

During a recent four-month period the program operated with only two caseworkers. One caseworker had been on unpaid leave to take care of an ailing relative. As a result the agency saved about $12,000 in staff salaries.

Joanne M. decided to use the savings to purchase computer equipment that she could use in her own home for, she said, work-related purposes. The funding guidelines, however, prohibited use of the funds for capital expenditures. In her annual accounting and report to the state public welfare department, Joanne M. did not report the one caseworker's four-month leave of absence. She also did not report that the federal and state funds were used to purchase computer equipment. The unauthorized appropriation of funds was uncovered in a random audit by the state auditor general's office. The deputy auditor general then informed Joanne M. that the auditor general was considering taking both civil and criminal action against her.

Although administrators can often justify reallocation of funds to meet agency needs, they must abide by funders' guidelines concerning changes made after the initial allocation. Some funders provide administrators with a margin of flexibility, for example, a 5 percent shift of funds among specified categories, such as personnel or equipment lines. Some funders, however, prohibit any allocation changes without formal authorization. Of course, no funders would permit administrators to siphon funds for their personal use. Any departure from established funding guidelines and administrative practices may expose a social work administrator to civil suits and/or criminal charges. According to the NASW *Code of Ethics,* "Social workers should be diligent stewards of the resources of their employing organizations, wisely conserving funds where appropriate and never misappropriating funds or using them for unintended purposes" (standard 3.09[g]).

DECEPTION AND FRAUD MOTIVATED BY ALTRUISM

In some instances social workers engage in deceit and fraud primarily to help clients. For example, they may eschew damaging diagnostic labels on insurance claim forms to avoid stigmatizing clients. In addition to documenting the extent of overdiagnosis, as described earlier, Kirk and Kutchins (1988) gathered evidence that social workers sometimes underdiagnose, presumably to benefit clients. Some practices observed and reported by Kirk and Kutchins's sample suggest that professionals often misdiagnose in order to help clients, that is, to avoid labeling them. For example, most respondents (87 percent) indicated that a less serious diagnosis than clinically indicated was used frequently or occasionally to avoid labeling clients. Seventy-eight percent reported that they frequently or occasionally used only the least serious of several appropriate diagnoses on official records. Most (82 percent) acknowledged that they frequently or occasionally used the diagnosis of adjustment disorder when a more serious diagnosis might be more accurate.

Social workers might intentionally deceive to benefit clients in other ways as well. Imagine, for example, a social worker who has been providing counseling services to a client, a forty-one-year-old woman, who had been manifesting relatively modest anxiety symptoms. On occasion the client experienced panic attacks, although the attacks tended to be rather mild. The client originally sought counseling from the social worker to help her cope with a conflict-ridden divorce.

After being in counseling with the social worker for about four months, the client one day asked the social worker to write a letter in support of her application for disability benefits. The client said that she was "sick and tired" of her job as a store manager and was finding it difficult to work during the divorce proceedings. The client told the social worker that she—the social worker—would probably need to embellish her letter in order to make a convincing case for disability. The client conceded that a candid report from the social worker would not be helpful, in light of the client's rather mild anxiety symptoms.

The social worker wanted to be supportive of her client and decided to write a convincing, albeit largely embellished, letter to the client's disability insurer. Shortly thereafter an insurance company representative contacted the social worker and at first politely challenged the social worker's assessment of her client's disability. Toward the end of the conversation the insurance company representative told the social worker that she had substantial evidence that the client was not in fact disabled and that the insurance company was concerned that the social worker was helping the client to perpetrate a fraud. The insurance company representative ended the conversation by saying that according to company policy she was obligated to refer the case to the local insurance fraud investigation unit.

Although the social worker was merely trying to be helpful, the embellished letter exposed her to considerable risk. Social workers must be careful to include in letters written on clients' behalf only those details that practitioners can document and substantiate. To do otherwise, even for altruistic reasons, is quite risky.

Social workers should exercise similar caution and reserve when writing reference letters on behalf of agency staff members who may be pursuing positions elsewhere. On occasion social workers will inflate their evaluations of a colleague in the agency to help that individual secure employment. Here too social workers incur considerable risk if they knowingly attest to skills and qualifications that the subject of the letter does not have. The other agency could hire this individual in part because of the social worker's recommendation. If that individual ends up engaging in some negligent action that might have been avoided if the individual had actually had the skills endorsed in the social worker's recommendation letter, the author of the letter could be at risk. While it may seem unlikely that the social worker who wrote the reference letter would be named as a defendant in a lawsuit, this is not a risk worth taking. To be on the safe side social workers should include in recommendation or reference letters only those details they know to be true or have good reason to believe are true.

One final form of deception and fraud concerns social work administrators who fabricate research or program evaluation results to enhance the likelihood of obtaining or retaining funding from some outside source (Wells and Farthing 2008). Social work administrators whose agencies depend on outside funding are under substantial pressure. They have a considerable incentive to present as positive a picture as possible about the agency's efficiency and effectiveness. However, such pressure can prove the downfall of an otherwise competent social work administrator.

Roland M., MSW, was the executive director of the Strathmore Substance Abuse Treatment Center. Strathmore was a private nonprofit agency that was about to begin its seventeenth year of service. The agency received about 60 percent of its revenue from the local Community Fund. The remaining funds were obtained from the state mental health agency's substance abuse division (25 percent) and client fees (15 percent).

One year earlier the Community Fund implemented new guidelines for member agencies. For the first time in its history the Community Fund was insisting on program evaluation data to demonstrate the effectiveness of services provided with its money. Member agencies were to collaborate with Community Fund staff to determine an acceptable program evaluation strategy. Most consisted of relatively simple outcome measures using primary and secondary data. In Strathmore's case the Community Fund wanted program staff members to collect data on lengths of stays in the residential component of the program, relapse rates, and costs per unit of service.

Roland M. was nervous about the program evaluation. Given that he depended on the Community Fund for such a large portion of his budget, he felt he could not afford unfavorable results. At the suggestion of the Community Fund's staff, Roland M. and his board of directors retained an outside evaluator, a consultant from the local school of social work. The consultant conducted the study over a nine-month period. Some of the most significant results were disappointing and unflattering. Roland M. was especially concerned about the discouraging data on relapse rates and program dropouts.

Unbeknown to the consultant, Roland M. modified several facts and figures in the consultant's final report in order to shed a more favorable light on the agency. However, an astute Community Fund staff member noticed a couple of inconsistencies in the report and telephoned the consultant for an explanation. The consultant and the Community Fund staff shortly found that Roland M. had altered some results. As a consequence Strathmore lost its Community Fund subsidy, and the Community Fund threatened to sue to recover a portion of the current year's allocation that was based in part on the report's results.

Relatively few social workers actively engage in deceit and fraud. Among those who do, some are motivated primarily by self-interest and greed. Their sleight of hand is designed to exploit others in order to line their own pockets or advance their own careers.

Others, however, have more altruistic intentions. These social workers may be moved by clients' plights or genuine concern about the financial stability and future of the agency that they administer. Their more noble motives do not excuse whatever deceit and fraud they engage in, of course. Nonetheless these social workers' actions contrast markedly with those of their self-centered colleagues whose deceit and fraud are driven essentially by self-interest.

And, human nature being what it is, in many instances social workers' deceitful and fraudulent activities depend on mixed motives. That is, social workers are inspired by simultaneous concern about themselves and others. An example of this phenomenon is social workers who submit fraudulent diagnoses to insurance companies to help clients obtain needed services and to enhance their own income.

Whatever the motives—whether singularly self-interested or altruistic, or mixed—social workers need to be cognizant of deceit and fraud in the ranks. They must avoid whatever temptation exists in their own work to deceive and defraud—if for no other reason than to avoid the accompanying liability risks—and they must engage in preventative efforts to discourage deception and fraud elsewhere in the profession.

8

Termination of Service

MANY MALPRACTICE AND LIABILITY RISKS also arise in relation to the termination of services. In my experience the most frequent problems concern allegations that professionals failed to terminate services properly, failed to continue needed services, or were unavailable to clients who were in need of care. Improper termination of service might occur, for instance, when a social worker transfers to a new position or moves out of town without adequately preparing a client for the termination or without referring a client to a new service provider. Or, a social worker might terminate services abruptly to a client who is noncompliant or because a client is unable to pay for the care. The advent of online and other long-distance counseling services introduces novel termination risks when social workers are not available to assist clients they never meet in person (Kraus, Stricker, and Speyer 2011; Reamer 2012c, 2013b). Social workers also risk liability when they are unavailable and fail to properly instruct clients about how to handle emergencies that may arise.

THE CONCEPT OF ABANDONMENT

A substantial portion of claims regarding termination of services involves allegations of abandonment. Abandonment is a legal concept that refers to instances when a professional is not available to a client when needed. Once a social worker begins to provide service to a client, whether in person or remotely (for example, using online or other distance counseling services), he incurs a legal responsibility to sustain that service or to properly refer a client to an alternative service provider. Social workers are not, of course, obligated to serve every individual who requests assistance. The social worker might not have room for a new client or may lack the specialized expertise a particular client may need.

However, once a social worker begins service, she cannot terminate it abruptly. Rather social workers are obligated to conform to the profession's standard of care regarding termination of service and referral to other providers in the event the client is still in need (Edwards, Edwards, and Wells 2012). As Schutz suggests with respect to termination of psychotherapy services, "Once a patient makes a contact with a therapist and the therapist agrees to see him, he is that therapist's patient. The therapist then assumes the fiduciary duty not to abandon the patient. At the very least, therefore, he must refer the patient to another therapist if he elects to terminate the relationship" (1982:50).

Social workers have to be careful not to extend services to clients beyond the point where they are warranted, clinically or otherwise. According to the NASW *Code of Ethics,* "Social workers should terminate services to clients and professional relationships with them when such services and relationships are no longer required or no longer serve the clients' needs or interests" (standard 1.16[a]). But as the case that follows illustrates, social workers sometimes fail to terminate services when termination is in the client's best interest.

Scott N., MSW, was in solo private practice. He had begun his private practice approximately six months earlier after working for seven years at a local community mental health center. Scott N. decided to begin his private practice to enhance his autonomy and to get away from what was beginning to feel like onerous bureaucracy at the community mental health center.

Scott N. knew that building up his client base would take a number of months and that his income would be modest during this period. He was concerned, however, about the relatively small number of referrals and inquiries that he had been receiving. The stagnant local economy exacerbated the problem because fewer people could afford private social work services, and the relatively high unemployment rate in the community meant that fewer people had third-party coverage for mental health services.

With two children in college Scott N. was getting more and more nervous about being able to pay his bills. One consequence was that he avoided terminating three clients who clinically were ready for termination. Scott N.

intentionally prolonged their treatment in order to sustain the revenue that these clients generated.

Two different insurance companies, both of which had contracts with managed-care firms, covered the services for these clients. At specified junctures in the treatment process Scott N. had to telephone the managed-care companies to seek approval for additional sessions with these clients. In his conversations with the managed-care representatives, Scott N. had to exaggerate their symptoms to make the case for such approval.

A social worker who fails to terminate properly and in the process attempts to deceive an insurance company obviously incurs risk. Clients may be upset about the prolonged treatment, and third-party payers may sue to recover fees that they paid the practitioner. Thus social workers must be particularly careful to avoid extending services beyond what is warranted, clinically or otherwise.

PREMATURE TERMINATION

More common, however, are instances in which the social worker terminates service to a client prematurely. Premature termination can occur for several different reasons. First, clients may initiate the termination of services, perhaps against the advice of social workers and other professionals involved in their care. Second, the social worker or other professional might initiate the termination, as when the practitioner finds that a particular client is not making adequate progress or is unable to pay for services. In addition social workers who find a particular client too difficult to handle are at risk of terminating services inappropriately. Clients who object to a social worker's decision to terminate services may file a lawsuit or licensing board complaint.

Client-Initiated Termination

Clients in residential and nonresidential programs sometimes decide unilaterally that they do not want to continue receiving services. Clients may leave residential programs against professional advice or may decide not to return for outpatient services.

In a South Dakota case, for example, a psychiatric patient who had a history of violence was taken on an outing and escaped, thereby terminating service. No one notified police of the man's dangerousness for about twelve hours after the escape. The patient broke into a home and killed a woman and her daughter. The plaintiff alleged that allowing the patient to go on the outing and not notifying law enforcement officials that the man was dangerous constituted negligence on the part of the psychiatrists in charge of the patient. The case was settled for $950,000 ("Patient Escapes" 1990:6).

In *Boles v. Milwaukee County* (1989) a woman with a history of mental illness was brought to a hospital emergency room after her sister observed her striking herself repeatedly. Because of this self-destructive behavior emergency room personnel placed the woman in restraints. Within less than thirty minutes the patient told a nurse that she felt better and wanted to return home. Before a psychiatrist arrived for a consultation, the woman left the hospital, shouted at cars, struck them with her hands, and was struck and killed by a car when she ran into the street.

The woman's children sued the hospital, claiming that staff failed to properly detain her in order to make an appropriate assessment. The appellate court affirmed the lower court's finding in favor of the family, concluding that the hospital's failure to detain the patient until completion of the psychiatric examination was "palpably negligent" ("Hospital Liable for Failing to Detain" 1990:4).

However, a Texas jury did not hold a hospital liable for injuries sustained by a patient who essentially terminated his own services by fleeing from the hospital. The plaintiff, a voluntary psychiatric patient at the hospital, and two other patients fled the building and were pursued by hospital employees. The plaintiff climbed a fence and ran along the shoulder of a highway, attempted to cross the lanes, tripped, and was hit by a truck. The plaintiff's leg was shattered and required extensive and repeated surgery. He argued that the hospital staff breached the standard of care in pursuing a voluntary patient and attempting to restrain him against his will ("Psychiatric Patient Injured" 1990:5).

Social Worker-Initiated Termination

In contrast a social worker's decision to terminate a client might result in premature termination. In residential programs, for example, staff members may terminate a client prematurely because they find that the client is not making adequate progress, they want to open up a bed for a client who will generate a higher reimbursement rate because of insurance coverage, or the client's insurance benefits have run out. Of course, premature termination sometimes occurs because of poor clinical judgment about the client's readiness for community-based living.

In 1981 a Kansas man sued a hospital and its doctors, claiming that his son was discharged prematurely. The son had been involuntarily admitted to a state hospital after an assault on his grandparents. During his stay at the state hospital staff members decided that the son should be transferred to a hospital in Salem, Oregon. However, the Kansas hospital's clinical director, who had never had contact with the patient, sent a note to the leader of the treatment team at his hospital stating that the patient is "physically healthy and suffers from a character disorder and . . . furthermore is not motivated for treatment. It rather looks to me that we should discharge this patient." The patient was discharged and killed his mother and brother.

The defendants in the suit disagreed about the reason for the discharge. The clinical director testified that the patient was discharged because he demonstrated no motivation for treatment; the treatment team, however, stated that he was discharged because he was "doing so well."

The federal district court in Kansas held that the hospital and doctors were negligent in discharging the patient prematurely and in not conducting an adequate assessment to determine his readiness for discharge. The court awarded the father $67,300 in damages (Austin, Moline, and Williams 1990:215–17).

A 1991 New York case raised similar issues. The plaintiff, a young woman, sued the New York City Health and Hospitals Corporation, alleging that a city hospital prematurely released and terminated services to a seriously disturbed woman who subsequently injured the plaintiff. The plaintiff had been waiting on a subway platform in New York City when the disturbed woman, released from the hospital the previous month, pushed the plaintiff in front of an oncoming train. The plaintiff sustained serious injuries, including blindness in one eye and various other head injuries; she experienced memory loss and permanent injury to her head, face, arms, legs, a hip, and abdomen.

In her lawsuit the plaintiff claimed that the hospital had discharged her attacker prematurely. The week before her release the disturbed woman had been restrained in a straitjacket after various acts of violence against herself and others. Just before her release the hospital kept the woman in the

highest form of security, and her treating physician noted her lack of understanding and concern about her treatment program upon release. The physician stated that he doubted the woman could succeed in her treatment
program. A jury awarded the plaintiff $1.5 million ("Government Liable"
1992:4).

A Texas jury also entered a judgment against a hospital in the case of a
son who killed his father. The father had sought emergency psychiatric care
and detention for his son. The son had been hospitalized four times and
had been diagnosed with chronic schizophrenia. The son was prescribed
neuroleptic (antipsychotic) medication but was released before anyone
administered the medication or monitored for its effectiveness. The next
morning the son killed his father. The plaintiffs claimed that the hospital
was negligent because it failed to detain the son and follow through with
proper treatment ("Man Murdered" 1992:6).

An Indiana man sued an agency after he was discharged and then
injured himself. The plaintiff had been admitted to a state hospital after a
suicide attempt and was discharged the following day. Later the same day
he attempted suicide again by pouring flammable substances over his body
and igniting them. He suffered extensive burns. The case was settled, with
the State of Indiana's Patient Compensation Fund paying him $300,000
and the doctor's insurance company paying $100,000 ("Man Claims
Improper Discharge" 1990:6).[1]

In a Pennsylvania case the plaintiff was a woman who had a history of
self-destructive behavior and had been hospitalized for treatment of severe
mental illness. She was then released to another individual's custody. The
plaintiff locked her custodian out of her own house and then drank or
ingested lye. In her lawsuit the plaintiff alleged that she had been released
inappropriately, particularly given that the hospital and other defendants
were aware of her history of mental illness, destructive behavior, and suicidal tendencies. The jury awarded $140,000 in damages against the hospi-
tal ("Patient Released" 1989:3).

Courts do not always find social service staff and agencies liable when
discharged clients subsequently harm another individual or themselves.

For example, in North Carolina a mental health center and one of its
psychiatrists were sued after a recently discharged client killed a fifty-eight-
year-old man in a knife fight. The client, who had been admitted to the

center in an intoxicated state, had been discharged after being examined by a staff psychiatrist. The plaintiffs alleged that releasing the client and terminating services to him constituted negligence. The defendants argued that they had no legal justification to continue involuntary commitment of the client. In 1989 a jury found in the defendants' favor ("Mental Health Facility" 1990:2).

A California court also found a hospital and its staff were not liable in injuries sustained by a patient injured in a suicide attempt. The plaintiff, a nineteen-year-old survivor of incest who had a history of suicide attempts and severe depression, was admitted voluntarily to the psychiatric unit of a local medical center. Shortly after admission, however, staff learned that the woman's insurance coverage would not cover the admission. The woman was discharged despite her adamant request to remain; she had promised to borrow the money to enable her to stay hospitalized.

Several hours after discharge the woman attempted suicide by driving her automobile off a cliff. She suffered severe injuries that required hospitalization for three and one-half months. The woman claimed that her psychiatric treatment was inadequate and was inappropriately terminated in light of her suicidal symptoms. Hospital staff, however, argued that the woman's financial status was unrelated to reasons for discharge and that termination of service was consistent with the standard of care ("Woman Claims She Was Improperly Discharged" 1989:2).

The liability risks associated with premature discharge when a patient's insurance benefits have been exhausted are addressed in a North Carolina case. The parents of a sixteen-year-old boy sued the hospital, claiming that their son's suicide was the result of premature discharge when the insurance coverage ran out. The boy had been admitted to the psychiatric hospital and remained there until two days after his insurance coverage was exhausted. Two weeks after discharge the boy committed suicide by taking a drug overdose.

The parents argued that they received no warning that their son was suicidal, that family therapy was not provided, and that the agency to which the hospital had referred the boy for follow-up care did not receive adequate information about his condition.

The psychiatrist involved in the case settled out of court for $90,000. A jury awarded the parents $7.09 million against the hospital ($1.09 million in compensatory damages and $6 million in punitive damages), although the trial judge reduced the compensatory damage award slightly (to $1.03 million) ("Teenager Commits Suicide by Taking Drug" 1992:1).

In another North Carolina case a twenty-five-year-old man was admitted to a hospital for treatment of suicidal ideation. The hospital determined that the man's insurance would cover a twelve-day stay. The patient expressed concern about being discharged but was released when his insurance coverage ran out. The next day the man shot and killed himself. The plaintiffs alleged that the man had been discharged only because his insurance coverage ran out and not because of his clinical status. The parties reached a $3 million settlement ("Man Discharged from Psychiatric Facility" 1994:4).[2]

Social workers in private agency-based practice and other outpatient settings have been known to terminate clients prematurely when they find them resistant, hostile, uncooperative, or otherwise difficult to handle. I am familiar with a case in which a social worker was sued by a former client who claimed that the social worker terminated her relationship with the client abruptly and precipitously. The severely disabled woman had sought counseling from a social worker who specialized in treatment of people with physical disabilities. After several months of intervention the social worker found it extremely difficult to relate to the client. She claimed that the client was excessively demanding and hostile and was consuming inordinate amounts of her professional time. The social worker said that the client telephoned her frequently and left angry messages when the social worker did not return the call promptly.

The social worker became more and more resentful of the client and during one particularly heated conversation told the client that she would no longer be able to serve her. The client mailed the social worker a certified letter asking for an explanation, but the social worker refused to accept the letter. In addition the social worker made no attempt to provide the client with names of other practitioners whom she could contact for assistance.

Although the social worker's frustration in this case may be understandable, her virtual abandonment of her client, including her refusal to accept the client's letter, is not. According to the NASW *Code of Ethics,*

> Social workers should take reasonable steps to avoid abandoning clients who are still in need of services. Social workers should withdraw services precipitously only under unusual circumstances, giving careful

consideration to all factors in the situation and taking care to minimize possible adverse effects. Social workers should assist in making appropriate arrangements for continuation of services when necessary.

(standard 1.16[b])

Social workers who anticipate the termination or interruption of services to clients should notify clients promptly and seek the transfer, referral, or continuation of services in relation to the clients' needs and preferences.

(standard 1.16[e])

As R. Cohen states,

No doctor in private practice is legally compelled to accept any patient for treatment. The mental health professional may feel that he does not have the expertise to deal with a particular problem; he may not have the number of hours needed to provide adequate services; he may not see himself as able to establish a good enough rapport with the patient; the patient may not be able to pay the doctor's fee, etc. But while there are any number of perfectly acceptable reasons for refusing to treat a patient, there is *no* reason to justify abandonment of a patient once treatment begins. Before accepting a new patient, the mental health professional would be wise to schedule an initial consultation for the purpose of a mutual evaluation of suitability. If a doctor accepts a patient but some time later believes he can no longer be of value (because, for example, he has discovered factors operating that are beyond his competence to deal with), "following through" would mean advising this patient of the state of affairs and referring him to an appropriate mental health professional.

(1979:273)

The reasons for termination of care were the central issue in a Missouri case. A thirteen-year-old boy was being seen as an outpatient at a state hospital. According to the plaintiffs—the boy's parents—they met with the treating physician two and one-half weeks before their son committed suicide, and informed the doctor of their son's suicide threats. A psychiatric resident who had seen the boy had referred the parents to the physician. The physician diagnosed the boy's condition as panic anxiety accompanied by a preoccupation with death. He saw the boy during the next two days, prescribed medication, and removed himself from the case five days after his consultation with the boy's parents.

The resident's notes, however, did not indicate that the other physician had removed himself from the case or that he had transferred the boy back to the original treatment team at the state hospital. Two original team members were no longer available (one had left the job and another was on vacation).

After discharge the boy committed suicide, just as he had threatened, by driving a car into a concrete embankment. Four teenage passengers in the car also died. The boy's family alleged, among other claims, that the treating physician's termination of his involvement in the case was improper. The doctor argued that he removed himself from the case because he thought the care provided by the treatment team would be adequate. He also claimed that his withdrawal from the case was not the proximate cause of the boy's death, that the death resulted from an accident, not suicide, and that the parents were at fault in allowing the boy to have access to car keys and in their monitoring of his medication. The jury awarded the parents $750,000 but under the doctrine of comparative negligence reduced the award by 25 percent because of fault by the parents ("Parents Allege Failure" 1990:4).

Social workers in managed care settings need to be particularly careful about the ways in which they terminate services. If clients' insurance companies refuse to authorize services or an extension of services, social workers should be sure to advise clients of their right to appeal the decision and offer to assist the client with the appeal process. Otherwise social workers may expose themselves to allegations that they abandoned their clients (Corcoran and Vandiver 1996; Edwards, Edwards, and Wells 2012; Reamer 2001c; Strom-Gottfried 1999). According to Madden:

> The provider's duty is to give all of the care that is necessary to the client, regardless of the decision of the managed care company to authorize payment for the services. Although this may seem unduly burdensome on clinicians, particularly those in a private practice setting, these are important legal guidelines that protect clients while not causing undue financial hardship to the clinician. The decision to terminate treatment must be based on clinical evidence, not managed care authorization (Corcoran & Vandiver 1996). The duty of the clinician is to seek approval, through any and all

appeals processes, if continued treatment is indicated. Further, the clinician should try to make arrangements with the client for payment including such options as reduced fee/sliding scale options. Alternatively, the clinician may refer the client to an agency that provides reduced fee or free services. As noted above, the referral process should be carefully attended to so as to ensure that the client actually receives the services. This issue comes down to a decision by the mental health care provider to decide whether to run the risk of a malpractice suit by not providing treatment that is judged to be necessary by the clinician but not by the managed care company.

(1998:141–42)

Also, social workers should be scrupulous about the ways in which they handle clients who have not paid overdue bills for services rendered. In general social workers assume considerable risk if they let clients accumulate large debt. As the case of *Geis v. Landau* (1983) illustrates (see chapter 3), courts have been critical of practitioners who have allowed clients to build up large unpaid bills. However, social workers can, in principle, terminate services to clients who have not paid their debts, so long as the practitioners do so ethically. According to the NASW *Code of Ethics,* "Social workers in fee-for-service settings may terminate services to clients who are not paying an overdue balance if the financial contractual arrangements have been made clear to the client, if the client does not pose an imminent danger to self or others, and if the clinical and other consequences of the current nonpayment have been addressed and discussed with the client" (standard 1.16[c]).

Social workers can also be liable for abandonment if they fail to provide clients with sufficient instructions about what to do when the social worker is unavailable because of vacation, illness, or emergencies. This also applies to social workers who provide long-distance counseling services online or through other remote means, for example, video counseling or telephone counseling (Reamer 2013b). Social workers should always provide clients with clearly stated information, including whom to call and how to handle emergencies. I always recommend that social workers provide these instructions to clients in writing and include in the case record a copy of the instructions, signed by the clients to acknowledge that they received the instructions and that the instructions were explained to them.

Social workers should be especially careful to arrange for competent coverage when they know that they will not be available for a period of time. The colleagues who are to provide coverage should be given information about clients' status sufficient to enable them to provide adequate care should the need arise (after obtaining clients' consent to the release of such information, of course).

In light of modern technology social workers should also be careful about checking their own telephone voice mail. To avoid abandonment claims social workers must frequently review messages left by clients. Using remote access to voice mail can facilitate this. It is important to refer clients to a colleague if they need immediate help and the social worker is unavailable. Failure to retrieve messages and provide proper referral could result in a liability claim alleging abandonment.

PREVENTION STRATEGY

Edwards, Edwards, and Wells (2012), Austin, Moline, and Williams (1990), Schutz (1982), and Woody (1997) recommend a number of procedures that social workers can follow to avoid charges of abandonment:

- Provide clients with the names, addresses, and telephone numbers of at least three appropriate referrals when it is necessary to terminate services.
- Follow up with a client who has been terminated. If the client does not go to the referral, write a letter to him about the risks involved should the client not follow through with the referral.
- Clients who will be terminated should be given as much advance warning as possible.
- When clients announce their decision to terminate prematurely, explain to them the risks involved and suggestions for alternative care. Include this information in a follow-up letter.
- Carefully document in the case record all decisions and actions related to termination of services.
- In cases involving discharge of clients from a residential facility, be sure that a comprehensive discharge plan has been formulated and significant others have been notified of the client's discharge (clients should be informed of this). In cases involving clients held in a residential facility by court order, seek legal consultation and court approval before terminating care.
- Provide clients with clear instructions to follow and telephone numbers to use in the event of an emergency. Include a copy of the instructions in

the client's case record. Clients should be asked to sign this copy, affirming that they received the instructions and that the instructions were
explained to them.

- When away from the office for an extended period of time, call in regularly
for messages. Social workers who are away from the office should leave an
emergency telephone number with a secretary, an answering service, or an
answering device. Social workers who anticipate that certain clients may
need assistance during their absence should refer those clients to a colleague with appropriate expertise.

- Social workers who provide online or other long-distance counseling services should ensure that clients understand what steps they should take if
they need emergency assistance.

- Social workers who are leaving an employment setting (for example, to start
a new job) should inform clients of appropriate options for continuation of
services (such as transferring to another service provider or continuing with
the social worker in her new employment setting) and of the benefits and
risks of the options (see NASW *Code of Ethics* [standard 1.16(f)]).

- Consult with colleagues and supervisors about a decision to terminate
services. In some cases addressing relevant issues can prevent termination.
For example, social workers may be able to address a client's reason for not
paying an overdue balance and develop a workable payment plan. Social
workers whose clients are not making reasonable progress may be able to
modify their intervention to enhance the client's progress.

9

Responding to Lawsuits and Ethics Complaints

THE ROLE OF PREVENTION

LEGAL LIABILITY AND LICENSING BOARD complaints are unfortunate risks associated with professional practice. They are also relatively rare occurrences. The vast majority of social workers will never be named as defendants in lawsuits or respondents in licensing board complaints. As I discussed in chapter 1, however, the number of claims against social workers has increased, as has the monetary value of related out-of-court settlements and judgments. In light of this trend social workers need to anticipate the possibility, however remote, that they will be named in a lawsuit or licensing board complaint. Although this book discusses various causes and sources of risk, social workers should also be acquainted with conventional advice about how to respond if they are named as a defendant or respondent, or retained as an expert witness (Barsky and Gould 2002; Bernstein and Hartsell 2004; S. Brodsky 1996, 1999; R. Cohen 1979; Edwards, Edwards, and Wells 2012; Meyer, Landis, and Hays 1988; Rome 2013; Saltzman and Proch 1990; Slater and Finck 2012).

IN THE EVENT OF A LAWSUIT OR LICENSING BOARD COMPLAINT

Assuming a social worker named in a lawsuit holds a liability insurance policy—which every modern social worker should—the insurance company will appoint an attorney to handle the case. Most popular liability insurance companies also cover legal costs associated with licensing board complaints. Social workers who lack liability coverage should consult an

attorney as well; although this can be expensive, social workers who pro-
ceed without skilled legal counsel do so at their own peril. Skilled attorneys familiar with health-care law, litigation, and licensing boards can be
remarkably helpful. When selecting a lawyer, social workers would do well
to follow Besharov's sound advice:

> Basically, selecting a lawyer is like selecting a doctor or a therapist. Personal
> recommendations from friends and colleagues are the best way to identify a
> qualified professional. Ask around. Find social workers or others who have
> been sued, find out who represented them, and ask whether they were sat-
> isfied with the representation they received. Do not be shy. Ask what the
> result was, and ask how expensive the lawyer was. Even workers who were
> represented by counsel provided by insurance companies can provide help-
> ful leads. Most lawyers who handle insurance cases also handle individual
> clients. . . .
>
> As potential lawyers are being identified, the social worker will have to
> decide whether to hire a general practitioner or a specialist. Many lawyers
> still maintain general practices, handling a variety of commercial, tax, fi-
> nancial, real estate, and torts cases. In smaller communities, there may be
> no choice but to hire a general practitioner. In larger communities, though,
> there will be a wide choice of specialists. (In fact, some lawyers specialize in
> plaintiff's tort work, while others specialize in defense work.)
>
> A specialist is more likely to do a satisfactory job handling the case than
> is a generalist unfamiliar or only marginally familiar with the relevant area
> of the law. This is crucial in the area of criminal law. *Under no circumstances
> should a lawyer with no experience in criminal matters be retained to handle
> a criminal case.* A lawyer who has never before handled a criminal case—or
> who has insubstantial experience—is simply incompetent to do so. In fact,
> an ethical lawyer conscious of this reality should decline to represent a per-
> son charged with a crime. The stakes are too high to have the lawyer learn
> while doing.
>
> (1985:199–200)

In many instances a social worker's employer (for example, a government or private agency) will retain an attorney to handle the lawsuit. The
social worker should be sure to talk with the attorney about whether the
attorney is planning to represent the social worker or only the agency.

Social workers who have been sued may be wise to retain their own lawyer because the attorney retained by the employer may be obligated, first and foremost, to protect the employer's interests. This could create a conflict of interest, particularly if the employer believes that the social worker, not the employer, was somehow negligent. Having one's own malpractice and liability policy—apart from the policy held by one's employer—provides access to an attorney whose sole mission is defending the social worker.

For a social worker sued or named in a licensing board complaint, reacting as calmly and thoughtfully as possible is important. This can be difficult, of course, given the traumatizing nature of legal proceedings. Ultimately a carefully planned response will be more effective than an impulsive one.

The first step is to notify the insurer of the lawsuit or complaint. The best course is to make a telephone call and to follow this with a certified letter and a copy of the letter sent by the plaintiff's attorney or, in the case of a licensing board complaint, the complainant. Although it is often tempting to talk with the client (or whoever the plaintiff or complainant is) about the lawsuit, the social worker should refrain from doing so. In fact discussing the case with anyone other than the attorney retained to defend the social worker is generally a mistake.

The plaintiff's attorney usually asks for copies of case record material and other relevant documents. As I discussed in chapter 7, social workers must not alter records to fill in gaps or create false impressions. Not only is this wrong but the plaintiff's attorney may have already seen unaltered copies of this material and will find the alteration. This would of course be disastrous.

A social worker named in a lawsuit commonly is asked to give a deposition, a sworn statement obtained in question-and-answer form before the trial (the discovery phase of litigation). A key goal of depositions is to promote settlement and minimize trial time. Some depositions are conducted remotely using videoconferencing technology, particularly when witnesses live a considerable distance from the lawyers' location. The plaintiff's attorney poses a series of questions, and the entire proceeding is recorded in order to prepare a transcript.

The primary purpose of a deposition is to obtain the social worker's version of what happened in the case and to provide leads that may be relevant. Of course, the social worker's attorney also has the option to depose the plaintiff and other parties who may be involved in the case (for example, family members of the client, colleagues of the social worker, or expert witnesses whose specialized knowledge may be drawn on by the plaintiff or defendant). R. Cohen offers a series of helpful guidelines for handling a deposition (some of this discussion also pertains to testimony in court or a licensing board hearing):

1. The first rule is to be honest. You are under oath and should be telling the truth at all times. If you do not tell the truth you may be subject to criminal charges. Additionally, if it can be demonstrated that there are falsehoods in your sworn testimony on any point (however minor), then your credibility on other points will be called into question.

2. Do not answer any question unless you are absolutely certain that you understand it fully. Do not be embarrassed to ask for as much clarification as you need or to say "I don't know."

3. If you are uncertain of your facts, state them as forthrightly as possible. On the other hand, if you are asked a question to which you really are not 100 percent certain of the facts it is all right to use qualifiers such as, "My best recollection is . . . "; "As best as I can recall . . . "; and "I believe. . . ."

4. If you are concerned about how to answer the examiner on some sensitive aspect of the case, or you believe that your answer might prove to be embarrassing, discuss the issue fully with your attorney before the deposition. Together you can decide if the matter is relevant to the case and, if so, what position to take.

5. The examiner may ask you what patient charts, documents, textbooks, or other sources you have consulted in preparing for your deposition. If you are a witness appearing on someone else's behalf he will probably ask you about the financial arrangements that have been made concerning your appearance at the deposition and your participation in the case. Be prepared for such questions by discussing them in advance with your attorney.

6. At any time during the deposition you may ask to have a private conference with your attorney. Similarly, you may at any time ask for a break if you are becoming fatigued or uncomfortable.

7. The well-known Army rule "never volunteer" is most appropriate as regards making a deposition. Do not volunteer any information that you are not specifically asked. Short answers—"yes" or "no" when possible—are best. Do not volunteer to look anything up, obtain any records, or do anything at all unless your attorney has advised you to do so. Do not volunteer

the name of someone who might know the answer to a question, and do not volunteer opinions if you are not asked for them.

8. Be cautious about deciding on which patient charts, notes, documents, or other memoranda you wish to bring with you into the deposition room, as the examiner may ask to look at such materials. It is therefore a good idea to have your attorney approve whatever it is you wish to bring with you.

9. If the examiner has in his possession a patient's chart or some other document and he asks you questions about it, read it over carefully before replying.

10. It is usually a good idea to wait a moment or two before answering any question during the deposition (as opposed to the trial). The brief pause will provide you with additional time to get your answer the way you want it, and it will provide your attorney with the time to raise any objections he might have to the question. If your attorney instructs you not to answer the question do not answer it, even if you think it will help your case to do so.

11. Speak slowly when answering all questions, and stop talking if your attorney interrupts. You may ask for some time to think about an answer to a question if the question is particularly difficult or complicated. Remember, the written transcript of your deposition will not reflect how long it took you to answer any questions, so do not feel pressured into giving quick answers.

12. If the opposing lawyers get into an argument, stay out of it. You should, however, listen carefully to what is being said and be particularly attentive to the point that your own counsel is trying to make. Such disagreements may alert you to an aspect of the case to which you may not have given due consideration before the deposition.

13. Some examiners may try to provoke you to the point where your judgment and memory is [sic] somewhat clouded. Methods of rattling you will vary, but a common technique is to accuse you of being inconsistent in your testimony. Alternatively, the examiner may refer to some document or record that your testimony supposedly contradicts. Be prepared for such contingencies, and do not let the examiner succeed in his goal. Be courteous and professional at all times.

14. Some examiners may appear to be exceptionally concerned, friendly, and understanding. In some instances this is a ploy designed to obtain

more from you than you are willing to give. The examiner is not your buddy. During the deposition the examiner will probably be sizing you up in terms of where your weak spots are as a witness on the stand. Therefore, you should be cordial but not overly friendly or anxious to please. If you are there to impress the examiner with anything, it is your credibility and self-confidence as a witness.

15. At some point in the deposition the examiner may attempt to summarize what you have said. Listen carefully to what he says when he is supposedly paraphrasing your testimony. Do not let him put words in your mouth. If what he is saying is not what you meant to say, do not hesitate to say so. Also, be aware of the fact that you can have any portion of your testimony read back to you at your request.

(1979:277–78)

One of my attorney friends also offers these suggestions:

- Remember, you can't win a case in a deposition—you can only lose. Be a goalie.
- Depositions are not normal conversations. Everything counts.
- Do not show your anxiety by answering quickly. Pause before answering, and do not offer any visual cues to your uncertainty.

After the court reporter has prepared the deposition transcript, the social worker should read a copy and correct any errors before signing it. It is wise to review the transcript again before going to court to testify, should the case get that far.

While many suggestions concerning depositions also apply to actual courtroom testimony, some do not. For example, many trial attorneys believe that pausing or hesitating too much can raise doubt in a jury's mind about a witness's credibility. Also, how the social worker appears at a trial—with regard to dress (conservative professional dress is usually recommended) and manner—counts much more than it does at a deposition. Jurors often react to subtleties related to a witness's physical appearance, gestures, and mannerisms.

On the witness stand the social worker must be careful not to use too much professional jargon or to appear cocky, cavalier, arrogant, condescending, insincere, crude, overly technical, or overbearing. When responding to a question that is difficult to answer, saying simply "I don't know" is fine and often desirable. Contriving an answer in order to sound knowledgeable can backfire.

Maintaining composure on the witness stand, despite an opposing attorney's best efforts to be provocative, is especially important. Social workers need to be aware that litigation is an adversarial process, and the job of opposing attorneys is to do their best to challenge and discredit the witness's testimony.[1]

As Saltzman and Proch observe,

> Attorneys use a variety of tactics to discredit witnesses and their testimony during cross examination. They use leading questions which require a yes or no answer when no such simple answer is possible or when it would be misleading. They may be condescending, attacking, or overly friendly. They may ask repetitious questions in an attempt to make you answer inconsistently or they may badger you. They may reverse your words. And they may question you about your personal beliefs and your personal life to show possible bias or prejudice or motive to lie. For example, in a child custody case involving a gay father, you may be asked your sexual preference, if you believe in the Bible, or if you know anyone who died of AIDS.
>
> The important point to remember when faced with such tactics is that this is part of the system and not something that is happening to just you. Your best defense is to remain alert and calm. Resist being lulled into a false sense of security when an attorney seems overly friendly and resist becoming defensive or hostile when an attorney seems to be attacking you.
>
> (1990:61)

A special problem sometimes arises when a social worker who is on the witness stand attempts to characterize a former client as having a major mental illness. This might occur if a former client sues a social worker and during the trial the social worker attempts to convey the impression that the client is unstable. R. Cohen refers to this as the "What's-wrong-with-that?" phenomenon:

> Many mental health professionals, to their detriment, make what might be termed "What's-wrong-with-that? (WWT)" errors in their court testimony. When a supposedly revealing statement about a patient's pathology compels

the majority of the jury to ask themselves, "What's wrong with that?" a WWT error has been made.

For example, suppose "Mr. Citizen," the patient, is forcibly taken from his home by the police, handcuffed, and packed into a police car in full view of his friends and neighbors. And suppose "Dr. Smith," a psychiatrist, testifies that the patient was verbally abusive and hostile to the therapist on admission. Jury members are likely to ask themselves, "What's wrong with that? Who wouldn't be verbally abusive and hostile under such conditions?" This is especially true if Mr. Citizen appears to be composed and "normal" in the courtroom. Smith may compound his WWT error by going on to say something like, "Further, Mr. Citizen denied that he was mentally ill." Again, jury members—who are more likely to identify with a patient than a psychiatrist—are likely to ask themselves, "What's wrong with that? I would deny it under the same circumstances."

To weaken his testimony still further, Smith might testify that the patient's denial of mental illness demonstrated lack of insight, which was evidence of mental illness. Although all of Smith's statements might make sense to experienced mental health professionals, they will probably not make much sense to the lay people of the jury. WWT errors can be avoided with some forethought, factual documentation, and practice in presenting professional opinion to lay audiences.

(1979:280–81)

Social workers need to be completely candid with their attorney to enable the attorney to prepare the strongest defense possible. Attorneys hate nothing more than surprises in the courtroom or licensing board hearing, particularly when the opposing attorney reveals damaging information that the attorney's client failed to disclose ahead of time. It is important to be forthright with your own attorney.[2]

THE ROLE OF THE EXPERT WITNESS

Social workers sometimes serve as expert witnesses. In litigation social workers may be expert witnesses on behalf of plaintiffs or defendants. In licensing board cases social workers may be expert witnesses on behalf of respondents (social workers accused of violating licensing standards) or a licensing board.

An expert witness is a witness, who by virtue of education, training, skill, or experience, is believed to have expertise and specialized knowledge in a particular subject beyond that of the average person. This expertise and specialized knowledge should enable others to officially and legally rely upon the witness's specialized (scientific, technical, or other) opinion about an evidence or fact issue within the scope of her expertise to assist the fact finder (judge, jury, or licensing board).

In U.S. courts, under Federal Rule of Evidence 702, an expert witness must be qualified on the topic of testimony. In determining the qualifications of the expert, the Federal Rules of Evidence require that the expert have specialized education, training, or practical experience in the subject matter relating to the case. More specifically Rule 702 states:

> A witness who is qualified as an expert by knowledge, skill, experience, training, or education may testify in the form of an opinion or otherwise if:
>
> (a) the expert's scientific, technical, or other specialized knowledge will help the trier of fact to understand the evidence or to determine a fact in issue;
>
> (b) the testimony is based on sufficient facts or data;
>
> (c) the testimony is the product of reliable principles and methods; and
>
> (d) the expert has reliably applied the principles and methods to the facts of the case.

Most courts of law follow what is known as the *Daubert* standard regarding the admissibility of testimony from an expert witness. The trial judge uses the *Daubert* standard to make a preliminary assessment of whether an expert's scientific testimony is based on reasoning or methodology that is scientifically valid and can properly be applied to the facts at issue. Under this standard the factors that may be considered in determining whether the methodology is valid are (1) whether the theory or technique in question can be and has been tested; (2) whether it has been subjected to peer review and publication; (3) its known or potential error rate; (4) the existence and maintenance of standards controlling its operation; and (5) whether it has attracted widespread acceptance within a relevant scientific community.[3] Although the *Daubert* case is binding only on federal courts, the majority of state courts have adopted the *Daubert* reasoning for trials in their jurisdictions.

PREVENTING LAWSUITS AND LICENSING BOARD
COMPLAINTS: GOOD PRACTICE

As I said in the preface, it is unfortunate that this book is necessary. Everyone in the field would prefer that social workers merely go about their noble business of helping people in need. No practitioner wishes to be distracted by the annoying, burdensome, and distressing problems of professional malpractice and liability.

As in all professions, however, these phenomena are a reality in social work. And much of the malpractice and liability risk in social work is preventable. Throughout this discussion I have reviewed a variety of practical ways in which social workers can reduce the chances of being sued. Examples include avoiding hallway conversations when discussing clients, managing digital and online communications carefully, complying with standard informed-consent procedures, understanding local privileged communication statutes, avoiding inappropriate dual relationships, documenting services provided to clients and supervision provided to staff, terminating services carefully, and seeking consultation when issues arise that are outside your range of expertise.

These and the many other practical suggestions that appear throughout this discussion can certainly go a long way toward preventing social work malpractice and liability. By themselves, however, they constitute a rather shortsighted approach to prevention. Rather, knowledge of these specific ways to prevent malpractice and liability are but supplements to a firm grasp of two essential components of competent social work: good practice and good ethics.

In my experience with respect to malpractice and liability problems in the profession, I have been struck by the frequency with which good practice would have avoided lawsuits and licensing board complaints. Certainly in some cases good practice by itself would not prevent a complaint. A social worker who is sued by a former client for having divulged confidential information to protect a third party from imminent violence threatened by the former client has not necessarily engaged in bad practice. In fact the social worker may very well have demonstrated good practice skills and made the right decision in deciding to breach confidentiality. That the client chose to sue the social worker for the breach may simply be unfortunate.

Similarly a social worker who is sued or named in a licensing board complaint for improper referral of a client to a specialist may have practiced good social work. He may have followed proper referral procedures, including giving the client the names of several well-known colleagues. However, one colleague may have sexually abused the client. The referring social worker may have had no way to know that his colleague would violate a client in such a way; the perpetrator's behavior may not have been well known in the professional community. In fact the assault may have been the first such occurrence in his career. Although the outcome was tragic, the referring social worker may have been in no way at fault. Clearly social workers can be competent practitioners and still get sued or named in a licensing board complaint.

Nonetheless social workers who understand sound practice principles and carry them out every day substantially reduce their chances of being sued. Social workers who have a firm understanding of confidentiality and privileged communication issues, the assessment process, intervention techniques, termination and boundary issues, and the nature of supervision, consultation, and referral, for example, minimize the likelihood that they will make the sort of mistake that could trigger a complaint. Skillful practice is the most powerful preventative. As Besharov appropriately asserts, in the event of a lawsuit "good practice is the best defense" (1985:168).

In addition, however, solid grounding in professional ethics is essential in order to prevent malpractice and liability. This is often the missing link in social workers' armamentarium.

PREVENTING LAWSUITS AND LICENSING BOARD COMPLAINTS: GOOD ETHICS

Social work values and ethics have always been a central ingredient in the profession. Ever since social work's formal inauguration in the late nineteenth century, practitioners have been concerned about the values of the profession. Historical accounts of the profession's development routinely dwell on the compelling importance of social work's values and ethical tenets. Over time beliefs about social work's values and ethics have served as the principal organizing theme of the profession's mission and as the normative linchpin in the profession's foundation.

Although the theme of values and ethics has endured in the profession, social workers' conceptions of what these terms mean, and of their bearing on practice, have changed considerably. Only recently, in fact, have social workers devoted serious attention to ethical issues as they pertain to professional malpractice and liability.

In the late nineteenth century, for example, the concern about the morality of the client was much greater than the concern for the morality or ethics of the profession or its practitioners. Organizing relief and responding to the "curse of pauperism" (Paine 1880) were the profession's principal missions. This preoccupation often took the form of paternalistic attempts to strengthen the morality or rectitude of the poor, whose wayward lives had gotten the best of them.

Concern about the morality of the poor waned considerably—although not entirely—during the rise of the settlement house movement in the early twentieth century, when the aims of many social workers shifted from concern about the morality, or immorality, of the poor to the need for dramatic social reform designed to ameliorate a wide range of social problems related, for example, to housing, health care, child care, sanitation, employment, poverty, and education (Reamer 1980, 1990, 1992c, 2013a).

Concern about the morality of the client continued to recede somewhat during the next several decades of the profession's life, as practitioners engaged in earnest attempts to establish and polish their intervention strategies and techniques, training programs, and schools of thought. Over time concern about clients' morality was overshadowed by debate about the profession's future, that is, the extent to which social work would stress the cultivation of expertise in psychosocial and psychiatric casework, psychotherapy, social welfare policy and administration, community organization, or social reform.

By the late 1940s and early 1950s, however, concern about the moral dimensions of social work practice had intensified although in rather different form. Unlike the earlier preoccupation with the morality of the client, this midtwentieth-century concern focused much more on the morality or ethics of the profession and of its practitioners. This was a significant shift. Nearly a half-century after its formal inauguration, the profession began to develop ethical guidelines to enhance proper conduct among practitioners— the sorts of guidelines that help to reduce malpractice and liability risks. In 1947, after several years of debate and discussion, the Delegate Conference of the American Association of Social Workers adopted a code of ethics. The profession's journals also began to publish articles on the subject with greater frequency.

Thus the period surrounding the 1950s marked the onset of serious scholarly interest in the subject of professional ethics. Not surprisingly in the 1960s social workers shifted considerable attention toward the ethical constructs of social justice, rights, and reform. The public and political mood of this turbulent period infused social work training and practice with concern about social equality, welfare rights, human rights, discrimination, and oppression (Emmet 1962; H. Lewis 1972; Plant 1970; Vigilante 1974). In 1960 the National Association of Social Workers adopted its first code of ethics.

The early 1980s marked yet another significant transition in social work's concern with value and ethical issues. During the 1970s interest in the broad subject of professional ethics surged dramatically. Professions as diverse as medicine, law, business, journalism, engineering, nursing, and criminal justice began to devote sustained attention to the subject. Large numbers of undergraduate and graduate training programs added courses on ethics to their curricula, professional conferences witnessed a substantial increase in presentations on the subject, and the number of publications on professional ethics increased dramatically (Callahan and Bok 1980; Reamer and Abramson 1982; Reamer 2001b, 2013a).

Since the late 1970s a major focus in ethics scholarship, training, and education has been on the phenomenon of ethical dilemmas. This development has especially important bearing on social workers' efforts to reduce malpractice and liability risks in the profession. Professionals have become increasingly interested in the analysis of ethical dilemmas that require practitioners to make difficult choices among competing professional duties or obligations.

Especially since the early 1980s social workers have been introduced to the subjects of ethical decision making and ethical theory, particularly as they pertain to the dilemmas encountered in day-to-day practice (Banks 2012; Barsky 2010; Levy 1976; Loewenberg and Dolgoff 1992; Reamer 1982a, 1983a, 1983b, 1987a, 1987b, 1989a, 1990, 1992c, 1993a, 1995, 2013a; Reamer and Abramson 1982; Rhodes 1986). There has also been some renewed interest in reexamining the content of social work's values (Banks 2012; Billups 2002; Siporin 1982, 1989; Specht and Courtney 1997).

Although firm grounding in social work's enduring values can go a long way toward preventing professional malpractice and licensing board complaints—after all, social workers who firmly grasp the obligation to respect clients' dignity are much less likely to exploit them sexually, financially, or otherwise—social workers must refine their understanding of, and ability to analyze, ethical dilemmas that arise in practice.

Many malpractice risks and licensing board complaints stem from decisions that social workers make in these circumstances. For example, whether a social worker should divulge confidential information against a client's wishes to prevent harm to a third party or how a social worker who lives and works in a small community manages complex boundaries requires keen understanding of the nature of ethical dilemmas and various ways of addressing them. Although reasonable people may disagree with a social worker's particular decision in the case, a practitioner who can explain to a court or licensing board how she went about examining and addressing this ethical dilemma may prevent a judgment against her. Being able to demonstrate such familiarity with literature and concepts in ethical decision making, consultation with experts on the subject, and documentation of efforts in this regard may convince a jury that the social worker acted in a manner consistent with the profession's standard of care. Moreover familiarity with the general subject of professional ethics, ethical dilemmas, and ethical decision making can, by itself, enhance the likelihood that social workers will make sound judgments—which may, after all, be the most powerful preventative of malpractice claims and licensing board complaints.

ETHICAL DILEMMAS AND DECISION MAKING

In many instances social workers' ethical responsibilities are clear and uncomplicated. Ordinarily social workers understand their duty, for example, to respect clients' right to confidentiality and to protect the general welfare of members of society. These ethical principles are set forth rather clearly in the NASW *Code of Ethics* (2008), and support for them in social work literature and practice is long standing.

On occasion, however, such duties conflict in ways that might generate a lawsuit or licensing board complaint. A social worker whose client informs him during a counseling session that she plans to harm her estranged spouse must make a difficult choice between the client's right to confidentiality and protection of a third party. Assuming clinical intervention fails to resolve the issue and evidence exists that the client plans to carry out her threat, the social worker must choose between two competing duties that social workers are ordinarily expected to fulfill.

Hence ethical dilemmas in social work include those instances in which practitioners face conflicting duties or obligations. Three categories of dilemmas are particularly relevant to social work practice and to malpractice and licensing board risks. The first includes ethical dilemmas related to intervention with individuals, families, and groups. Prominent dilemmas in this area concern issues of confidentiality, boundaries and dual relationships, client self-determination, paternalism, and truth telling (Reamer 1980, 1982b, 1983b, 1987a, 1990, 2013a). As I have discussed, with regard to confidentiality social workers need to understand the extent of clients' rights and the limits of confidentiality, particularly when clients threaten to harm themselves or a third party (Arnold 1970; Barsky 2010; Dickson 1998; Promislo 1979; M. Reynolds 1976; Wilson 1978). Under what circumstances should social workers breach clients' right to privacy in order to protect third parties or the clients from themselves?

Similar dilemmas arise with regard to clients' right to self-determination. Ordinarily social workers respect clients' right to self-determination and help them pursue goals that are meaningful to them (S. Bernstein 1960; Keith-Lucas 1963; McDermott 1975; Perlman 1965; Reamer 1983b). Instances arise, however, in which social workers must consider limiting clients' right to self-determination because such actions threaten to harm them or third parties.

Consider, for example, a social worker whose client is a battered woman. After a period of separation from her abusive partner, who has beaten the client on several previous occasions, the client informs the social worker of her intention to once again live with her partner. The social worker feels strongly that the client is quite likely to be abused again. Empirically based literature on the phenomenon also supports the worker's hunch. To what extent should the worker respect the client's right to self-determination and help her pursue her chosen goal, as opposed to actively attempting to dissuade her from her plans to move in again with her partner? Understanding these issues may help to prevent a lawsuit or licensing board complaint alleging improper treatment or inappropriate use of coercion.

Further, how should social workers respond to severely mentally or physically disabled clients who have decided to end their lives because of the chronic emotional or physical pain that they experience? Should social workers summarily reject the possibility of "rational suicide" and discourage clients from further consideration of the possibility? Is it ever defensible for social workers to respect the decision of a distressed but competent client who has decided to commit suicide? Social workers' answers to these complex questions may have important bearing on the likelihood that they will be sued or named in a licensing board complaint for causing or failing to prevent a client's suicide.

Debate concerning the limits of clients' right to self-determination in instances in which their actions seem self-destructive inevitably leads to discussion of the concept of professional paternalism. Whether social workers acted assertively enough with clients who harmed themselves is a common issue in lawsuits and licensing board complaints.

Paternalism is ordinarily defined as interference with an individual's intentions or mental state in order to protect the individual from herself (Buchanan 1978; Carter 1977; Dworkin 1971; Feinberg 1971; Gert and Culver 1976, 1979; Husak 1980). Common examples of paternalism include prohibiting swimming at beaches when lifeguards are not on duty, requiring members of certain religious groups to receive life-saving blood transfusions, permitting involuntary civil commitment to a psychiatric facility, and legislating against suicide. The general presumption in social work is that social workers should respect clients' right to self-determination and that interference with this right requires truly exceptional circumstances where clients pose a serious threat of harm to themselves or others. According to the NASW *Code of Ethics,* "Social workers respect and promote the right of clients to self-determination and assist clients in their efforts to identify and clarify their goals. Social workers may limit clients' right to self-determination when, in the social workers' professional judgment, clients' actions or potential actions pose a serious, foreseeable, and imminent risk to themselves or others" (standard 1.02).

Social workers concerned about preventing lawsuits and licensing board complaints, in addition to protecting clients, face several types of ethical dilemmas involving paternalism (Reamer 1983b, 2013a). First are those instances in which social workers decide whether to physically interfere with clients for their own protection. Should a social worker require a resourceful but troubled homeless individual to go to a shelter against his wishes when the temperature is below freezing? How a social worker handles this predicament may affect the chances of being sued for false imprisonment.

Second are those instances in which social workers decide whether to withhold information from a client because of a belief that the client's knowledge of that information will be harmful. Is it justifiable, for example, for a hospital-based social worker to withhold from a critically ill patient the information that his child was just killed in an automobile accident? Is paternalism, in the form of withholding personally relevant information, justified in order to protect the hospital patient from harm?

Third are those instances in which social workers decide whether to deliberately give clients inaccurate information, or to lie to clients, in order to protect clients from harm. Is it justifiable on paternalistic grounds for a social worker to lie to a child about the reason for her father's arrest by the police in order to preserve as much as possible the child's relationship with her father? Is it permissible to give inaccurate information to a suicidal client in an effort to prevent suicide? Would such actions breach the standard of care in the profession and expose a social worker to a liability claim or licensing board complaint?

Dilemmas involving paternalism frequently raise issues concerning truth telling. Although social workers are typically inclined to be truthful with clients, truth telling may seem to be harmful at times (Bok 1978). Whether deception can ever be justified is an important matter to debate.

The second major category of ethical dilemmas in social work pertains to the ways in which practitioners design and administer social welfare policies and programs (Reamer 1987a, 1990, 2000a, 2013a). Social workers also encounter dilemmas concerning their duty to obey laws, agency rules, and public or private agency regulations. In all states, for example, social workers are required to report suspected cases of child abuse and neglect to protective service officials. Despite this mandate, however, social workers sometimes do not report such cases on the ground that they are in a better position than public officials to intervene effectively or that they do not want to betray the client's trust. As I have discussed, social workers who fail to report suspected abuse or neglect risk being sued for failure to consult a specialist.

Complicated ethical dilemmas also arise with respect to compliance with regulations and agency policy. Many social service agencies, for instance, depend on reimbursement for their services from insurance carriers or other third-party payers. To receive reimbursement agency staff members typically need to provide insurers with documentation of reimbursable services provided. Because some of the agency's services may not be reimbursable under the insurer's guidelines, social workers may struggle with their obligation to provide truthful claims information. The viability of the agency and its services may be at stake. Of course, a social worker who decides to submit bogus information to obtain reimbursement risks criminal charges and a lawsuit filed by the insurer.

The third broad category of ethical dilemmas involves relationships among professional colleagues. The most common, perhaps, concerns instances in which social workers encounter impaired or incompetent colleagues. These circumstances—when a social worker has evidence that a colleague is abusing alcohol, drugs, or clients, for example—involve troubling ethical issues in regard to whistle-blowing (Barry 1986; Bok 1980; Nader, Petkas, and Blackwood 1972; Peters and Branch 1972; Reamer 1984, 1990, 1992a, 1992b, 2012a, 2013a; Siegel 1992). Under what circumstances is whistle-blowing (for example, notifying an employer or licensing board about an impaired colleague) justifiable? What conditions should first be met? How much professional and personal risk should the whistle-blower be willing to assume? On the one hand are liability risks if a social worker fails to confront an impaired employee who subsequently injures a client. On the other hand, confronting an impaired colleague in the presence of third parties and discussing the problem with other agency staff may lead to a defamation-of-character lawsuit or licensing board complaint.

Ethical dilemmas can also arise in relationships among colleagues with respect to the use of deception. Social service providers may be competitors, and such competition may sometimes tempt administrators to engage in deceptive practices to win new grants or undermine competitors' advantage in order to ensure their own agency's fiscal health or survival. Deception may also be contemplated in order to surreptitiously gather information to document suspected wrongdoing by colleagues.

Social workers today have greater access to literature and instruction on ethical decision making. Especially since the mid-1970s the growth in literature and teaching on ethical decision making has been substantial. Social workers can consult a wide range of resources that provide useful introductions to, and overviews of, various ethical theories and frameworks for ethical decision making and for analyzing ethical dilemmas in practice (Banks 2012; Barsky 2010; Congress 1999; Reamer 1989a, 1990, 2013a; Rhodes 1986).

No precise formula for resolving ethical dilemmas exists. Reasonable, thoughtful social workers can disagree about the ethical principles and criteria that ought to guide ethical decisions in any given case. But ethicists generally agree on the importance of approaching ethical decisions systematically, by following a series of steps to ensure that all aspects of the ethical dilemma are addressed. Following a series of clearly formulated steps allows social workers to enhance the quality of the ethical decisions they make. In my experience social workers attempting to resolve ethical dilemmas find these steps helpful:

1. Identifying the ethical issues, including the social work values and duties, that conflict
2. Identifying the individuals, groups, and organizations likely to be affected by the ethical decision
3. Tentatively identifying all viable courses of action and the participants involved in each, along with the potential benefits and risks for each
4. Thoroughly examining the reasons in favor of and against each course of action, considering relevant
   a. Codes of ethics and legal principles
   b. Ethical theories, principles, and guidelines
   c. Social work practice theory and principles
   d. Personal values (including religious, cultural, and ethnic values and political ideology), particularly those that conflict with one's own
5. Consulting with colleagues and appropriate experts (such as agency staff, supervisors, agency administrators, attorneys, and ethics scholars)
6. Making the decision and documenting the decision-making process
7. Monitoring, evaluating, and documenting the decision

CONDUCTING AN ETHICS AUDIT

One of the most effective ways to prevent malpractice and licensing board complaints is to conduct an ethics audit (Reamer 2000b, 2001a, 2013a). An ethics audit provides practitioners and agencies with a framework for examining and critiquing the ways in which they address a wide range of ethical issues. More specifically an ethics audit provides social workers with an opportunity to

- Identify pertinent ethical issues in their practice settings that are unique to the client population, treatment and intervention approach, setting, program design, and staffing pattern
- Review and assess the adequacy of their current ethics-related policies, practices, and procedures
- Design a practical strategy to modify current practices, as needed, to prevent lawsuits and ethics complaints
- Monitor the implementation of this quality assurance strategy

Conducting an ethics audit involves several key steps:

1. In agency settings a staff member should assume the role of chair of the ethics audit committee. Appointment to the committee should be based on demonstrated interest in the agency's ethics-related policies and practices. Ideally the chair would have formal education or training related to professional ethics. Social workers in private or independent practice may want to consult with knowledgeable colleagues or a peer supervision group.
2. Using the list of major ethical risks as a guide (client rights, confidentiality and privacy, informed consent, service delivery, boundary issues and conflicts of interest, documentation, defamation of character, client records, supervision, staff development and training, consultation, client referral, fraud, termination of services, practitioner impairment), the committee should identify specific ethics-related issues on which to focus. In some settings the committee may decide to conduct a comprehensive ethics audit, one that addresses all the topics. In other agencies the committee may focus on specific ethical issues that are especially important in those settings.
3. The ethics audit committee should decide what kind of data it will need to conduct the audit. Sources of data include documents and interviews conducted with agency staff that address specific issues contained in the audit. For example, staff may examine the forms the agency uses to explain clients' rights and informed consent. In addition staff may interview or administer questionnaires to key personnel in the agency about such matters as the extent and content of ethics-related training that they have received or provided, specific ethical issues that need attention, and ways to address

compelling ethical issues. Committee members may want to consult a lawyer about legal issues (for example, the implications of federal or state confidentiality regulations and laws or key court rulings) and agency documents (for example, the appropriateness of agency informed-consent and release-of-information forms). Also, committee members should review all relevant regulations and laws (federal, state, and local) and ethics codes in relation to confidentiality, privileged communication, informed consent, client records, termination of services, supervision, licensing, personnel issues, and professional misconduct.

4. Once the committee has gathered and reviewed the data, it should assess the risk level associated with each topic. The assessment for each topic has two parts: policies and procedures. The ethics audit assesses the adequacy of various ethics-related policies and procedures. Policies may be codified in formal agency documents or memoranda (for example, official policy concerning confidentiality, digital and online communications, informed consent, dual relationships, conflicts of interest, and termination of services). Procedures include social workers' actual handling of ethical issues in their relationships with clients and colleagues (for example, concrete steps that staff members take to address ethical issues involving confidentiality or boundaries, routine explanations provided to clients concerning agency policies about informed consent and confidentiality, ethics consultation obtained, informed-consent forms completed, documentation placed in case records in ethically complex cases, and supervision and training provided on ethics-related topics).

5. The committee should assign each topic addressed in the audit to one of four risk categories: no risk—current practices are acceptable and do not require modification; minimal risk—current practices are reasonably adequate, but minor modifications would be useful; moderate risk—current practices are problematic, and modifications are necessary to minimize risk; and high risk—current practices are seriously flawed, and significant modifications are necessary to minimize risk.

6. Once the ethics audit is complete, social workers need to take assertive steps to make constructive use of the findings. Social workers should develop a plan for each risk area that warrants attention, beginning with high-risk areas that jeopardize clients and expose social workers and their agencies to serious risk of lawsuits and ethics complaints. Areas that fall into the categories of moderate risk and minimum risk should receive attention as soon as possible.

7. Establish priorities among the areas of concern, based on the degree of risk involved and available resources. Spell out specific measures that need to be taken to address the problem areas identified. Examples include reviewing all current informed-consent forms and creating updated versions; writing new comprehensive confidentiality policies; creating a client rights statement; inaugurating training of staff responsible for supervision; strengthening staff training on documentation and on boundary issues; and preparing detailed procedures for staff to follow when terminating services to clients.

8. Identify all the resources needed to address the risk areas, such as agency personnel, publications, staff development time, appointment of a committee or task force, legal consultants, and ethics consultants.

9. Identify which staff will be responsible for the various tasks, and establish a timetable for completion of each. Have a lawyer review and approve policies and procedures to ensure compliance with relevant laws, regulations, and court opinions. Identify a mechanism for following up on each task to ensure its completion and for monitoring its implementation.

10. Document the complete process involved in conducting the ethics audit. This documentation may be helpful in the event of a lawsuit alleging ethics-related negligence (in that it provides evidence of the agency's or practitioner's conscientious effort to address specific ethical issues).

Agency administrators can also conduct a "management audit" (Kurzman 1995; Houston-Vega, Nuehring, and Daguio 1997) to ensure the agency's compliance with widely embraced standards. The typical management audit verifies that

- The agency's government licenses (such as those from the department of mental health, division of substance abuse, department of human services) are in good standing.
- The agency's papers of incorporation and bylaws fully authorize the current scope of practice and service.
- The state licenses and current registrations of all professional staff are active.
- Protocols for handling emergencies (e.g., fire drills, involuntary client hospitalization, staff safety, unusual incident reporting) are well known and updated.
- Premiums for all forms of casualty insurance are paid and current, and the coverage for programs, staff, and settings is adequate.

- Procedures for maintaining and safeguarding client records are sound.
- Staff evaluations are conducted and reviewed regularly.
- Records for fiscal disbursements are properly authorized and maintained.
- Insurance reimbursement forms are completed in a timely fashion and are authenticated in accordance with contractual requirements.

Although social workers might prefer to avoid the topic of professional malpractice and risk management, practitioners need to understand the risks involved and ways to mitigate them. Given the complexity of the legal and practice issues involved, the tendency may be for social workers to become preoccupied with the technical aspects of professional malpractice and liability. These high-anxiety issues often lead social workers to dwell on the trees—the mechanics of lawsuits and licensing board complaints, and the mistakes, oversights, and improprieties that may give rise to them—rather than on the forest, the need to engage in good and ethical practice. In the final analysis, however, skillful and ethical practice is the most effective way to prevent and manage risk. This is also the hallmark of a professional.

Sample Forms

Note: These are sample forms. Social workers and agencies should use these only as a general guide. Revisions may be necessary based on practitioners' and agencies' specific settings, client populations, and services. Agencies that serve clients who have difficulty with English should translate these forms into languages that their clients can understand. Several forms contain blank lines followed by a direction in square brackets that is addressed to the agency or independent practitioner; that is, the agency or practitioner should insert the information before asking the client to read and sign the form.

Client Rights

We want you to know that as a client of this agency you have certain rights. ABC Social Service Agency treats all people with dignity and respect. ABC Social Service Agency does not discriminate on the basis of race, ethnicity, national origin, color, sex, sexual orientation, gender identity or expression, age, marital status, political belief, religion, immigration status, and mental or physical disability. In addition, you have the following specific rights:

1. You have the right to privacy and confidentiality. All information that you disclose to agency staff members will be kept confidential in accordance with federal and state laws and relevant court orders. [*Note:* Agencies and social workers may wish to add specific details concerning the confidentiality of information related to, for example, substance abuse treatment, HIV/AIDS, abuse and neglect, threats to third parties, electronic records, minors, court orders, and disclosure of information to insurers.]

2. You have the right to know that information about you may be shared among staff members for the purposes of service planning, service coordination, and referral.

3. You have the right to receive information and to be informed in a language that you understand. If ABC Social Service Agency is unable to provide services in a language that you understand, we will do our best to refer you, with your permission, to an agency that can provide services in your language.

4. You have the right to know the title and professional qualifications of the staff members who provide services to you.

5. You have the right to be informed about decisions that staff members make concerning services provided to you. You have the right to participate in those decisions whenever feasible.

6. You have the right to ask for a second opinion concerning your services and decisions made about you.

7. You have the right to appeal decisions about you made by agency staff.

8. You have the right to refuse services in accordance with federal and state laws and relevant court orders.

9. You have the right to ask for a referral to another agency or practitioner.

10. You have the right to receive a copy of the client handbook. This handbook includes descriptions of this agency's services, staff, confidentiality guidelines, emergency services, and other important information.

11. You have the right to be informed of the cost of services. ABC Social Service Agency charges fees that are fair and reasonable. ABC Social Service Agency will take into consideration your ability to pay.

12. You have the right to ask to review the information in your agency record.

13. You have the right to refuse permission for agency staff to use technology such as one-way mirrors, video recorders, tape recorders, and still cameras.

14. You have the right to refuse to participate in any research or evaluation project that ABC Social Service Agency conducts or sponsors.

Client signature _____

Parent/Guardian signature _____

Date _____

Consent for Release of Confidential Information

Client name _____ Date of birth _____

I hereby authorize ABC Social Service Agency to:

___ Release the record of my care to: _____

[specify agency, practitioner, facility and address]

This information may be released via:

___ U.S. Mail

___ Telephone

___ Fax

___ E-mail

___ Other (specify): _____

___ Obtain the record of my care from: _____

[specify agency, practitioner, facility and address]

___ Speak verbally regarding my care to: _____

[specify agency, practitioner, facility and address]

The information to be released shall include:

___ Assessments ___ Treatment plans ____ Treatment provided

____ Consultation reports ___ Medication records ___ Verification of attendance ____ Discharge plan

___ HIV/AIDS information (specify) _____

___ Substance abuse treatment (specify) _____

___ Other information (specify)_____

Pertaining to services on or about _____

[specify date(s)].

This information is needed for the following purpose(s):

___ Treatment/continued care

___ Consultation

___ Legal purposes

___ Application for insurance

___ Payment of insurance claim

___ Disability determination

___ Other (specify) _____

I understand that my records are protected under [specify relevant state and local laws] and cannot be disclosed without my written consent except as otherwise specifically provided by law. I also understand that if my records involve alcohol or drug abuse issues, treatment, or services, they are processed according to Federal Regulation 42 C.F.R. Part 2 (1987), Confidentiality of Alcohol and Drug Abuse Patient Records. A general authorization for disclosure of medical or other information is not sufficient for this purpose.

I understand that I may revoke this consent at any time before the ABC Social Service Agency releases the information that I have authorized herein. This authorization expires [specify date or time period].

I have read this statement carefully, it has been explained to me in a language that I can understand, and I have had an opportunity to ask questions about it.

Client signature _____

Parent/Guardian signature _____

Signature of witness _____

Date _____

Guidelines for Group Confidentiality

As a member of this therapy group, I understand that I have an obligation to respect the privacy and confidentiality of other group members. I agree to keep confidential all information shared by other group members. I will not talk with others outside the group about what is shared during group discussions.

Further, I understand that there is a risk of disclosure to people outside the group by people in the group. I agree to hold ABC Social Service Agency harmless from any claims or liability resulting from any disclosure of confidential information, by me or other group members, to parties outside the group.

Client signature _____

Parent/Guardian signature _____

Date _____

Social Media and Electronic Communications Policy

In order to clarify our use of electronic modes of communication during your treatment, I have prepared the following policy. This is because the use of various types of electronic communications is common in our society, and many individuals believe this is the preferred method of communication with others, whether their relationships are social or professional. Many of these common modes of communication, however, put your privacy at risk and can be inconsistent with the law and with the standards of my profession. Consequently, this policy has been prepared to assure the security and confidentiality of your treatment and to assure that it is consistent with ethics and the law.

If you have any questions about this policy, please feel free to discuss this with me.

E-mail Communications

I use email communication and text messaging only with your permission and only for administrative purposes unless we have made another agreement. That means that email exchanges and text messages with my office should be limited to things like setting and changing appointments, billing matters and other related issues. Please do not email me about clinical matters because email is not a secure way to contact me. If you need to discuss a clinical matter with me, please feel free to call me so we can discuss it on the phone or wait so we can discuss it during your therapy session. The telephone or face-to-face context simply is much more secure as a mode of communication.

Text Messaging

Because text messaging is a very unsecure and impersonal mode of communication, I do not text message to nor do I respond to text messages from anyone in treatment with me. So, please do not text message me unless we have made other arrangements.

Social Media and Social Networking

I do not communicate with, or contact, any of my clients through social media platforms like Twitter and Facebook. In addition, if I discover that I have accidentally established an online relationship with you, I will cancel that relationship. This is because these types of casual social contacts can create significant security risks for you.

I participate on various social networks, but not in my professional capacity. If you have an online presence, there is a possibility that you may encounter me by accident. If that occurs, please discuss it with me during our time together. I believe that any communications with clients online have a high potential to compromise the professional relationship. In addition, please do not try to contact me in this way. I will not respond and will terminate any online contact no matter how accidental.

Websites

I have a website that you are free to access. I use it for professional reasons to provide information to others about me and my practice. You are welcome to access and review the information that I have on my website and, if you have questions about it, we should discuss this during your counseling sessions.

Web Searches

I will not use web searches to gather information about you without your permission. I believe that this violates your privacy rights; however, I understand that you might choose to gather information about me in this way. In this day and age there is an incredible amount of information available about individuals on the Internet, much of which may actually be known to that person and some of which may be inaccurate or unknown. If you encounter any information about me through web searches, or in any other fashion for that matter, please discuss this with me during our time together so that we can deal with it and its potential impact on your treatment.

Recently it has become fashionable for clients to review their health care provider on various websites. Unfortunately, mental health professionals cannot respond to such comments and related errors because of confidentiality restrictions. If you encounter such reviews of me or any professional with whom you are working, please share it with me so we can discuss it and its potential impact on your counseling. Please do not rate my work with you while we are in treatment together on any of these websites. This is because it has a significant potential to damage our ability to work together.

(adapted from Kolmes 2013)

1. PROFESSIONAL RISK MANAGEMENT: AN OVERVIEW

1. Unless otherwise noted, all references to the NASW *Code of Ethics* are to the 2008 edition, which is the most recent.
2. See "Patient Falls to Death" (1995:2), "Psychiatric Nurse Hangs Self" (1995:4), and "Woman Claims Improper Sexual Conduct" (1996:3) for additional discussion of comparative negligence.
3. Readers should be aware that lower-court decisions do not constitute legal precedents that are necessarily applicable in other court cases. Only appellate cases are controlling in this way. Nevertheless I have included a number of lower-court decisions that provide valuable illustrations of conceptual points addressed throughout the book.

2. CONFIDENTIALITY AND PRIVILEGED COMMUNICATION

1. Many practitioners refer to *Tarasoff* as the "duty to warn" case. In fact this phrase is misleading. The court noted practitioners' duty to protect, not their duty to warn. Warning a potential victim is one way, but not the only way, to protect potential victims. Notifying law enforcement officials of a threat and seeking psychiatric hospitalization of a dangerous client are other ways practitioners can attempt to protect potential victims. *Tarasoff* is better described as the "duty to protect" case that led to current confidentiality standards.
2. The original *Tarasoff* case was decided by the California Supreme Court in 1974. The court then withdrew its first published opinion and in 1976 issued its second opinion, commonly known as *Tarasoff II,* which recognized a duty to protect third parties under certain circumstances.
3. Also see "Patient's Threats Disclosed" (1993); "Psychiatrist and Psychologist Revealed Patient's Threat" (1995); "Psychologists Owed Duty to Protect

Child" (1996); "Counselor Had No Duty to Warn" (1997); "Counseling Center Did Not Violate" (1997); "Lack of Physician-Patient Relationship" (1998); "Defendant's Admission to Therapist Not Protected" (1999); "Psychiatrist's Testimony About Patient's Threats" (1999); "Psychologist Immune from Liability" (2001); "Hospital Had Duty to Protect" (2001).

4. See also *Perreira v. State* (1989); *Schuster v. Altenberg* (1988); and *Naidu v. Laird* (1988)).

5. Also see "Hospital Has No Duty to Protect" (1993); "Chemical Dependency Counselor" (1993); "Claim for Injuries" (1994); "Therapists Have No Duty" (1996); "No Duty to Warn" (1999).

6. ATLA refers to the Association of Trial Lawyers of America. The citation is to the organization's law reporter.

7. Also see "Psychiatrist Did Not Owe Duty to Protect" (1995).

8. The Missouri Court of Appeals overruled a lower court's order compelling a wife to disclose medical records of her treatment for substance abuse and psychological and psychiatric test results for use in divorce proceedings. The appellate court found that under federal law the identity, diagnosis, or treatment of any patient that is maintained in connection with substance abuse treatment is confidential. See Missouri *ex rel.* C.J.V. v. Jamison (1998) and "Wife Not Compelled" (1999). Also see *In re* W.H., in which a lower court ruled that the records of the parent's treatment were not subject to disclosure in a child neglect proceeding ("Substance Abuse Program Records Confidential" 1994).

9. In 1998 the U.S. Supreme Court ruled that lawyers cannot be forced to reveal their clients' confidences even after the client dies, rebuffing the independent counsel Kenneth W. Starr's effort to obtain notes made by the lawyer for Vincent W. Foster Jr. shortly before the deputy White House counsel committed suicide (Marcus and Schmidt 1998).

10. See *Sanfiel v. Department of Health* (1999) for discussion of issues related to a practitioner's disclosure of confidential information to the media. The Florida District Court of Appeal held that a psychiatric nurse's intentional disclosure of confidential psychiatric treatment records to the media constituted unprofessional conduct ("Psychiatric Nurse's Disclosure" 2000).

11. In rare instances social workers may obtain authorization from a judge, or may be ordered by a judge, to disclose confidential information related to the investigation of an extremely serious crime. See, for example, the federal regulation Confidentiality of Alcohol and Drug Abuse Patient Records.

12. In an unusual case involving testimony by a social worker concerning child abuse, the Wisconsin Court of Appeals ordered a case retried because the testimony of a social worker, which was protected by physician-patient privilege, should not have been admitted into evidence. The social worker, a community mental health employee, disclosed that the client had told her that he had problems with an uncontrollable sex drive and pedophilia. The client argued that he had believed that his discussion of the issue was confidential. See *Wisconsin v. Locke* (1993).

13. Also see "Hospital Releases Woman's Psychiatric Records" (2000); "Woman Sues Hospital" (2001); and "Psychologist Violates Confidentiality" (2001).

14. A federal district court in Wisconsin held that the psychotherapist-patient privilege did not protect a man's statements to two Alcoholics Anonymous volunteers who advised him to go to a detoxification center. The man claimed that he thought the volunteers were counselors; the volunteers ended up contacting the police and sharing information with them about a gun in the man's possession. The court ruled that the man's disclosure did not fall under the state's law that permits patients to refuse to disclose confidential information shared with licensed clinicians or people believed to be such ("Statements . . . [to] Volunteers Not Protected" 1997).

3. THE DELIVERY OF SERVICES

1. I recently consulted on a case involving a social worker whose position was split between clinical and research responsibilities (the case is discussed in Mannix 2012). The social worker was named in a licensing board complaint involving the suicide of a research project participant who was being treated for schizophrenia. Differences in standards of care pertaining to the social worker's clinical and research roles were critically important.

2. See "Alcoholic Physician's Medical Records" (2001:6) for discussion of issues involving a clinician who completed a release-of-information form *after* the client had signed it.

3. Also see "Man Discharged from Psychiatric Facility" (1994); "Man on One-to-One Watch" (1996); "Teenager Commits Suicide after Evaluation" (1996); "Man Hangs Self" (1997); "Psychiatrist Takes Patient Off Suicide Watch" (1998); "Negligent Supervision of Patient" (1998); and "Claimant Wins Decision" (1999).

4. Also see "Court Denies Summary Judgment" (1996); "Misdiagnosis of Multiple Personality Disorders" (1997); and "Woman Sues Psychologist" (1998).

5. Also see Madden (1998).

6. Also see "Theory of Repressed Memories Valid" (1996); "Woman Claims Nurse Therapist Implanted" (1996); "Plaintiff Claims Repressed Memories" (1997); "Plaintiffs Claim Therapist Planted" (1997); "Recovered Memories . . . Not Admissible" (1998); and "Court Refuses to Dismiss" (1998).

7. In a Ohio case the state licensing board disciplined a social worker for giving a client two significant sums of money (State of Ohio 2009).

8. See *Aronoff v. Board of Registration in Medicine* (1995) and "Psychiatrist Censured" (1996:6) for discussion of issues involving a therapist's "commercial transactions" with a client.

9. Also see "Man Commits Suicide after Evaluation" (1994); "Woman Claims Husband Improperly Allowed" (1994); "Plaintiffs Claim Failure to Continue Hospitalization" (1994); "Man Claims Hospital Fails to Restrict" (1994).

10. Also see "Psychiatric Ward Fails" (1999) for another illustration of the need to remove dangerous objects from suicidal clients.

11. Also see *Welk v. Florida* (1989).

12. Also see *Rouse v. Cameron* (1966) and *Eckerhart v. Hensley* (1979).

13. Also see "Psychologist Who Failed to Follow Procedures" (1993).

14. Also see "Counselor Properly Reports" (1995) and "Statements Made to Therapist" (1996).

15. See *Rosenberg v. Helinski* (1992), a lawsuit that alleged that a psychologist who repeated his in-court testimony to a television reporter had defamed the father in a sex abuse case. The Maryland appellate court ruled that the psychologist "enjoyed a legal privilege to defame" and therefore could not be sued for defamation ("Psychologist in Sex Abuse Case" 1993:1).

4. IMPAIRED SOCIAL WORKERS

1. Also see *Palmer v. Board of Registration in Medicine* (1993); "Woman Claims Psychologist Began Sexual Relationship" (1994); "Woman Receives $7.1 Million Verdict" (1994); "Psychologist Has Romantic Relationship" (1994); "Psychiatrist Has Sexual Relations with Patient" (1995); "Therapist Sleeps with Patient" (1996); "Therapist's Sexual Misconduct" (1996); "Woman Blames Psychological Problems" (1997); "Improper Sexual Contact" (1997); "Court Upholds Revocation" (1997); "Court Upholds Law" (1998); "Mental,

Emotional Anguish Blamed" (2000); "Psychiatrist Engages in Sex with Patient" (2001).

2. Also see "Psychiatrist Dates Patient" (1997) and "Psychiatric Patient Claims Improper Sexual Contact" (2000).

5. SUPERVISION: CLIENTS AND STAFF

1. Also see *Siklas v. Ecker Center* (1993) and "Mental Health Center Could Be Held Liable" (1994:2) for discussion of issues related to supervision of clients.

2. Also see "Psychiatric Patient Leaps" (1992:2); "Court Dismisses Patient's Personal Injury Claim" (1994:6); "Man Commits Suicide in Hospital" (1996:3); and *Johnson v. New York* (1993).

3. Also see "No Liability for Injury" (1993:3).

4. Also see *Tabor v. Doctors Memorial Hospital* (1990).

5. Also see *Stropes v. Heritage House* (1989).

6. See "Psychologist Who Had Sex with Patient" (1997) and "Clinic Not Liable for Negligence of Therapist" (2001) for additional discussion of claims that sexual misconduct by the practitioner was negligent and violated employers' administrative policy.

7. See "Therapist Begins Personal Relationship" (1994) for discussion of negligence attributed to a practitioner who referred a married couple to a colleague and allegedly failed to supervise properly. The referring psychologist supervised his colleague's treatment of the couple for a period of time during which the primary therapist began a personal relationship with the wife.

6. CONSULTATION, REFERRAL, DOCUMENTATION, AND RECORDS

1. Also see "Patient Can Not Bring Malpractice Action" (2000:1).

2. Also see "Woman Comes Under Care of Psychotherapist" (1996:2).

3. The act, 740 Ill. Comp. Stat. 110, may be found at the website of the Illinois Legislative Reference Bureau, http://www.ilga.gov/legislation/ilcs/ilcs3.asp?ActID=2043&ChapterID=57 (accessed July 8, 2013).

4. The grammarian Theodore Bernstein offers several humorous examples that should underline how serious punctuation errors in a case file could prove to be. "It makes a difference," Bernstein notes, "whether you write, 'She went to the little boy's room' or 'She went to the little boys' room.'" He also quotes a gem from a news story: "Mrs. Anna Roosevelt Boettiger, only daughter of

the late President Roosevelt, disclosed today plans for her third marriage to Dr. James Addison Halstead." He drily adds: "Surely she was not marrying the same man for the third time. A comma is necessary after 'marriage'" (Bernstein 1965:357, 361).

8. TERMINATION OF SERVICE

1. Also see *Goryeb v. Pennsylvania* (1990).
2. See "Patient Commits Suicide After Release" (1995:1) and *Muse v. Charter Hospital* (1995) for additional discussion of negligence issues involving termination of services and hospital discharge when a client is unable to pay. In this case a North Carolina court ruled in favor of the estate of a patient who committed suicide two weeks after being released from a hospital against his treating physician's medical judgment. The court said that the estate could pursue a wrongful death action against the hospital for willful and wanton misconduct because the decision to release the man was based on the expiration of his insurance coverage. The court held that the hospital had a duty not to interfere with the medical judgment of its treating physician.

9. RESPONDING TO LAWSUITS AND ETHICS COMPLAINTS: THE ROLE OF PREVENTION

1. Consider the story told about F. E. Smith, the first earl of Birkenhead (1872–1930), who was a British barrister. Smith once cross-examined a young man who was claiming damages for an arm injury caused by the negligence of a bus driver. "Will you show us how high you can lift your arm now?" Smith asked. The young man gingerly raised his arm to shoulder level, his face distorted with pain. "Thank you," Smith said. "And now, please will you show us how high you could lift it before the accident?" The young man eagerly shot his arm up above his head. He lost his case (Fadiman 1985:513).
2. The lawyer for Russell Sage, the famous U.S. financier, was delighted by the case that Sage had presented to him. "It's an ironclad case," he exclaimed with confidence. "We can't possibly lose." "Then we won't sue," Sage said. "That was my opponent's side of the case I gave you" (Fadiman 1985:485).
3. The *Daubert* standard was established in *Daubert v. Merrell Dow Pharmaceuticals* (509 U.S. 579 (1993)), in which two minor children and their parents alleged that the children's serious birth defects had been caused by the mothers'

prenatal ingestion of Bendectin, a prescription drug marketed by a pharmaceutical company. The district court granted the company summary judgment based on a well-credentialed expert's affidavit concluding, upon reviewing the extensive published scientific literature on the subject, that maternal use of Bendectin has not been shown to be a risk factor for human birth defects. Although the plaintiffs had responded with the testimony of eight other well-credentialed experts, who based their conclusion that Bendectin can cause birth defects on animal studies, chemical structure analyses, and the unpublished reanalysis of previously published human statistical studies, the court determined that these experts were basing their testimony on evidence that did not meet the applicable "general acceptance" standard and so could not be considered by the court. The district court's decision later was upheld by the U.S. Supreme Court.

REFERENCES

Abbott, J. M., B. Klein, and L. Ciechomski. 2008. "Best Practices in Online Therapy." *Journal of Technology in Human Services* 26:360–75.

Alabama State Board of Social Work Examiners. 1999. "In re Sally Baker." http://www.socialwork.alabama.gov/pdfs/Baker%20disciplinary%20action.pdf (accessed December 22, 2013).

——. 2003. "In the Matter of Shirley Carter." http://www.socialwork.alabama.gov/pdfs/Carter%20Decision.pdf (accessed December 23, 2013).

——. 2006. "In the Matter of Michael Beddingfield." http://www.socialwork.alabama.gov/pdfs/Beddingfield.pdf (accessed December 22, 2013).

——. 2009. "In the Matter of Sharon J. Jones." http://www.socialwork.alabama.gov/pdfs/S.%20Jones%20Discip.%20doc.pdf (accessed December 23, 2013).

"Alcoholic Physician's Medical Records Improperly Released." 2001. *Mental Health Law News* 16 (10): 6.

Alexander, R. Jr. 1997. "Social Workers and Privileged Communication in the Federal Legal System." *Social Work* 42 (4): 387–91.

"Alleged Sexual Misconduct by Psychotherapist Causes Stress Disorder." 1994. *Mental Health Law News* 9 (8): 6.

Antler, S. 1987. "Professional Liability and Malpractice." In *Encyclopedia of Social Work*. 18th ed., 346–51. Silver Spring, MD: National Association of Social Workers.

Arkansas Social Work Licensing Board. 2013. "Disciplinary Action." http://www.arkansas.gov/swlb/pdfs/Disciplinary_Action_Descending_Order.pdf (accessed December 22, 2013).

Arnold, S. 1970. "Confidential Communication and the Social Worker." *Social Work* 15 (1): 61–67.

"Attorney Suffers Psychotic Breakdown from Lifespring Training." 1991. *Mental Health Law News* 6 (7): 1.

Austin, K. M., M. E. Moline, and G. T. Williams. 1990. *Confronting Malpractice: Legal and Ethical Dilemmas in Psychotherapy.* Newbury Park, CA: Sage.

Austin, M. J. 1981. *Supervisory Management for the Human Services.* Englewood Cliffs, NJ: Prentice-Hall.

Ballou, B. R. 2007. "Licensing of Hospital Officials Under Review: Resume at Issue, Official Resigns." *Boston Globe,* June 8. http://www.boston.com/news/local/massachusetts/articles/2007/06/08/licensing_of_hospital_officials_under_review/?page=full (accessed July 11, 2013).

Banks, S. 2012. *Ethics and Values in Social Work.* 4th ed. Basingstoke, UK: Palgrave Macmillan.

Barak, A. and J. M. Grohol. 2011. "Current and Future Trends in Internet-supported Mental Health Interventions." *Journal of Technology in Human Services* 29:155–96.

Barak A., L. Hen, M. Boniel-Nissim, and N. Shapira. 2008. "A Comprehensive Review and a Meta-analysis of the Effectiveness of Internet-based Psychotherapeutic Interventions." *Journal of Technology in Human Services* 26:110–60.

Barker, R. L. and D. M. Branson. 2000. *Forensic Social Work.* 2d ed. New York: Haworth.

Barnett, J. E. 2005. "Online Counseling: New Entity, New Challenges." *Counseling Psychologist* 33:872–80.

Barr, D. 1997. "Clinical Social Worker Disciplined by State, Sued over Patient Relations." *(Harrisonburg, Va.) Daily News-Record,* November 14, 19.

Barry, V. 1986. *Moral Issues in Business.* 3d ed. Belmont, CA: Wadsworth.

Barsky, A. 2010. *Ethics and Values in Social Work.* New York: Oxford University Press.

Barsky, A. and J. Gould. 2002. *Clinicians in Court: A Guide to Subpoenas, Depositions, Testifying and Everything Else You Need to Know.* New York: Guilford.

Barton, W. E. and C. J. Sanborn, eds. 1978. *Law and the Mental Health Professions.* New York: International Universities Press.

Berg, J. W., P. S. Appelbaum, C. W. Lidz, and L. S. Parker. 2001. *Informed Consent: Legal Theory and Clinical Practice.* 2d ed. New York: Oxford University Press.

Bergstresser, C. 1998. "The Perspective of the Plaintiff's Attorney." In Lifson and Simon, *Mental Health Practitioner and the Law,* 329–43.

Berliner, A. K. 1989. "Misconduct in Social Work Practice." *Social Work* 34 (1): 69–72.

Bernard, J. and C. Jara. 1986. "The Failure of Clinical Psychology Students to Apply Understood Ethical Principles." *Professional Psychology: Research and Practice* 17 (4): 316–21.

Berner, M. 1998. "Write Smarter, Not Longer." In Lifson and Simon, *Mental Health Practitioner and the Law*, 54–71.

Bernstein, B. 1981. "Malpractice: Future Shock of the 1980s." *Social Casework* 62 (3): 175–81.

Bernstein, B. and T. Hartsell. 2004. *The Portable Lawyer for Mental Health Professionals*. 2d ed. Hoboken, NJ: John F. Wiley & Sons.

Bernstein, S. 1960. "Self-determination: King or Citizen in the Realm of Values?" *Social Work* 5 (1): 3–8.

Bernstein, T. 1965. *The Careful Writer: A Modern Guide to English Usage*. New York: Athenaeum.

Besharov, D. J. 1985. *The Vulnerable Social Worker: Liability for Serving Children and Families*. Silver Spring, MD: National Association of Social Workers.

Billups, J. O., ed. 2002. *Faithful Angels: Portraits of International Social Work Notables*. Washington, DC: NASW Press.

Bissell, L. and P. W. Haberman. 1984. *Alcoholism in the Professions*. New York: Oxford University Press.

Bissell, L., L. Fewell, and R. Jones. 1980. "The Alcoholic Social Worker: A Survey." *Social Work in Health Care* 5:421–32.

Board of Social Work of the State of Idaho. 2012. "In the Matter of Natalie Montross." http://www.idph.state.ia.us/IDPHChannelsService/file.ashx?file=FC7595BF-3B2B-4DA0-A9C4-C09006AF88E7 (accessed December 23, 2013).

Bok, S. 1978. *Lying: Moral Choice in Public and Private Life*. New York: Pantheon.

———. 1980. "Whistleblowing and Professional Responsibility." *New York University Education Quarterly* 11:2–10.

Bradley, L., B. Hendricks, and D. R. Kabell. 2012. "The Professional Will: An Ethical Responsibility." *Family Journal* 20 (3): 309–14.

Brodsky, A. M. 1986. "The Distressed Psychologist: Sexual Intimacies and Exploitation." In Kilburg, Nathan, and Thoreson, *Professionals in Distress*, 153–71.

Brodsky, S. 1996. *Testifying in Court: Guidelines and Maxims for Testifying in Court*. Washington, DC: American Psychological Association.

———. 1999. *The Expert Expert Witness: More Maxims and Guidelines for Testifying in Court*. Washington, DC: American Psychological Association.

Buchanan, A. 1978. "Medical Paternalism." *Philosophy and Public Affairs* 7:370–90.

Buchanan, A. E. and D. W. Brock. 1989. *Deciding for Others: The Ethics of Surrogate Decision Making*. Cambridge: Cambridge University Press.

Bullis, R. K. 1995. *Clinical Social Worker Misconduct*. Chicago: Nelson-Hall.

Calfee, B. E. 1997. "Lawsuit Prevention Techniques." In *The Hatherleigh Guide to Ethics in Therapy,* 109–25. New York: Hatherleigh.

Callahan, D. and S. Bok, eds. 1980. *Ethics Teaching in Higher Education.* New York: Plenum Press.

Campbell, J. M. 2006. *Essentials of Clinical Supervision.* Hoboken, NJ: John F. Wiley & Sons.

Carroll, R., ed. 2011. *Risk Management Handbook for Healthcare Organizations.* Hoboken, NJ: John F. Wiley & Sons.

Carter, R. 1977. "Justifying Paternalism." *Canadian Journal of Philosophy* 7:133–45.

Caspi, J. and William Reid. 2002. *Educational Supervision in Social Work.* New York: Columbia University Press.

Celenza, A. 2007. *Sexual Boundary Violations: Therapeutic, Supervisory, and Academic Contexts.* Lanham, MD: Aronson.

"Chemical Dependency Counselor Who Disclosed Client's Threats Immune from Liability." 1993. *Mental Health Law News* 8 (10): 2.

Chenneville, T. (2000). "HIV, Confidentiality, and Duty to Protect: A Decision-making Model." *Professional Psychology: Research and Practice* 31 (6): 661–70.

"Claim for Injuries from Escaped Patient Dismissed: Claimant Not Readily Identifiable Victim." 1994. *Mental Health Law News* 9 (1): 3.

"Claimant Wins Decision on Liability for Failure to Prevent Suicide." 1999. *Mental Health Law News* 14 (6): 1.

"Clinic Not Liable for Negligence of Therapist Who Had Sex with One of His Patients." 2001. *Mental Health Law News* 16 (3): 2.

Cohen, B. Z. 1987. "The Ethics of Social Work Supervision Revisited." *Social Work* 32 (3): 194–96.

Cohen, R. J. 1979. *Malpractice: A Guide for Mental Health Professionals.* New York: Free Press.

Cohen, R. J. and B. DeBetz. 1977. "Responsive Supervision of the Psychiatric Resident and Clinical Psychology Intern." *American Journal of Psychoanalysis* 37:51–64.

Cohen, R. J. and W. E. Mariano. 1982. *Legal Guidebook in Mental Health.* New York: Free Press.

Congress, E. P. 1999. *Social Work Values and Ethics.* Chicago: Nelson-Hall.

Coombs, R. H. 2000. *Drug-impaired Professionals.* Cambridge, MA: Harvard University Press.

Corcoran, J. and J. Walsh. 2010. *Clinical Assessment and Diagnosis in Social Work.* 2d ed. New York: Oxford University Press.

Corcoran, K. and V. Vandiver. 1996. *Maneuvering the Maze of Managed Care.* New York: Free Press.

Corey, G. and B. Herlihy. 1997. "Dual/Multiple Relationships: Toward a Consensus of Thinking." In *The Hatherleigh Guide to Ethics in Therapy,* 183–94. New York: Hatherleigh.

"Counseling Center Did Not Violate Patient's Confidentiality When It Disclosed Her Death Threats." 1997. *Mental Health Law News* 12 (5): 1.

"Counselor Begins Sexual Relationship with Client." 1991. *Mental Health Law News* 6 (4): 1.

"Counselor Had No Duty to Warn Ex-wife of Patient Who Later Shot Her." 1997. *Mental Health Law News* 12 (11): 1.

"Counselor Properly Reports Child's Alleged Sexual Abuse by Mother." 1995. *Mental Health Law News* 10 (10): 5.

"Counselor Who Suspected Child Abuse Not Liable for Interfering with Family Rights." 1990. *Mental Health Law News* 5 (5): 4.

"Court Affirms Suspension of Psychologist's License for Sexual Misconduct." 1997. *Mental Health Law News* 12 (12): 3.

"Court Denies Summary Judgment on Most Claims Against Therapist." 1996. *Mental Health Law News* 11 (11): 4.

"Court Dismisses Patient's Personal Injury Claim." 1994. *Mental Health Law News* 9 (6): 6.

"Court Refuses to Dismiss Negligence Claims Against Therapist." 1998. *Mental Health Law News* 13 (10): 3.

"Court Reinstates False Imprisonment Suit." 1993. *Mental Health Law News* 8 (7): 4.

"Court Upholds Law Used to Convict Therapist for Sexual Misconduct." 1998. *Mental Health Law News* 13 (3): 2.

"Court Upholds Revocation of Psychologist's License Because He Had Sex with Patient." 1997. *Mental Health Law News* 13 (2): 6.

Cowles, J. 1976. *Informed Consent.* New York: Coward, McCann and Geoghegan.

Crombie, D. 1989. "Social Worker Sentenced in Assaults." *Providence (RI) Journal-Bulletin,* April 20, B3.

"Defendant's Admission to Child Molestation Not Protected by Therapist-Client Privilege." 1999. *Mental Health Law News* 14 (2): 2.

"Defendant's Admission to Therapist Not Protected: Expressed Threat of Future Criminal Conduct." 1999. *Mental Health Law News* 14 (9): 4.

DePanfilis, D. and M. K. Salus. 2003. *Child Protective Services: A Guide for Caseworkers.* Washington, DC: U.S. Department of Health and Human Services.

Deutsch, C. 1985. "A Survey of Therapists' Personal Problems and Treatment." *Professional Psychology: Research and Practice* 16 (2): 305–15.

Dickson, D. T. 1995. *Law in the Health and Human Services.* New York: Free Press.

——. 1998. *Confidentiality and Privacy in Social Work.* New York: Free Press.

——. 2001. *HIV, AIDS, and the Law: Legal Issues for Social Work Practice and Policy.* New York: Aldine de Gruyter.

"Doctor Who Conducted Training Had Duty to Warn or Prevent Resident from Abusing Patient." 1999. *Mental Health Law News* 14 (4): 4.

Donnelly, J. 1978. "Confidentiality: The Myth and the Reality." In Barton and Sanborn, *Law and the Mental Health Professions,* 185–205.

"Drug Treatment Counselor Has Affair with Patient's Mother." 1992. *Mental Health Law News* 7 (1): 3.

Dudley, J. R. 2009. *Social Work Evaluation: Enhancing What We Do.* Chicago: Lyceum Books.

Dworkin, G. 1971. "Paternalism." In R. A. Wasserstrom, ed., *Morality and the Law,* 107–26. Belmont, CA: Wadsworth.

Edwards, L. L., J. S. Edwards, and P. K. Wells. 2012. *Tort Law for Legal Assistants.* 5th ed. Clifton Park, NY: Delmar.

Emmet, D. 1962. "Ethics and the Social Worker." *British Journal of Psychiatric Social Work* 6:165–72.

"Employer May Be Held Liable for Psychotherapist's Sexual Misconduct." 1990. *Mental Health Law News* 5 (11): 1.

"Employer Not Vicariously Liable for Therapist's Sexual Misconduct." 1989. *Mental Health Law News* 4 (10): 1.

Epstein, R. 1994. *Keeping Boundaries: Maintaining Safety and Integrity in the Psychotherapeutic Process.* Washington, DC: American Psychiatric Press.

Fadiman, C., ed. 1985. *The Little, Brown Book of Anecdotes.* Boston: Little, Brown.

"Failure to Refer to Psychiatrist and to Hospital Alleged in Suicide." 1995. *Mental Health Law News* 10 (5): 6.

Farber, B. A., ed. 1983. *Stress and Burnout in the Human Service Professions.* New York: Pergamon.

Farber, B. A. and L. H. Heifetz. 1981 "The Satisfaction and Stresses of Psychotherapeutic Work: A Factor Analytic Study." *Professional Psychology: Research and Practice* 12 (5): 621–30.

Fausel, D. F. 1988. "Helping the Helper Heal: Codependency in Helping Professionals." *Journal of Independent Social Work* 3 (2): 35–45.

Feinberg, J. 1971. "Legal Paternalism." *Canadian Journal of Philosophy* 1:105–24.

"Female Therapist Engages in Same-Sex Relationship with Patient." 2000. *Mental Health Law News* 15 (6): 3.

Finn, J. 2006. "An Exploratory Study of Email Use by Direct Service Social Workers." *Journal of Technology in Human Services* 24:1–20.

Fisher, M. A. 2013. *The Ethics of Conditional Confidentiality: A Practice Model for Mental Health Professionals.* New York: Oxford University Press.

"$570,841 Judgment Returned; Man Committed Suicide After Leaving Psychiatric Facility." 1991. *Mental Health Law News* 6 (2): 3.

Flexner, A. 1915. "Is Social Work a Profession?" In *Proceedings of the National Conference of Charities and Correction,* 576–90. Chicago: Hildman.

Florida Board of Clinical Social Work, Marriage and Family Therapy and Mental Health Counseling. 2001. "Department of Health vs. Deborah A. Hulbert." http:// ww2.doh.state.fl.us/FinalOrderNet/folistbrowse.aspx?LicId=4410&ProCde=5201&discpln=DISCPLN (accessed February 6, 2013).

Francis, D. D. and J. Chin. 1987. "The Prevention of Acquired Immunodeficiency Syndrome in the United States." *Journal of the American Medical Association* 257:1357–66.

Freudenberger, H. J. 1986. "Chemical Abuse Among Psychologists: Symptoms, Causes, and Treatment Issues." In Kilburg, Nathan, and Thoreson, *Professionals in Distress,* 135–52.

Gartrell, N., J. Herman, S. Olarte, M. Feldstein, and R. Localio. 1986. "Psychiatrist-Patient Sexual Contact: Results of a National Survey." *American Journal of Psychiatry* 143 (9): 1126–31.

Gechtman, L. and J. Bouhoutsos. 1985. "Sexual Intimacy Between Social Workers and Clients." Paper presented at the annual meeting of the Society for Clinical Social Workers, University City, California.

Gelman, S. R. and P. J. Wardell. 1988. "Who's Responsible? The Field Liability Dilemma." *Journal of Social Work Education* 24:70–78.

Gert, B. and C. M. Culver. 1976. "Paternalistic Behavior." *Philosophy and Public Affairs* 6:45–57.

——. 1979. "The Justification of Paternalism." *Ethics* 89:199–210.

Gifis, S. H. 2010. *Law Dictionary.* 6th ed. Hauppauge, NY: Barron's.

Giordano, P. C. 1977. "The Client's Perspective in Agency Evaluation." *Social Work* 22 (1): 34–39.

Goby, M. J., N. J. Bradley, and D. A. Bespalec. 1979. "Physicians Treated for Alcoholism: A Follow-up Study." *Alcoholism: Clinical and Experimental Research* 3:121–24.

Gottlieb, M. C. 1995. "Avoiding Exploitive Dual Relationships: A Decision-Making Model." In D. N. Bersoff, ed., *Ethical Conflicts in Psychology*, 242–43. Washington, DC: American Psychological Association.

Gould, D. 1998. "Listen to Your Lawyer." In Lifson and Simon, *Mental Health Practitioner and the Law*, 344–56.

"Government Liable for Premature Release of Psychiatric Patient." 1992. *Mental Health Law News* 7 (3): 4.

Graffeo, I. and D. La Barbera. 2009. "Cybertherapy Meets Facebook, Blogger, and Second Life: An Italian Experience." *Annual Review of CyberTherapy & Tele-medicine* 7: 108–12.

Gray, L. A. and A. K. Harding. 1988. "Confidentiality Limits with Clients Who Have the AIDS Virus." *Journal of Counseling and Development* 66 (5): 219–23.

Greenwood, E. 1957. "Attributes of a Profession." *Social Work* 2 (3): 45–55.

Grossman, M. 1978. "Confidentiality: The Right to Privacy Versus the Right to Know." In Barton and Sanborn, *Law and the Mental Health Professions*, 137–84.

Gutheil, T. G. and G. O. Gabbard. 1993. "The Concept of Boundaries in Clinical Practice: Theoretical and Risk-Management Dimensions." *American Journal of Psychiatry* 150 (2): 188–96.

Gutheil, T. G. and R. I. Simon. 2005. "E-mails, Extra-therapeutic Contact, and Early Boundary Problems: The Internet as a 'Slippery Slope.'" *Psychiatric Annals* 35:952–60.

Guy, J. D., P. L. Poelstra, and M. Stark. 1989. "Personal Distress and Therapeutic Effectiveness: National Survey of Psychologists Practicing Psychotherapy." *Professional Psychology: Research and Practice* 20 (1): 48–50.

Hahn, Robert A. 1982. "Culture and Informed Consent: An Anthropological Perspective." In President's Commission, *Making Health Care Decisions*, 37–62.

Hamilton, G. 1936. *Social Case Recording.* New York: Columbia University Press.

——. 1946. *Principles of Social Case Recording.* New York: Columbia University Press.

——. 1951. *Theory and Practice of Social Case Work.* New York: Columbia University Press.

Harkness, D. 2008. "Consultation." In *Encyclopedia of Social Work.* 20th ed., 420–23. New York and Washington, DC: Oxford University Press and NASW Press.

Herrington, R. E., D. G. Benzer, G. R. Jacobson, and M. K. Hawkins. 1982. "Treating Substance-Use Disorders Among Physicians." *Journal of the American Medical Association* 247:2253–57.

Hester, D. M. and T. Schonfeld, eds. 2012. *Guidance for Healthcare Ethics Committees.* New York: Cambridge University Press.

Hinkelman, M. 2010. "Two Social-Service Administrators Get Long Jail Terms in Danieal's Death." *Philadelphia Inquirer,* June 11. http://articles.philly.com/2010–06–11/news/24966642_1_danieal-kelly-social-services-long-jail-terms (accessed July 11, 2013).

Hogan, D. B. 1979. *The Regulation of Psychotherapists: Volume I—A Study in the Philosophy and Practice of Professional Regulation.* Cambridge, MA: Ballinger.

"Hospital Had Duty to Protect Mother of Patient with Psychiatric Impairments. 2001. *Mental Health Law News* 16 (9): 1.

"Hospital Has No Duty to Protect Unforeseeable Third Party Whom Patient Assaulted." 1993. *Mental Health Law News* 8 (5): 1.

"Hospital Liable for Employee's Sexual Assault on Psychiatric Patient." 1992. *Mental Health Law News* 7 (10): 6.

"Hospital Liable for Failing to Detain Mentally Ill Emergency Room Patient." 1990. *Mental Health Law News* 5 (1): 4.

"Hospital Liable for Failure to Admit Suicidal Patient Who Killed Himself." 1991. *Mental Health Law News* 6 (8): 4.

"Hospital Liable for Failure to Prevent Suicide of Psychiatric Patient." 1990. *Mental Health Law News* 5 (2): 2.

"Hospital Liable for Suicide of Psychiatric Patient." 1990. *Mental Health Law News* 5 (5): 2.

"Hospital Not Negligent in Supervising Patient Who Attacked Another Patient." 1992. *Mental Health Law News* 7 (1): 3.

"Hospital Releases Woman's Psychiatric Records to Ex-Husband: $385,000 Verdict." 2000. *Mental Health Law News* 15 (7): 5.

Houston-Vega, M. K., E. M. Nuehring, and E. R. Daguio. 1997. *Prudent Practice: A Guide for Managing Malpractice Risk.* Washington, DC: NASW Press.

Hu, J., H. Chen, and T. Hou. 2010. "A Hybrid Public Key Infrastructure Solution (HPKI) for HIPAA Privacy/security Regulations." *Computer Standards & Interfaces* 32:274–80.

Husak, D. N. 1980. "Paternalism and Autonomy." *Philosophy and Public Affairs* 10:27–46.

"Improper Sexual Contact Blamed for Further Psychological Problems." 1997. *Mental Health Law News* 12 (6): 4.

"Inadequate Psychiatric Treatment Blamed for Woman Killing Son." 1994. *Mental Health Law News* 9 (10): 2.

Iowa Board of Social Work. 2013. "In the Matter of Brian C. Nedoba." http://www.idph.state.ia.us/IDPHChannelsService/file.ashx?file=B5221FE3-D8F1-4A02-B595-8C8878F8173A (accessed December 22, 2013).

"Issuer of Degrees Pleads to Fraud." 1997. *NASW News,* February, 9.

Jayaratne, S. and W. A. Chess. 1984. "Job Satisfaction, Burnout, and Turnover: A National Study." *Social Work* 29 (5): 448–55.

Jayaratne, S., T. Croxton, and D. Mattison. 1997. "Social Work Professional Standards: An Exploratory Study." *Social Work* 42 (2): 187–99.

Johnson, M. and G. L. Stone. 1986. "Social Workers and Burnout." *Journal of Social Work Research* 10:67–80.

Jones, G. and A. Stokes. 2009. *Online Counseling: A Handbook for Practitioners.* New York: Palgrave Macmillan.

Joseph, M. V. 1989. "Social Work Ethics: Historical and Contemporary Perspectives." *Social Thought* 15 (3/4): 4–17.

"Juvenile's Communications to Psychologist and Social Worker Not Privileged." 2001. *Mental Health Law News* 16 (8): 5.

Kadushin, A. 1976. *Supervision in Social Work.* New York: Columbia University Press.

——. 1977. *Consultation in Social Work.* New York: Columbia University Press.

——. 1992. *Supervision in Social Work.* 3d ed. New York: Columbia University Press.

Kagle, J. D. 1987. "Recording in Direct Practice." In *Encyclopedia of Social Work.* 18th ed., 463–67. Silver Spring, MD: National Association of Social Workers.

Kagle, J. D. and P. N. Giebelhausen. 1994. "Dual Relationships and Professional Boundaries." *Social Work* 39 (2): 213–20.

Kagle, J. D. and S. Kopels. 2008. *Social Work Records.* 2d ed. Long Grove, IL: Waveland Press.

Kain, C. D. 1988. "To Breach or Not to Breach: Is That the Question?" *Journal of Counseling and Development* 66 (5): 224–25.

Keith-Lucas, A. 1963. "A Critique of the Principle of Client Self-Determination." *Social Work* 8 (3): 66–71.

Kilburg, R. R., F. W. Kaslow, and G. R. VandenBos. 1988. "Professionals in Distress." *Hospital and Community Psychiatry* 39:723–25.

Kilburg, R. R., P. E. Nathan, and R. W. Thoreson, eds. 1986. *Professionals in Distress: Issues, Syndromes, and Solutions in Psychology.* Washington, DC: American Psychological Association.

Kirk, S. A., ed. 2005. *Mental Disorders in the Social Environment: Critical Perspectives.* New York: Columbia University Press.

Kirk, S. A. and H. Kutchins. 1988. "Deliberate Misdiagnosis in Mental Health Practice." *Social Service Review* 62 (2): 225–37.

Kitchener, K. S. 1988. "Dual Role Relationships: What Makes Them So Problematic?" *Journal of Counseling and Development* 67 (4): 217–21.

Kliner, D. J., J. Spicer, and P. Barnett. 1980. "Treatment Outcome of Alcoholic Physicians." *Journal of Studies on Alcohol* 41 (11): 1217–20.

Knuth, M. O. 1979. "Civil Liability for Suicide." *Loyola of Los Angeles Law Review* 12:967–99.

Knutsen, E. 1977. "On the Emotional Well-Being of Psychiatrists: Overview and Rationale." *American Journal of Psychoanalysis* 37:123–29.

Koeske, G. F. and R. D. Koeske. 1989. "Work Load and Burnout: Can Social Support and Perceived Accomplishment Help?" *Social Work* 34 (34): 243–48.

Kolmes, K. 2012. "Social Media in the Future of Professional Psychology." *Professional Psychology: Research & Practice* 43 (6): 606–12.

——. 2013. "My Private Practice Social Media Policy." http://www.drkkolmes.com/docs/socmed.pdf (accessed July 19, 2013).

Kopels, S. and J. D. Kagle. 1993. "Do Social Workers Have a Duty to Warn?" *Social Service Review* 67 (1): 101–26.

Kraus, R, G. Stricker, and C. Speyer, eds. 2011. *Online Counseling: A Handbook for Mental Health Professionals,* 2d ed. London: Elsevier.

Kurzman, P. A. 1995. "Professional Liability and Malpractice." In *Encyclopedia of Social Work.* 19th ed., 1921–27. Washington, DC: NASW Press.

"Lack of Physician-Patient Relationship Did Not Provide Psychiatrist with Defense." 1998. *Mental Health Law News* 3 (4): 1.

Lakin, M. 1988. *Ethical Issues in the Psychotherapies.* New York: Oxford University Press.

Laliotis, D. A. and J. H. Grayson. 1985. "Psychologist Heal Thyself: What Is Available for the Impaired Psychologist?" *American Psychologist* 40:84–96.

Lamb, D. H., C. Clark, P. Drumheller, K. Frizzell, and L. Surrey. 1989. "Applying *Tarasoff* to AIDS-Related Psychotherapy Issues." *Professional Psychology: Research and Practice* 20 (1): 37–43.

Lamb, D. H., N. R. Presser, K. S. Pfost, M. C. Baum, V. R. Jackson, and P. A. Jarvis. 1987. "Confronting Professional Impairment During the Internship: Identification, Due Process, and Remediation." *Professional Psychology: Research and Practice* 18 (6): 597–603.

Lambert, T. F. 1996. "Tom on Torts." *Law Reporter* 39:228–31.

Landers, S. 1992. "Ethical Boundaries Easily Trespassed." *NASW News,* October, 3.

Levy, C. S. 1973. "The Ethics of Supervision." *Social Work* 18 (3): 14–21.

——. 1976. *Social Work Ethics.* New York: Human Sciences Press.

Lewis, H. 1972. "Morality and the Politics of Practice." *Social Casework* 53 (7): 404–17.

Lewis, M. B. 1986. "Duty to Warn Versus Duty to Maintain Confidentiality: Conflicting Demands on Mental Health Professionals." *Suffolk Law Review* 20 (3): 579–615.

Lifson, L. and R. Simon, eds. 1998. *The Mental Health Practitioner and the Law: A Comprehensive Handbook.* Cambridge, MA: Harvard University Press.

Litan, R. E. and C. Winston, eds. 1988. *Liability: Perspectives and Policy.* Washington, DC: Brookings Institution.

Litan, R. E., P. Swire, and C. Winston. 1988. "The U.S. Liability System: Background and Trends." In R. E. Litan and C. Winston, eds., *Liability: Perspectives and Policy,* 1–15. Washington, DC: Brookings Institution.

Lloyd, J. D., ed. 2001. *Family Violence.* San Diego: Greenhaven.

Loewenberg, F. and R. Dolgoff. 1992. *Ethical Decisions for Social Work Practice.* 4th ed. Itasca, IL: F. E. Peacock.

Louisiana State Board of Social Work Examiners. 2013a. "In the Matter of Donald Henry." http://www.labswe.org/lms/Files/625.pdf (accessed December 22, 2013).

——. 2013b. "In the Matter of Jennifer Gordon." http://www.labswe.org/lms/Files/580.pdf (accessed December 22, 2013).

——. 2013c. "In the Matter of Kristin Richards." http://www.labswe.org/lms/Files/606.pdf (accessed December 22, 2013)

Luepker, E. and L. Norton. 2002. *Record Keeping in Psychotherapy and Counseling: Protecting Confidentiality and the Professional Relationship.* New York: Brunner-Routledge.

Madden, R. G. 1998. *Legal Issues in Social Work, Counseling, and Mental Health.* Thousand Oaks, CA: Sage.

——. 2003. *Essential Law for Social Workers.* New York: Columbia University Press.

"Malpractice: How to Sidestep the Pitfalls." 1997. *NASW News,* February, 5.

"Man Claims Hospital Fails to Restrict Dangerous Psychiatric Patient." 1994. *Mental Health Law News* 9 (9): 3.

"Man Claims Improper Discharge Following Suicide Attempt." 1990. *Mental Health Law News* 5 (11): 6.

"Man Claims Inadequate Observation in Psychiatric Ward; Falls from Window." 1994. *Mental Health Law News* 9 (11): 3.

"Man Commits Suicide After Evaluation at a VA Hospital: $200,000 Settlement." 1994. *Mental Health Law News* 9 (2): 6.

"Man Commits Suicide in Hospital; Bed Checks Fail to Discover Death." 1996. *Mental Health Law News* 11 (2): 3.

"Man Discharged from Psychiatric Facility Commits Suicide: $3 Million Settlement." 1994. *Mental Health Law News* 9 (8): 4.

"Man Hangs Self After Being Referred for Outpatient Therapy." 1997. *Mental Health Law News* 12 (6): 3.

"Man in Joint Counseling Did Not Waive Patient-Psychotherapist Privilege." 1995. *Mental Health Law News* 10 (4): 3.

"Man Kills Woman, Then Commits Suicide: $1 Million Settlement on Claim of Failure to Diagnose." 1994. *Mental Health Law News* 9 (5): 3.

"Man Murdered by Son Following Son's Dismissal from Hospital After Evaluation." 1992. *Mental Health Law News* 7 (3): 6.

"Man on One-to-One Watch Allowed to Leave Floor Without Required Clearance: Falls from Window." 1996. *Mental Health Law News* 11 (3): 4.

Mannix, A. 2012. "U of M Paid Legal Bills of Former Employee Sanctioned over Dan Markingson case." *City Pages,* November 19. http://blogs.citypages.com/blotter/2012/11/u_of_m_paid_legal_fees_dan_markingson_case.php (accessed June 12, 2013).

Marcus, R. and S. Schmidt. 1998. "Attorney-Client Privilege After Death Is Upheld." *Washington Post,* June 26. http://www.washingtonpost.com/wp-srv/politics/special/clinton/stories/foster062698.htm (accessed July 21, 2013).

"Marriage Therapist Has Affair with Patient." 1990. *Mental Health Law News* 5 (4): 3.

Martelle, S. 2009. "Broken Trust." *Hour Detroit,* August. http://www.hourdetroit.com/Hour-Detroit/August-2009/Broken-Trust/ (accessed December 21, 2013).

Maryland Board of Social Work Examiners. 2012. "In the Matter of Ava Barron-Shasho." http://dhmh.maryland.gov/bswe/Docs/Orders/Shasho-1735.pdf (accessed December 22, 2013).

——. 2013. "In the Matter of Lachandra Colbert." http://dhmh.maryland.gov/bswe/Docs/Orders/colbert-1775.pdf (accessed December 23, 2013).

McAdams, C. R. and K. L. Wyatt. 2010. "The Regulation of Technology-assisted Distance Counseling and Supervision in the United States: An Analysis of Current Extent, Trends, and Implications." *Counselor Education and Supervision* 49:179–92.

McArdle, E. 1994. "New Cause of Action May Stem from California Verdict: Father Wins $500,000 for Daughter's 'False Memory' of Abuse." *Lawyers Weekly USA,* June 6, B3.

McCrady, B. S. 1989. "The Distressed or Impaired Professional: From Retribution to Rehabilitation." *Journal of Drug Issues* 19:337–49.

McDermott, F. E., ed. 1975. *Self-determination in Social Work.* London: Routledge and Kegan Paul.

"Member Blows Whistle on Rx Refills." 1990. *NASW News,* June, 11.

"Mental, Emotional Anguish Blamed on Improper Sexual Contact During Treatment." 2000. *Mental Health Law News* 15 (2): 5.

"Mental Health Center Could Be Held Liable for Breaching Duty to Exercise Reasonable Care." 1994. *Mental Health Law News* 9 (5): 2.

"Mental Health Center's Failure to Conduct Tests for Brain Tumor Make It Liable for Patient's Death." 1992. *Mental Health Law News* 7 (5): 2.

"Mental Health Facility Not Liable for Release of Patient." 1990. *Mental Health Law News* 5 (4): 2.

"Mental Patient Escapes and Is Struck by Car." 1990. *Mental Health Law News* 5 (11): 3.

Meyer, R. G., E. R. Landis, and J. R. Hays. 1988. *Law for the Psychotherapist.* New York: W. W. Norton.

Midkiff, D. M. and W. J. Wyatt. 2008. "Ethical Issues in the Provision of Online Mental Health Services (E-therapy)." *Journal of Technology in Human Services* 26:310–32.

Miller, I. 1987. "Supervision in Social Work." In *Encyclopedia of Social Work.* 18th ed., 748–56. Silver Spring, MD: National Association of Social Workers.

Millon, T., C. Millon, and M. Antoni. 1986. "Sources of Emotional and Mental Disorder Among Psychologists: A Career Development Perspective." In Kilburg, Nathan, and Thoreson, *Professionals in Distress,* 119–34.

"Misdiagnosis of Multiple Personality Disorders: $2.4 Million Settlement." 1997. *Mental Health Law News* 12 (6): 6.

Moline, M. E., G. T. Williams, and K. Austin. 1998. *Documenting Psychotherapy: Essentials for Mental Health Practitioners.* Thousand Oaks, CA: Sage.

Morgan, S. and C. Polowy. 2011. "Social Workers and Skype: Part I." *NASW Legal Defense Fund, Legal Issue of the Month.* November. www.socialworkers.org/ldf/legal_issue (accessed July 6, 2013).

Morse, R. M., M. A. Martin, W. M. Swenson, and R. G. Niven. 1984. "Prognosis of Physicians Treated for Alcoholism and Drug Dependence." *Journal of the American Medical Association* 251:743–46.

Munson, C. E. 1983. *An Introduction to Clinical Social Work Supervision.* New York: Haworth.

——. 2001. *Handbook of Clinical Social Work Supervision.* 3d ed. New York: Haworth.

Nader, R., P. J. Petkas, and K. Blackwood, eds. 1972. *Whistle Blowing.* New York: Grossman.

NASW (National Association of Social Workers). Commission on Employment and Economic Support. 1987a. *Impaired Social Worker Program Resource Book.* Silver Spring, MD: Author.

——. 1987b. "'Signing Off' Fraud Charge Warns Kentucky Clinicians." *NASW News,* June, 1.

——. 1994. *Guidelines for Clinical Social Work Supervision.* Washington, DC: Author.

——. 2008. *Code of Ethics.* Rev. ed. Washington, DC: Author.

NASW and ASWB (National Association of Social Workers and Association of Social Work Boards). 2005. *Standards for Technology and Social Work Practice.* Washington, DC, and Culpeper, VA: Authors.

National Conference of State Legislatures. 2013. "Mental Health Professionals' Duty to Protect/Warn." *NCSL,* January. http://www.ncsl.org/research/health/mental-health-professionals-duty-to-warn.aspx (accessed December 21, 2013).

"Negligent Care of Mental Patient Alleged in Suicide Death; $317,500 Verdict." 2001. *Mental Health Law News* 16 (2): 2.

"Negligent Supervision of Patient on Suicide Watch Blamed for Hanging Death." 1998. *Mental Health Law News* 13 (9): 3.

New Jersey State Board of Social Work Examiners. 2000. "In the Matter of Daniel Cruz." http://www.state.nj.us/lps/ca/action/20000216_44SW01452900.pdf (accessed December 22, 2013).

——. 2004. "In the Matter of Paul Steffens." http://www.state.nj.us/lps/ca/action/20040123_44SW00652000.pdf (accessed December 23, 2013).

Nicholson, K. 2001. "'Rebirth' Therapists Get 16 Years." *Denver Post,* June 19. http://www.denverpost.com (accessed June 19, 2001).

"No Duty to Warn Without Direct Threat of Specific Act Against Identifiable Victim." 1999. *Mental Health Law News* 14 (3): 6.

"No Liability for Injury to 'Escaped Person.'" 1993. *Mental Health Law News* 8 (5): 3.

"Note: Social Worker–Client Relationship and Privileged Communications." 1965. *Washington University Law Quarterly,* 362–95.

"No 'Trust Relationship' Between Patient and Counselor." 1991. *Mental Health Law News* 6 (12): 4.

"No Violation of Confidentiality in Communicating Patient's Arson Confession." 1990. *Mental Health Law News* 5 (4): 4.

"Nursing Home Liable in Attempted Suicide." 1990. *Mental Health Law News* 5 (1): 1.

"Official of Alcohol Center Entered into Sexual Relationship with Woman One Month After She Left Program." 1990. *Mental Health Law News* 5 (7): 5.

Olarte, S. W. 1997. "Sexual Boundary Violations." In *The Hatherleigh Guide to Ethics in Therapy,* 195–209. New York: Hatherleigh.

Paine, R. T. Jr. 1880. "The Work of Volunteer Visitors of the Associated Charities Among the Poor." *Journal of Social Science* 12:113.

"Parents Allege Failure to Document Treatment Withdrawal from Case Contributed to Son's Suicide." 1990. *Mental Health Law News* 5 (12): 4.

"Patient Admitted to Hospital for Detoxification; Attempted Suicide Results in Brain Damage." 1990. *Mental Health Law News* 5 (7): 2.

"Patient Can Not Bring Malpractice Action Against Psychologist Who Consulted with Patient's Therapist." 2000. *Mental Health Law News* 15 (3): 1.

"Patient Commits Suicide After Release; Claim Stated for Wrongful Death." 1995. *Mental Health Law News* 10 (9): 1.

"Patient Escapes and Commits Murder." 1990. *Mental Health Law News* 5 (10): 6.

"Patient Falls to Death from Hospital Window; $563,500 Settlement." 1995. *Mental Health Law News* 10 (3): 2.

"Patient Improperly Treated for Panic Disorder and Agoraphobia." 1992. *Mental Health Law News* 7 (7): 6.

"Patient Jumps from Hospital Window." 1989. *Mental Health Law News* 4 (12): 2.

"Patient Raped by Fellow Patient." 1989. *Mental Health Law News* 4 (11): 6.

"Patient Released from Mental Hospital Ingests Lye." 1989. *Mental Health Law News* 4 (11): 3.

"Patient Sexually Abused by Psychologist." 1990. *Mental Health Law News* 5 (12): 3.

"Patient's Threats Disclosed: Right to Privacy Not Violated." 1993. *Mental Health Law News* 8 (2): 6.

Patti, R. J. 1983. *Social Welfare Administration: Managing Social Programs in a Developmental Context.* Englewood Cliffs, NJ: Prentice-Hall.

Pearson, M. M. 1982. "Psychiatric Treatment of 250 Physicians." *Psychiatric Annals* 12:194–206.

Pearson, M. M. and E. A. Strecker. 1960. "Physicians as Psychiatric Patients: Private Practice Experience." *American Journal of Psychiatry* 116 (10): 915–19.

Pecora, P. J., J. K. Whittaker, A. N. Maluccio, R. P. Barth, and D. Panfilis. 2009. *The Child Welfare Challenge: Policy, Practice, and Research.* 3d ed. Piscataway, NJ: Aldine-Transaction.

Perlman, H. H. 1965. "Self-determination: Reality or Illusion?" *Social Service Review* 39 (4): 410–21.

Pernick, M. S. 1982. "The Patient's Role in Medical Decision Making: A Social History of Informed Consent in Medical Therapy." In President's Commission, *Making Health Care Decisions,* 1–35.

Peters, C. and T. Branch. 1972. *Blowing the Whistle: Dissent in the Public Interest.* New York: Praeger.

Peterson, M. R. and R. L. Beck. 2003. "E-mail as an Adjunctive Tool in Psychotherapy: Response and Responsibility." *American Journal of Psychotherapy* 57:167–81.

"Physician Fails to Properly Treat Depression or Make Timely Referral." 1992. *Mental Health Law News* 7 (10): 2.

Pinals, D. A. and D. Mossman. 2012. *Evaluation for Civil Commitment.* New York: Oxford University Press.

"Plaintiff Claims Repressed Memories Implanted by Psychiatrist; $2.4 Million Settlement." 1997. *Mental Health Law News* 12 (11): 2.

"Plaintiffs Claim Failure to Continue Hospitalization Led to Murder, Then Suicide: $363,000 Verdict." 1994. *Mental Health Law News* 9 (4): 2.

"Plaintiffs Claim Therapist Planted False Memories in Patient." 1997. *Mental Health Law News* 2 (11): 6.

Plant, R. 1970. *Social and Moral Theory in Casework.* London: Routledge and Kegan Paul.

Polowy, C. I. and C. Gorenberg. 1997. *Client Confidentiality and Privileged Communications: Office of General Counsel Law Notes.* Washington, DC: National Association of Social Workers.

Pope, K. S. 1988. "How Clients Are Harmed by Sexual Contact with Mental Health Professionals: The Syndrome and Its Prevalence." *Journal of Counseling and Development* 67 (4): 222–26.

Pope, K. S., B. G. Tabachnick, and P. Keith-Spiegel. 1987. "Ethics of Practice: The Beliefs and Behaviors of Psychologists as Therapists." *American Psychologist* 42:993–1006.

President's Commission for the Study of Ethical Problems in Medicine and Biomedical and Behavioral Research. 1982. *Making Health Care Decisions: The Ethical and Legal Implications of Informed Consent in the Patient-Practitioner Relationship,* vol. 3. Washington, DC: U.S. Government Printing Office.

Price, D., K. Duodu, and N. Cain. 2009. *Defamation: Law, Procedure, and Practice.* 4th ed. London: Sweet & Maxwell.

"Privilege Did Not Protect Defendant's Letter to Therapist Admitting Sexual Abuse of Daughter." 1993. *Mental Health Law News* 8 (8): 1.

Prochaska, J. and J. Norcross. 1983. "Psychotherapists' Perspectives on Treating Themselves and Their Clients for Psychic Distress." *Professional Psychology: Research and Practice* 14 (5): 642–55.

Promislo, E. 1979. "Confidentiality and Privileged Communication." *Social Work* 24 (1): 10–13.

"Psychiatric Nurse Hangs Self While Patient in Hospital." 1995. *Mental Health Law News* 10 (9): 4.

"Psychiatric Nurse's Disclosure of Confidential Treatment Records Justified License Suspension." 2000. *Mental Health Law News* 15 (8): 3.

"Psychiatric Nurse Seduced Woman into Lesbian Relationship; $460,000 Verdict." 1995. *Mental Health Law News* 10 (9): 3.

"Psychiatric Patient Claims Improper Sexual Contact; $217,373 Verdict." 2000. *Mental Health Law News* 15 (2): 6.

"Psychiatric Patient Has Sexual Relationship with Psychiatrist." 1989. *Mental Health Law News* 6 (11): 4.

"Psychiatric Patient Injured Trying to Flee Hospital." 1990. *Mental Health Law News* 5 (4): 5.

"Psychiatric Patient Leaps from Hospital Window, Suffers Paraplegia; $1.32 Million Verdict." 1992. *Mental Health Law News* 7 (12): 2.

"Psychiatric Patient Not Properly Monitored While Eating Chokes to Death." 1990. *Mental Health Law News* 5 (11): 4.

"Psychiatric Patient Raped by Fellow Patient." 1989. *Mental Health Law News* 4 (3): 4.

"Psychiatric Ward Fails to Prevent Suicide: $1 Million Verdict." 1999. *Mental Health Law News* 14 (7): 4.

"Psychiatrist and Psychologist Revealed Patient's Threat: No Invasion of Privacy." 1995. *Mental Health Law News* 10 (6): 1.

"Psychiatrist Censured for Engaging in Commercial Transactions with Patient." 1996. *Mental Health Law News* 11 (3): 6.

"Psychiatrist Dates Patient Who Had Been in Detox Program; $2.3 Million Verdict." 1997. *Mental Health Law News* 12 (4): 6.

"Psychiatrist Did Not Owe Duty to Protect Prospective Victims of Former Patient." 1995. *Mental Health Law News* 10 (10): 4.

"Psychiatrist Did Not Owe Duty to Warn Patient's Sister About Risk." 1989. *Mental Health Law News* 4 (10): 3.

"Psychiatrist Engages in Sex with Patient; Inadequate Monitoring of Prescription Drugs." 2001. *Mental Health Law News* 16 (1): 4.

"Psychiatrist Has Sexual Relations with Patient; $1.45 Million Verdict." 1995. *Mental Health Law News* 10 (10): 2.

"Psychiatrist Has Sex with Patient." 1989. *Mental Health Law News* 4 (11): 6.

"Psychiatrist Not Negligent in Misdiagnosing and Releasing Patient Who Killed Third Party." 1992. *Mental Health Law News* 7 (10): 1.

"Psychiatrist's Crime Tip Did Not Violate Physician-Patient Privilege." 1990. *Mental Health Law News* 5 (3): 1.

"Psychiatrists Liable for Patient's Attempted Suicide." 1991. *Mental Health Law News* 6 (3): 1.

"Psychiatrist's License Suspended Six Months for Having Sexual Relations with Patient." 1993. *Mental Health Law News* 8 (3): 4.

"Psychiatrists Not Liable for Discharging Patient Who Later Committed Suicide." 1989. *Mental Health Law News* 4 (10): 2.

"Psychiatrist's Testimony About Patient's Threats Not Protected by Psychotherapist-Patient Privilege." 1999. *Mental Health Law News* 14 (12): 3.

"Psychiatrist Sued; Recovered Repressed Memories of Patient's Childhood." 1995. *Mental Health Law News* 10 (4): 6.

"Psychiatrist Takes Patient off Suicide Watch to Go on Outing; He Plunges to His Death." 1998. *Mental Health Law News* 13 (9): 3.

"Psychiatrist Who Discloses Confidential Information About Patient Liable for Damages." 1994. *Mental Health Law News* 9 (4): 1.

"Psychiatry Resident Has Improper Sexual Contact with Child." 1999. *Mental Health Law News* 14 (10): 3.

"Psychological Counselor Refers Patients to Unqualified 'Colleague.'" 1991. *Mental Health Law News* 6 (8): 6.

"Psychologist Breaches Psychologist-Patient Privilege by Providing Testimony." 2000. *Mental Health Law News* 15 (2): 4.

"Psychologist Did Not Maintain Proper Records." 1992. *Mental Health Law News* 7 (1): 6.

"Psychologist Encourages Sexual Misconduct Between Patient and Psychiatrist." 1989. *Mental Health Law News* 4 (3): 2.

"Psychologist Has Romantic Relationship with Patient; Patient Returns to Abusive Husband and Attempts Suicide." 1994. *Mental Health Law News* 11 (10): 2.

"Psychologist Immune from Liability for Warning About Threats." 2001. *Mental Health Law News* 16 (8): 1.

"Psychologist in Sex Abuse Case Cannot Be Sued for Defamation." 1993. *Mental Health Law News* 8 (6): 1.

"Psychologist-Patient Privilege Did Not Protect Statements by Spouse During Counseling." 1994. *Mental Health Law News* 10 (7): 2.

"Psychologist's License Properly Revoked for Deception in Application." 1991. *Mental Health Law News* 6 (5): 6.

"Psychologists Owed Duty to Protect Child from Sexual Abuse." 1996. *Mental Health Law News* 11 (4): 3.

"Psychologist's Unorthodox Treatment for Personality Disorder Results in $325,000 Settlement." 1995. *Mental Health Law News* 10 (3): 1.

"Psychologist Violates Confidentiality Privileges." 2001. *Mental Health Law News* 16 (7): 4.

"Psychologist Who Failed to Follow Procedures for Reporting Child Abuse Not Immune from Liability." 1993. *Mental Health Law News* 8 (6): 3.

"Psychologist Who Had Sex with Patient May Have Acted Within Scope of Employment." 1997. *Mental Health Law News* 12 (4): 1.

"Psychotherapist Has No Duty to Warn Third Party of Patient's Threat of Violence." 1992. *Mental Health Law News* 7 (2): 3.

"Psychotherapist May Not Be Sued for Erroneous Child Abuse Diagnosis." 1992. *Mental Health Law News* 7 (11): 4.

Quinsey, V. L., G. T. Harris, M. E. Rice, and C. A. Cormier. 2005. *Violent Offenders: Appraising and Managing Risk.* Washington, DC: American Psychological Association.

Reamer, F. G. 1979. "Protecting Research Subjects and Unintended Consequences: The Effect of Guarantees of Confidentiality." *Public Opinion Quarterly* 43 (4): 497–506.

——. 1980. "Ethical Content in Social Work." *Social Casework* 61 (9): 531–40.

——. 1982a. *Ethical Dilemmas in Social Service.* New York: Columbia University Press.

——. 1982b. "Conflicts of Professional Duty in Social Work." *Social Casework* 63 (10): 579–85.

——. 1983a. "Ethical Dilemmas in Social Work Practice." *Social Work* 28 (1): 31–35.

——. 1983b. "The Concept of Paternalism in Social Work." *Social Service Review* 57 (2): 254–71.

——. 1984. "Enforcing Ethics in Social Work." *Health Matrix* 2 (2): 17–25.

——. 1987a. "Values and Ethics." In *Encyclopedia of Social Work*. 18th ed., 801–9. Silver Spring, MD: National Association of Social Workers.

——. 1987b. "Ethics Committees in Social Work." *Social Work* 32 (3): 188–92.

——. 1987c. "Informed Consent in Social Work." *Social Work* 32 (5): 425–29.

——. 1989a. "Toward Ethical Practice: The Relevance of Ethical Theory." *Social Thought* 15 (3/4): 67–78.

——. 1989b. "Liability Issues in Social Work Supervision." *Social Work* 34 (5): 445–48.

——. 1990. *Ethical Dilemmas in Social Service*. 2d ed. New York: Columbia University Press.

——. 1991a. "AIDS: The Relevance of Ethics." In F. G. Reamer, ed., *AIDS and Ethics*, 1–25. New York: Columbia University Press.

——. 1991b. "AIDS, Social Work, and the 'Duty to Protect.'" *Social Work* 36 (1): 56–60.

——. 1992a. "The Impaired Social Worker." *Social Work* 37 (2): 165–70.

——. 1992b. "Should Social Workers Blow the Whistle on Incompetent Colleagues?" In E. Gambrill and R. Pruger, eds., *Controversial Issues in Social Work*, 66–78. Boston: Allyn and Bacon.

——. 1992c. "Social Work and the Public Good: Calling or Career?" In P. N. Reid and P. R. Popple, eds., *The Moral Purposes of Social Work*, 11–33. Chicago: Nelson-Hall.

——. 1993a. *The Philosophical Foundations of Social Work*. New York: Columbia University Press.

——. 1993b. "Liability Issues in Social Work Administration." *Administration in Social Work* 17 (4): 11–25.

——. 1995. "Malpractice and Liability Claims Against Social Workers: First Facts." *Social Work* 40 (5): 595–601.

——. 2000a. "Administrative Ethics." In R. Patti, ed., *The Handbook of Social Welfare Management*, 69–85. Thousand Oaks, CA: Sage.

——. 2000b. "The Social Work Ethics Audit: A Risk Management Strategy." *Social Work* 45 (4): 355–66.

——. 2001a. *The Social Work Ethics Audit: A Risk Management Tool*. Washington, DC: NASW Press.

——. 2001b. *Ethics Education in Social Work*. Alexandria, VA: Council on Social Work Education.

——. 2001c. "Ethics and Managed Care Policy." In N. W. Veeder and W. Peebles-Wilkins, eds., *Managed Care Services: Policy, Programs, and Research*, 74–96. New York: Oxford University Press.

——. 2002. "Risk Management." In A. Roberts and G. J. Greene, eds., *Social Workers' Desk Reference,* 70–75. New York: Oxford University Press.

——. 2004. "Ethical Decisions and Risk Management." In M. Austin and K. Hopkins, eds., *Supervision as Collaboration in the Human Services,* 97–109. Thousand Oaks, CA: Sage.

——. 2005. "Documentation in Social Work: Evolving Ethical and Risk Management Standards." *Social Work* 50 (4): 325–34.

——. 2006. *Ethical Standards in Social Work: A Review of the NASW Code of Ethics.* 2d ed. Washington, DC: NASW Press.

——. 2009. *The Social Work Ethics Casebook: Cases and Commentary.* Washington, DC: NASW Press.

——. 2012a. *Boundary Issues and Dual Relationships in the Human Services.* New York: Columbia University Press.

——. 2012b. "Essential Ethics Education in Social Work Field Instruction: A Blueprint for Field Educators." *Field Educator* 2 (2). http://fieldeducator. simmons.edu/article/essential-ethics-education-in-social-work-field-instruction/ (accessed February 25, 2014).

——. 2012c. "The Digital and Electronic Revolution in Social Work: Rethinking the Meaning of Ethical Practice." *Ethics and Social Welfare* 7 (1): 2–19.

——. 2013a. *Social Work Values and Ethics.* 4th ed. New York: Columbia University Press.

——. 2013b. "Social Work in a Digital Age: Ethical and Risk Management Challenges." *Social Work* 58 (2): 163–72.

Reamer, F. G. and M. Abramson. 1982. *The Teaching of Social Work Ethics.* Hastings-on-Hudson, NY: Hastings Center.

Reaves, R. R. 1986. "Legal Liability and Psychologists." In Kilburg, Nathan, and Thoreson, *Professionals in Distress,* 173–84.

"Recovered Memories of Prior Sexual Abuse Not Admissible." 1998. *Mental Health Law News* 13 (2): 2.

Recupero, P. R. and S. E. Rainey. 2005. "Informed Consent to e-therapy." *American Journal of Psychotherapy* 59:319–31.

Reid, W. H. 1999. *A Clinician's Guide to Legal Issues in Psychotherapy.* Redding, CT: Zeig, Tucker and Theisen.

"Resident at Hospital for Mentally Retarded Receives Award for Negligent Treatment." 1989. *Mental Health Law News* 4 (3): 4.

Reynolds, B. C. 1942. *Learning and Teaching in the Practice of Social Work.* New York: Farrar.

Reynolds, M. M. 1976. "Threats to Confidentiality." *Social Work* 21 (2): 108–13.

Rhodes, M. 1986. *Ethical Dilemmas in Social Work Practice.* London: Routledge and Kegan Paul.

Rieman, D. W. 1992. *Strategies in Social Work Consultation.* New York: Longman.

Robinson, G. W. Jr. 1962. "Discussion." *American Journal of Psychiatry* 118 (9): 779–80.

Robinson, V. 1936. *Supervision in Social Case Work.* Chapel Hill: University of North Carolina Press.

——. 1949. *The Dynamics of Supervision Under Functional Controls.* Philadelphia: University of Pennsylvania Press.

Rome, S. H. 2013. *Social Work and the Law: Judicial Policy and Forensic Practice.* Upper Saddle River, NJ: Pearson.

Rothblatt, H. B. and D. H. Leroy. 1973. "Avoiding Psychiatric Malpractice." *California Western Law Review* 9:260–72.

Rozovsky, F. A. 1984. *Consent to Treatment: A Practical Guide.* Boston: Little, Brown.

St. Germaine, J. 1993. "Dual Relationships: What's Wrong with Them?" *American Counselor* 2:25–30.

——. 1996. "Dual Relationships and Certified Alcohol and Drug Counselors: A National Study of Ethical Beliefs and Behaviors." *Alcoholism Treatment Quarterly* 14:29–44.

Saks, E. R. 2002. *Refusing Care: Forced Treatment and the Rights of the Mentally Ill.* New York: Oxford University Press.

Saltzman, A. and K. Proch. 1990. *Law in Social Work Practice.* Chicago: Nelson-Hall.

Santhiveeran, J. 2009. "Compliance of Social Work E-therapy Websites to the NASW Code of Ethics." *Social Work in Health Care* 48:1–13.

"Schizophrenic Patient Hangs Self." 1991. *Mental Health Law News* 6 (3): 6.

Schoener, G. R. 1995. "Assessments of Professionals Who Have Engaged in Boundary Violations." *Psychiatric Annals* 25:95–99.

Schoener, G. R. and J. Gonsiorek. 1988. "Assessment and Development of Rehabilitation Plans for Counselors Who Have Sexually Exploited Their Clients." *Journal of Counseling and Development* 67 (4): 227–32.

"School and Staff Not Liable for Injuries Sustained When Retarded Resident Was Attacked." 1994. *Mental Health Law News* 9 (5): 3.

Schutz, B. M. 1982. *Legal Liability in Psychotherapy.* San Francisco: Jossey-Bass.

Sears, R., J. Rudisill, and C. Mason-Sears. 2006. *Consultation Skills for Mental Health Professionals.* Hoboken, NJ: John F. Wiley & Sons.

"Sexual Relationship Between Patient and Unlicensed Mental Health Worker Results in Lawsuit." 1995. *Mental Health Law News* 10 (5): 3.

Sheffield, A. E. 1920. *The Social Case History: Its Construction and Content.* New York: Russell Sage Foundation.

Shore, J. H. 1982. "The Impaired Physician: Four Years After Probation." *Journal of the American Medical Association* 248:3127–30.

Shulman, L. 1987. "Consultation." In *Encyclopedia of Social Work.* 18th ed., 326–31. Silver Spring, MD: National Association of Social Workers.

——. 2008. "Supervision." In *Encyclopedia of Social Work.* 20th ed., 186–90. New York and Washington, DC: Oxford University Press and NASW Press.

Sidell, N. L. 2011. *Social Work Documentation: A Guide to Strengthening Your Case Recording.* Washington, DC: NASW Press.

Siebert, D. 2006. "Personal and Occupational Factors in Burnout among Practicing Social Workers: Implications for Researchers, Practitioners, and Managers." *Journal of Social Service Research* 32:25–44.

Siegel, D. H. 1992. "Should Social Workers Blow the Whistle on Incompetent Colleagues?" In E. Gambrill and R. Pruger, eds., *Controversial Issues in Social Work,* 66–78. Boston: Allyn and Bacon.

Simon, R. I. 1995. "The Natural History of Therapist Sexual Misconduct: Identification and Prevention." *Psychiatric Annals* 25:90–94.

——. 1998. "Litigation Hot Spots in Clinical Practice." In Lifson and Simon, *Mental Health Practitioner and the Law,* 117–39.

——. 1999. "Therapist-Patient Sex: From Boundary Violations to Sexual Misconduct." *Forensic Psychiatry* 22:31–47.

Simone, S. and S. M. Fulero. 2005. "*Tarasoff* and the Duty to Protect." *Journal of Aggression, Maltreatment, and Trauma* 11 (1/2): 145–68.

Siporin, M. 1982. "Moral Philosophy in Social Work Today." *Social Service Review* 56 (4): 516–38.

——. 1989. "The Social Work Ethic." *Social Thought* 15 (3/4): 42–52.

Slater, L. K. and K. R. Finck. 2012. *Social Work Practice and the Law.* New York: Springer.

Slavin, S., ed. 1982. *Applying Computers in Social Service and Mental Health Agencies.* New York: Haworth.

Slovenko, R. 1978. "Psychotherapy and Informed Consent: A Search in Judicial Regulation." In Barton and Sanborn, *Law and the Mental Health Professions,* 51–70.

"Social Worker Engages in Sexual Relationship with Patient." 1999. *Mental Health Law News* 4 (5): 2.

Sonnenstuhl, W. J. 1989. "Reaching the Impaired Professional: Applying Findings from Organizational and Occupational Research." *Journal of Drug Issues* 19 (6): 533–39.

Specht, H. and M. E. Courtney. 1997. *Unfaithful Angels: How Social Work Has Abandoned Its Mission.* New York: Simon and Schuster.

Stadler, H. A., K. Willing, M. G. Eberhage, and W. H. Ward. 1988. "Impairment: Implications for the Counseling Profession." *Journal of Counseling and Development* 66 (6): 258–60.

"State Disciplines Psychiatrist for Making Improper Referral." 1992. *Providence (RI) Journal-Bulletin,* December 1, B3.

State of Ohio Counselor and Social Worker Board. 1996. "In the Matter of Charlea M. Harbert." http://cswmft.ohio.gov/DiscLic/S0001133.pdf (accessed December 23, 2013).

——. 2008. "Consent Agreement between Beth Adkins and the State of Ohio Counselor, Social Worker, and Marriage and Family Therapist Board." http://cswmft.ohio.gov/DiscLic/S0023843.pdf (accessed December 21, 2013).

——. 2009. "Consent Agreement between Robert J. Carson and the State of Ohio Counselor, Social Worker, and Marriage and Family Therapist Board. http://cswmft.ohio.gov/DiscLic/I0009744.pdf (accessed December 23, 2013).

"Statements Made to Alcoholics Anonymous Volunteers Not Protected by Privilege." 1997. *Mental Health Law News* 12 (3): 1.

"Statements Made to Therapist by Man Charged with Sexual Abuse Not Protected." 1996. *Mental Health Law News* 11 (12): 2.

Stoesen, L. 2002. "Recovering Social Workers Offer Support." *NASW News,* July, 3.

Strom-Gottfried, K. J. 1999. "Professional Boundaries: An Analysis of Violations by Social Workers." *Families in Society* 80:439–49.

Substance Abuse and Mental Health Services Administration. 2011. "Facebook Provides First-of-a-Kind Service to Help Prevent Suicides." http://www.samhsa.gov/newsroom/advisories/1112125820.aspx (accessed June 13, 2012).

"Substance Abuse Program Records Confidential." 1994. *Mental Health Law News* 9 (5): 6.

"Suicidal Patient Not Restrained by Defendant Hospital." 1990. *Mental Health Law News* 5 (2): 3.

Syme, G. 2003. *Dual Relationships in Counselling and Psychotherapy.* London: Sage.

"Teenager Claims No Probable Cause for Confinement in Psychiatric Hospital." 1994. *Mental Health Law News* 9 (9): 1.

"Teenager Commits Suicide After Evaluation with Social Worker." 1996. *Mental Health Law News* 11 (4): 4.

"Teenager Commits Suicide by Taking Drug Overdose After Hospital Discharge." 1992. *Mental Health Law News* 7 (4): 1.

"Testimony from Social Worker and Psychologist Not Privileged." 1996. *Mental Health Law News* 11 (10): 6.

Texas Department of State Health Service. 2013. "Texas State Board of Social Worker Examiners Enforcement Actions—Disciplinary Actions." http://www.dshs.state.tx.us/socialwork/sw_cmp.shtm (accessed December 22, 2013).

"Theory of Repressed Memories Valid for Purposes of Introducing Evidence." 1996. *Mental Health Law News* 11 (10): 3.

"Therapist Begins Personal Relationship with Wife While Still Seeing Husband." 1994. *Mental Health Law News* 9 (6): 4.

"Therapist Sleeps with Patient and Makes Her Pregnant." 1996. *Mental Health Law News* 11 (4): 5.

"Therapists Fail to Notify or Take Action Against Abuse of Group Home Residents." 2001. *Mental Health Law News* 16 (8): 2.

"Therapists Have No Duty to Control Outpatients from Harming Unidentified Third Parties." 1996. *Mental Health Law News* 11 (9): 1.

"Therapist's Sexual Misconduct Would Result in Physical Harm, Mental Illness." 1996. *Mental Health Law News* 11 (11): 6.

Thoreson, R. W. and J. K. Skorina. 1986. "Alcohol Abuse Among Psychologists." In Kilburg, Nathan, and Thoreson, *Professionals in Distress*, 77–117.

Thoreson, R. W., M. Miller, and C. J. Krauskopf. 1989. "The Distressed Psychologist: Prevalence and Treatment Considerations." *Professional Psychology: Research and Practice* 20 (3): 153–58.

Thoreson, R. W., P. E. Nathan, J. K. Skorina, and R. R. Kilburg. 1983. "The Alcoholic Psychologist: Issues, Problems, and Implications for the Profession." *Professional Psychology: Research and Practice* 14 (5): 670–84.

"Three Sentenced to Prison for Scheme to Defraud Medicare." 2011. Press release. U.S. Attorney's Office, Middle District of Louisiana. http://www.justice.gov/usao/lam/press/press1101.html (accessed July 11, 2013).

Towle, C. 1945. *Common Human Needs*. Washington, DC: U.S. Government Printing Office.

——. 1954. *The Learner in Education for the Professions.* Chicago: University of Chicago Press.

"Treating Therapist Falsely Reports Father's Molestation of Young Daughter." 1997. *Mental Health Law News* 12 (9): 4.

Trice, H. M. and J. M. Beyer. 1984. "Work-Related Outcomes of the Constructive Confrontation Strategy in a Job-Based Alcoholism Program." *Journal of Studies on Alcohol* 45 (5): 393–404.

Tsui, M. 2005. *Social Work Supervision: Contexts and Concepts.* Thousand Oaks, CA: Sage.

Twemlow, S. W. and G. O. Gabbard. 1989. "The Love-Sick Therapist." In G. O. Gabbard, ed., *Sexual Exploitation in Professional Relationships,* 71–87. Washington, DC: American Psychiatric Press.

U.S. Department of Health and Human Services. 1989. *Bibliography and Resource Guide on Alcohol and Other Drugs for Social Work Educators.* Rockville, MD: Author.

U.S. National Center on Child Abuse and Neglect. 1981. *National Study of the Incidence and Severity of Child Abuse and Neglect.* Washington, DC: Department of Health and Human Services.

Vaillant, G. E., J. R. Brighton, and C. McArthur. 1970. "Physicians' Use of Mood-Altering Drugs." *New England Journal of Medicine* 282:365–70.

VandeCreek, L., S. Knapp, and C. Herzog. 1988. "Privileged Communication for Social Workers." *Social Casework* 69 (1): 28–34.

VandenBos, G. R. and R. F. Duthie. 1986. "Confronting and Supporting Colleagues in Distress." In Kilburg, Nathan, and Thoreson, *Professionals in Distress,* 211–31.

Vigilante, J. 1974. "Between Values and Science: Education for the Profession or Is Proof Truth?" *Journal of Education for Social Work* 10:107–15.

Watson, A. S. 1972. "Levels of Confidentiality in the Psychoanalytic Situation." *Journal of American Psychoanalytic Association* 20 (1): 156–76.

Wells, F. and M. Farthing, eds. 2008. *Fraud and Misconduct in Biomedical Research.* 4th ed. London: Royal Society of Medicine Press.

White, B. 1994. *Competence to Consent.* Washington, DC: Georgetown University Press.

Whittaker, R., S. Merry, K. Stasiak, H. McDowell, I. Doherty, M. Shepherd, E. Dorey, V. Parag, S. Ameratunga, and A. Rodgers. 2012. "A Mobile Phone Depression Prevention Intervention for Adolescents: Development Process and Post-program Findings on Acceptability from a Randomized Controlled Trial." *Journal of Medical Internet Research* 14 (1). http://www.jmir.org/2012/1/e13/ (accessed July 16, 2013).

"Wife Kills Self; Had Been Hospitalized for Earlier Suicide Attempt." 1995. *Mental Health Law News* 10 (2): 3.

"Wife Not Compelled to Turn Over Medical Records for Use in Divorce Proceedings." 1999. *Mental Health Law News* 14 (1): 3.

Wigmore, J. H. 1961. *Evidence in Trials at Common Law.* Edited by J. T. McNaughton. Rev. ed. Vol. 8. Boston: Little, Brown.

Wilson, S. J. 1978. *Confidentiality in Social Work.* New York: Free Press.

———. 1980. *Recording: Guidelines for Social Workers.* 2d ed. New York: Free Press.

Wisconsin Department of Safety and Professional Services. 2012. "In the Matter of Disciplinary Proceedings against Jackie M. Morter." https://online.drl.wi.gov/decisions/2012/ORDER0001302–00006751.pdf (accessed December 22, 2013).

———. 2013. "In the Matter of Disciplinary Proceedings against Cheryl K. Rotherham." 2013. https://online.drl.wi.gov/decisions/2013/ORDER0002561–00008687.pdf (accessed December 22, 2013).

"Woman Blames Psychological Problems on Psychologist's Sexual Relationship with Her." 1997. *Mental Health Law News* 12 (8): 2.

"Woman Claims Husband Improperly Allowed to Leave Hospital When Suicidal: $800,000 Verdict." 1994. *Mental Health Law News* 9 (2): 6.

"Woman Claims Improper Sexual Conduct by Psychologist." 1996. *Mental Health Law News* 11 (2): 3.

"Woman Claims Nurse Therapist Implanted False Memories of Sexual Abuse." 1996. *Mental Health Law News* 11 (4): 2.

"Woman Claims Psychological Counselor Implanted Memories of Satanic Rituals and Parental Incest." 1995. *Mental Health Law News* 10 (7): 3.

"Woman Claims Psychological Problems Following 'Seminar Training.'" 1992. *Mental Health Law News* 7 (2): 6.

"Woman Claims Psychologist Began Sexual Relationship; $650,000 Verdict." 1994. *Mental Health Law News* 9 (4): 6.

"Woman Claims She Was Improperly Discharged from Psychiatric Ward Due to Inadequate Insurance." 1989. *Mental Health Law News* 4 (11): 2.

"Woman Comes Under Care of Psychotherapist Who Suffers from Psychiatric Disorder." 1996. *Mental Health Law News* 11 (1): 2.

"Woman Evicted and Taken to Hospital Charges False Imprisonment." 1993. *Mental Health Law News* 8 (3): 6.

"Woman Falsely Imprisoned After Seeking Rape-Crisis Counseling at Mental Health Facility." 2001. *Mental Health Law News* 16 (2): 1.

"Woman Has Sexual Relationship with Therapist; $123,500 Award." 1999. *Mental Health Law News* 14 (12): 5.

"Woman Receives $7.1 Million Verdict for Abuse and Prescription of Drug by Psychiatrist." 1994. *Mental Health Law News* 9 (11): 2.

"Woman Sues Hospital for Disclosing Records: Did Not Waive Privilege by Failing to Object." 2001. *Mental Health Law News* 16 (8): 3.

"Woman Sues Psychologist for Use of Unorthodox Therapies." 1998. *Mental Health Law News* 13 (2): 4.

Wonnacott, J. 2012. *Mastering Social Work Supervision.* London: Jessica Kingsley.

Wood, B. J., S. Klein, H. J. Cross, C. J. Lammers, and J. K. Elliott. 1985. "Impaired Practitioners: Psychologists' Opinions About Prevalence, and Proposals for Intervention." *Professional Psychology: Research and Practice* 16 (6): 843–50.

Woody, R. H. 1997. *Legally Safe Mental Health Practice.* Madison, CT: Psychosocial Press.

Worchel, D. and R. E. Gearing. 2010. *Suicide Assessment and Treatment: Empirical and Evidence-Based Practices.* New York: Springer.

Zur, O. 2007. *Boundaries in Psychotherapy: Ethical and Clinical Explorations.* Washington, DC: American Psychological Association.

Abille v. United States, 482 F. Supp. 703 (N.D. Cal. 1980).

Addington v. Texas, 441 U.S. 418 (1979).

Alberts v. Devine, 479 N.E.2d 113 (Mass. 1985).

Alexander v. Knight, 177 A.2d 142 (Pa. 1962).

Almonte v. New York Medical College, 851 F. Supp. 34 (D. Conn. 1994).

Aronoff v. Board of Registration in Medicine, 652 N.E.2d 594 (Mass. 1995).

Baker v. United States, 226 F. Supp. 129 (D. Iowa 1964).

Bellah v. Greenson, 146 Cal. Rptr. 535 (Cal. Ct. App. 1978).

Belmont v. California State Personnel Board, 111 Cal. Rptr. 607 (Cal. Ct. App. 1974).

Berry v. Moench, 331 P.2d 814 (Utah 1958).

Birkner v. Salt Lake County, 771 P.2d 1053 (Utah 1989).

Boles v. Milwaukee County, 443 N.W.2d 679 (Wis. Ct. App. 1989).

Boyer v. Tilzer, 831 S.W. 2d 695 (Mo. Ct. App. E.D. 1992).

Boynton v. Burglass, 590 So. 2d 446 (Fla. Dist. Ct. App. 1991).

Brady v. Hopper, 570 F. Supp. 1333 (D. Colo. 1983).

Bramlette v. Charter-Medical-Columbia, 393 S.E.2d 914 (S.C. 1990).

Cabrera v. Cabrera, 23 Conn. App. 330 (Conn. App. Ct. 1990).

Caesar v. Mountanos, 542 F.2d 1064 (9th Cir. 1976).

Cairl v. State, 323 N.W.2d 20 (Minn. 1982).

California v. Cabral, 15 Cal. Rpt. 2d 866 (Cal. Ct. App. 1993).

California v. Gomez, 185 Cal. Rpt. 155 (Cal. Ct. App. 1982).

California v. Kevin F., 261 Cal. Rptr. 413 (Cal. Ct. App. 1989).

Cameron v. Montgomery County Welfare Services, 471 F. Supp. 761 (E.D. Pa. 1979).

Carr v. Howard, Massachusetts, Norfolk County Super. Ct., No. 94–97, March 5, 1996.

Chatman v. Millis, 517 S.W.2d 504 (Ark. 1975).

Chrite v. United States, 564 F. Supp. 341 (D. Mass. 1983), Civ. No. 81–73844.

Cohen v. State, 382 N.Y.S.2d 128 (N.Y. App. Div. 1976).

Corgan v. Muehling, 574 N.E.2d 602 (Ill. 1991).

Currie v. United States, 644 F. Supp. 1074 (M.D.N.C. 1986).

Cutter II v. Brownbridge, 228 Cal. Rptr. 545 (Cal. Ct. App. 1986).

Darrah v. Kite, 301 N.Y.S.2d 286 (N.Y. App. Div. 1969).

Davis v. Lhim, 124 Mich. App. 291 (Mich. Ct. App. 1983).

DeShaney v. Winnebago County Department of Social Services, 812 F.2d 298 (7th
    Cir. 1987), 109 S. Ct. 998 (1989).

Dill v. Miles, 310 P.2d 896 (Kan. 1957).

Doe v. Roe, 400 N.Y.S.2d 668 (N.Y. Sup. Ct. 1977).

Doe v. Samaritan Counseling Center, 791 P.2d 344 (Alaska 1990).

Dymek v. Nyquist, 128 Ill. App. 3d 859 (Ill. App. Ct. 1984).

Eckerhart v. Hensley, 475 F. Supp. 908 (Mo. 1979).

Elliott v. North Carolina Psychology Board, 485 S.E.2d 882 (N.C. Ct. App. 1997).

Estate of Davies v. Reese, 248 N.W.2d 344 (Neb. 1977).

Fedell v. Wierzbieniec, 485 N.Y.S.2d 460 (N.Y. Sup. Ct. 1985).

Ferrara v. Galluchio, 152 N.E.2d 249 (N.Y. 1958).

Force v. Gregory, 63 Conn. 167, 27 A. 1116 (1893).

Garamella v. New York Medical College, 23 F. Supp. 2d 153 (D. Conn. 1998).

Gares v. New Mexico Board of Psychologist Examiners, 798 P.2d 190 (N.M. 1990).

Geis v. Landau, 458 N.Y.S.2d 1000 (N.Y. Civ. Ct. 1983).

Goryeb v. Pennsylvania Department of Public Welfare, 575 A.2d 545 (Pa. 1990).

Green v. State, 309 So. 2d 706 (La. Ct. App. 1975).

Hague v. Williams, 181 A.2d 345 (N.J. 1962).

Hammer v. Rosen, 165 N.E.2d 756 (N.Y. 1960).

Hammonds v. Aetna Casualty & Surety Co., 243 F. Supp. 793 (N.D. Ohio 1965).

Heinmiller v. Department of Health, 903 P.2d 433 (Wash. 1995).

Hess v. Frank, 367 N.Y.S.2d 30 (N.Y. App. Div. 1975).

Holt v. Nelson, 523 P.2d 211 (Wash. Ct. App. 1974).

Horne v. Patton, 287 So. 2d 824 (Ala. 1974).

Hothem v. Fallsview Psychiatric Hospital, 573 N.E.2d 803 (Ohio Ct. Cl. 1989).

Hulsey v. Stotts, Barclay, Pettus, Moore, Whipple and Dugan, Inc., 155 F.R.D. 676
    (N.D. Okla. 1994).

Humphrey v. Norden, 359 N.Y.S.2d 733 (1974).

In re Estate of Bagus, 691 N.E.2d 401 (Ill. App. Ct. 1998).

In re Lifschutz, 467 P.2d 557 (Cal. 1970).

In re Quinlan, 355 A.2d 647 (N.J. 1976).

In re W. H., 602 N.Y.S.2d 70 (N.Y. Fam. Ct. 1993).

Jablonski v. United States, 712 F.2d 391 (9th Cir. 1983).

Jaffe v. Redmond, 116 S. Ct. 1923 (1996).

Jensen v. Conrad, 747 F.2d 185 (4th Cir. 1984).

Johnson v. New York, 603 N.Y.S.2d 852 (N.Y. App. Div. 1993).

Kavanaugh v. Indiana, 695 N.E.2d 629 (Ind. Ct. App. 1998).

Kleber v. Stevens, 249 N.Y.S.2d 668 (N.Y. 1964).

Kogensparger v. Athens Mental Health Center, 578 N.E.2d 916 (Ohio Ct. Cl. 1989).

Lake v. Cameron, 364 F.2d 657 (D.C. Cir. 1966).

Lee v. Alexander, 607 So.2d 30 (Miss. Supt. Ct. 1992).

Leedy v. Hartnett, 510 F. Supp. 1125 (M.D. Pa. 1981), Civ. No. 80–0201.

Lipari v. Sears, Roebuck, 497 F. Supp. 185, Civ. No. 77-0-458 (D. Neb. 1980).

Little v. Utah State Division of Family Services, 667 P.2d 49 (Utah 1983).

Lovett v. Superior Court, 203 Cal. App. 3d 521 (Cal. Ct. App. 1988).

Lux v. Hansen, 886 F.2d 1064 (8th Cir. 1989).

MacDonald v. Clinger, 446 N.Y.S.2d 801 (N.Y. App. Div. 1982).

Mammo v. Arizona, 675 P.2d 1347 (Ariz. Ct. App. 1983).

Marvulli v. Elshire, 27 Cal. App. 3d 180 (Cal. Ct. App. 1972).

Mavroudis v. Superior Court, 162 Cal. Rptr. 724 (Cal. Ct. App. 1980).

McIntosh v. Milano, 168 N.J. Super. 466, 403 A.2d 500 (N.J. 1979).

McNamara v. Honeyman, 546 N.E.2d 139 (Mass. 1989).

Meier v. Ross General Hospital, 445 P.2d 519 (Cal. 1968).

Merchants National Bank v. United States, 272 F. Supp. 409 (D. N.D. 1967).

Minnesota v. Andring, 342 N.W.2d 128 (Minn. 1984).

Minogue v. Rutland Hospital, 125 A.2d 796 (Vt. 1956).

Missouri ex rel. *C.J.V. v. Jamison*, 973 S.W.2d 183 (Mo. Ct. App. 1998).

Missouri v. Beatty, 770 S.W.2d 387 (Mo. Ct. App. 1989).

Missouri v. Edwards, 918 S.W.2d 841 (Mo. Ct. App. 1996).

Muse v. Charter Hospital of Winston-Salem, Inc., 452 S.E.2d 589 (N.C. Ct. App. 1995).

Naidu v. Laird, 539 A.2d 1064 (Del. 1988).

Narcarato v. Grob, 180 N.W.2d 788 (Mich. 1970).

Nelson v. Dahl, 219 N.W. 941 (Minn. 1928).

Norton v. Argonaut Insurance Co., 144 So. 2d 249 (La. 1962).

O'Connor v. Donaldson, 422 U.S. 563 (1975).

Palmer v. Board of Registration in Medicine 612 N.E.2d 635 (Mass. 1993).

Parker v. Miller 860 S.W.2d 452 (Tex. App. Ct. 1993).

Patterson v. Jensen, 17 N.W.2d 423 (Wis. 1945).

Perreira v. State, 768 P.2d 1198 (Colo. 1989).

Pisel v. Stamford Hospital, 430 A.2d 1 (Conn. 1980).

Porter v. Maunnangi, 764 S.W.2d 699 (Mo. App. 1988).

Pundy v. Illinois Department of Professional Regulation, 570 N.E.2d 458 (Ill. App. Ct. 1991).

Redding v. Virginia Mason Medical Center, 878 P.2d 483 (Wash. Ct. App. 1994).

Reif v. Weinberger, 372 F. Supp. 1196 (D. D.C. 1974).

Rennie v. Klein, 462 F. Supp. 1131 (D. N.J. 1978).

Renzi v. Morrison, 618 N.E.2d 794 (Ill. App. Ct. 1993).

Rogers v. South Carolina Department of Mental Health, 377 S.E.2d 125 (S.C. Ct. App. 1989).

Rosenberg v. Helinski, 616 A.2d 866 (Md. Ct. Spec. App. 1992).

Rouse v. Cameron, 373 F.2d 451 (D.C. Cir. 1966).

Rule v. Chessman, 317 P.2d 472 (Kan. 1957).

Runyon v. Smith, 730 A.2d 881 (N.J. Super. Ct. App. Div. 1999).

Salgo v. Stanford University Board of Trustees, 317 P.2d 170 (Cal. Ct. App. 1957).

Samuels v. Southern Baptist Hospital, 594 So. 2d 571 (La. Ct. App. 1992).

Sanfiel v. Department of Health, 749 So. 2d 525 (Fla. Dist. Ct. App. 1999).

Sayes v. Pilgrim Manor Nursing Home, 536 So. 2d 705 (La. Ct. App. 1988).

Schloendorff v. Society of New York Hospital, 211 N.Y. 125 (1914).

Schuster v. Altenberg, 424 N.W.2d 159 (Wis. 1988).

Sears v. U.S., 497 F. Supp. 185 (N.E.D. Neb. 1980).

Seavy v. State, 250 N.Y.S.2d 877 (N.Y. App. Div. 1964), 216 N.E.2d 613 (N.Y. 1966).

Shaw v. Glickman, 415 A.2d 625 (Md. Ct. Spec. App. 1980).

Siklas v. Ecker Center for Mental Health, Inc., 617 N.E.2d 507 (Ill. App. Ct. 1993).

Simonsen v. Swenson, 177 N.W. 831 (Neb. 1920).

Sisson v. Seneca Mental Health/Mental Retardation Council, Inc., 404 S.E.2d 425 (W. Va. 1991).

Smith v. Yohe, 194 A.2d 167 (Pa. 1963).

Snyder v. Mouser, 272 N.E.2d 627 (Ind. Ct. App. 1971).

Stovall v. Harms, 522 P.2d 353 (Kan. 1974).

Stropes v. Heritage House Children's Center of Shelbyville, Inc., 547 N.E.2d 244 (Ind. 1989).

Superintendent of Belchertown v. Saikewicz, 370 N.E.2d 417 (Mass. 1977).

Suslovich v. New York State Education Department, 571 N.Y.S.2d 123 (N.Y. App. Div. 1991).

Tabor v. Doctors Memorial Hospital, 563 So. 2d 233 (La. 1990).

Tarasoff v. Board of Regents of the University of California, 529 P.2d 553 (Cal. 1974, also known as *Tarasoff I*); 551 P.2d 334 (Cal. 1976, also known as *Tarasoff II*).

Thompson v. County of Alameda, 614 P.2d 728 (Cal. 1980).

Underwood v. United States, 356 F.2d 92 (5th Cir. 1966).

Vassiliades v. Garfinckel's, 492 A.2d 580 (D.C. 1985).

Vaughn v. North Carolina Department of Human Resources, 252 S.E.2d 792 (N.C. 1979).

Vineyard v. Craft, 828 S.W.2d 248 (Tex. Ct. App. 1992).

Walker v. Parzen, 24 Ass'n. of Trial Lawyers of America L. Rep. 232 (June 1983).

Welk v. Florida, 542 So. 2d 1343 (Fla. Dist. Ct. App. 1989).

Whitree v. State, 290 N.Y.S.2d 486 (N.Y. Ct. Cl. 1968).

Winfrey v. Citizens & Southern National Bank, 254 S.E.2d 725 (Ga. Ct. App. 1979).

Wisconsin v. Locke, 502 N.W.2d 891 (Wis. Ct. App. 1993).

Wofford v. Eastern State Hospital, 795 P.2d 516 (Okla. 1990).

Wood v. Samaritan Institution, 26 Cal. 2d 847, 853, 161 P.2d 556 (1945).

Yorsten v. Pennell, 153 A.2d 255 (Pa. 1959).

CPSIA information can be obtained
at www.ICGtesting.com
Printed in the USA
JSHW012249140123
36291JS00002B/170